B2B and Beyond

B2B and Beyond

New Business Models Built on Trust

Harry B. DeMaio

*With contributions from Partners,
Directors, Managers, and Consultants of
Deloitte & Touche and Deloitte Consulting*

John Wiley & Sons, Inc.
New York • Chichester • Weinheim • Brisbane • Singapore • Toronto

Library of Congress Cataloging-in-Publication Data:

DeMaio, Harry B.
    B2B and beyond : new business models built on trust/Harry B. Demaio.
      p. cm.
    Includes index.
    ISBN 0-471-05466-6 (cloth : alk.paper)
      1. Electronic commerce—Security measures. 2. Business networks—Computer networks—Security measures. 3. Electronic data interchange—Security measures. 4. Computer security. 5. Data protection. 6. Trust. I. Title: Business to Business and beyond. II. Title

HF5548.32 .D46 2001
658′.0558—dc21   2001045311

Printed in the United States of America.
10 9 8 7 6 5 4 3 2 1

About the Author

Harry B. DeMaio is a firm director specializing in secure e-Business technology within Deloitte & Touche's Enterprise Risk Services Practice. He was formerly president of Deloitte & Touche Security Services LLC (DTS), a wholly owned subsidiary of Deloitte & Touche.

He has extensive experience in advising major organizations on security policies, practices, and organization, as well as security architecture, design, and the application of security and contingency technology, especially in B2B environments. He has a significant background in the installation and management of information systems, and application and system software development.

He joined Deloitte & Touche in 1987 after 31 years with the IBM Corporation, where he held major management positions in marketing, systems engineering, software development, and information security. His last position with IBM was as Corporate Director of Data Security Programs, with worldwide responsibility for IBM's offerings, customer support, and external and government relations concerning information security, privacy protection, transborder data flow, and information trade.

Harry DeMaio has written many articles for major data processing and accounting journals and legal, business, and industry publications. His first book, *Information Protection and Other Unnatural Acts—Every Manager's Guide to Keeping Vital Computer Data Safe and Sound*, was published in 1992 in the United States and in 1995 in Japan. He is the author of a number of Deloitte & Touche management briefings, including "Information Protection, Your Business and The Internet" and "Client Server and Information Protection." He is a frequent guest speaker on television, radio, and at conferences.

He is a former Adjunct Professor of Information Systems, Graduate School of Business, Pace University. DeMaio is a former chairman of the Miami University (Ohio) Business Advisory Council. He is a former member of the Transborder Data Flow Policy Committee, U.S. State Department. He is a Certified Information Systems Security Practitioner (CISSP) and holds memberships in the Information Systems Audit and Control Association; the Information Systems Security Association; and I-4 (The International Information Integrity Institute). DeMaio holds a BA from Fordham University and an MBA from Pace University, and is a graduate of IBM's Systems Research Institute.

Yet again, to a very extraordinary bear

Contents

Acknowledgments

Many people have provided invaluable contributions and assistance in the development of this book—especially a global team of partners, directors, managers, and consultants from several Deloitte & Touche practices. Their names are listed below in alphabetical order. They are all highly experienced consultants with in-depth technical and e-Business knowledge. They have an extensive list of client service qualifications at many of the world's most prestigious corporations and institutions.

Because I have taken liberties in developing, combining, and modifying new content and existing contributions to meet the format and purpose of this publication, I have not made specific contributor citations. To the greatest degree possible, for ease of reading, I have also tried to embed references in the text rather than resort to footnotes. The responsibility for the accuracy, readability, and comprehensiveness of this text rests with me. If readers would like to pursue more in-depth discussions on any of the issues or subjects raised in this book, the author and publisher will make every effort to put them in contact with the appropriate Deloitte & Touche experts.

Deloitte & Touche Contributors and Reviewers

Don Ainslie	Mark Ford	Scott Kandel
Tejinder Basi	David Gautschi	Yag Kanani
Cathy Benko	Dahl Gerberick	Ami Kaplan
Jim Burns	Donna Gustafson	Dean Kingsley
Tom Buss	Sandy Herrygers	Bill Kobel
Doug Cale	Tom Haberman	Beth Larson
Kevin Calland	Todd Hjerpe	Bill Levant
Dean Clark	Pete Jensen	Eric Leighninger
Ted Dezabala	Robert Jervay	Steve Livingston
Bill Dziadyk	Ev Johnson	Brent Loebig
Don Elledge	Bill Kacal	Toni Marshall

John Marry   Sean Peasley   John Stacey
Tom McGinnis   Ian Perry   Trevor Stewart
Marc MacKinnon   Dennis Peters   Anne Taylor
Rena Mears   Debra Phelps   Ed van Essen
Adel Melek   Richard Punt   Stephen Wagner
Steve Michaud   Terry Ribb   Mike Wien
Chris Mitchell   Steve Ross   Jeff Willemain
Jorgen Moller   Bob Rothermel   Fiona Williams
Bill Murray   Irwin Siegel   Clay Young

A special acknowledgement to *Mary Ann McMahon,* Director of Marketing, Deloitte & Touche Enterprise Risk Services, for her energetic, efficient, consistent, good-natured, understanding, thought-provoking, and very necessary management and assistance in bringing this book to reality. It was actually fun, wasn't it, Mary Ann? Well, maybe.

I am also very grateful to:

- Several of my colleagues from I-4 (The International Information Integrity Institute) for their expert reviews, comments, and support:
  - Ben Asbury—EDS
  - Claire Hoyum—The St. Paul Companies, Inc.
  - Michael Leach—E.I. DuPont de Nemours & Co. Inc.
  - Bruce Moulton—Fidelity Investments
  - Eric Schansman—Rabobank International
  - Bill Whitehurst—IBM Corporation
- Grant Goldin, Durwin Sharp, and Rolf Smith of the Virtual Thinking Expedition Company for their guidance in scaling the cliffs of thinking and change.
- Jon Graff of NetReliance for his ideas and approaches to encryption.
- Fred Magner, CIO, Unocal Corporation, for his incisive observations on the energy industry.
- Julie Wantland, ExxonMobil Global Services Corporation, for her work and ideas on e-Trust in the petroleum market.

- Donn Parker, who was thinking thoughts on information integrity when most of us were still learning which was the lock and which was the key.
- Nelia Pozzuoli of the Nationwide Companies for her thoughts on quality and security in infrastructures.
- Jeffrey Ritter, Partner, Kirkpatrick & Lockhart LLP, for his help on privacy issues.
- Sherry Turkle, Ph.D., Professor of the Sociology of Science, Massachusetts Institute of Technology, for allowing me to adapt several of her innovative and perceptive concepts on how we use and interact with computers.
- Susan Swope, Tim Welsh, John Thurlow, Pat Gilmore, and Karen Worstell, of AtomicTangerine, for their continued professional insights.
- Tim Burgard and Louise Jacob, John Wiley & Sons, Inc., for keeping the ship afloat, on course, and on time.
- A very special thanks to my wife, Virginia, for her enthusiastic support of this project, her tolerance of my work habits, and her excellent suggestions and comments. Also for the exceptional help I received from my sons Mark and Andrew. All three shared experiences and perceptions from their extensive backgrounds as information systems professionals. This book is better for it.
- I have no doubt omitted vital names, and I apologize profusely. Please charge it to the faulty memory of the chronologically challenged and not to malice or slight.

Preface

In 1992, I wrote a book titled *Information Protection and Other Unnatural Acts*. It is out of print, although in its time it sold quite well, in spite of, or maybe because of, its title. (A Japanese translation, whose title and content I've never been sure of, did not do badly, either.)

Actually, the title was intended to be neither prurient nor misleading. *The point was that information protection, far from being a natural human trait, ran counter to our desires to communicate, our curiosity, and our inability to look at information as just another business asset. Business or institutional managers who expected that information protection would result from people just doing the right thing were in for a severe disillusionment. Guidance, protective measures, and enforcement were necessary.*

Almost 10 years later, not only does this basic principle still hold true, but it has been amplified by our full-scale, headlong stampede into the Information Age, exemplified by, but by no means limited to, the Internet, overwhelming computing power, the cell phone, wireless personal digital assistants, and an onslaught of visual, audio, and print materials.

So, obviously, in one sense, an update is overdue. In technology years, 1992 is somewhere between the Cretaceous and Mesozoic periods. 1992 not only predated all of those technologies but it also predated many of the relationships that are evolving in our social, political, and economic realms as a result.

However, this is not simply an update. It is a different view. In this text, we concentrate not just on protecting the information asset itself, but understanding and managing the new contexts, environments, and relationships in which information plays a crucial role. How do you establish multidimensional trust in e-based relationships? Like its predecessor, this book is about technology and behavior but it concentrates, not just on establishing individual protection, but on developing interactive trust. And as we shall see, that is a very different model. (I refuse to use the term—paradigm shift.)

Is this the last information protection model ever to be hauled out for analysis and dissection? Of course not! For example, read Ray Kurzweil's prophetic works on the evolution of intelligent machines, and you may envision an important shift in dominance between man and technology. In his future view, machines will *independently* (no direct human design, intervention, or control) manage and process much of our commerce and infrastructure support. Will it happen as he predicts? Possibly, but we have enough alligators in the current swamps to keep us more than busy right now. This book is not a futuristic excursion. It is about the here and now (and the next few years). So it, too, is doomed to obsolescence. I hope it is helpful during its short life.

WHAT IS THIS BOOK AND HOW IS IT ORGANIZED?

First, let's state what this book is not. It is not a diatribe on being good and avoiding evil. It is not the latest "you'd better watch out " advisory from your friendly auditor. It is not a self-defense manual. ("How to defend yourself when attacked by a NetExchange!!" "B2B: the End of Civilization as We Know and Love It.") Nor, we hope, is it another catalog of security and control do's and don'ts, although we do supply plenty of advice.

Rather, it is intended to assist enterprise managers who believe, as we do, that B2B either is or should be a major component in most business-growth strategies. It will demonstrate that trust, control, and security can often make or break an e-Business strategy, much more dramatically than in conventional business processes. It places great emphasis on the reciprocal and distributed nature of B2B—running an economic initiative cooperatively. It takes the view of both the "big kids in charge" and those who are "just participating, thank you." It points out strongly that in B2B, any one organization plays many different roles, and that reciprocal trust is a key to keeping the play moving successfully.

But it is not a naïve exercise in cheerleading. We understand full well that there are many serious issues associated with B2B, some of which can be lethal. We also believe that successful B2B environments do not spring forth immediately, automatically, or without transitional pain. Properly designed, developed, marketed, and managed, the rewards of B2B can be exceptional. Done poorly, you could not only damage yourself but a lot of other players with you. This is important material we're covering even if we sometimes are a bit breezy in our presentations. ("This is not just a matter of life and death, this is serious." Anonymous.) Serious stuff can still be fun, and in the interest of keeping you with us, we'll try to keep things light—but not light-weight. We hope you'll agree.

ORGANIZATION

We have taken the space shuttle approach to this subject. We start in Part I with a couple of turns in planetary orbit, setting out e-Business and e-Trust concepts and outlining "cosmic" positions and issues.

Next, in Part II, we lower the flight path and concentrate on e-Trust, business processes, technology functions, relations, examples, and some more detailed problems.

In Part III we come down to the deck with a series of chapters that describe in just enough detail for the interested business executive, new or modified trust approaches, tools, and techniques suited for use in the e-world. By that time we hope that we will have given you enough information and motivation to launch or enhance an existing, effective B2B trust program. Oh, incidentally, Deloitte & Touche would love to help you.

WHO SHOULD READ THIS BOOK, AND WHY?

This text is intended for a wide range of individuals concerned with trustworthy e-Business. We've tried to put equal stress on business, management, administrative, and technological issues. We assume you have a user's basic knowledge of the Internet. (You can log on and off, surf, and do e-mail.) We do supply some rather basic descriptions and definitions in several different chapters. Please control your ego, restrain your need to cut to the chase and your desire to get to the racy parts, and do read that descriptive and definitional material. For one thing, it will establish where we are coming from. Common vocabulary is essential for common communication. For another, there just might be one definition or nuance you hadn't thought about before. If not, see the cashier, and he/she will gladly refund your five minutes.

There are also a couple of technical chapters, both on the e-infrastructure and on security and controls tools and techniques. Some experienced technologists and in-depth security specialists will find only a few things they don't already know. However, they may find new and, we hope, useful ways of explaining what they do know to the "technically unenlightened." On the other hand, if we did this correctly, the "technically unenlightened" will find the specialized stuff easier going than they thought.

If nothing else, you'll be able to show off your newfound knowledge at cocktail parties and throw buzzwords around with the best of them. By the way, if you want to take the air out of a mnemonic spouting techno-snob, innocently ask what some arcane mnemonic stands for letter for letter. PCMCIA is a great one. (I'm not going to tell you.) The odds are heavily in your favor that he or she will not actually know or will have forgotten. This is especially effective in a group discussion where you are likely to get four or five versions for each term. (Oh, all right—**P**ersonal **C**omputer **M**emory **C**ard **I**nternational **A**ssociation, those network connection and special function cards you slip into the side of a laptop. I want half your winnings, if you bet.)

We are also making another, perhaps dangerous, assumption: *that you are more strongly motivated to achieve rewards than to simply avoid punishment.* The premise of this book is one of improvement and enhancement—not safety at all costs. If that is not your mindset, we may make you uncomfortable in places. This may sound strange coming from an "audit firm"—but you see, we actually see ourselves as business advisors.

While many sections of this book can be read independently and individual topics can be directly referenced, we believe you'll derive more benefit from reading it in its entirety and in front-to-back order. Until we publish the Japanese edition, please do not try to read it in reverse.

This is not a "how-to" manual. For example, in the chapters on technology, process and standards, we have sought a middle road between generality and detail. We warn the reader that e-Business technology is extremely volatile and product references and standards content will change rapidly and often. We present design characteristics and standards as they existed at the time of publication, but strongly urge the reader to seek primary sources for the most recent updates.

SEVERAL COMMENTS, CAVEATS, AND CONFESSIONS

I have tried to make this a global presentation. I hope that the style, language, and references used in this text will resonate well with readers both inside and outside the U.S. borders. In my successive careers with IBM and Deloitte & Touche, I have traveled extensively and worked with many international colleagues and clients. I like to think I am sensitive to international viewpoints and priorities. I ask the indulgence of my non-U.S. readers if the language or frame of reference displays a national or local bias.

The contributors, editors, and publisher have taken pains to distinguish provable facts, supportable opinion, and balanced conjecture in this text. We indulge in conjecture and identify it as such where there are several viable or as yet undeveloped alternatives that could have a significant impact on your investments and objectives.

We have made every effort to make this book helpful, readable, and enjoyable. We hope you agree. We welcome all comments and suggestions from our readers.

Several of the chapters in this book are extracted from previously published articles. Some content has been edited and modified from Deloitte & Touche's internal and published documents on the subjects of NetMarkets, ERP, e-Business, and security. The vast preponderance of the material is original for this publication.

See you inside.

Harry DeMaio

PART

I

Getting Comfortable with B2B and e-Trust

1

"Of Course, I Trust You!"

The original title of this book was "Of Course I Trust You—New Rules and Business Models for B2B and Beyond." Then the publisher's marketing department pointed out that this could easily get the book stocked in with self-help volumes like "How to Handle a Cheating Spouse" or "Giving Your Teen-Ager the Keys to the Ferrari." Pragmatism won out.

Still, the original title remains on the back cover and part of the front cover motif. It comes from a dimly remembered motion picture where a Mississippi riverboat gambler is about to play Poker with a dancehall queen. As he begins to deal, she touches his hand, looks soulfully into his eyes and purrs, "Of course I trust you, honey, but cut the cards."

That's the subject of this book:

- *The development within complex electronic environments*
- *of mutual trust*
- *based on each player's willingness and ability to continuously demonstrate*
- *to all the other players' satisfaction*
- *that the game is honest, open, following the rules, and properly controlled.*

Our game is e-Business, more specifically, Business to Business (B2B)— cooperative e-Business between business entities. Like poker, it's highly interactive. You need a winning strategy and tactics, plenty of resources, reflexes, skill, and yes, luck. Unlike poker, B2B is at its best when it is *not* a zero-sum game. It can be win–win, provided that all the players take cooperation seriously and come to the table prepared to play with shared goals and objectives. For many organizations, that's a new type of business experience, and it's not always comfortable. It may not even seem sensible. It certainly can be different.

DIFFERENT? YES, AS IN, WELL, DIFFERENT

Let us establish one strategic beachhead immediately. If you are taking your organization substantially, seriously, and extensively into B2B and Beyond, you are making a major commitment to being different. You won't stop at tweaking, although there will be plenty of fine-tuning as you move deeper into the e-world. But there might also be drama, emotion, risk, adventure, disappointment, triumph, and possibly, even violence (nothing fatal, we hope). In short, everything that makes life worth living. *In many cases, we are testing whether you can substitute e-Trust for direct ownership and control. As we see daily, traditional mergers, acquisitions, and vertical integration can be costly, painful, and seldom meet, much less exceed, expectations.* We will be discussing and suggesting large-scale change—but executed sensibly, gradually, patiently, and effectively.

Being different means thinking, looking, acting, and following a course that is at variance with your normal situation and that of your compatriots. That may sound inconsistent in a text that also claims that just about everyone is heading into the e-Business world. We really believe they are. But not at the same speed or on the same route, not with the same commitment, and probably not with the same results.

Before discussing e-Trust, let's spend a moment on *trust* itself. Exhibit 1.1 illustrates the major influences that establish trust in any mutual business situation, "e" or not. The relative weights will change with the players and the environment. Contrast in your mind orange growers, parts suppliers, credit institutions, and a hospital.

There's a very compelling marketplace reason for this shift in emphasis toward trust. Price is still the buyer's fundamental concern. But price is becoming a less powerful *differentiator.* Traditional corporate pricing strategies have less impact. Thanks especially to the Internet and technology in general, in both B2C (business to consumer) and B2B, brand differentiation and buyer loyalty are already far more difficult to capture and maintain. Customers have mouse-click choice and access.

Exhibit 1.1   Trust Diagram

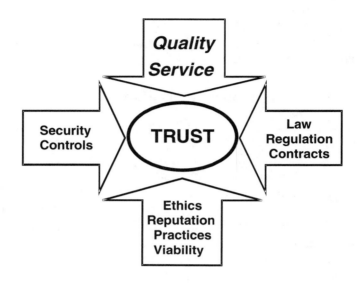

Price-bots, programs that scan the net searching for the best deal, are not restricted to e-tailing. Price wars are continuous and conducted at electronic speed. Auctions and reverse auctions are becoming the bidding mode.

Packaging, the other consumer and corporate product/service differentiator, has also been affected by the Web. The website is often a surrogate for the product or service package—it goes beyond appearance. If your site is low function, unreliable, slow, hard to navigate, or annoying—so is your image. Of course, the converse is also true.

In this environment, quality, service, and trust are emerging as the most powerful new enablers for successful branding, sustained differentiation, and customer loyalty—both at the consumer and business level. "Hey Supplier! I TRUST YOU!! Why else would I stick with you if you don't offer the currently lowest price?" For many organizations, maintaining the highest level of quality, service, and trust is a market survival strategy in the face of increasing price pressure.

One of the major differences in B2B will be the elevated position trust must occupy in your strategy, plans, design, and execution. We're going to spend a lot of time examining, parsing, poking at, and hopefully developing a profound understanding of e-Trust's critical role in the e-Business environment. It may well be the most important business difference you'll encounter in the age of "e". Trust us.

THE OTHER GUY'S EXPECTATIONS

As we said, trust is mutual and reciprocal in B2B. Throughout this book we'll be swapping around three basic, risk-related questions:

1. Can I trust the entities and infrastructures on whom I depend?
2. Can they trust me?
3. Together, can we trust our common infrastructure and processes?

Question 1 has been with us since the dawning of business and information protection. The overwhelming concern of business risk management is self-protection.

Question 2 has always been more implicit than explicit—until now. To avoid the risk of lost business, lost partners, or regulatory wrath, I must be trustworthy in traditional business relations (whatever that means in my marketplace). Now, however, B2B adds the further notion of continuous and extensive collaboration, cooperation, and interdependence—not just in the exchange of goods and services, but in the joint detailed conduct of business.

Consider "just-in-time" inventory management. FedEx, UPS, DHL, and a variety of other shippers have made their recent reputations (and a lot of money) by not simply transporting goods to destinations, but also by allowing businesses to cut back or eliminate inventories and their warehouse functions and *rely on* their shippers to get materials and finished products directly to their operational destinations, undamaged, ready-to-use, and on time. In short, the shippers meet an increasing part of the business customer's supply chain expectations. Most major shippers now have a very substantial logistics arm to further their direct penetration into the supply chain process.

If, sometimes virtually overnight (no pun intended) and for whatever reason, that trust is lost, both a business and an advanced operating concept may suffer. If you lose trust in your shippers, cavernous, high-cost warehouses and inventories could come hurtling back into your life, damaging your profits and those of your suppliers and customers. In a later chapter, we'll talk further about mobile warehousing. Like many things we'll discuss in this book, mobile warehousing is arriving on the scene slowly and sometimes awkwardly, but it's coming.

The answer to Question 3—together, can we trust our common infrastructure and processes?—is a variable, depending on how much common infrastructure and service sharing takes place in your B2B process. If a third-party servicer, systems integrator, or network manager provides infrastructure support in a totally outsourced mode, then Questions 1 and 2 primarily apply (seller/buyer). But another form of dependence is also prevalent in B2B—true sharing and co-management, sometimes in an informal consortium, sometimes not. In some respects, this is the trickiest of the lot because the lines of demarcation, the roles, and the rules are not always clear enough for the work to be done cost-effectively and the trust to be supported.

In any event, B2B and Beyond changes protective priorities. By all means, protect yourself first (just as in the event of a loss in cabin pressure, parents should put on their oxygen masks before their kids). Otherwise you and your partners will suffer. B2B heightens the potential that if your partner suffers because of you, eventually you will suffer, too—but it also enhances the opportunity for prospering in common, too, or else why do it?

You are going to have to pay more attention to your partners' expectations and frame of reference; understand them; try to modify them to your benefit. Decide if they're necessary and possible; alter your position or behavior; reach agreement, and then live up to it. Marketing folks have been doing this with customers for ages. Extend the same concept to your B2B partners and stakeholders. (As someone said recently, "The airlines and the FAA need to understand that when you're transporting paying passengers, on-time performance is not satisfied by same-day delivery.") Exceed expectations, live long, and prosper.

POINT TAKEN, SO WHAT?

For the moment, suffice it to say that we are not suggesting you throw your enterprise on the tender mercies of your partners and competition, new technologies, new business processes, and new world environments with no more than a naïve smile and crossed fingers. e-Trust is an unemotional, business-justified, and necessary condition for e-Business success. We would hardly claim that it is, in itself, a sufficient condition for success, but it's a biggie.

Throughout our excursion, you will hear plenty of references to *transitional hybrids* in organization, relationships, business processes, and technologies. As the name suggests, transitional hybrids are not, at least initially, intended as final states—but many of them hang around for an extraordinary period of time and in some cases become permanently institutionalized. They must be constantly rechecked and challenged for continued validity. Should the adjusters continue to tweak, massage, append, and fine tune, or has the time for bulldozers finally arrived? Please remember, age alone is not justification for replacement. (I sure hope not.) But, by all means, replace in the face of failure, increasing expense, inefficiency, or competitive disadvantage. But the new solution better be a better solution.

IS "E" REALLY FOR ME?

As this book was being prepared for publication in late 2000 and early 2001, the e-world was undergoing what will no doubt be the first of many shakeouts, course corrections, and culling of the flocks as we move from—Business as Usual, twentieth century style—to—Business to Be, 21st century style.

As a result of these shakeouts, instant zillionaires once again found financial reality, having to trade down their Lamborghinis for oh, at least a Lexus. Hot-shot startups, tap dancing on a "can't lose" value proposition and a volatile IPO, tripped over their own shoestrings. Now, some doomsayers have begun to scuttle the whole idea of a Web-based global economy. "It'll never fly, Orville." The problem with such apocalyptic thinking is simple: You can't go back, even if you want to. And it is hardly clear that we should.

We hope to demonstrate that a well planned, comprehensively designed, carefully executed, and *conscientiously controlled* transition into full-scale B2B is not only a major step forward in the growth of the world and individual enterprises, but a necessity. While there will be many hiccups, detours, and (hopefully few) outright disasters on the journey, the trip is worth making. Or in poker terms, it's the best game in town.

This book is not a defense of B2B itself. There are plenty of good expositions on that topic. Nor does it require that you have total faith in B2B's future (although we are believers). *Instead it provides what we hope is a strong rationale and helpful guidance for putting trust, controls, and security in paramount positions as we move more deeply into B2B.* This may seem self-evident to some, but it is not an operating characteristic for which the e-world has, as yet, become famous. We believe the following corollary is equally important: *The traditional ways of defining, designing, developing, deploying, and directing control structures and making business decisions based on them will no longer do in the B2B world.*

FOUR B2B PRINCIPLES WE'D LIKE YOU TO EXAMINE AND ACCEPT

Let us firmly anchor in your mind the four basic B2B principles on which this text is based:

1. **B2B is essentially an evolutionary process,** in spite of all of the prophetic and evangelical proclamations of the dawning of a new age powered by lightning-fast revolution. That's good news and bad. The good news is that the likelihood of runaway technology and catastrophic ventures is somewhat reduced. But, unfortunately, evolution can be slow, painful, and circuitous. And since many of the new B2B technologies and business processes offer significant opportunities for growth and success, we can't allow the evolution to become glacial. The trick is to get the benefits of these new opportunities at the most cost-effective pace, doing the least damage in the process. We will base our approach on assumptions of evolution, not revolution.

2. **Evolution creates transitional hybrids.**—These are entities and processes with one foot in the technological and operational past and one or more feet scrambling into the future. While we will present the glowing world of super extranets, NetExchanges, and NetMarkets as probable realities, they will not pop into being full-blown and mature. We will spend much more time in this book on "How do you get there from here?" than in contemplation of e-nirvana. Obviously to do that, we must understand the nature and differences of the farther-out future and apply them to a closer-in perspective. Even if your enterprise is not on the leading edge of "everything starts with an e," you should understand the implications of dealing with enterprises that are true believers, and you should know enough to avoid painting yourself into operational or strategic corners that

will keep you from playing with the other kids when they come to call.

3. **Transitional hybrids are the most difficult business environments to manage and control but they dominate the e-landscape.** Besides the obvious state of flux they all share, the important thing about transitional hybrids is, *Not only do they differ from what generally was the norm in the past and what is commonly foreseen for the future—They differ from each other.* This may be e-Business heresy. Many enthusiasts believe that the Internet and B2B, especially in the form of NetMarkets and NetExchanges, will be the great unifying and homogenizing forces in the future world of commerce. But in a competitive marketplace, the push for enterprise differentiation will always outrun desire for unity. However, at least one major contributor to more rational control and trust exists—the technical infrastructure can be made to look and act more unified. "Technology? You're kidding!" No, we'll see how later.

   However, as the colors, patterns, number, and position of each B2B leopard's spots uniquely changes, the usefulness of *untailored, generalized* best practices, standards, benchmarks, and traditions diminishes, and in some cases does damage. It has always been popular with business management to put controls and security in the category of "Tell me what the rest of the relevant world is doing to comply with the standards and then show me how I can get in the middle of the pack so I can then forget it and get on with the more important stuff." But borrowing the other guy's approach or slavishly following public standards will only work if you can assure yourself that they truly and fully apply to you. You're different—or at least that's what you're telling the world. So you're going to have to develop and then continue to develop and maintain individualized trust, security, and control strategies and processes customized to your own environments.

   You must do this while still maintaining compatibility with your constituencies, at least at the points of business and technical interface. In short, as your world gets more complex, either invest more time and attention before the fact to your enterprise's unique control needs or get ready to waste more and more time and effort cleaning up messes or recovering from near-death experiences.

4. **Company's coming! The essence of the world of B2B is deep, comprehensive, and high-speed corporate interaction.** We will spend much of our time discussing the crucial differences between the traditional, introspective, and defensive security and control strategies of the past and the mutual, interdependent trust requirements sitting on our doorsteps. They are fundamentally different in philosophy, strategy, technology, and execution. But again, they must be developed in a transitional hybrid environment. Enough on principles. On with the show.

SO, JUST WHAT IS E-BUSINESS?

There are 2.74568 very precise definitions of e-Business for every player in the field. Mapping the nature, structures, and differences between e-Commerce and e-Business has become a subculture all its own. We really don't want to get into an etymological war.

OK, if you insist, here's what we believe is the major difference between e-Commerce and e-Business. e-Commerce uses the Internet primarily as a means of conducting sales transactions, especially for consumers. e-Business leverages new and existing technologies to interact, transact, and collaborate with members of the organization's entire value chain. That can involve a lot of folks, inside and out, and it's not restricted to B2B. We no doubt will get many arguments about both definitions and the distinctions between them, but we will be true as we can to those statements through the remainder of this text.

HOW DOES E-TRUST PLAY INTO THIS?

Below the surface of our discussions lies a subtle but critical question. Can businesses change their personalities? Can we move from an atmosphere of knee-jerk suspicion and litigation to one that is more cooperative, supportive, and mutually dependent. Can we shift from one form of control to another—one that is based on trust? Notice, please, we said nothing about giving up control. We said a "different" form of control—one that is necessary if you really want to take advantage of what B2B and Beyond can offer.

Now, let's get serious. Is competition really going to disappear, and are lions and lambs really going to lie down together? I don't think soooo! But that doesn't mean the law of the jungle cannot and should not be modified to enhance the interests of all the creatures. I think it was my alma mater, the IBM Corporation, who coined the phrase *co-opetition*. If not, I apologize to the true author. The term captures the essence of today's turbo-charged information environment. Two or more business entities may simultaneously be each other's customer, supplier, ally, and competitor.

Diplomats will no doubt say, "So what else is new? Nations have been doing that for centuries. We wrote the book on co-opetition." True, but Machiavelli and the Rothschilds didn't have to deal with multidirectional, nanosecond, global transactions. High speed co-opetition is new for both nations and businesses. How we handle it will be key, and trust is at the crux of our success.

E-TRUST DOES NOT MEAN LOSS OF CONTROL

Quite the contrary, it means having to exert different, more complex, mutually developed, and agreed-upon control measures. No one is asking you to roll over and expose your throat to the rest of the wolf pack. However, understand that mutually developed *anything* comes at a cost in time, effort, and yes, compromise. It is this point of compromise that concerns many managers and executives who are used to thinking of themselves as the exclusive masters of their own universe. Realistically, it's been a long time since any of us have been true and absolute rulers. Next time you get on a plane, even if you're your own pilot, consider the degree to which you're in charge. As a former pilot, I can tell you—you've got lots of company. Get used to mutuality but remember that mutuality means change of, not absence of, controls.

NICE PHILOSOPHY, BUT THIS IS BUSINESS!

Building global e-Trust communities may sound idealistic and academic. Actually, it's as pragmatic as you can get. As an increasing proportion of the world's population and enterprises become e-enabled, each commercial sector—service, nontangible good, and even tangible good—is becoming more fluid. Except perhaps for agriculture and the extractive industries that are tied directly to a geographic base, sources of materials, goods, and services, as well as markets are becoming more mobile, especially in the virtually driven world. You can conduct most e-Business transactions from anywhere.

However, as an enterprise's market reach expands dramatically through electronics, there is a corresponding price to pay in volatility. More goods and services are becoming commoditized. So, how to keep a customer or client? How to keep your price structure intact? B2B provides some excellent opportunities to capitalize on quality, service, and trust, because many e-based organizations have demonstrated exactly the opposite because they didn't adjust to the market's expectations. More on this anon.

THE COST VIEW

One of the few things I still remember from Business School is that maximum sustained profits result from an optimum combination of increased revenues and decreased costs over time. Don't be frightened, I'm just a humble MBA.

If your plans for B2B are postulated on significant cost reductions, then consider that the new process should be capable of replacing or significantly reducing the old. One of the financial traps of Web-based processes to date has been the inability of organizations to achieve their cost-cutting objectives. Why? In part, because Web-based processes are not yet very good at standing alone as pure plays. In fact, one of the factors leading to the demise of many e-tailers was their inability to provide a complete shopping, purchasing, and fulfillment experience entirely through the Web, much less as a single transaction. Tried to return any merchandise to an e-tailer or question a charge or an error in shipment? In many cases, it's not a lot of fun. Were you upset because each transaction unleashed a barrage of promotional e-mails from the site and countless other sites? How long before you found what you wanted? Was the transaction secure? How do you know?

I wish I had a lire for every person who has asked me if it's really safe to give credit card information over the net. I would be fabulously wealthy. This is from people who routinely hand over their credit card to an unknown store clerk for exactly the same transaction. And many e-tail transactions really are as safe or safer than their conventional counterparts. (Plus, the credit card company has primary liability for paying off any fraudulent damages.) So, what's the hang up? Is this just unpredictable, inconsistent, and intractable human nature? The e-tailer better hope not. We all better hope not. A major part of the problem is aggravated by the industry's inability or unwillingness to build the consumer's trust and comfort level in a new mode, even if it as safe or safer than the old. Many e-tailers have had to resort to or hold on to full-time call centers and even bricks-and-mortar stores to shore up the relationship. So long, margin. So long, venture. In B2C, trust and comfort is crucial.

"BUT I THOUGHT WE WERE TALKING ABOUT B2B."

We are—mostly. As we'll note again later, B2B and B2C are rather artificial dividing lines, and we should be able to draw warnings, lessons, and ideas from each arena. Is there a comparable lesson for B2B? I think so. Let's look at it.

In B2B, the trust pattern can come in a number of ways, each subtly different. There is the *extranet,* in which one party opens its inner processes *directly* to a wider range of outside partners in the interest of saving time or cost, facilitating business growth, protecting against competition, improving service image, improving accounting or record keeping, reducing duplication of effort, or mutually building toward a more comprehensive relationship. (I'm sure there are a million more motivations but you get the idea.) We are not talking about arms-length electronic payments, although they are a good first step. We're talking about integrating partners directly into selected internal processes of our business—shipping, order tracking, parts and product availability, prices, payables and receivables, marketing, and executive compensation (just checking to see if you're paying attention) that vary with the industry, the partners, and the level of trust.

Now let's move to the next two models—NetExchanges and their more comprehensive siblings, NetMarkets. Could a stock exchange provide multibillion-share trading service to its members and the investing public if each member acted totally independently? Would the exchange be anything more than a convenient address? Since the first transactions under the buttonwood tree in Wall Street or the Paris Bourse, more and more transaction-related functions have been transferred to intermediaries—third parties—to enhance speed, volume, specialization, record keeping, infrastructure management, transfer and settlement, rule making, self regulation, overall service, and oh yes, trust.

More often than not, that third party has been the stock exchange itself or some entity under contract to it, such as SIAC (Securities Industry Automation Company). SIAC is owned by several exchanges. But any number of independent quotation and rating services, reporting systems, and international linkages also exist. Which brings us to the NetMarket. Consider all the world's stock exchanges (or a large population) not just communicating but supported by a common set of transaction services, for exactly the same reasons an exchange's members would seek common support. The principle behind the NetExchange and the NetMarket are the same. They differ in scope, membership, and impact. Did I hear someone say trust?

Now extrapolate that same image to whatever industry, sector, region, or environment you choose. No more competition? Are you kidding? The human genome project has a long way to go to get rid of that gene. We are not talking about mere connection—we are raising the image of an interoperating but still competitive environment involving mutual support, mutual investment, and mutual trust. There's that word again.

BUSINESS IS BUSINESS, SECURITY IS SECURITY, TRUST IS TRUST!

We hope, by the time you finish this book, you will accept that statement only at its most generic level. Certainly, war may be war, but Julius Caesar and Norman Schwartzkopf would have serious disconnects when it comes to strategy, tactics, and weapons. Most people who make these blanket simplifications about e-Business, e-Security, and e-Trust either do not comprehend the important changes in our society, economies, and technologies or are in a state in denial. Either attitude is dangerous.

Exhibit 1.2 is adapted from an August 2000 article in *Business Week*. I call it The Evolving Enterprise. The evolution is broad and deep. Examine each row. Some changing characteristics, like hourly inventory turns (just-in-time management) and real-time financials have profound impacts on our information processes, to say nothing of corporate governance and stewardship. Some, like global reach, virtual integration, Web organization, and changes in worker makeup, change the very fundamentals of the enterprise. In fact, the term *enterprise* as we use it today is something of a misnomer for the business entities that we see forming (slowly and with some pain), such as the NetMarket and NetExchange. The column labeled "Now" is my addition. It reflects the fact that integration into a single, seamless business entity is being displaced, at least for the immediate future, by interoperation and interconnection of dissimilar entities. The transitional hybrid rules.

True homogenization is difficult, costly, and can be politically lethal. Examine the low success rate of new mergers and acquisitions over the past few years. Consider the mortality rate of the executives

Exhibit 1.2   The Evolving Enterprise

Characteristics	20th Century	Now	Soon
Organization	Pyramid	Hybrid	Web–Network–Exchange
Focus	Internal	Hybrid	External
Style	Structured	Hybrid	Flexible
Strength	Stability	Hybrid	Change
Structure	Self-sufficient	Hybrid	Interdependent
Resources	Physical assets	Hybrid	Information
Operations	Vertical integration	Hybrid	Virtual Integration
Products	Mass production	Hybrid	Mass Customization
Reach	Domestic	Hybrid	Global
Financials	Quarterly	Hybrid	Real-Time
Inventory turns	Months	Hybrid	Hours
Strategy	Top-down	Hybrid	Bottom Up
Workers	Employees	Hybrid	Employees /Free Agents
Improvement	Incremental	Hybrid	Revolutionary

involved. Acquisition, corporate absorption, total transformation, and digestion often result in the business equivalent of antibody rejection. Looser, cooperative hybrid structures more accurately reflect the dynamics of our restless business environment. Add, subtract, transfer, adapt. Each hybrid is in itself different from its fellows and continues to change.

There are enough differences in business directions today to warrant major rethinking at every level. And there are enough serious differences in our information processes and usage to warrant the time and attention of even the most experienced executive, business manager, technologist, auditor, security specialist, and concerned citizen.

IMPACT ON INFORMATION PROTECTION, TRUST, AND CONTROL

If these and other changes are enveloping us, why should we expect the concepts and constructs of security, control, and trust to stay the same? In information processing today, protection, trust, and control are driven by business requirements. 'Twas not ever thus! In the pre-Internet computer days, the computing device itself forced a sameness on our approach to security. "Here's how you protect a computer!" And one computer from a protective standpoint looked very much like another of its own class. One type of device, one type of protection. Sounds great, but it's fundamentally flawed.

You see, the idea of the computer and its infrastructure as primary objects of protection was always an aberration. It began that way because they were so expensive, large, and difficult to replace. Today, we throw them away. *We are returning our attention to where protection, trust, and control should always have been—the processes and the information that make up the landscape we manage.* The parts inventory database that once nestled physically in a single, well-protected array of disk drives is now living a dynamic and virtual life housed on any number of interconnected servers and workstations. If anything, that database is more important than it ever was but it now requires increasingly sophisticated virtual as well as physical protection. We'll see how shortly.

NEW APPROACHES FOR NEW ENVIRONMENTS

We can and do, of course, use the computer itself as a control tool, but we are now dealing with a very broad array of environments, processes, users, relationships, and threats. Adopting one-size, one-type protection will either leave embarrassing exposures or create expensive, unnecessary, and often counterproductive overkill. We must tailor to the hybrid, using the business requirements as our primary source of direction.

Through networking, we are connecting and adapting old and new processes and technologies and only selectively tearing down and rebuilding to a single image. As long as the interfaces between processes are compatible and interoperable, reconstructing what goes on behind them becomes a matter of particular corporate need, priority, and timing.

"WHOA, THERE! WHAT ABOUT TRANSFORMATION AND INTEGRATION?"

They are very much alive, well, and occupying their front row seats in the sun. Thanks for asking. As you know, these two terms are used somewhat ambiguously in the literature. Let's clarify what they mean in our context so you can see that there is little or no conflict between them and the type of hybrids we're describing.

Transformation, as it is most commonly used, describes a procedure that takes disparate but related business applications throughout (or in major parts of) an enterprise and reconstructs and harmonizes them under a common business process umbrella. The most common are ERP—enterprise resource planning (e.g., SAP or JD Edwards); human resource management (e.g., PeopleSoft); corporate financial systems (e.g., Oracle Financials); and a variety of others that are more industry specific.

I realize that such rebuilding of business process systems sure looks like a complete replacement strategy and it can be—for one or more of the B2B partners. ERP and its kindred systems can bring major parts of the business information process out of a cobbled, techno-churn chaos and create order and reason. For that purpose alone, it is worth the time and effort. But the benefits far exceed orderliness. Quality, speed, cost-effectiveness, control, service, and stability come to mind for starters.

But must every member of a proposed extranet, NetExchange, or NetMarket adopt or adapt an ERP system in order to participate? If so, many of these B2B communities will be much slower in developing. If not, then a baseline business and technological interface structure needs to be developed so that the players at different stages of transformation can participate. For example, we'll talk a bit later about issues surrounding EDI and newer e-Business transaction systems. Can they and should they coexist? At what cost?

Today, there are few purebred, totally exclusive, enterprise-wide implementations of SAP, PeopleSoft, Oracle Financials, and the like. In fact, as the marketplace progresses, each of these suppliers is being called upon to enrich and expand its external interface capabilities (such as MySAP) to work with outside systems. B2B interconnection is not a cheap substitute for transformation. It opens new business relationships that may eventually create prospects for advanced transformation where and when it makes sense.

Integration, as we're using it, simply refers to business processes, systems, applications, and technologies working together appropriately and cost-effectively. It does not mean building a one-vendor shop. In B2B, integration will be more logical than physical—that is, rather than thinking in terms of converging and concentrating physical data centers and disk farms, or adopting a single vendor philosophy, we begin to think in Web and Internet terms where the rules of identity and access management manage the relationships. A 200-terabyte e-Business database may be in one physical place or distributed over a hundred places (on or off the Web). The choices will be based on a very long list of issues ranging from bandwidth to legal requirements. We'll examine most of them in future chapters.

GETTING THERE

We'll see, as we progress through the following chapters, that old and new protective models must be made to co-exist, if for no other reason than economics. Many new business approaches come on stream initially as low or no margin ventures. Instead of replacing function, they often become add-ons to the existing process, and the enterprise must accommodate and constrain the extra cost.

Obviously, we all hope these redundancies are temporary. But how many organizations have dropped their service call centers even though they now have an extensive Web-based capability? Few to none. Why? Because the Web is not now and may never be fully mature enough and trusted enough to cover the entire B2C or B2B experience. There are times I want—or need—to talk to a person. There are things I can't do through an ATM or a web connection. Or—and this is crucial, I can still do them more easily and with more confidence over the phone, by fax, or in mixed mode. The e-tail universe is full of users who get all the way to the end of Web-based shopping experience and then pick up a phone and complete the transaction. They're seeking reassurance, confidence, and trust. The current mode for success is not necessarily eliminating but rather rebalancing and realigning transaction support functions to form a profitable mix (in other words, hybrids). How long we stay this way is anyone's guess but as you know, many temporary situations develop permanent status.

On the other hand, the B2B world could actually transit to stand-alone Web-based processing faster than some B2Cs. Many B2B organizations have cut their teeth on electronic funds transfer or EDI and are more disposed to using interactive electronics in the pure state. The B2B populations are usually smaller than B2C, and as a result of ongoing relationships are better known to each other. But the stakes are usually higher. Even when a new B2B process goes live on the Internet, the training wheels may stay on for quite a while and the hybrid remains.

HELP FROM AN UNEXPECTED SOURCE

A short digression: Another positive contributor to the B2B transition can be all the work we put into Y2K. Aside from the big benefit that nothing much happened—which was no accident—one of the most significant side effects from all the auditing, inventory taking, and conversion work we did to ensure that cockeyed calendars didn't do us in was this: For one brief, shining moment, we probably had the most up-to-date, comprehensive, nearly correct, and useful view of our information processing environment ever.

In many cases, we also converted the mystic ramblings of the ancient computing druids like me into something approximating understandable code, and we consolidated virtuoso pieces and duct tape add-ons into suites of compatible process. Now we are trying to bury Y2K as an anomaly that shouldn't have happened. PLEASE DON'T. Use the inventory and base of information and the updated and newly consolidated processes you established back then as a control platform for easing transition to B2B.

If you gleefully created a bonfire for all the Y2K data you'd collected on your systems, sift through the ashes. If you didn't, drag the data and the skills you developed out of the attic and make them usable again. In B2B, the more stable and well understood each environment is before interconnection and interoperation, the fewer hassles and false starts. Good Y2K-based information won't get you there alone, but it may make one or two major side trips unnecessary.

SURVEYING THE LANDSCAPE

The same evolutionary, hybrid approach we project for B2B is true of its trust, security, and control measures. Expensive, cosmic new protection schemes are seldom in the cards. I get especially concerned when a large multinational client announces a global replacement strategy for its security mechanisms. "Let's completely convert to digital certificates and get rid of passwords once and for all." Not a bad strategic objective. Usually a very difficult tactical exercise! Business-driven transitions (and changing security and controls are in that category) should be built to *ultimately* achieve strategic objectives but should be implemented around tactical business and technological realities. They should also begin producing some tangible benefits as they go on stream. We'll keep returning to this point throughout our journey.

We're going to concentrate on questions like, What will your voyage into and through B2B look like? What are some of the key B2B variants? How safe will the journey be? How do you manage and prosper in a sea of partnerships and alliances? Whom do you trust, and why? What trust tools and procedures do you need? What do you do with them, and when? As far as security, control, and trust are concerned, what is enough and what may be overkill, and how do you tell the difference? What skills and management structures do you need? Where can you get help? What is the meaning of life? (Just kidding.)

We are trying to present a balanced view of the trust, security, and control realities, implications, and prospects associated with the development of e-Business both today and in the reasonably foreseeable future. This book presents issues and problems, *but* it is not a doomsday scenario. It suggests solutions and approaches, *but* it is not a step-by-step cookbook. We hope to give you a clear, readable, and concise view of what it will take to carry off trustworthy e-Business, especially B2B and Beyond, over the next few years. In this rapidly evolving arena, the "next few years" is the only horizon we can professionally address with any real confidence.

And that's our intention—to provide you with a higher level of confidence as you move, happily or otherwise, into the "e-Business and NetMarket Cosmos." That is definitely the business community's ultimate destination, but you can strongly influence your own course and speed and how painful or profitable the passage is for you, your company, your business partners, customers, and stakeholders.

In the interest of keeping this book and your exhaustion within bounds, we are going to concentrate our discussions of e-Trust primarily on the broadly defined information aspects of the business relationships. We openly admit that the basic sources of e-Trust or any kind of business trust are the quality, value, timeliness, and appropriateness of the goods or services being supplied coupled with the business reputation of the organizations involved. The press is full of product and service failures. Nifty information systems aren't always the answer. The best reservation system in the world won't compensate for dirty airplanes, poor on-time performance, or surly staff.

But since our purpose is to concentrate on establishing and maintaining trust in extranets and evolving NetExchanges and NetMarkets, the most sensible approach is to focus on what is or should be different from the more conventional aspects of business.

IN OTHER WORDS, E-TRUST!!

The letter "e" is rapidly progressing from the most used to the most overused letter in the English language. Unfortunately, at least for the present, it is also a convenient form of shorthand for the Internet-based, electronically driven environment into which the 21st century finds itself moving. So with very e-mpathetic apologies to those of you who are totally sick of e-everything, we're going to stay with the e-convention rather than try to invent an equally annoying substitute.

Instead, let's concentrate on the word *Trust*. Not security! Not control! *Trust*. We chose it carefully, because it is the real essence of relationships in the e-universe. Security is a state. Control is a process. *But trust is an ongoing interaction that establishes and maintains confidence between or among entities.* Trust requires security and control but it goes beyond them. It depends on technology and protective mechanisms, but it also involves reputation, contracts, law, openness, familiarity, fair business practices and ethics, quality, timeliness, and a host of other relationship characteristics.

NO BLINDFOLDS

As we said earlier, we are *not* talking about *blind* trust. You know, "Sorry about that, but that ice sure looked solid enough to skate on!" However, there are very few instances of totally assured trust, either. Phrases like, "Take it on trust" or "you'll just have to trust us" imply that there is a point in many transactions beyond which tangible proof and control mechanisms won't work, aren't available, or have minimum incremental value.

There is an acute balance to be maintained. In the words of Chris Argyris: "If trust is high, precision can be low, if trust is low, precision must be high." This is not an argument for ditching controls or taking unwarranted risks. It is an argument for not treating all of your partners, customers, and suppliers as prima facie thieves and bounders or every support environment as one step from catastrophe. It is an argument for developing processes to support the conclusion that the game is honest and I don't have to scrupulously check each deal. In short, if I can establish rational and appropriate trust, I may actually be able to dispense with some expensive and redundant controls. I'm sure I've made some of my colleagues and part of the reading audience uncomfortable with that last comment. I haven't taken complete leave of my senses. But let's face it. You will not be able to control your B2B e-universe alone. You are going to need partner support, and therefore, reciprocal partner trust. Besides, controls and security operate on a sliding scale of cost effectiveness and only paranoids and fools go for the absolute all-or-nothing extremes, except in a few instances where there is no other alternative.

But you are still not blind. Beyond the point of tangible control, your own past experience or a knowledgeable third-party's recommendation are probably your most reliable guides. Let's call it lightly protected trust. The trick is to use those guides without developing business paranoia, doing damage to the relationship, losing the benefits of high-speed, high-volume interaction, or burdening the process with excess direct and indirect cost. There is a finite limit to the practical value of security and control mechanisms in any situation, and this has never been truer than in e-environments.

THE OUTER LIMITS

So, where are the limits to this discussion on e-Trust? It's a tough call. Quality plays a large role. If product failure data were properly gathered and interpreted and honestly communicated and acted upon, would some injuries, death, and lawsuits be avoided? Of course! Business ethics, law, morality, and national culture are all crucial to creating and maintaining trust. In this book, although we will speak to the entire spectrum of trust, we are definitely putting a technology spin on our exploration. Primarily, we want to give you a rational view of what security and control technologies can and cannot do, and at what cost, to support trust. We will recommend approaches and supplements. We will present, demonstrate, explain, and try to persuade. After that, the commitment, decisions, effort, and results are up to you. We'll be coming back to this point repeatedly in our discussions.

By the way, it's going to take a little while yet for us to get down and dirty in detailing e-Trust issues, policies, procedures, and technologies. We want to be sure you have a full appreciation of how different some aspects of e-Business can be—and therefore, how different e-Trust can be. The deceptive part of e-Trust is you'll often hear and use many of the traditional language, tools, and techniques, but not necessarily in traditional contexts or structures. Conversely, you may not appreciate the true value of some of the newer protective technologies like encryption and digital certificates until you understand why some of the older technologies are losing their effectiveness. But first. . . .

2

Scoping Out the Topic

Our first order of business is to describe and circumscribe our topic. "Scoping it out," in consultant speak. Notice, we said, "describe and circumscribe"—not define. We are trying for comfortable understanding, not laser precision. Of course, from time to time we will also offer some specific definitions, mostly from accepted external sources. We will circumscribe our scope with the following statement:

We're going to concentrate on the trust, control, and security aspects of e-Business to Business (B2B) interaction.

We'll focus on the following, now and for the near future:

- Business modes and models
- Application and infrastructure designs
- Hardware and software technologies
- Business procedures required to create, collect, transmit, *process*, record, store, display, and *act upon* business related information

The term *process* covers a wide range of activities, including calculation, transmission, storage, identification, authentication, manipulation, combination, evaluation, management, protection, and many others.

Act upon is a key differentiator between previous computer-supported and newer e-Business models. Implicit but fundamental to the value proposition of true e-Business is the end-to-end information stream between business entities resulting in the *fully completed, interactive transaction.* Most prior interactive models triggered a set of processes of variable duration, with the user getting an immediate message acknowledgement but no or few usable results. Today, we are working toward a goal of online, on the spot, real-time closure of the transaction for the user. That doesn't mean a car magically appears in your driveway when you log off an order screen. It does mean that your stock sale is executed and confirmed.

This approach includes but is hardly limited to

- Verified, just-in-time production and delivery of virtual or tangible goods or materials
- Agreed upon and verified exchange of monetary or intellectual property or value
- Finalized and propagated decisions or opinions
- Approval and delivery of medical, legal, accounting, or other professional services
- Commercial, information, travel, entertainment, and similar services

A MAJOR "BUT"—B2B IS NOT JUST TRANSACTIONS

My very astute colleague, Michael Leach of DuPont, in reviewing a pre-publication version of this book pointed out, with some justice, that I might be giving the impression that transactions, and transactions alone, are the mainstream of B2B. This is certainly not the case nor was such an impression intentional on my part. In fact, the collaborative nature of B2B suggests quite the opposite. B2B is NOT just a newer version of Electronic Data Interchange—EDI. (We'll have more to say on EDI later.)

B2B involves a much richer combination of cooperative activities, not the least of which is the sharing of data, services, applications, and infrastructure by an ever-widening sphere of partners. It is this networked sharing that enhances the global potential of B2B, especially if the Internet and Web are the vehicles of choice. The synergy of shared resources and business power is a key differentiator of the B2B environment and is a major component of its fundamental Value Proposition.

However, this same synergistic sharing is also the cause of many of the most profound and knotty e-Trust issues that arise in B2B. Privacy, intellectual property, accountability, anonymity, and operational security all take on more complex and situational characteristics as the B2B environment expands. Consider this point strongly as we review our examples in Chapter 10 on industry characteristics. Consider the social, economic, and regulatory forces we address in Chapter 12 or Identity Management in Chapter 15. Consider the organizational and assurance issues in Chapters 20 and 21. In every case, the traditional modes of inter-company transaction control will no longer suffice. In every case, although it will greatly assist, enhanced security and control technology is not the total solution. Relationships and practices are the focal points.

As the name suggests, B2B is all about interaction but interaction in the very broadest sense of the term. Technology enables, businesses share, and businesses execute. Businesses and their stakeholders trust.

BUT WHAT ABOUT OUR HERITAGE?

Internet-related technology and process has claimed a significant beachhead in e-Business territory. But we will not ignore so-called legacy processes and systems. Indeed, they are very important players in the hybrid security worlds we'll be exploring. Nor will we ignore "back-end" systems. They often make the difference between success and failure in the "click and mortar" universe. We'll move around in the supply chain arena and talk about enterprise resource planning (ERP), but primarily as it relates to the trusted e-Business/NetMarkets. We'll also investigate financial structures and processes.

NAVIGATING E-JARGON

To get more comfortable with e-Business jargon, let's define or describe a few terms. Even if you think you know all of them, please take a brief moment to read through them so you know what *we* mean when *we* use them (definitions courtesy of Webopedia.com).

Internet

A global network connecting millions of computers. At the end of 2000, the Internet had more than 400 million users worldwide, and that number is still growing rapidly. More than 100 countries are linked into exchanges of data, news, and opinions, with the sharpest growth in Asia and Latin America.

Unlike some earlier online network services that are centrally controlled, the Internet is decentralized by design. Each Internet computer, called a *host,* is independent. Its operators can choose which Internet services to use and which local services to make available to the global Internet community. Remarkably, this anarchy by design works exceedingly well. It's not total democracy. A few large hosts act as concentrated switching systems for the Internet, but no one of them has exclusive control over the routing. The internet is a multi-path environment.

Why use the Internet? Here are some reasons most commonly given by advocates. Like most enthusiastically supported sales points, they are generally true but may need some further scrutiny.

- Ubiquity—Macro (global reach) and micro (each individual)
- Relative speed of deployment
- Transaction unit cost—Price/performance
- End user ease of use
- Market expectation/competitive pressure
- Widespread advocacy
- Widely available technology
- Widely accepted processes
- Scalability, portability, future growth potential
- It may be the only alternative!

For example, consider Internet ubiquity in either form—macro or micro—and ask that question kids ask worldwide. "Are we there yet?" Then listen for the equally recognizable answer—"Not yet, but pretty soon." And at the moment, it's better than whatever's in second place. Similarly, the other advantages should be scrutinized for their specific value to your organization.

There are a variety of ways to access the Internet. Most online services, such as America Online, offer additional services besides connection. However, it is still possible to get uncluttered, basic connection through a "vanilla" commercial Internet Service Provider (ISP—see below). Nevertheless, pure-play ISPs are becoming fewer and fewer.

World Wide Web

I'm sure you know this, but it might bear repeating. The Internet and the World Wide Web are not synonymous. The simplest definition of the World Wide Web is " a subset of Internet servers that support specially formatted documents." The Web was designed to make graphical presentation and overall navigation easy on the Internet. Without it, you'd be living with a complex, text-only environment much like the old PC-DOS operating systems, for those of you old enough to remember them. No pictures, no mice. Odds are, because of navigation difficulties, you wouldn't be using the Internet at all.

There are three components that are crucial to the Web user.

1. The **browser** is a special program (Netscape, Microsoft Internet Explorer, to name the two most popular) that acts as a translator, navigator, presenter, and facilitator between the user and other Web-enabled Internet sites.

2. The browser, in turn, uses a special protocol, **Hyper Text Transfer Protocol (HTTP),** to communicate and activate its functions. (As any diplomat will tell you, a protocol is simply a standardized way of doing something.) As you point and click, the browser acts as an intermediary. Next time you use the Web, notice at the top of your browser screen in the address bar space, that the address of the location you are seeking will have the format— "http://www.someplace.com." This tells the local Internet server to which you are connected that this is a Hypertext-formatted address and the location is a Web-enabled location. Web addresses (URLs—Uniform Resource Locators) are only one of several forms of Internet address. If you look at the bottom of the screen, depending on how your browser is set up, you may see a string of numbers interrupted by dots. This is the actual Internet address (like a phone number).

3. The URL (address, domain name) format is one part of the **HyperText Markup Language (HTML)** rules that are used to build Web pages, and to program and communicate through the HTTP protocol. HTML and many of its derivative languages support links to other documents, as well as graphics, audio, and video files. The website developer's use of HTML allows you to click on specially highlighted links on a Web page to take you somewhere else. The browser translates the link URL, initiates and monitors the Internet call, and assists you in navigating to and on the new site. The browser also keeps a temporary history of where you've been so you can navigate by simply using the Back and Forward buttons.

A Brief Digression on Domain Names

What's a domain name? A domain name is a unique alphanumeric name that is used to identify your presence on the Internet. For U.S.-based sites, the domain name normally ends with the suffix .com, .net, .edu., or .org (for example, www.mybusiness.net). More suffixes are coming. The domain name is the part of a URL that identifies your primary Web server. Like an office building address, it often requires additional floor and suite locations to get you precisely where you want to go. Again, while you browse, you will see in the address bar extensions being added to the primary URL as you zero in on a specific screen. For our purposes, though not strictly correct, we will use the terms URL and domain name as meaning roughly the same thing.

You don't actually "own" a domain name, even if it sounds or looks like your own corporate identification. I'm not kidding. Domain name registration grants the right to use the domain name exclusively, but not to own it. Irritating, huh? Someone else can and often will use your organization ID as its domain name, if you're not careful. Originally the National Science Foundation (NSF) handled Internet IP address and domain-name registration. Today, Network Solutions, Inc. (NSI) is the official registrar of domain names for the U.S.-based Internet's .com, .org, .net, .edu, and .gov domains. (There are other domains, especially country identifiers like .ru or .fr not covered by NSI. Under its contract with the NSF, its domain-name registrations are done by NSI through InterNIC, the Internet Network Information Center. Is that enough abbreviations for you?)

For a fee, InterNIC registers domain names, maintains the master domain-name registration database, and builds and distributes the master domain-name files to the Internet's root domain-name servers. When you request a particular Internet domain, it is passed on to an Internet root domain-name server that, in turn, points and connects to that host server (computer) where the domain is stored or hosted. In addition to creating a domain in the first place, registering domain names also includes the responsibility for changing, deleting, and re-registering them. *For the suffixes named above, domain names do not exist until one is requested from InterNIC.*

BTW (e-mail talk for By the Way), domain-name management has become a strange but important aspect of being on the Web. Until recently, when domain-name assignments finally became a bit more orderly and controlled, there was a thriving and shady, "get rich quick" business in buying up unused domain names that sounded like or were the names of real people or enterprises and selling them back at outrageous prices to buyers eager to protect the company's image. Some controls have been put in place to prevent domain names from being bought for speculative resale or blackmail, and not for actual use. This does not prevent a disreputable site or a competitor from actually using a domain name it registers. One of the most frequently registered domain names on the Web is some variant of Pamela Anderson's name. The lady does not own or manage all those sites.

All Web servers are on the Internet. Not all Internet servers are Web enabled. SMTP—Simple Mail Transfer Protocol-based e-mail—some forms of video/music streaming, and file transfer (FTP) are three examples of non-Web Internet technologies, although they may have additional Web interfaces for ease of use. Your e-mail address probably does not have "http://www." in it. That means it's not using the Web, even though your Web browser got you there. Confused? Don't be. Your browser on your computer can hook you up to other Internet services besides the Web. FTP is a far more effective way of moving bulk files around the Internet than the Web.

Another BTW. Like it or not, everyday usage continues to mix up the Web and the Internet. In most discussions, it doesn't really matter very much. We'll be careful where we have to be, but you don't have to unless you're making important service-related decisions requiring some precision or are dealing with a techno-pedant. We discuss the Web and other technologies further in Chapter 13, and we refer to it throughout the book. If you think of the Internet as the global supporting transfer mechanism and the Web as your primary but not necessarily exclusive communication and control vehicle on it, you'll be close enough to the truth for our purposes. Did you really need to know all that? If you recognize it passively the next time it comes up, that's all we wanted.

The next several definitions apply to how the Internet can be configured and managed. Understanding the differences is important. These configurations may support Web and non-Web services.

Intranet

An **intranet** *is a network, based on Internet data and transmission protocols, belonging to an organization, often a corporation, and accessible only by the organization's members, employees, or others such as contractors with authorization.* An intranet's websites look and act just like any other website, but firewalls and other security technologies surrounding an intranet fend off unauthorized access.

Like the Internet itself, intranets are used to share information but only among chosen and authorized participants. Secure intranets are now the fastest-growing business segment of the Internet because they are much less expensive to build and manage than private networks based on proprietary protocols and technologies.

Extranet

An extranet is an intranet that is partially accessible to authorized outsiders. Whereas an intranet resides behind a firewall and other controls and is accessible only to people who are members of the same company or organization, an extranet provides various levels of accessibility to outsiders. You can access an extranet only if you have a valid username and password, and your identity determines which parts of the extranet you can traverse. Extranets are becoming a very popular means for business partners to exchange information. Caution: Converting or supplementing an intranet to take on extranet characteristics takes a good deal more than simply reconfiguring a few firewalls. There are major business relationships as well as other technical structures to consider, design, deploy, and control. More later.

The Ps—ISPs, ASPs, Portals, Content Providers, CSPs

An **Internet Service Provider (ISP)** *is a company that provides access to the Internet.* For a monthly fee, the service provider gives you a connectivity software package, username, password, and access phone number. Equipped with a telephone modem, cable modem, or DSL (digital subscriber line) connection, you can then log on to the Internet and among other things, browse the World Wide Web, chat rooms, and USENET, and send and receive e-mail. ISPs also serve large companies, providing a direct connection from the company's networks to the Internet. ISPs themselves are connected to one another through Network Access Points (NAPs). ISPs are also called IAPs (Internet Access Providers).

Application service providers (ASPs) *are third-party entities that centrally manage and distribute software-based services and solutions to customers across a wide area network.* In essence, ASPs are a way for companies to outsource some or almost all aspects of their information technology needs.

ASPnews.com breaks ASPs down into these five subcategories:

1. Enterprise ASPs deliver high-end, global business applications.
2. Local/regional ASPs supply a wide variety of application services for smaller businesses in a local area.

3. Specialist ASPs provide applications for a specific need, such as website services or human resources.
4. Vertical market ASPs provide support to a specific industry such as Healthcare.
5. Volume business ASPs supply general small/medium-sized businesses with prepackaged application services in volume.

ASPs may be commercial ventures that cater to customers, or not-for-profit or government organizations, providing service and support to end users.

A **Web Portal** is *a website or service that offers a broad array of resources and services, such as e-mail, forums, search engines, and online shopping malls.* Some may be closed environments, however. This may make certain types of interoperability and exchange with other services difficult. The first Web portals were online services, such as AOL, that provided both access to the Web and expanded search-engine facilities. They have expanded dramatically into much broader service suppliers. By now, most of the surviving Web search engines have transformed themselves into Web portals to attract and keep a larger audience.

The term **content provider (CP)** *unfortunately is widely used and abused. Its scope and meaning varies from industry to industry.* In entertainment and news reporting, for example, it refers to those entities that create or develop the music, programs, features, games, photos, and news items for the electronic distributors (in our parlance, service providers). Generally, most content providers do not directly distribute. But, sometimes they do. As usual, the functions to be performed are easier to distinguish than the business entities that perform them. For example, what is Disney in this context?

In manufacturing, content from a CP may include catalogs, patents, codes, or regulations. In the distribution industry, you'd find shipper IDs and shipping codes, logistics services, air, rail, water, and over-the-road schedules and services. For healthcare, it ranges from pharmaceutical catalogs to health encyclopedias, practitioner and service provider directories to health benefits, and FDA regulations. CPs and CSPs are critical components of both the goods and service sectors and represent a major part of the value of e-marketplaces. A CP may or may not also be a CSP.

Content Service Providers (CSP) *usually do not participate directly in business transactions (ASP) or network function support (ISP). Instead, they provide key intellectual materials to facilitate the process.* They may or may not actually create or generate the intellectual property they supply. Examples are catalog services, performance and satisfaction rating services, and credit rating services. As the name suggests, a catalog service supports e-Business by obtaining or developing, updating, cross referencing, and distributing catalog content for specific industries, commodities, services, marketplaces, or areas. Content providers (CPs) and their distributors (CSPs) may be tightly coupled or deliberately separated to avoid potential conflict (such as performance ratings services). In the future, many CSP functions will no doubt be an integral part of NetExchange and NetMarket structures.

HARDWARE AND SOFTWARE PROVIDERS

These are the folks who supply processors, operating system, network, data storage and management, display, application, and an almost infinite array of specialized function that make up the infrastructure of the "e" arena. We'll talk about them in several places, especially in Chapter 11. It's easy to take this group for granted in the midst of all our conversations on new entities and relationships. A bit like taking tires on a vehicle for granted until. . . . A bit later in this book we'll discuss the trust responsibilities these organizations have and the fact, frankly, that they are not always holding up their end. We are only beginning to see a landscape of industrial-strength, reliable, secure infrastructures required to carry off B2B. Too many e-Businesses today are running (or trying to run) on consumer strength products.

NETEXCHANGES AND NETMARKETS

From a structural standpoint, what are **NetExchanges** and **NetMarkets?** They are extranets on steroids. This time we provide description, not definition.

NetExchange

A very good analogy for a NetExchange can be derived from the financial or, more specifically, the securities arena. If you parse out the workings of a typical stock exchange:

- The roles and relationships among buyers, sellers, and the intermediary role of the exchange itself;

- The nature of the transactions—buying, selling, trading, adjusting, reporting;
- The information infrastructure required to support the processes and players; and
- The speed, volume, value, and often, irrevocability of the process; and apply them to other business venues:
  - Manufacturing
  - Banking and other financial services
  - Telecommunications
  - Healthcare
  - Travel, hospitality , and entertainment
  - Distribution and retail

you can get a good idea of the NetExchange model. Buyers and sellers with common interests use an intermediary environment to facilitate their business interactions.

One important point to remember in Exhibits 2.1 and 2.2: The buyer and supplier are transaction-related roles, not actual business entities. Corporation X may be a buyer one minute and a supplier the next. Rapidly shifting roles are key to e-Business.

Exhibit 2.1   The NetExchange

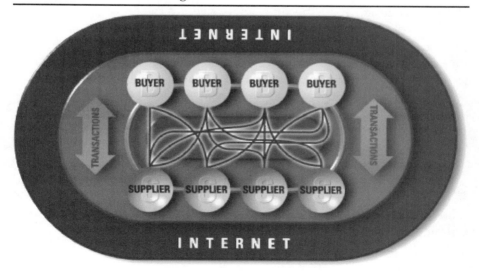

Exhibit 2.2   The NetMarket

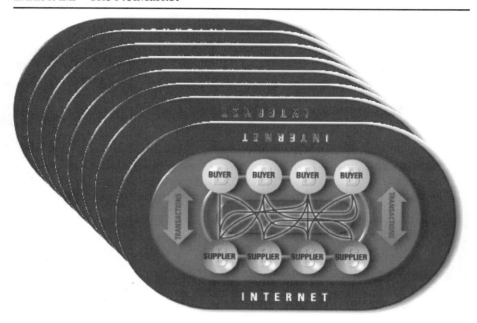

NetMarkets

To get a similar idea of a NetMarket, let's expand the securities exchange example we've just discussed. We'll go beyond a single exchange to a larger securities market, or even to the entire global securities market. Here we see exchanges dealing with other exchanges, differentiated perhaps by geography, types of financial instruments, or membership. Also tied in are related financial entities such as banks, regulators, and insurance. It is also surrounded by a massive number of support systems such as quote services and market reports. Now, once again, apply this extended model to other industries and, more importantly, to entire economic sectors—transportation, construction, food supply, energy.

One NetMarket for All?

Consider the ongoing interaction required to maintain the flow and balance of the high-technology sector. It ranges from raw-material development to chip and component design; from software through firmware to hardware; from research to service delivery; from manufacture to distribution; from marketing to government relations. Consider the spectrum of players, events, dependencies, and information flow. It stretches across just about every industry, sector, and area of interest—public and private. Could one virtual NetMarket serve this complex? Would it be desirable? It's not clear, but a lot of intelligent folks are examining the eventual possibility. If it can't, the primary reasons will not be technological.

Consider managing energy supply for an area, country, or region. In the United States with deregulation, price crises, and the rising search for alternative sources, the once-quiet public utility and fuel arenas are now competitive and political hotbeds. It is not uncommon for bid and ask prices and negotiation on future electric generation to look very much like any other commodity market. Synchronized with that commodity trading is the actual power grid management required to deliver the power.

Often, as in the case of oil tankers or grain carriers, cargo ownership can be transferred dynamically. As you know, a tanker load of oil may change owners and final destinations several times while in transit from the point of origin. In the JIT delivery world, this phenomenon will be spreading to other commodities and raw materials.

Think of a "virtual moving warehouse" that stores and dynamically redirects containerized goods while in transit—on the road, on rails, in the air, or at sea. These virtual warehouses will supplement, and in some few cases totally replace, conventional warehouses and goods storage. It takes more than the Internet to make this happen, and we discuss some of the processes and technologies involved a bit later. These could all be managed by a complex of NetExchange or NetMarket mechanisms. Think about some of the security and trust issues that arise when the touch of a computer key can change ownership and destinations on a physical asset you've never seen. (How do you handle customs issues on virtually reassigned goods? Virtually.)

In a typical NetMarket, any number of industries will intersect and interact to provide a wide variety of related and required goods, services, and information. You can begin to see how the e-Business to NetExchange to NetMarket progression works. (We dedicate a major chapter to filling out these descriptions and relationships.)

TRADING AND PRICE AGREEMENT MECHANISMS

There are two main mechanisms for arriving at agreed-upon trade in the e-Business environment:

1. Direct bid
2. Open auctions
   a. Standard auction—single seller, multiple buyers
   b. Reverse auction—single buyer, multiple sellers
   c. Ascending price ("English")
   d. Descending price ("Dutch")
   e. Fixed point of time
   f. Continuous

QUERY: WHERE ARE EDI AND EFT IN B2B E-BUSINESS?

Good question. Let's discuss electronic data interchange (EDI) first. EDI is a set of protocols, standards, and conventions under which businesses can exchange transactions in common. It speaks to format, structure, and general procedures. It has brought much order to the chaotic world of invoices, bills of lading, purchase orders, adjustments, and acknowledgements. EDI has made it far easier for companies to begin and then maintain a first-time electronics-based business relationship. Many large manufacturers, wholesalers, and retailers will only accept transactions in EDI format. But protocol and format alone do not make a process or a relationship. B2B goes well beyond EDI and speaks to the development of a structure based on alliances of mutual support by separate entities. In the set of definitions that follow, I hope you observe that speaking a common business language and observing the rules of etiquette are only the first steps toward conducting interactive, high-speed business in a co-opetitive mode.

Electronic funds transfer (EFT) has blossomed into a rich environment of financial transactions underpinning e-Commerce, e-Business, and individuals through the intermediation of the global banking system. Whereas EDI can be viewed as an early movement toward fuller B2B relationships and activities, EFT is actually an integral part of the B2B structure and is growing, changing, and expanding as e-Business and e-Commerce change.

Putting it another way, EDI conventions can assist in getting a B2B relationship off the deck more rapidly and cost effectively but it is not a necessary condition for B2B success. EFT in one form or another absolutely is. We will make the point over and over in this book. Don't confuse entities with function. Today's banks as we know them (or think we know them) will undoubtedly continue to morph into different types, shapes, sizes, and colors. Regardless of how the industry churns and financial institutions move toward crossover acquisition, disintermediation, or spinoff, the EFT *process* must live a long and robust life. Otherwise . . . well, there is no otherwise.

Now let's get back to our array of B2B functions and players.

MORE B2B NOMENCLATURE

To fully appreciate B2B we can further break it down into four basic functional parts, modes, or *sides*—buy, sell, inside-common, infrastructure. I believe the Oracle Corporation first coined these valuable concepts. We'll describe them further in just a few moments. But let's level set for a moment. This topography applies to most B2B environments—extranets, NetExchanges, NetMarkets, and any other animal that may appear in the B2B food chain.

Be careful here. We are describing e-Business roles, functions, or processing modes. We are not suggesting that individual companies, enterprises, or organizations belong to only one of these categories. (Yes, I know, a few might.) With the exception of the retail consumer, most players in B2B or B2B2C will be involved to varying degrees in all four. It is important, especially relating to e-Trust, to keep focusing on the structure, transaction, or process under discussion and the current role of the enterprise or players involved. As the roles change, so do the responsibilities and impacts. We will find ourselves saying such things as, "Company X in the role of buyer uses the following buy-side functions. Now in the role of seller, that same Company X will use these sell-side functions."

The overall trust, security, and control strategy of Company X is a composite of its requirements, responsibilities, and activities in all of the modes in which it operates. That composite will change over time as company-to-company relationships and processes are newly established, altered, or shut down.

By the way, as you enter a B2B discussion, make sure everybody is using these terms the same way. Much time can be wasted and many tempers strained if you don't. Coming to think of it, this warning applies to the entire e-Business environment. Unlike the in-depth "techie" worlds, where the terminology is often arcane and obscure, e-Business parlance often takes a familiar business word or phrase and gives it new and subtly different meaning. Therein lies potential chaos.

THE B2B "SIDES"

Considering how quickly terms, concepts, and phrases are created, adapted, and modified in the e-world, it should not be surprising that there are two descriptive constructs that share "side" terminology. They actually serve somewhat different purposes. *The first, Exhibit 2.3, looks at the terrain from a business process ownership, agency, responsibility, and interaction viewpoint.* It sees the world from a buy side, sell side, inside, and outside view. Buy and sell match with inside and outside to form four *combinations.* So buy functions happen both inside and outside the enterprise. Inside is the enterprise itself. Outside would be ASPs, partners, third parties, auction sites, market makers and so on. You have a similar arrangement for sell. Sell inside, sell outside. Of course, you can also parse the universe from the opposite view—Outside buy and sell, inside buy and sell.

OK, now that you have that straight, that's **NOT** the model we are using in this book. Since you'll see it used by other sources we felt we should present both variations. *The view we're going to use, Exhibit 2.4, has been designed to concentrate on application function, interfaces, and technical architecture and design. Each element is distinct and independent.* Buy and sell include all locations and variations. Inside-common used here means shared supporting applications and middleware. If you prefer "common," use it. We'll hyphenate it most of the time. Infrastructure speaks to

Exhibit 2.3

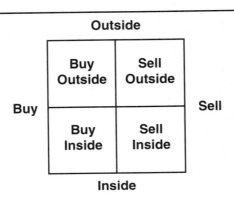

Exhibit 2.4

Buy	Sell
Inside-Common	Infra-Structure

the underlying technology, especially the network and platforms. It's essentially the application and technology view.

Why are we using a technology-centric view in a business book? Web-based security and control is somewhat easier to explain in this view. And this book is about techno-business. Both views serve different purposes and are equally valid. Unfortunately, they both have too large an established basis of use to make either one go away. Let's explain the version we'll be using more fully.

1. **Buy side**—The functions required to find, evaluate, "purchase," procure, receive, and take ownership of an item of property (tangible or intellectual) or a right to some service or status. The buy side has a strong genetic tie to the industrial procurement process but remember, we are talking about a wider range of goods and services as well as B2B2C characteristics. We have "purchase" in quotes because there are other modes of exchange such as barter or mutual transfer of rights that go beyond simple transfer of currency for possession of goods.

2. **Sell side**—"Well, obviously, this is the inverse process to buy side." Yes, but that's not a very helpful description. Included in this function is a wide range of activities, including website design and presentation, portal and service linkages, advertising, customer relationship management (CRM), market analysis, sales, fulfillment, service and returns, and a good, healthy reach into supply chain and distribution management.

3. **Inside-Common**—The business processing gearbox between buyer and seller which, depending on the number and nature of the parties and transactions, may be very complex. Inside

membership varies with industry. Here we might find all of
the dynamic and static records transfer, reconciliation, record
keeping, payment, financial settlement, and billing functions
between entities. These are processes, applications, and
functions that *support* several or many separate and distinct
processes or applications.

You will also hear the term *middleware* used here.
Middleware is a subset of *inside.* It is software that *connects*
two otherwise separate applications. For example, there are a
number of middleware products that link a database system
to a Web server. This allows users to request data from the
database using forms displayed on a Web browser, and it
enables the Web server to return dynamic Web pages for
conversion to transaction or query form based on the user's
requests and profile.

Middleware is used to describe separate products that serve as
the glue between applications. It is, therefore, distinct from
import and export features that may be built into one of the
applications. Middleware is sometimes called *plumbing* because
it connects two sides of an application and passes data between
them. But the pipes appellation is also often applied to
infrastructure and networks, so once again, check what the real
topic of the conversation is (thanks to webopedia.com).

Inside-common does not necessarily mean inside a single
enterprise. It means inside the extranet, NetExchange, or
NetMarket structure. Go back to our stock market
comparison and think about clearing and reconciliation. If
you have even a rudimentary understanding of how financial
markets work, you can create a comfortable analogy.

4. **Infrastructure**—The technological underpinnings that support
   items 1 through 3. The most obvious is a complex,
   interoperable network. But also consider, as a trust-related
   example, the directory service and encryption key management
   processes that may be necessary to support this process.

Many sell, buy, inside-common, and infrastructure functions can be and
are supplied by third-party specialists. Remember this as we explore
trust responsibilities and roles.

Does all this nomenclature really matter? Yes, it does. Most of us
have grown up believing that these business and technology functions

are encapsulated within a single company structure, with the possible addition of a few contract organizations.

In Exhibit 1.2, The "Evolving Enterprise" in Chapter 1, we saw major transitions taking place on all fronts. In fact, we may someday be hard pressed to define just what an enterprise is, and what functions it performs. A corporate office, a board, a charter, a stock symbol, a logo, and what else? Are holding companies the model of the future enterprise? In some industries will the NetExchanges and NetMarkets be the new scene of all traditional enterprise transactions? Someone else can write that book.

However, the structures and relationships are truly changing. Perhaps not as rapidly, profoundly, or successfully as many enthusiasts would have you believe. This can be and will remain rocky terrain. But change is upon us, and the danger in subtle, evolutionary transition is the likelihood that some of the essentials (such as control) may be overlooked until too late. We will base much of our subsequent discussions about e-Trust on these four B2B divisions. Make sure you're comfortable with these functions and with the fact that they may have lives independent of any one of the individual organizations involved.

DISINTERMEDIATION OR TRANSINTERMEDIATION?

At about this time in discussions like these, the term *disintermediation* usually rears its unpronounceable head. In the disintermediation scenario, banks, travel agents, brokers, and manufacturers' representatives are all headed for the scrap heap as the end parties in a business relationship shed the middlemen and reach out to each other in direct electronic embrace. The brave new disintermediated world will be greatly consolidated, simplified, and streamlined as the overhead and baggage disappear. OK, conclusion jumpers, let's be careful here.

For one thing, getting rid of the middleman may not always be efficient or desirable. Many e-Business value propositions justified primarily on disintermediation-based savings will disappoint. The demise of these intermediaries has often been vastly over-predicted, just as their price/performance has been undervalued. But even assuming these entities disappear or are drastically downscaled, the services and functions they perform will still remain in large part and must be performed, facilitated, and controlled somewhere.

Since most of the functions the intermediaries performed will simply be transferred to other parties or transformed, maybe *transintermediation* is a better but equally unpronounceable term? The point for our discussions is that the need for control, security, and trust is built around functions as well as entities. That need doesn't disappear with the intermediary unless the function also disappears. (Seldom!) The exclusion of a supplier does not always decrease the complexity or enhance the control of the processes involved. It may have the opposite effect.

VIRTUAL COMMUNITIES

The concept of virtual communities is key to the e-Business environment. Essentially, a virtual community is one that shares common interests, goals, processes, and characteristics and is brought together primarily through Internet connection. Of course, there will often be concomitant physical interaction, especially if the community is involved in the exchange of physical goods or nonelectronic services.

Obviously not all virtual communities are business oriented. Just wander around on the Web or USENET areas of the Internet and you will see how many affinity groups exist. Of course, the major purpose behind NetExchanges and NetMarkets is to construct, maintain, and grow virtual business communities. These communities may be extremely complex and dynamically expand or contract. In the construction of successful B2B environments, the business architecture—the structure, nature, and interaction of the business communities involved—must be the driving influence of the technical architecture, not the other way around.

We will discuss the virtual business communities that populate the B2B landscape in greater detail in Part II. There are two terms we should address now:

1. **Seller sites**—These are companies that focus on direct-to-buyer commerce such as Amazon.com and eBay for consumers or Grainger for consumers and businesses.

2. **Market makers**—B2B market makers are third-party intermediaries whose primary purpose, in most cases, is to match corporate buyers and sellers. They typically take a fee, make a spread, or receive commissions for their services. They may be the corporate identity and structure behind a NetMarket or NetExchange.

The differences between these entities are not always clear. A seller site could also act as an intermediary for other entities. Airline reservation systems have been doing this for years.

It's important to remember that all of these communities are still in formative stages. It is not clear what levels of service aggregation and differentiation will occur as the e-marketplace matures.

For example, consider the functions of catalog provision and management. Is that CSP a viable standalone business, or will it be a sub-function within a seller site or market maker environment? In a highly fragmented market, with a large number of suppliers and a large inventory of alternative items, bringing order to the potential chaos of floor-to-ceiling catalogs (literally and figuratively) may indeed be a worthwhile pure play, especially if other features like supplier service ratings and price guidance are included. Combination of services is and will continue to be a business imperative for all the usual reasons (one-stop shopping, economy of scale, competitive advantage). But it's also important to keep the nature and purposes of the individual services clear and distinct, because not all entities will combine the same way. Although it may be initially uncomfortable, in the interest of clarity, whenever we can, we will continue to refer in this book to services to be supplied rather than the service entity itself.

TRUST COMMUNITIES AND ENVIRONMENTS

The terms *trust communities* and *environments* in this text represent *a type of virtual community in which a high level of mutual trust is a critical or mandatory success factor.* Although few, if any, communities can survive without some level of acceptable trust, there are many (healthcare, transportation, most finance, public safety, and essential services) where the level of trust must demonstrably exceed "normal" expectations. It is usually the participants themselves, with the help of laws, regulations, professional standards, and public opinion, that set these expectations. We will devote significant time in later sections exploring what these trust communities should look like and how they should be designed, deployed, and supported technologically.

As we explore e-Trust communities, bear in mind that each organization may play a somewhat different trust role within any given community and may also be a member of more than one trust community. For example, a medium-size distributor may simultaneously control its own extranet, involving warehouses, truckers, and suppliers, while being part of a larger manufacturing exchange or another organization's extranet. This may result in more complex or, worst case, conflicting security and control requirements being imposed on individual trust community players. In subsequent chapters, we will attempt to sort out some of these requirements by industry and by type of player—ASP, CSP, ISP, NetExchange, or NetMarket and, of course, the extranet owner/manager.

Some B2C and a relative handful of B2B entities may currently look and act as if they are following the behavior codes of Attila the Hun, but the future of e-Business (expanded extranets, NetExchanges, and NetMarkets) depends on orderly, cooperative, well understood, practical, and cost-effective mechanisms and procedures tailored to provide appropriate e-Trust in each community.

E-BUSINESS FACILITATORS

What are the basic and common facilitating characteristics of all of these environments including Business to Consumer (B2C)? Here's a typical but nonexhaustive list:

- global interconnection
- bandwidth
- breadth of function
- ease of use
- speed
- capacity
- interoperability
- accuracy
- accessibility
- durability
- common community
- trust

Without constant expansion and acceleration of all these facilitators, the e-universe would not be possible. These facilitators are enhanced by increasingly powerful hardware and software technologies that help create, collect, transmit, process, record, store, display, and act upon business-related information. They also interact with trust.

THERE IS A DARK SIDE

Although most of these same facilitators and technologies can be major contributors to trust and safety, they can also contribute to the downfall of the system.

Internally, as scale, speed, load, and complexity within the system increase, so do potential negative consequences. A Formula One racecar at top speed is tougher to drive than a Volkswagen Beetle. Simplicity is always desired but seldom attained in e-Business interconnections.

Externally, as networks grow, the size and attractiveness of the target and its potential vulnerabilities also increase. Just as large jet aircraft and associated air traffic management are astoundingly safe for the functions they perform, when a big jet goes down or is taken down, the results are usually catastrophic. So, too, with large nets. (In searching for an ongoing illustrative model to which most business and nonbusiness readers can easily relate, I've decided to frequently refer to air travel. It has many e-Business characteristics, and it's familiar—often too familiar. We will discuss other industries in detail, but if the examples, similes, and metaphors have a commercial aviation bias, it's in the interest of common understanding.)

In addition, dependence on single sources of support can have widespread consequential damage and economic impact in the event of failure. Using our air transport example, remember the last airline strike or any blizzard at O'Hare Airport in Chicago? (Europeans can choose Charles De Gaulle or Heathrow.) Alternatives can be few, impact can be staggering. As we'll see, NetExchanges and, to a greater degree, NetMarkets share the same characteristics. Although they amplify and enrich the business process, they can also amplify negative consequences of an incident, often by orders of magnitude.

Let's clean up a few loose ends before we leave this chapter.

WHAT ABOUT BUSINESS TO CONSUMER (B2C)?

Roughly described, B2C refers to e-environments where an individual consumer is *directly* involved in one part of the transaction, usually, but not always, in the role of buyer. Auction processes, for example, can reverse the role. Obviously, part of the separation between B2B and B2C is artificial. Track back or forward far enough in B2B and there is a consumer on the end or at the beginning. The converse holds true for B2C. Consumers buy, finance, insure, rent, fuel, evaluate, litigate, navigate, drive, wreck, replace, and bring in for service the products around which several major automotive B2B NetExchanges and NetMarkets are developing. Actually, there are very few absolute B2Bs. There are B2B2Cs, B2B2B2Cs, and any number of other combinations. But for the sake of clarity and managing the topic, we're going to restrict our view to *intercorporate* B2B characteristics wherever we can without distorting the landscape or arriving at misleading conclusions.

WHAT ABOUT DOT.COMS?

The term *dot.com* has evolved into a creature of the media and investment communities. In most current usage, it describes a type of e-Business enterprise that is entrepreneurial, fast growth, innovative, high risk, and technocentric (and pages of additional adjectives.) Many, but by no means all, dot.coms occupy the B2C space. Most are pure Internet plays—for example, a dot.com e-tailer usually does not offer stores or telephone call centers. Increasingly, dot.coms as a class are taking it on the economic and public image chin. Unfortunately, many of the viable and valuable B2Cs are being unfairly herded in with the turkeys. The term dot.com itself provides little additional or distinctive value to our discussions on security and trust, except in the obvious case that go-go enterprises often put security on a back shelf as they dedicate themselves to quick entry and market share growth. Dot.coms, in the daily spotlight, may also have a disproportionate negative impact on public, regulatory, and legislative opinion about e-Business in general. We won't completely ignore the term, but you won't see it very often in this text.

SECURE E-BUSINESS

Like you, we believe that *secure* e-Business, NetExchanges, or NetMarkets are the only acceptable models. But that statement begs many questions. In this risk-oriented age of crashing day traders, thrill rides (on and off the stock market), high-flying ventures, and negative margin enterprises, how safe does safe really have to be? At what direct or indirect cost? Is too much safety also dangerous? In a volatile world of shifting demands and techno-churn, how long can you expect to stay safe without significant change and update? A wide range of variables, constraints, trade-offs, and risks must be taken into account in planning, developing, implementing, and managing secure e-Business and NetExchange/NetMarket environments. We'll discuss them in some detail in later chapters.

As far as security solutions go, let's dispose of the silver bullet theory immediately. There is no single process, design, or product that can, by itself, totally support the wide variety of e-Business security and controls requirements today or in the foreseeable future. You'll hear this statement again. There are good, recommended, composite solutions and suites available, but even they have not reached plug-and-play or one-stop status. They demand understanding and balanced implementation, and unfortunately, some assembly and concern for interoperability is still required.

Thanks for staying with us during the definition and scoping. There'll be a chapter later describing in some detail the major technologies of e-Business. Sorry, but this is a complex area with lots of similar sounding buzzwords. We'll try to keep things as clear and simple as possible.

3

The e-World: To B2B and Beyond

OK, get it out of your system, the universal pun: 2B or not 2B? That is the question. Feel better? In this chapter we're going to indulge in and reflect on some unabashed utopianism. We want you to see some of the prerequisites, constraints, and implications of the hyperconnected world that is postulated by Internet enthusiasts for the future. We are not naysayers. We actually believe you can get there from here. Just pack enough underwear. It's a longer trip than you may have been led to believe.

One of the most important principles to remember when you analyze the social, artistic, and commercial potential for new technologies (and their corresponding trust characteristics) is that the earliest applications are almost always extensions and variations on the current and familiar world (think of *horseless* carriage, *central* heating, *indoor* plumbing, *talking* pictures).

First-generation television was *illustrated* radio with pictures as a supplement. Radio professionals dominated. They produced talking heads in static situations. Then, as the medium was populated with people from other backgrounds—theater, motion pictures, sports—and the technology of the medium improved—greater portability, sensitivity, resolution, color, high-speed transmission—television developed characteristics that are uniquely its own. (Radio also changed to the portable, on-the-move-talk-tunes-news environment we now "enjoy.")

Today we see war and death as it is happening. Global sports events reach audiences in the billions. Japanese cooking contests fascinate

American viewers. People vie for millions of dollars by getting married or trying to survive or keep their relationships intact on a desert island in front of worldwide audiences. Motion pictures like *The Truman Show* suggest that unwitting players can be tracked from cradle to grave by an increasingly invasive TV medium and audience. Computer-generated graphics create animals talking in lip-synch, celebrities resuscitated from the dead, nonexistent buildings, vehicles, storms and backgrounds, and now video-generated game and TV personalities. (Want to join the Lara Croft fan club?) You can supply an immense number of additional examples.

The point is that no one could predict in the 1950s how video (not just television) would evolve by the start of the 21st century. Even more important, we don't know now how video technology will improve, morph, and converge by the end of this century.

NOW HOW ABOUT THE INTERNET? IS THE WEB JUST A PRELIMINARY STEP?

We ain't seen nothin' yet. As data transmission becomes more ubiquitous, wider band, cheaper, portable, faster, clearer, and with fewer outages, and computer/storage/data entry/display technologies still obey Moore's law, doubling in capacity and speed every 12 to 18 months, the possibilities go off the scale. But the Internet as we currently know it will not always be the only game in town.

We already have Internet 2, a separate heavy-duty, high-speed, ultra-bandwidth environment being sponsored, developed, and managed by a consortium of universities and research groups. Internet 2 is a reaction to the congestion, attacks, breakdowns, and the lower level of service and accessibility on the primary Internet. In a very real sense, Internet 2 is a special form of high-performance *Intranet*. If there is already an Internet 2, can 3, 4, or 5 be far behind—developed by interest groups whose capacity, quality, stability, and security requirements exceed what's publicly available?

Consider, as we talk further about NetMarkets and NetExchanges, whether these facilities will develop and flourish on the baseline Internet or become totally separate network domains restricted to specific participants and activities with limited, if any, external interfaces. In other words, the current single, homogenizing Internet environment will begin to fragment. This has interesting trust consequences. In some cases, the best thing to do to maintain high levels of trust may simply be to pick up your bat and ball and go play somewhere else. Is this a step backward? Not necessarily. Not all Internet technology-based environments need or want ubiquitous public access. As we've said, one size will not continue to fit all, and one pattern and color will not please all.

Today, the question is whether the Web players—institutions, businesses, governments, and individuals—will have the vision, ethical concerns, willingness to change, and the ability to distinguish between fads and progress to optimize newer technology's potential to enhance trust.

Let's apply the generational yardstick to the Internet. We are definitely in the first generation of Internet usage—possibly even pre-first. *Today, first-generation players are using the Internet as a channel to sell their current information, products, and services to consumers at the lowest possible price* (sometimes zero, and these dot.coms are often dying in the process).

In B2C today, the seller's view dominates. But that seller may not be the most intelligent player. Dot.coms rise and fall. (There may be more pet supply sites than there are pets.) Focused sites proliferate and coexist alongside and within generic portals. Results are often mediocre. Many sites are navigational nightmares, overloaded with animated ads that distract and annoy and without adequate infrastructure to support the sales and fulfillment process. More money and effort is spent on advertising than on designing, building, and managing the site and its offerings. Auctions, price surfing, price bots, and price wars at microsecond speed commoditize goods and services and decimate profits, if any. User trust is at best lukewarm.

WOE IS US?

Does all of this mean the Web is a disaster area destined for self-destruction? No, it means we're still in the first generation, still groping for what works and what doesn't—adjusting, adapting, creating, destroying, overkilling, and overreacting in the process. But we are moving forward.

In the "second" generation, we believe consumers and businesses will use the Internet as a personal or group resource that delivers a real-life virtual experience by blending the world's diverse resources into personal or group solutions to achieve personal or group goals. Historians will, no doubt, look back and define a third, fourth, and nth generation but in a real sense, we are in a perpetual state of Generation 1.x. The transitioning hybrid is our steady state. The pure second or third generation will be apparent only in retrospect.

ALL IS TRANSITION, AND THE HYBRID IS KING

There's an important social, business, and technological design point here. Jumping directly, uncompromisingly, and exclusively to "next generation" design objectives works only in "from scratch" and isolated environments. Of these, there are few indeed. For compatibility, cost control, and transitional ease, the "to-be" design must always accommodate the "currently as-is." Transition is invariably a hybrid and compromise affair. So while we can be wilder in our speculations, let's be a bit more modest in our expectations.

EVOLVING B2B AND B2C

Actually, as we evolve toward the second generation and beyond, the artificial barriers between B2C and B2B will become porous and in many cases will disappear. These two classifications are handy for maintaining some referential sanity, but don't be pedantic about them. They don't stand up to much pressure or scrutiny. Plus, in either environment, the dominance of the supplier or the buyer will reach a teetering equilibrium because an increasing population of Internet players will carry both roles, switching back and forth as personal, business, or institutional needs require. The NetExchanges and NetMarkets we will be examining shortly are only the first steps toward this next generation. We will never completely reach the second generation as we're currently describing it, though. Too many unpredicted variables will intervene. Our point is not to produce a predictive timetable as much as to illustrate probable trends and their impact on security, control, and trust.

Even though financial services, manufacturing, communications, and healthcare may be the industries that dominate the infant NetExchange/NetMarket universe, let's take our first illustration from the travel environment because most people (and all consultants) are familiar with it. We realize that parts of the examples that follow are from B2C as well as B2B situations. However, the following detailed illustrations are designed to get you thinking along NetExchange/NetMarket lines, not analyzing specific service environments. That comes in Part II. We've deliberately overdone the particulars here to make a point. In B2B, success is in the details.

You will probably recognize the following scenarios all too well.

THE TRAVEL-SUPPORTED EXPERIENCE

Very few of us travel for its own sake. That is, we travel to get somewhere, see someone or something, experience something or someplace, do something, reach some agreement, and so on. With the exception, perhaps, of cruise ships, touring, or long-distance running, the trip is seldom an end in itself. Flying on a new type of aircraft for its own sake will interest me—once. I'm writing this paragraph in an airport, and as an experience in itself, I don't care if I ever see one again. Nevertheless, in today's parlance, we frequently speak of traveling as if it were an end, not a means. I have sometimes felt that business meetings are just annoyances that get squeezed between my last and next flight. Many of our meetings start with the question, "What time is your plane?"

So, if it's only a means to an end, why does it dominate our landscape? Primarily because it's complicated, difficult, unpredictable, costly, and frustrating. And the interesting part is that actual movement from place to place occupies only a small part of the travel picture. Arrangements, visas, reservations, confirmations, resolving conflicts, altering itineraries, reacting to cancellations, tracking luggage, keeping score of frequent flier and other affinity awards, communications—that's the bulk of the travel experience today.

In this first generation, the Internet is a tool for carrying out some of those individual processes with some questionable "enhancements." It's an alternate mode of communication and transaction, but it has not yet reached the point where it is more than a very basic first step toward a widely preferred, integrated, value-added environment.

Why do airlines and other services offer discounts for booking on the Internet? Because the average user has yet to see sufficient value. Even though I am a Web enthusiast, I still prefer to interact with a live travel specialist because we can rapidly and mutually examine alternatives. Today's Web sites are still too passive and are constructed to present information, not manage an experience or a relationship. They'll grow up.

As we move toward the second generation, the concept of travel will be displaced by the travel-assisted experience. In other words, travel—instead of being a dominant and worrisome process—will become what it should be: a supporting activity to achieve more important purposes—visiting family, meeting clients, seeing places, attending events.

THE ONE-STOP, CONTINUOUS SUPPORT, FLAWLESS, NO-SWEAT TRAVEL-ASSISTED EXPERIENCE

I'll start taking the concept of Internet-based, travel-assisted experience seriously when I can continuously and interactively combine my calendar activities (meet with Client X or visit the Hong Kong office) with instant travel alternatives, including lodging, air, and ground transport, even eating and after-hours entertainment. I want composite cost comparisons to see if the trip is worth it. Maybe a video conference or on-line Web meeting makes more sense. What can I combine to optimize time, minimize cost, and enhance the associated experience, like having one more day with the family?

If a rental car makes sense at all, then I want the system to acknowledge my preferences for a mid-size car (not an SUV) and provide preprogrammed GPS facilities for all the terrain I will cover. Best-price flights are a foregone conclusion, but I want refund capabilities because business appointments change. No red-eye flights, if possible. Upgrades are to be sought vigorously. I want the system to intuitively and automatically assume that as a nonsmoker, I want a nonsmoking room, nonsmoking restaurant seats, and, on international flights, a nonsmoking airline. In a hotel I want a king-size bed and a computer-friendly desk and phone system.

I want the system to make judgments on choosing alternative airports or hotel locations within the same city based on the address, name, or stored business card of the individual I'm going to see and also based on airport and airline delay statistics. (In New York, should we use LaGuardia, JFK, Newark, or Westchester?)

I want to combine and check all these arrangements with those of my participating colleagues, and when we're mutually satisfied, I want to lock in the whole thing with a single credit transaction and a single "travel-experience identifier" instead of twenty confirmation numbers, tickets, and boarding passes. I want to be able to change routes, timing, and facilities, and to have the system search and update all affected processes.

For noncredit transactions, I want electronic money deposited in a smart card wallet in whatever foreign currencies, amounts, and denominations I will need based on the parameters of the trip. It must, of course, enable the production of hard currency as needed, through ATMs or similar devices.

I want the experience to be as automatic and in-the-background as possible, but I want to be able to intervene easily if I have to. (Do not book me on Kamikaze Airlines or in Hovel Hotels based on prior experiences. I do want to make a side trip to catch the annual Running of the Reindeer in Talinn, Estonia.) I want the system to learn from prior performance and optimize on the basis of my and its own evaluations.

Needless to say, I want to participate in this experience from a hand-held (implanted?), wireless, voice-activated, and voice-recognition-capable personal digital assistant that doubles as a phone, personal and business organizer, book, entertainment, and business tool. *And here's the kicker. I want to be able to trust the system implicitly.*

(Is the above scenario B2C or B2B? Actually both. Do we care? They're convenient current descriptors and categories that we will continue to use throughout this text, but don't expect reality, especially future reality, to be too scrupulous about preserving the boundaries.)

Yes, I know I want a lot, but I am presenting a tangible and—believe it or not, probably conservative—example of the consumer-driven second-generation Web-based travel system. The reason for presenting this scenario in what you might currently consider to be overkill mode is to drive home the business relationship issue. Business relationships, not technology, will determine whether this can indeed happen. Interestingly enough, there are few, if any, technological show stoppers or not-yet-inventeds in the mix. Certainly, this scenario has a rapacious hunger for bandwidth and network efficiency, storage, and processing power, and it presents a massive software development requirement. It could be an operational nightmare. User-friendly design must dominate. Safety, quality, and trust are critical. But in the last analysis, how well we change the business landscape will be the final determinant.

USERS MUST ADAPT, BUT HOW ABOUT THE SUPPLIERS?

As we noted, a large population of users/consumers have some serious adjusting to do as we move toward the next generations. (How well do you currently handle a cell phone or PDA?) The user will often be the initial gating factor in the move to interactive transactions. However, a much more difficult issue is the dramatic institutional and business transformation that must take place to realize the requirements outlined above. As a background for our upcoming consideration of Net-Exchanges and NetMarkets, let's explore the business and institutional side of our second generation travel experience. I hasten to point out that NetMarkets as currently implemented do not come close to meeting all our second-generation objectives stated above. But if you look hard enough, you can see many of them on the horizon.

The travel support system will be rather complex and will require the invention of new entities or at least, providing new capabilities to existing entities to intermediate the process. Exactly how they will actually evolve is anyone's guess since there are so many possible commercial and institutional combinations. Concerns about mergers, service domination, monopolies, and national and international restrictions can seriously affect how this environment will emerge. Can anyone make a profit in this structure? Is it worth the effort? We don't know yet, but even with the backslide of many B2C ventures, B2B and the Net-Market structure are still being actively pursued. So let's concentrate on functions to be performed with the assumption that some may never make it as pure play suppliers and any number of enterprise and organizational options are possible.

THE TRAVEL-ASSISTED EXPERIENCE NETEXCHANGE AND NETMARKET

We've seen what the buyer (or at least one buyer) wants. How will those services be offered and supplied? Again, we will not try to clearly define future business entities. What is Amazon.com, eBay, or Priceline.com today? What will they be tomorrow? Will they exist at all? Their volatility is one of their major characteristics. We can, however, predict some of the major business process and technological functions that will be required to fulfill the buyer's requirements for the travel-assisted experience.

The desired services outlined in the travel-assisted experience above go well beyond the traditional carrier/agent functions we know today.

To begin with, we need a sophisticated and constantly active parsing function that breaks down, organizes, and tracks the components of the experience the user wishes to have. That function can be on an ASP or a Web portal and must have high levels of business and technological interoperability with all of the processing constituencies that will be involved. Most likely, the parsing that is visible to the consumer will initially be carried out through the consumers' "wireless PDA plus" or wireless laptop, a family server, and the portal or ASP function. The family server may be replaced by a family Web site. However, the marketing, information service, and transaction fulfillment structures are far more complex. This is not your simple (sometimes) "booking a round trip between Cincinnati and Chicago."

The following example may seem trivial, but it drives mega-billions of dollars a year in trade, commerce, and economic growth. It is that family trip that always sounded like a good idea until it came time to actually do it.

AN EXAMPLE FROM ALL-TOO-REAL LIFE

Let's go to Grandma's for her 70th birthday.

- Who's going? Dad, Mom, Sarah (13), Junior (8), Baby (6 Mos.)
- Who's not going? The dog
- Where's the start point? Home (Atlanta), except for Sarah, who will be in Indianapolis at an Indoor Soccer Tournament and will join the family en route
- Where is Grandma's? 60 miles west of St. Paul, Minnesota

- When is her birthday? February 8th (cold, snowy, and generally yucky)
- What are we bringing? Dad and Mom's luggage; Sarah's luggage and soccer equipment; Junior's luggage and toys; Baby's car seat, stroller, and an infinite amount of infant paraphernalia. Presents for Grandma, Grandpa, and Aunt Clara, who's very sensitive about being left out. Mom's diet food. Formal attire for the black-tie birthday party. Reading material, computer games, and a ton of snacks.
- What are we bringing back? All of the above except the presents plus the results of one day's shopping at The Mall of America and replenished snacks.

OK, that's enough. The Trip from Hell? That's up to our system to determine.

The above information is entered by Mom and maintained on the "always-on" family server or Web site through a series of menus. Dynamic update takes place between the server/site and Mom's, Dad's, and Sarah's "always-on" PDAs. The family server/site, in turn, resolves or at least identifies intrafamily gaps and conflicts (that soccer tournament). When it has things sufficiently organized it begins to communicate with the Internet-based "travel experience" portal. The portal goes into action communicating with the family's server/site and the potential seller exchanges and NetMarkets, as well as other information services.

Step one is to clearly define the experience required and to create a minimized and prioritized set of options on which the family can decide. This can be done using a variety of parameters—least cost, least time, best experience, least risk, and so on.

As we explore this experience, give primary consideration to the processes being performed and the interoperation required on the buy side, sell side, inside-common, and infrastructure.

First, the "experience" is analyzed and deconstructed into components that will be assembled into prioritized scenarios. This process will take place between the portal, the family server/Web site, and the personal PDAs.

Baseline costs and functions (things that change little or not at all from option to option):

- Gifts—Refer to Grandma's preestablished gift preference profile within cost parameters. This could be on the family server or registered at an Internet site. Decide with each travel option selected whether to send gifts directly to Grandma's, send them to the family's home for them to bring, or have the gifts travel separately to a pickup point near their final destination.

- Dog kennel—Services, availability, costs, the dog's needs and sensitivities. The time/cost spent in the kennel will vary somewhat with each possible solution. Is getting the neighbor's daughter to dog-sit a better alternative?
- Mom's diet food supply—type, amount, send ahead?
- Mom's new formal dress—Show available shops and current prices, including any markdown sales. But since a fitting will no doubt be required, she will probably not buy direct from Web.
- Dad's tux rental—will order direct from Web.

Other pertinent parameters

- Dad's available vacation time—look up Dad's calendar for vacation balance.
- Time constraints—Mom must be back by the 12th for the plumbers. Dad must be in New York on the 13th.
- Permissible out of school time for Sarah and Junior—2 days
- Preferable out of school time for Sarah and Junior—0 days
- Other decision factors—Baby gets carsick (call pediatrician) but if, on the other hand, a car is available en route and at Grandma's, then side trips, luggage handling, and shopping is facilitated. Sorry, Baby! Even more sorry, Mommy!

Transportation and lodging options:

- *Option 1* Drive family car
  - Route—Atlanta to St. Paul, with side trip for Sarah in Indianapolis
  - Basic transit cost—Current gas prices × mileage + depreciation and oh, yes, snow tires.
  - Intermediate lodging and food—Yes. Cost??
  - Time—Two days each way plus stay over in St. Paul.
- *Solution 1*
  Calculate route and any construction delays, bad weather probability, time, cost, and comfort factors. Download GPS

maps. Note cell phone dead spots. Calculate fastest and most economical routes. Identify stopover hotels or other options. Calculate best start and stop times. Hold results for comparison with other options.

- *Information suppliers and processors for solution 1:*
  - AAA—Route and conditions
  - Cell phone supplier—Area coverage and dead spots
  - National Weather Service—Projected conditions through period (These first three will probably be a single, related service.)
  - Lodging NetExchange—En route lodging availability and cost
  - Automotive supplies NetExchange—Snow-tire availability and costs
  - Fuel cost bulletin board
  - Soccer tournament schedules
  - Airlines (for time and cost comparison)
  - Kennels of America reservation system
  - Pediatrician, directly or through managed care service
  - International gift exchange
  - Credit, banks, and settlement institutions
  - Fulfillment and delivery services
  - Atlanta School System—Exam and homework assignments
  - Plumber exchange confirmation system
  - (You can name at least five more. Go ahead and try.)
    By the way, will the end user be conscious of the different entities involved? Only where decisions and transactions surface. Lots of paddling will be going on beneath the serene surface.

Solution 1A

Same as 1 but substitute car or van rental for family car. What changes occur on the supplier side?

Solution 2

Fly entire family. Try listing the suppliers and processes. Don't forget airport parking costs. Don't forget Sarah in Indianapolis.

Solution 3

Fly-Drive. Calculate best combinations.

Solution 4

Stay home and establish interactive streaming video hookup of entire family singing Happy Birthday as precisely timed gifts arrive from FedEx or UPS. (Aunt Clara is not happy but secretly, Grandma is relieved.) Store, edit, package, and then transmit copy of video to all concerned via the Special Days Captured Forever NetExchange.

- *Choose solution:*
  Based on optimization of priority factors (cost, time, safety, convenience, Aunt Clara)
- *Activate chosen solution:*
  - Validate choice.
  - Trigger travel experience identity code and open files in all servers and PDAs.
  - Generate security authentication processes for all players.
  - Initiate reservations and resolve conflicts. Measure against optimum cost, time, and convenience parameters.
  - Update PDAs appropriately. Sarah just gets times and places. Mom and Dad also get costs and supplier IDs.
  - Initiate required purchases of goods and services (e.g., gifts, clothing, and snow tires, if option 1 is chosen).
  - Initiate and complete credit or debit charges in optimum sequence and at optimum points of time:
    - 21 days for best air prices
    - Car rental according to best contract
    - Gifts and other purchases according to family payment strategy
    - Kennel and hotels as necessary to lock in reservations
    - Suppliers, agency functions, credit card system, transfer transactions, and data to support process.
  - Create master active file encrypted under travel experience ID on family server and at portal, and scan at prescribed intervals for any changes entered by buyers or suppliers.
  - Recalculate and reconstruct the components of the travel experience as necessary.
  - Continue to monitor through the "experience" period. Save results for future reference, performance evaluation, and optimization.
  - Initiate credit card payments and reconcile.

- Process gift return from Aunt Clara.
  At each site, NetExchange, or composite NetMarket, similar
  supplier-side transaction history is being recorded for fulfillment
  tracking; payment debit/credit processing; return or refund
  process, if necessary; affinity credits (Frequent Flyer Miles, store
  and hotel credit points); future marketing and statistical analysis,
  regulatory oversight, future contract negotiations between
  suppliers, tax payments, and so on.

ENOUGH, ALREADY!

If your eyes didn't glaze over somewhere in the middle of this exercise,
you now have some idea of the complexities associated with the second
generation. Most of these services already exist. It's the dynamic, managed, and controlled interaction that will make the difference. New entities and new business rules must be developed. The technologies exist but
are not yet deployed in robust, economic, or sufficiently capacious form to
support what we described. A mountain of *interoperable* application and
infrastructure software must be developed, deployed, maintained, and
updated. There is a process-oriented skills base and management group
that must further emerge. And. . .we have to get the trust approaches
agreed upon, designed, and implemented as the environment grows.

Is this example unique or overblown? We don't think so. Some of
the manufacturing, financial services, healthcare, and distribution scenarios that fill the literature are every bit as rich and complex. Later
we'll discuss a healthcare scenario. Once again, we believe these cases
can happen but they will be progressively managed into existence, just
as talking pictures have become digital streaming video over time.

A SIDE COMMENT ON DIS/TRANSINTERMEDIATION

In our travel example, it's tough to tell who or what has been transin-
termediated because we tried to keep specific company identity to a
minimum (fulfillment groups, settlement agencies, credit functions).
But who has been disintermediated? Oddly enough, in a real sense, it is
the end users. They are disintermediated from all of the "schlepping,"
waiting on hold, searching, tracking, and frustration. If our example or
some reasonable subset really works, the users' experiences are truly
enhanced and their intervention is reduced dramatically. If it doesn't
deliver as promised, watch out. The result may be aggravated chaos,
with partially empowered automated systems unable to deal with

unusual circumstances. Anyone who has tried to reschedule a cancelled flight when all they have is an e-ticket knows what I mean.

A LITTLE COLD WATER ON OUR OVERHEATED UTOPIA, PLEASE

Can this type of hyperconnected, real-time drama really happen? Well, a lot of intelligent, practical people and enterprises are spending good money, time, and effort to move toward these kinds of environments. Do we really want them? What are the downsides? Do I hear privacy concerns? Do I hear audit trail and reconciliation problems? Legal liability issues? Tax venue questions? (The Internet will not be tax-free forever.) Reliability and service level demands? Competitive and monopoly concerns? Labor problems? Technological interoperability issues? Local, national, and international jurisdictional issues? Can the players involved make a profit in this environment?

Are these issues insurmountable? Is this type of exchange/market going to be the electronic Tower of Babel? Should you start hiding gold and jewelry under the mattress in preparation for the e-Depression?

We don't think so. After all, we are steely eyed, hard-headed, battle-scarred veterans who still believe in the e-future. But do not underestimate the power of these and similar issues to slow, limit, distort, suboptimize, and otherwise alter, redirect, reprioritize, or stop parts of our utopian vision. ("When are you going to stop with the lists?" Well, there are twelve conditions that must first be met. Kidding.)

Some processes, especially in the economic and social realms, can be glacial. For example, as we will illustrate further in Chapter 12, we are still battling many of the same basic privacy issues 20 years later in the age of the connected PC. Warning: technology is seldom the primary gating factor. Technology can enable, but it can seldom create success on its own. Be prepared to actively and continuously deal with the soft sides of e-business as well. In your planning and implementation, do not separate the "soft" social, political, cultural, and business issues from the "hard" technological and operations functions. They are interdependent.

So much for Generation 2. Back to the present and immediate future. Throughout the rest of this book, we'll try to keep a tighter rein on reality. But, for now. . . . .

4

The Fable (Part 1)

No self-respecting, 21st-century business book can show its cover in public unless it contains a fable or illustrative tale. Ours follows. There are no mice or cheese. Like most fables, it is deeply rooted in reality.

Once upon a time, not too very long ago, in a land not too far away, there lived a very powerful queen who ruled over Mystical Queendom with great foresight and wisdom—well, sometimes. Her name was Queen Tessence III or "Good Queen Tess" as she was known to her friends, if she had any. She had the usual royal family and retinue:

- Binky, her prince consort
- Nit, her son, the crown prince
- Max, her archwizard
- Minnie, her court witch
- Smedley, her lord high chancellor

There were also assorted princesses and princelings, lords, ladies, retainers, an Army and Navy, a modest Air Force, Royal Explorers, traveling minstrels, and an executioner.

At the beginning of this tale, Smedley was also the royal data center manager. You see, the queen loved technology and was into computers BIGTIME. Unfortunately, in the beginning, the machines her wizard Max designed and built were big in size, big in cost, big in power consumption, but very small in usefulness. Indeed, it was hard work for them to even open and close the royal drawbridge. But the queen valued her computers

Exhibit 4.1   e-Business, Phase 1

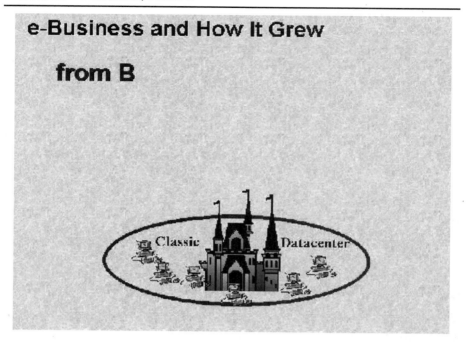

highly and kept them in a very secure dungeon with guards and thick walls, surrounded by a very deep moat (Exhibit 4.1). There were very nasty creatures in the moat, but that's another story.

*   *   *

(The Guild Bylaws of the Writers of Network Computing Studies insists that any author who employs the fable as an illustrative device must clearly and frequently explain its meaning. This does not imply, gentle reader, that you are a dullard, incapable of grasping the delicious allusions, incisive irony, or delicate nuance of the tale. It does mean that you are probably multitasking as you read this and are easily distracted, or are sitting in an airport bombarded by new announcements of delays and cancellations, as well the suffocating din of neighboring cell-phone conversations. We shall make our running commentaries brief.)

It was in the earliest mainframe years, the 1950s and 1960s (Believe me. I was there.), when the time honored moat mentality first took hold. As we indicated earlier, computers didn't do all that much, but they sure did cost a lot. Protective physical cordons for the devices and, incidentally, their contents became the custom, and they have followed us to this day although the cordons are now more virtual (like firewalls) than physical. There's nothing wrong with cordons. They're just not sufficient or totally suitable for some networks. Our fable continues.

*   *   *

Time went by and her majesty, Max, Smedley, and her computers all got a lot smarter. The queen began to realize that they could be used to help run Mystical Queendom—collecting taxes, counting the royal treasure, paying the Army and Navy, updating the heraldry and family tree, and other dull stuff like that. Speaking of dull, Prince Consort Binky spent most of his time in the royal wine cellars. The queen despaired of his ever being useful.

Then Max came up with a splendid idea. "Majesty," he intoned, "would it not be a grand and wondrous thing to build a second data center at the other end of your vast Mystical Queendom? You would have much closer control of those rebellious peasants, an awesome edifice to impress your neighbors and . . . you could send the prince consort to run it."

The queen saw the value immediately and told Max and Smedley to make it so. "But, madam," Smedley, ever the cautionary, expostulated, "Think of the risks. Sending Prince Consort Binky, who, begging your pardon, is not the brightest candle on the Christmas tree, off to manage a data center at the remote and barely civilized other end of the Queendom could be dangerous indeed. How will we manage and protect it . . . and him, of course?"

"Oh, Smedley," riposted the queen, "Sometimes I wonder about you. We will erect another huge dungeon and moat just like this one; we'll make copies of all the computers and programming stuff; we'll send out all of my least favorite courtiers to staff it, and then . . . we'll connect the place to an armor-covered leased data line (invented and managed by the Royal Semaphore Corps) and control it from here (Exhibit 4.2). Do you honestly think I'd let Binky run anything complicated?"

And so it was done. In honor of his forthcoming great adventure, the queen asked the prince consort to name this great achievement. He called it multisite computing. We told you he was dull.

*   *   *

Hi again, this time a little demythologizing about leased lines and remote computing! Although there are actual living examples of the queen's "armor-plated," physically isolated leased lines, primarily for military and intelligence use, the average leased line is neither armored nor physically isolated. Webopedia.com defines a leased line as: "A permanent telephone connection between two points set

Exhibit 4.2   e-Business, Phase 2

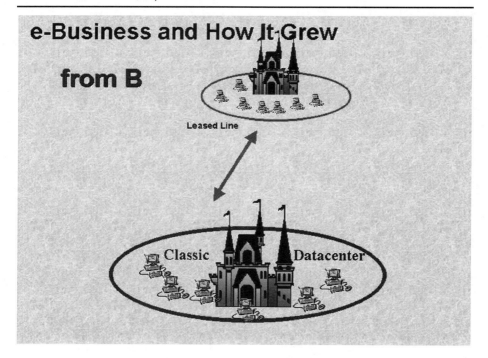

up by a telecommunications carrier. Typically . . . to connect geographically dis-
tant offices. Unlike normal dial-up connections, a leased line is always active."
The primary purpose for leased or "dedicated" lines is accessibility and performance, not security. Security, in the shape of partial isolation, is a side effect.

Today, a leased line may well be a set of multiplexed channels, part of a sub-
divided wide-band transmission system guaranteed by the carrier to be constantly
available to you and of a certain speed and capacity. Your traffic is logically but not
necessarily physically isolated unless you specify it as such . . . and pay extra for it.
There can be downsides to physical isolation, such as creating a single point of failure. If the physically dedicated line goes out, so do you. If a logically dedicated line
fails, the multiplexed channels are moved, if possible, to a still active line.

A word on remote or multisite computing. Today that nomenclature is almost meaningless in the sense that it no longer says anything definitive about
how processes are controlled. In the earlier days of remote computing, the remote site was under the direct, computer-based control and administration of
the master site. You cannot safely draw the same conclusion when and if the
term is used today. Ask for more detail. Back to our "Tale of Two Sites."

*   *   *

One day, Crown Prince Nit, now in his endearing twelfth year, raged at his mother, the queen, "Mo-o-om!! Smedley won't let me use the computers to catalog my polo ponies, or keep my collection of jousting cards, or play solitaire or anything. Make him do it!"

The queen, sensing yet another crisis du jour or in the prince's case, du millisecond, decided in her great wisdom to have Max create a small, separate, computer system especially for Nit.

The crown prince had other ideas. "Mo-o-om! I don't want any of Max's dumb mainframe stuff. I want my personal witch, Minnie, to build me a whole new bunch of her special super dooper, teeny weeny, magic machines and put them all over the castle so I can play with them whenever and wherever I want."

The queen gave in and, to both Max's and Smedley's consternation, commissioned Minnie to build this new collection of devices, which they called a LAN. Officially, LAN means local area network, but palace insiders knew it was named after the crown prince, the loathsome, arrogant nitwit. (Exhibit 4.3). Then she told Smedley to connect it to the Multi Computing Datacenter.

The Wizard Max went off to soothe his damaged ego, but Chancellor Smedley, who had now also been designated manager of information systems, protested. "Madam, you know full well that Minnie and Max have never done anything the same way. It's an affair of perverse honor between them never to agree. If we connect that Minnie monstrosity, it will be bedlam. The moats will be breached. We will lose control. The crown prince and his playmates will be all over both of the Datacenters. Binky, your prince consort out there in the hinterlands, will never know what hit him."

The queen considered the prospect and smiled (a frightening sight, indeed). "Smedley, must I do everything around here? Build a separate moat around the LAN (the Net, not the Nit) and put a gateway between it and the Datacenters."

And so it was done. Smedley added another title to his honorifics—Keeper of the Imperial Interface, right behind Lord Keeper of the Privy Princely Password and Woyal Worry Wart.

*   *   *

You no doubt immediately caught the subtle symbolism of the names, Max and Minnie. Here, gentle reader, is the beginning of the age of transitional hybrids. (Late 1970s and 1980s.) Yes, before this, there were different types of mainframes and different types of magnetic tapes and punched cards (round hole-rectangular hole. Let's not talk about chads.) However, those

Exhibit 4.3

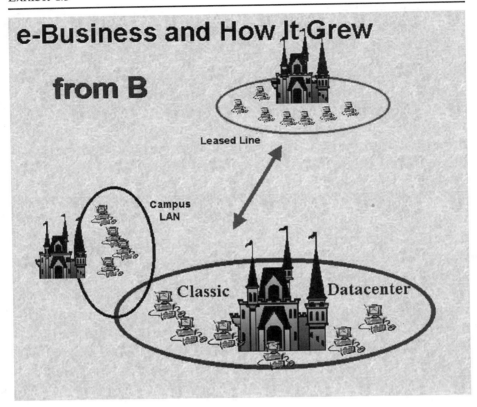

corporate systems were mostly standalone or from a single manufacturer's family.

But as the mini-computer (not the PC yet) came upon the scene, so too did new network and system architectures, (ethernet, token ring) and even different modes of computing and storage. Operational as well as technological incompatibility now reared its head in a serious way. The other important aspect of the local area network was distribution of function. Instead of a single mainframe being in charge of all activities, functions were now allocated to specific processors or servers—file servers, print servers, network management servers, application servers, security servers. This was not a headless democracy but a distributed oligarchy of cooperating (hopefully)

functions allowing smaller, cheaper, networked devices to more flexibly in-
terconnect as individual workstations or servers. This approach was not
without compatibility issues. Not every mini looked or talked alike—to each
other, much less to mainframes. Why didn't the industry standardize? Why
are there so many religions?

Actually, the potential chaos was taken in hand. The interface where two
or more systems came together became the point of technical, operational, and
standards concentration, and is very likely to remain so. The interface is where
data content translation, data format transformation, protocol mediation, and
many other layered functions are adjusted for communication and interopera-
tion between unlike systems and applications. Security and control functions
are no exception. They, too, must be mediated and translated—with possible
reduction of effectiveness. More on this, anon. Once again, it's showtime!
Bring on our players.

*   *   *

Time passed and a traveling roadshow of actors, musicians, troubadors, merchants, and magicians came to the palace—asking to entertain the court and maybe do a little business while they were there. The queen, bored out of her mind with all the spare time she now had as a result of her smoothly running, if rather expensive, MIS (Majestic Information System), issued a royal proclamation entitled, "Why Not!"

That evening, during the entertainments and revelries, a strange-looking merchant and magician with oddly focused eyes, frizzy hair and unkempt beard, wearing sandals and a long, frayed shirt with a strange cabalistic motto (TCP/IP for Me) asked to approach the queen. "Careful, madam," whispered Smedley. "He looks wild and danger-ous." The queen said, "Get a grip, Smed," and issued another royal proclamation: "Why Not II !"

The slovenly merchant and magician (M&M) approached with a brightly shining box in his trembling hands and said, "Oh, great queen, have I got a deal for you! How would you like to be hooked real time into everything that's happening in Mystical Queendom; have imme-diate answers to your most ticklish questions; buy all your crown jew-els wholesale; play war games and get daily updates from your colonies and military; in bazillion colors and super high resolution on this glit-tering screen—all for the price of a local call?"

The queen knew when she was being had and beckoned the royal executioner. "Bring your noose and your axe," she cooed. "No, No,

Majesty," said the M&M. "I mock thee not. Here, I'll write you a contract I wouldn't even give my own mother. A free, six-month trial at my own expense, subject to our usual terms and conditions."

"No," said the queen, "subject to *my* terms and conditions. If it works and I like it, I'll keep it and you keep your head. If not, we'll both suffer a small loss."

"Oh, naturally, Majesty," said the wild-eyed Tekkie (for he was a member of that shadowy and mysterious tribe that hovered on the fringes of known civilization). "I'm so glad you explained it."

"What is this magic called?" the queen queried.

"It is commonly known as the Internet, but we tribesmen call it the "Whirled, White Wedge" after our sacred Frisbee altar stone," he rejoined.

"Work on the name," said the queen "and have this net thing ready by sunup. And, oh yes, make one for Prince Consort Binky. Maybe it will keep him out of the wine cellars."

"Oh boy," said the Tekkie. "Oh brother," said Smedley.

And so it was done (Exhibit 4.4).

*   *   *

In order to ensure that you don't nod off before this bedtime story is complete, we've compressed several events: the arrival of the personal computer and its evolution from a standalone personal device to a connected workstation. We've also elided the development of the Internet and the World Wide Web.

As you know, the PC comes in two major flavors, IBM compatible (DOS/Windows) and MAC compatible. There are a few other forms of specialized exotica. However, most of the minis (Sun, Digital, HP, IBM) use operating systems from the Unix family. As you might suspect, there are many Unix dialects. Minis and PCs could communicate with each other across networks but not without some heavy interfacing. Security and control design in these different operating systems was, and still is . . . different. Different approaches and design, different technology and language.

We described the Internet and the Web in Chapter 2 and we revisit them several more times. Notice in our diagram, we show separate connection to the Internet from two separate locations. Could the primary and secondary centers talk through the leased line to each other's Internet links? Yes, but hang on a few minutes. The game is still afoot.

*   *   *

Exhibit 4.4

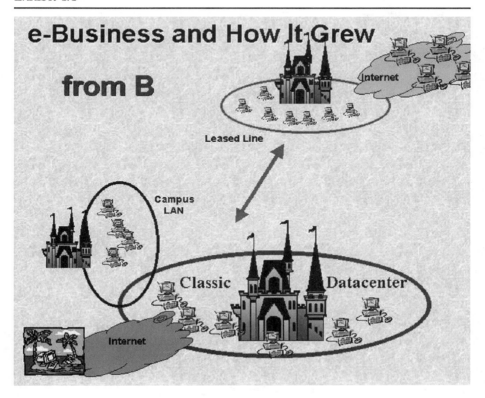

Well, gentle reader, as you can well imagine this was the beginning of a whole new era in the Mystical Queendom. The queen, after a couple of sovereign snits, got the hang (oops, sorry, M&M) of it, and soon the entire court was surfing and browsing and clicking and scrolling and jumping and hyperlinking day and night. "Whee," said the queen (using the Royal Whee, of course). "This is fun, Smedley, and you know what I like most about it?"

Expecting the worst, because that's what he usually got, Smedley bowed his head, raised his eyebrows in query, and waited. "It's dirt cheap," said her majestic self. "It's got some way to go yet in performance and it hangs up now and then, but I like it. I can talk to the colonies and the explorers and order up exotic stuff and keep the generals and admirals in line for next to nothing. Tell the Royal Semaphore Corps to close down the leased lines and use the Internet. And tell that Tekkie I want to buy a big piece of his company at a ridiculously low price."

Smedley was in high twitter as he cried, "Your majesty, think of the dangers. All of those hackers and ne'er do wells are salivating at the thought of getting into the royal databases. The Internet is public and very treacherous."

"So build me an "Intra" Net, reserved only for selected members of the court. I want a VPN—very private network. (Actually VPN means *virtual private network*. The queen wasn't very good at mnemonics.) Build firewalls. Use Crypto—whatever that is."

"But madam . . ."

"Who's queen?"

And so it was done (see Exhibit 4.5).

*   *   *

Exhibit 4.5

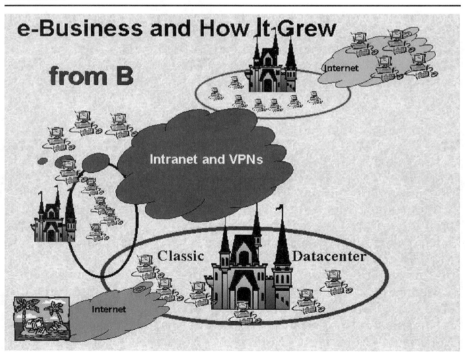

As we noted in Chapter 2, intranets use Internet protocols and services but employ firewalls and a system of passwords or other identifiers to restrict access and usage to a known and approved population. (We discuss firewalls and password technologies in Part III.) Why are we still showing the two external Internet connections as well? Because those connections are still there to allow access to the outside world. Does that mean that someone could traverse from the outside connection, through one of the datacenters and into the intranet? If the protective system isn't comprehensively coordinated and administered, yes!

A word about VPNs, although we also discuss them in Part III. Virtual private networks are the Internet equivalents of the leased line arrangement (with, as usual, some differences). They are set up by hardware/software combinations at each end (gateway) of the specific link to be protected and provide a transparent encrypted channel (tunnel) for transmitting and receiving data. The user, by calling up the intranet URL, gets the immediate benefit of the VPN. Depending on the logon process of the system being used, an additional password may or may not be necessary, but no further user action is required during the session. VPN protection does not extend past the gateways into the supporting systems and servers. It is called gateway-to-gateway. Protection from user workstation to user workstation requires additional support. This is called end-to-end protection. They are not the same. Now, the calm before the storm.

*   *   *

Believing that the queen had at last settled in after her orgies of technological and organizational shape shifting, Grand Chancellor Smedley, now also CIO of the realm, went to an ASP/CSP/ISP convention. Splurging on a spectacular spending spree and sportively splashing at his splendid spacious spa, he was speechless as the spokesman (enough with the SPs) from the court broke the news. The crown prince, his Nitwitship, had come of age. As was the custom, notices had been posted on all the matrimonial Web sites. A perfect princess had been found for the perfect prince.

Poor Smedley. The princess came from an old, distinguished, and very, very prosperous kingdom, and the two empires were to be joined, nay, homogenized. Yes, a royal merger was on—guaranteed dynamite. His worst nightmare had arrived wearing a wedding dress.

"Your majesty, I, of course, offer my sincere felicitations to you and the Nit, er prince, but I should like to draw your attention to some delicate differences that may make this merger messy. They do not speak our language, or we theirs. They use meters and we use feet. They use DC and we use AC. They're merchants and we're scientists. Our technology spans decades, they're newcomers. Their computers count by five and ours count by two. Our currency is decimal, theirs is chaos. "They say potayto and we say potahto, they say tomayto and we say tomahto, potayto, potahto, tomayto, tomahto, let's call the whole thing off."

The queen who, in her furs and gown of gold, was happily going over the overflowing inventory of the recently merged treasuries, shifted on her newly acquired throne of ivory and sapphires, sipped from her ruby-studded goblet of rare oriental wine, readjusted her 40-carat mother of the groom ring, smiled at Smedley, and asked, "And your point is?"

Thus, dear reader, the extranet (Exhibit 4.6) was born.

Exhibit 4.6

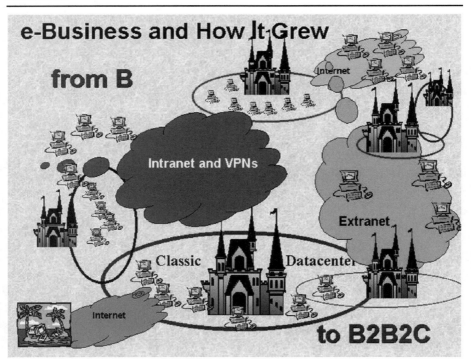

*   *   *

One last aside. I'm beginning to feel like that smirking paper clip or super-perky dog that keeps popping up in Windows applications. The extranet comes in different shapes, types, and sizes. It may be no more than a controlled opening in an intranet for individual user access or, and that's what we're illustrating here, it may be the coming together of two star systems on their way to becoming a galaxy. The point is that an extranet could, depending on design and control, provide access for all merged parties to all merged services and vice versa (including those hanging outside on Internet links). Is that what you want? If not, how do you want it configured from an optimized business process viewpoint? How sure are you about its current state?

So here it is. One form of the transitional hybrid. Addition, adaptation, some deletion. Nothing much has been tossed away since the beginning of our example, except perhaps the leased line. But by a series of connections and combinations, a complex environment of old and new, multitechnologies, multistandards, multiapplications, and mega-multiusers has emerged. Why was it created? How well was it planned? How well controlled? How will it be maintained and administered? If it's transitional, where is it going? If it's a hybrid, is some genetic adjustment needed? No two networks, enterprises, NetExchanges, or NetMarkets will answer the same way.

*   *   *

Our story doesn't end there. A commission was set up to name this new empire. Smedley suggested BigBang. "It has a powerful, creative sound." "How about To The Max," volunteered Max, modestly. The prince consort contributed White Lightning, no doubt bringing his vast experience and proclivities to bear. The crown prince, demonstrating once again the acuity for which he was famous, proclaimed, "We are combining a Queendom and a Kingdom—let's call it Dom-Dom." "Yes, you are, my liege," they all agreed. The new crown princess liked Planetary Bank (or any bank). Minnie said, "Let's call it Dizney!" The queen, as usual had the last word. "No, my dears, let's keep it very simple for the men in the family. We'll call it B2B2C. We all know what that means."

And they all lived happily ever after, or at least until the next chapter.

5

The Fable (Part 2) and Wrapping Up Part I

I hope you recognized, directly or through hearsay, people and situations in the fable in Chapter 4. But if there are any controls specialists, MBA candidates, experienced executives, professors, network aficionados, or consultants in the audience, you know the fable (case study) can't possibly end there. I mean, a two-realm extranet is hardly worth getting excited about. An extranet, by and of itself, is neither beneficial nor harmful. We need more information. It's time for the follow-on scenarios. They appear in no order of author preference, objective probability, or pedagogic value. Each is cunningly constructed, however, to illustrate some of the principles we will be examining throughout the rest of our excursion. I'm sure you will recognize most of them immediately. But pay attention; this counts toward the final exam.

FOLLOW-ON SCENARIO 1—OOPS!

No sooner did the dust settle around the Royal B2B2C extranet when a foreign venture capital group called Realms R Us (RRU) started to market the concepts of NetExchanges and NetMarkets planet-wide. Smedley, Max, and Minnie quit the Mystical Queendom to take a ground-floor equity stake in RRU and signed on to build, operate, and manage Trulydom.com, a NetMarket designed to allow all rulers to interactively negotiate and deal with each other on a global basis. As of this writing, they are on their fifth business plan and have had to withdraw

their IPO twice. However, in one broad stroke, the queen's source of technical and managerial expertise all but disappeared.

The newly expanded Queendom, as predicted by Smedley, started almost immediately to show signs of uncontrolled and uncoordinated expansion, internal conflict, and lack of consistent, hands-on management. To say nothing of controls! Realm performance measurement, such as it was, was on the verge of being handed back to the soothsayers. They seemed to be the only ones with the temerity to claim they understood what was going on. Realm burn rate (not to be confused with the number of subjects burned at the stake) seemed to be going out of sight, but no one was sure. Rumors of major layoffs rattled through the castle keep. This was not a community of trust.

On the technology front, things weren't much better. *Interface resolution* and *standards harmonization* became code words for massive mutual finger pointing. While it was difficult to prove, there were strong suspicions that certain persons both inside and outside the realm were taking advantage of the situation to exploit the gaps and mismatches for their own nefarious gain.

It didn't help that the crown princess's dowry had been seriously overstated (but then, so too had the crown prince's intelligence). There was serious talk by the two royal families of dissolving the union. This did not please the members of the nobility and merchant class, who had staked much of their resources and future prosperity on promises of great new opportunities. The taxpaying subjects were fearful. Needless to say, the queen was not happy and as they say, when the queen's not happy, ain't nobody happy.

(We could say something here about the queen bringing in a professional services firm to help sort things out and rebuild but that would be self-serving. So we won't.)

Optional Exercise

How could these problems have been detected, avoided, or mitigated before things went too far awry? Have you noticed that the queen, for all of her micromanagement tendencies, didn't seem to pay much attention to the potential downside of any of her initiatives? Besides Smedley, she didn't seem to have any knowledgeable staff members who were willing to push back. Where was the auditor general and the chancellor of the exchequer? Craft a doctoral thesis on what went wrong and how it could have been avoided. Fully document your conclusions with in-depth citations and forward to the publisher of this book. We'll take it from there.

SCENARIO 2—IN YOUR DREAMS

Scenario 2 was going to be "They Lived Happily Ever After in Perfect Harmony and Bliss." You know how likely that is. So let's move on to Scenario 3.

SCENARIO 3—REAL WORLD

At this point, your patience must be wearing thin with cutesy stuff, so let's abandon the fable. The third and final scenario is actually the real-world situation we're going to consider for the rest of this book. The extranet keeps on growing and changing and connecting and joining with some false moves, disappointments, mistakes, backtracking, recovery, and occasional hand wringing. But it continues, on balance, to flourish and provide significant value.

Extranets, NetMarkets, and NetExchanges can and will succeed and produce significant benefits. But they can't succeed without these features:

- A strong foundation of rational, specific, and attainable business and technical expectations with plenty of provision for downside events. Beware the Nirvana value proposition.
- Careful study and evaluation before establishing partnerships, alliances, service relationships, and dependencies. Once you're in, you may not be able to get out again without a lot of grief.
- A healthy skepticism about the potential market and a realistic view about potential competitors.
- A major, ongoing business and technical planning program that facilitates incremental deployment and is flexible enough to stand up to course corrections.
- A timeline that matches resources and costs.
- A conservative technology approach. State of the Art often isn't.
- Vendors, servicers, and consultants who clearly demonstrate skill, experience, flexibility, staying power, and a strong sense of cooperation and responsibility. No technology or concept fanatics, please.
- An adequate and stable financing plan with good contingency provisions.
- A strong risk-management mentality. Notice I did not say risk aversion. This stuff is risky, but if the business expectations are right, it should be worth taking.

- Honest and comprehensive performance measurement and evaluation laced with healthy skepticism.
- Strong, experienced management at all levels. Yes, I know this is new territory, and new technology and youth is important, but starting with a blank sheet of paper doesn't mean you start with blank expressions. Old dogs can also learn and manage these new tricks. Go for a mix.
- Conservative staffing, balanced with third-party outsourcing.
- Equal involvement by business, technical, and controls management in the planning, design, and evaluation of the program.
- Planning controls and security as you plan systems, applications, and procedures.

WRAPPING UP PART I

Before we change our orbital flight plan and head into the lower elevations of Part II, let's go back for one more high-level look at the evolving B2B information protection context—Exhibit 5.1.

The primary targets to be protected changed a long time ago from the centralized computer centers to widely distributed information and its associated processes. The multimillion-dollar mainframes are still a part of the information economy but generally we have instilled more value into the information than the silicon and wire that's processing it. Personal computers lose their value so rapidly that we sometimes hope someone will steal them because you can't give them away.

We all know this intuitively, and yet many corporate security strategies still have at their heart the concept of the moat—physical and virtual. Batten down the hatches and keep out all incoming traffic. The

Exhibit 5.1   Information Protection Is Changing Enormously

Then	Now
— Intra-enterprise	— Multienterprise extranets & beyond
— Perimeter control	— What perimeter?
— System centric	— Ubiquitous
— Siloed applications	— Distributed—third party
— One technology fits all	— Are you kidding?
— Proprietary technology	— Open, closed, and in between

firewall perpetuates this thinking with some carefully monitored passageways. The moat is still an important component in many environments, but that's all it is—a component. It may not even be a major form of protection; in a few cases, it may be a major inhibitor.

The trusted relationship is becoming the bedrock of e-Business, and that is a transitive environment. Mutual trust for mutual business activities. Multidirectional (and in some cases, multidimensional) controls are in the cards. They're not as exotic as they sound and we'll try to give you greater insight in Parts II and III.

So, in our orbital excursion around the unfolding and rapidly rotating world of B2B and beyond, we hope we've given you enough appreciation for its structural, business, technical, and trust characteristics to feel comfortable coming in for a closer look. Perhaps what is most striking is that it's a maddening combination of the familiar and the strange—simultaneous déjà vu and where am I? I'm sure you're sick of the word *hybrid* by now, and we'll try to restrain its use through the rest of the text, but it does apply. Some synonyms for hybrid are cross, mixture, amalgam, fusion, and crossbreed.

WHAT'S NEXT? ON TO PART II

In Part II, we'll begin by parsing e-Trust in more detail. We'll take a closer look at B2B processes (the "sides") in industry contexts. We'll examine the security and trust requirements of each side, and we'll also look at the special needs of the major industry groups. We'll talk about the trust responsibilities of the Ps—ASPs, CSPs, and the rest. We'll look at the regulatory landscape. It's not very pretty.

PART

II

A Closer View

6

More on e-Trust

We have spent the last few chapters establishing the general B2B context. In Part II, we will move on to a closer examination of e-Trust characteristics, the e-Trust nature of the B2B "sides," and the needs of specific industries. We'll finish with a review of regulations as a point of transition into Part III, "Making It Happen," the e-Trust process, tools, and techniques.

But first, we should take a few moments to answer in a little more detail the question, "What is e-Trust?" You may recall in the Introduction that we described trust as an ongoing transaction that establishes and maintains confidence between or among entities.

You may also remember we said we were seeking "the development of mutual trust in complex electronic environments, based on each player's willingness and ability to continuously demonstrate to all the other players' satisfaction that the game is honest, open, following the rules, and properly controlled."

THE "E" MAKES A DIFFERENCE

Dr. Sherry Turkle, Professor of the Sociology of Science at MIT, has done some fascinating and extremely valuable work in exploring the changing relationships between people and computers, automated toys, and other forms of "opaque technologies." Although these technologies can appear to demonstrate some small level of personality, she explores how in order to enhance, manage, and increase our comfort with the relationship, we supplement that perception of personality and, in some cases, alter our perception of ourselves. She describes such relationships with these devices as being "taken at interface value."

With her permission, I've adapted several of her concepts to the e-Business environment. Why, in spite of immense investments, has the conduct of business on the Internet (B2B and B2C) not yet reached its anticipated levels? One reason may be that the human participants haven't yet adapted their own expectations and behavior to the environment. And the environment isn't helping enough. For example, what does *user friendly* really mean in a B2C situation, and how do I recognize it when I see it? Does it simply mean stop poking ads in my eye as I browse; help me navigate flexibly; respond to my last click with some meaningful suggestions? Or is there more?

We usually can handle a face-to-face and live telephone relationship. Mail has been with us for centuries, and e-mail is, in one sense, just a more rapid variant. Online chat bears more relation to a telephone conference than to an e-Business transaction. But browsing a website and conducting business through that site is still an uncomfortable hodgepodge of semi-familiar functions, expectations, and perceptions. Where we expect instant confirmation to an order, we often get a separate e-mail. If we reach an impasse, we must resort to the phone, seeking direct human contact. Oddly, the telephone itself with the addition of automated responses is becoming more opaque, especially where there is no human-contact option. "Dial 8 to have yourself ignored and totally disconnected."

Not to belabor the point, but as business takes more advantage of automatic and usually more opaque technologies, it cannot simply assume that the individual or process on the other end will properly adapt. Nor can it be certain what their perceptions and expectations are to begin with. For example, will the carefully prepared list of suggested services constructed by a Customer Relationship Management system hit the mark or repel the recipient as an arrogant and incorrect intrusion?

"Yes, but business has always been like that." True, but in the case of e-Business, the e-mode itself—with its opaque interface, speed, quirks, resistance to variations, and intolerance of errors—may be an even more powerful contributor to failure or success. Your transaction-based websites are a strong projection of your corporate image, in many cases far stronger than your advertising. In this environment, establishing trustworthiness is critical. Your success depends on earning and keeping the trust of not only your customers and clients, but also your partners, stakeholders, and other concerned parties. Let's focus in on the B2B aspects.

SO, WHAT MAKES e-TRUST *e-TRUST?*

Several characteristics *must* be evident if a B2B environment is to be considered trustworthy. They may not necessarily appear or dominate in non-B2B situations. They are different from most traditional scenarios.

The first is agreed-upon *reciprocity*—the willingness of all the players to extend protection not only to all the other players but also to the network-based environment itself—the common cause. This does not mean *equal* protection for all. It means *appropriate* protection for all. The degree to which this reciprocity is extended by any one entity to any other entity or to the network as a whole will be determined by the specific nature of the network and the players. This reciprocity should be a formal part of any B2B agreement and should be subjected to individual company management review both before joining the net, exchange, or market and throughout community membership, especially when the community changes profoundly (new members, services, liabilities, regulations).

The next characteristic derives from the first—*clarity of responsibility and liability*. Remember our conversation in Chapter 1 about partner expectations? Before you go off on a vast program of trust enhancement, determine what's expected of you and, in turn, what you expect. Such explicit conversations and agreements are rare in today's business communities, even among sophisticated, technology-driven industries. The cynics in the crowd are no doubt saying, "Let sleeping partners lie. You're just making trouble and expense for yourself."

Unless it is specifically transferred in the B2B agreement, individual members still retain primary responsibility for their own protection. However, reciprocity demands that whenever and wherever a transaction, data object, or processing function under your control affects me, you will extend the same, appropriate level of protection as you would if it only affected you. That doesn't mean you become my police force, fire department, and ambulance service. It means you have my interests as well as yours in mind in any joint situation. Very few B2B networks have yet fully achieved this level of mutual understanding and support, especially since, as we pointed out in the fable in Chapters 4 and 5, many of them have evolved rather than formally strategized and planned their way into their relationships.

The third characteristic is *external demonstrability*. Here is the *defining difference* between conventional information security and e-Trust. In conventional security practices, we normally do not reveal the nature or extent of our security capabilities. Indeed, to do so is considered an act of compromise. Are we suddenly suggesting guided tours of the vaults and dungeons? Certainly not! What we are suggesting is a series of external signs and representations that will meet the expectations and support the confidence of our fellow players.

Demonstrability comes in various forms:

- Adoption of reciprocal protective technologies and processes that are, in themselves, rigorously and demonstrably secure (e.g., certain forms of encryption, VPNs)
- Assessment and attestation by disinterested, appropriately skilled third parties
- A suitable physical, virtual, and operational infrastructure that can be certified as such, whenever necessary, by agreed-upon third parties
- External commitment to standards of good practice and technology
- Active and supportive membership in associations and groups committed to advancing the state of the art
- Periodic self-assessments with results that are confidentially shared with partners with a "need to know"
- Exclusive use of third-party service vendors whose trustworthiness and commitment to and performance of secure practices can be demonstrated
- Public statements committing to security policies and intent
- Binding contractual agreements with appropriately severe sanctions for security and control misfeasance, malfeasance, or dereliction
- Public licensing, where appropriate
- Published demonstration of awareness, understanding, and compliance with pertinent regulations and laws
- A published program for hiring and retaining key management and process personnel with suitable skills in and attitudes toward trust, security, and control
- Appropriate levels of background checks, bonding, and testing of key personnel
- Demonstrable trust, security, and control training programs for all involved personnel

- Performance evaluation criteria that clearly and forcefully specify trust, security, and control requirements
- A program of appropriate openness in public and stockholder relations dealing with responses to failures, breaches, compromises, and outages
- Visible and consistent demonstration by senior management of all parties that e-Trust is a fundamental, key, and inviolable component of e-Business

None of these steps, taken singly, will suffice. But a uniquely tailored composite program, agreed upon by all the participants, including, as necessary, the public and external authorities, should produce an atmosphere of sufficient trust that only the most paranoid would fail to find assurance.

Standardization of processes, interfaces, and technologies is the last characteristic of a trustworthy B2B. I'm sure some security and control experts would have put this in the number one position, and I will no doubt hear from them. I have no disagreement that standards are essential, especially when they affect the serious matters we are considering. Quite the contrary, we can't live or work without them.

However, depending too heavily on public or industry standards as the yellow brick road to e-Trust is dangerous and can cause delays and disappointments. Like it or not, formal (de jure) standards evolve—slowly, tortuously, and politically—often well in the rear of the parade of environments and events they address.

I have served on enough public, private, and corporate standards bodies and sat through enough frustrating sessions to realize that, especially when an established but no longer adequate body of practice already exists, it's going to be a long, slow pull to reach a new standard that the majority (forget unanimity) will support. Most de jure standards evolve from ad hoc standards and practices.

Nor is the standards community a single-minded environment. The security and control standards arenas affecting e-Trust are numerous, complex, and often have conflicting agendas. These bodies range from professional service to technology; international to local; industry specialized to globally applicable; government to private; technical to procedural; cosmic subject matter to nits and lice.

Some standards are developed to be deliberately exclusionary. Others are built for universal applicability. There is a false aura of permanence and market validation about standards. They do change. They don't always catch on. They are recalled.

Standards are necessary to avoid total chaos but perfect order is never in the cards. Do not create unreasonable expectations for the standards communities. Waiting for a unanimously accepted, consistent, comprehensive, complete, and coherent set of standards before pursuing a specific objective or situation will lead to missed opportunities and market paralysis. Oddly, it will deprive the standards communities of real-life experience upon which to build their guidance.

The ad hoc standard that gradually evolves from market acceptance is often the best pragmatic result we can expect. But the ad hoc standard is not always the technical or procedural best. Witness VHS or high-definition television. Sometimes, suboptimal technology turns out to be the most cost-effective. However, it does provide a platform for "getting on with it."

If you are intent on getting on with it, standards will not fully protect you with an impervious barrier to e-risk. Be prepared to scuttle certain approaches, drop some technologies and techniques, lick a few wounds, and mourn a few losses . . . and spend more than you anticipated. By all means, participate and support, but do not create unreasonable expectations for the standards communities, especially in an area as complex and as yet undeveloped as e-Business. We'll give you illustrations of standards activities in Part III. You can judge for yourself.

MANAGING RISK VERSUS RISK AVERSION

"Get on with it!" I am assuming that you are reading this book because you or those you advise have some personal or corporate interest in e-Business, its nature, its opportunities, its pitfalls, and its overall likelihood of success. I am further assuming that you realize that e-Business is risky. Also, I assume that because you cross streets, take elevators, ride airplanes, get married, have children, and invest in the market that you are not totally risk-averse. (I suppose you could be risk-unconscious, a not too unusual state in business and life.) Finally, because only a few of you wrestle alligators, climb Mt. Everest, or collect used landmines, there is also a limit to your risk acceptance. Daredevils make for interesting motion-picture heroes/heroines but lousy enterprise managers. *Entrepreneur* is not a synonym for chute-less skydiver. Being risk averse can be a prudent attitude, provided it does not suffocate willingness to take justified risks. Total risk aversion is fatal. So, we have to find an appropriate level of risk for our environment, business, and culture, and manage to it (Management 101).

Clearly, the nature of the trusted environment is a critical factor. Levels of security and control approved for a wholesale distribution network would probably not be sufficient for a medical care environment (unless the distribution network is a peerless model). Privacy, confidentiality, and anonymity requirements will vary. System integrity requirements and intolerance for outages will be measured in terms of cost-effectiveness in non–life-threatening environments.

For the record, let's list some synonyms for trust: confidence, reliance, expectation, dependence, belief, and assurance. Each is slightly different in its connotations, but they all share common prerequisites. Rational trust (the only kind we'll discuss) requires security and control, but it goes beyond them. It depends on technology and protective mechanisms, but it also involves reputation, contracts, law, openness, familiarity, fair business practices and ethics, quality, timeliness, and a host of other relationship characteristics. e-Trust, as we're using the term, is the application of these principles to the extranet, NetExchange, and NetMarket environments (B2B and Beyond).

HOW MUCH IS ENOUGH?

e-Trust establishes the basis upon which two or more entities are willing to conduct e-Business with each other. In this sense, e-Trust is relative. The nature of the transaction, the prior and current relationships of the participants, and the rewards of mutual success or the impact of failure will, in large part, determine the level of trust required and granted by the parties involved. It is also affected by the willingness of those parties to take risks.

As we have noted, mitigating risk is hardly a new subject. Moral, legal, and regulatory requirements limit management's options and protect the public, stakeholders, and participants from foolhardiness or malice. Generic benchmarks and best practices can also provide operating guidelines. But, generally, the level of risk acceptance or aversion in an e-environment will be determined by the management of the enterprises. *e-Trust is fundamentally a business decision process.* The technology and application methods to support that process should be determined by the business requirements.

NEW PLAYERS, NEW GAME

The problem with e-Business of any kind is that there can be so many different business managements and environments involved. You need only examine the organizational structure of a typical extranet, NetExchange, or NetMarket to see this. This is more than an obvious academic point to be acknowledged and passed over. For true e-Trust to be established, substantial negotiation and mutual agreement on terms and conditions will often be necessary. At a minimum, carefully explore whether your current information-related terms and conditions are applicable and sufficient for the relationships into which you are entering. Too many new e-structures are established without this step, and the damage can be substantial. Get your lawyers, auditors, and business and labor relations specialists up to speed. I hope the fact that you're reading this means you're trying to get on top of the issues and possible solutions yourself.

It is dangerous to assume that switching from an existing, conventional business relationship to an e-Business relationship between or among the same entities is simply business as usual with a new technological twist. "We've been doing business for years. Why do we have to go through these trust formalities now?" In fact, in a few cases, you *may* not have to. But if you haven't already picked up some signals that this is different from your former ways of doing business, you're probably not yet moving toward the full potential of e-Business. When we examine e-Trust objectives in the next chapter, ask yourself what could change as a result of establishing an extranet, NetExchange, or NetMarket relationship.

TRUST COMMUNITIES AND ENVIRONMENTS

Let's repeat the definition of a trust community: *A type of virtual community in which a high level of mutual trust is a critical or mandatory success factor.* A business community of trust must provide the following, wherever and whenever required:

- Confidentiality of user information
- Privacy for data subjects
- Anonymity of buyers or sellers
- Fairness and self-regulation of pricing mechanism
- Stability and integrity of the market and its supporting processes
- Openness
- Neutrality and independence
- Interoperability; common standards
- Clearing and settlement; or fulfillment
- Reporting and transparency
- Enforcement of trading rules
- Regulated access to the market space
- Systems and data integrity

B2C VERSUS B2B(2C) e-TRUST

However, the specific trust models of B2B and B2C may often be quite different. Let's examine how and why simply transporting B2C protection to a B2B environment lock, stock, and barrel (or vice versa) is not a good idea. Nor is B2B2C just a simple exercise in appending B2B trust functions to B2C. Consider a manufacturer acquiring and revamping existing e-tail websites to establish a direct channel into the marketplace. There's the matter of business process and technology integration, readjusting responsibility, and comprehensive management, to name just a few. Let's compare the two arenas.

B2C e-TRUST

B2C usually involves these factors:

- A large number and very wide range of occasional buyers (or in the case of auctions, buyers or sellers) interoperate with one primary selling, buying, or market making entity. (Yes, I know there are exceptions.)
- Volume per buyer is low, but aggregate volume is expected to be quite high.
- Transaction value, viewed objectively, is medium to low.
- Privacy is often a major concern.
- Although potential fraud and consumer identification and authentication are significant issues, the credit card indemnification system backstops most transactions.
- With a few very significant exceptions, the temporary failure of a B2C environment can usually be weathered with minimum permanent damage.
- B2Cs appear, rise, fall, disappear, or mutate with astonishing speed and facility.
- Even when they are broadly implemented, most B2C security system designs are relatively straightforward and similar to each other.

There is certainly much to consider in B2C trust. The subject demands and already has books of its own. We'll cover B2C trust further only as it appears in B2B2C situations such as consumer finance, consumer product manufacture, and service.

SO, HOW DOES B2B TRUST DIFFER FROM B2C?

Trusted and secure B2B has many subtle (and not so subtle) differences from B2C, as well as from predecessor legacy-based business processing models. For example:

- Because of the number and nature of the participating enterprises, there is a much higher level of variability—but at the same time, interdependence—among technologies, users, organizational cultures, structures, and procedures. Specific control criteria can be complex. B2C usually works around one dominant environment. When it begins to mushroom, it becomes C2B2B2C. Isn't this fun?

- Alliances, partnerships, and formal third-party relationships abound in B2B. With them come the possibilities of security and control mismatches and differences in trust philosophy and priorities.

- In B2B, business process owners usually directly manage their individual part of the information chain, lowering the influence of centralized network security management and raising the likelihood of fewer standards and less rigorous enforcement.

- The process and technology interface is the primary but not exclusive venue for trust negotiation. You will hear the term, "DMZ—Demilitarized Zone." It refers to areas outside the participants' firewalls, uncovered by any protection except that which the transaction or data brings with it as it transits (e.g., encryption). The DMZ should not be a totally unmanaged void. To the contrary, as in warfare and diplomacy, its dimensions, description, management, and what happens out there can be critical to e-Trust success. We talk about DMZs again in Chapter 17.

Notice that although the technology can certainly be complex, many of these issues are organizational, business process, and procedural in nature. Terms, conditions, and restrictions are as important as communications protocols. B2B is not the exclusive province of the technologists.

Frankly, many business managers, auditors, and legal staffs are behind the power curve in understanding what all this can mean. You may choose to believe that this is just another Y2K: All bluster, hand wringing, and overkill. Y2K was a defense program against a possible technology-induced disaster that didn't happen. But that "disaster" was a nonevent thanks to a lot of preparedness. It was not, as some think, simply a wayward asteroid that changed its course unaided.

However, as we've been saying, B2B trust is not exclusively or even primarily defensive. It's designed to enhance business growth through electronics. It's intended to support service, quality, and loyalty and keep conflict, misunderstanding, costly repairs, and finger pointing to a minimum. It's the foundation of effective partnership.

Having said that, let's turn to the trust technology and design side. Hybrid and complex technologies at the network, application, platform, and data storage levels are usual in B2B. We'll take them up in some detail shortly.

There are some pluses:

- The size and volatility of the user community is generally lower than B2C. Many B2B environments are semi-closed, as opposed to wide-open B2Cs.
- Because the players are often known to each other, the need for strong individual authentication and authorization techniques may be less pressing.
- Encrypted paths and data may be more important than encrypted personal ID. For example, virtual private networks (VPNs) and gateway-to-gateway rather than end-to-end security may be sufficient to fill the need for trusted B2B information transfer if there is a robust internal security system already in place at each end.
- Personal privacy is normally a lower priority, but confidentiality, transaction integrity, and nonrepudiation often rank high. The tools to achieve these ends are discussed in Part III.
- There's no credit card issuer to indemnify the players, but a number of transaction guarantor services are entering the landscape—partner/service providers with their own technologies, viewpoints, and interests.

ARE YOU SAYING WE HAVE TO START FROM SCRATCH?

Certainly not! You can and should learn from others and replicate their approaches. Otherwise, we wouldn't be presenting this book to you. But don't get mesmerized with adopting generalized "best practices" and simply try to force-fit them to your environment without some close analysis and modification. Although there are many common generic issues and requirements in B2B, the combined effect of organization, culture, and technical complexity can make each B2B environment's security and control profile different, even in the same industries.

In a typical B2B environment, several or many institutions and enterprises, thousands of user applications, and a rich hybrid of changing technologies will be present. Each element can have a significant impact on the overall security of the process and few important security decisions should be taken without considering each of these aspects.

e-TRUST OBJECTIVES

We believe a B2B or any e-environment must supply *and demonstrate* appropriate objectives:

- Identity management
- Confidentiality, privacy, and anonymity
- Process integrity
- Integration security

- Infrastructure security
- Content quality and integrity
- Nonrepudiation
- Freedom from denial of service
- Auditability and accountability

We'll discuss them one by one in the next two parts, but remember: Not only are they interrelated; they are also served by many of the same tools. For example, we'll find out later that encryption can be an effective tool for integrity and auditability, as well as confidentiality. We'll also find that in order to achieve these objectives, you need a coordinated program of technology and procedures. As we've mentioned, just throwing responsibility and a checkbook into the laps of security technology specialists will not achieve overall e-Trust. All together now, once more!—e-Trust is primarily a business process.

TRUST PROCESSES AND TECHNOLOGIES

OK, what processes and technologies are we talking about? Again, we're just going to list them here. We'll devote considerably more attention to each in subsequent chapters.

- Identification–authentication–authorization
  - Identity management subsystems
  - Strong identification/authentication and single-use passwords
  - PKI, digital certificates / certificate and registration authorities, digital signatures, time stamps, encapsulation

- Single sign on
- Single points of security administration
- Smart cards, biometrics, intelligent agents
- Content protection
  - Encryption for integrity
  - Data cleansing
- Path and process protection
  - Firewalls and virtual private networks
  - "Trusted" hardware and software
  - Monitoring/reporting
- Design, development, and penetration tests
- Monitoring, audit, and continuous test
- Physical security
- Public and private defensive intelligence gathering
- Denial of service defenses
  - Antiviral
  - Mirroring, back-up, and recovery strategies
  - "Social engineering" defenses

A few sample trust issues:

- Trusted identities
  - Are we dealing with the correct participants?
  - Is it really them?
- Privacy—confidentiality
  - Is information restricted to only authorized individuals and organizations?
- Content integrity
  - Is the information being used accurate, timely, pertinent, complete, current, and uncorrupted?
- Integration integrity
  - Are all elements of the transactions fully and correctly processed throughout the entire processing environment?
  - Are the support and management processes designed for mutual trust?
  - Can we prove and demonstrate it to all concerned parties' satisfaction?

On to Chapter 7 and a closer look at e-Trust objectives, functions, and issues.

7

Focusing on Specific e-Trust Objectives

In the next few chapters, we will continue to examine e-Trust from a variety of angles and aspects. Only when you begin to get a good feeling for the distinctions you should make and the characteristics you can exploit will you be able to develop a strategy for tailoring your initiatives, solutions, and tools to your own individual requirements. Once again, one size does not fit all, and we are dealing with large, often unique, complex entities in states of transition. Let's start with some specific e-Trust objectives and move on from there. As usual, we are being more descriptive than definitive.

As we said earlier, *any information processing* environment must provide appropriate

- Confidentiality, privacy, and anonymity
- Process integrity
- Content integrity
- Nonrepudiation
- Freedom from denial of service
- Auditability and accountability

However, in B2B, the extra factors of *reciprocity* and *external demonstrability* make themselves felt. In addition, while they too belong in any processing environment, *clarity of responsibility* and *practical standardization* must extend throughout the full limits of the e-domain. So let's revisit each objective and concentrate on what's different or more critical in the B2B world.

NOTHING'S EVER NEAT AND CLEAN, IS IT?

These objectives overlap, and they are better viewed as different facets of the same environment. For example, a battle has raged (well, maybe fumed a little) since security specialists and backup and disaster recovery specialists have come into existence. Are these totally separate, related, or unified disciplines? I'm sure it's very important to the individuals whose job descriptions and livelihoods are being affected. It's also important to the entities being protected. But the fact is, if you draw a Venn diagram (you know, overlapping circles) of the two functions, there's a big center section covered by both and affected by common threats. When we talk about disruption of service shortly, you'll see what we mean.

However, this is not the only area of overlap. In fact, overlap is endemic to the whole e-Trust landscape. And it increases with networks and B2B. But overlap is not necessarily an indication of poor organization. (I'm going to be pilloried by the "separation of duties" supporters.) It's often the only pragmatic alternative. It may not always be possible or even make sense to eliminate commonality, especially where different companies and entities are involved. It does make sense—nay, it's critical—to manage and coordinate the overlap. Just don't go crazy trying to chart it all. Organization charts seldom reflect all of reality.

"Hold on there, Mr. Consultant. Right in the last chapter and a couple of paragraphs above, you said that clarity of responsibility and liability was critical to establishing e-Trust, especially as the environment gets more and more complex. Are you talking out of both sides of your mouth here?"

Clever of you to have picked that up, Gentle Reader, but clarity and sole source do not mean the same thing. There will be very few functions in B2B for which there is no shared responsibility. This is a community, and communities to a greater or lesser extent share responsibilities. Are the police the only ones responsible for law and order? OK. Enough of organizational dynamics! Let's talk about trust objectives.

CONFIDENTIALITY, PRIVACY, AND ANONYMITY— THE TANGLED TRIPLETS

If ever three terms were confused, misused, mangled, and mistaken, it's these. The problem, of course, is that they look alike and, to a certain extent, can be attained and assured by the same measures. To a certain extent! That's the problem, but don't worry. We are not about to launch into a detailed deconstruction of the terms and their implications for mankind. Instead, we're going to give you a few brief distinctions and point out why the distinctions are important. We're restricting ourselves to the use of these terms in information environments.

Confidentiality involves restricting access to, and the use of information to, an approved community under approved conditions. So does privacy. The differences rest in the subject matter being controlled, the restrictors and restrictees, and the specific circumstances and motivations for restriction. I'm sure that helped a lot. Let's go a little further.

Generally, we invoke *confidentiality* to protect information assets that have *both* inherent value in themselves as well as specific value to the individuals concerned. Intellectual property, processes, and techniques come to mind. Most people (with some glaring exceptions) recognize the needs for patents and copyrights. Possession and ownership plays a large role in confidentiality. *The data owner's rights dominate.*

Privacy is governed by a different rubric. The inherent value of the information is less important than the desires of the information subject. I don't want you to know my shoe size even if, to most of the world at large, it's a piece of useless data. *The subject's rights frequently overshadow the rights of the individual or entity in possession of, or seeking possession of, the information.* It is often conditioned by social attitudes—the movie star's right to privacy versus the public's right to know (and the media's right to tell).

Confidentiality requirements can often be adjudicated through property-related law, contracts, and the like (China notwithstanding). Privacy is an ill-defined human right and is interpreted differently throughout the world. It can be adjudicated by common law, specific legal provisions, codes of ethics, agreements, or knock-down, drag-out fights.

"So what's the big deal? Slap on some access management technology and kill two birds with one stone. We've been doing it for years." Yes, but! As we move further into the realm of cooperative protection called for by e-Business, who and what you protect and restrict is taking on more importance than simply how you go about protecting.

An Example: Customer Relationship Management

Let's take an example from the very center of sell-side e-Business, customer relationship management (CRM). We'll outline it briefly here and then explore it more deeply in a following chapter. CRM is one of the strongest sell-side engines. As we said earlier, price is becoming a less reliable horse to ride if you want to stay ahead of the pack. Service, quality, and trust are pulling ahead, and to maintain those, you have to know your customers as well as you know your product. The better you understand your market and respond to your customers, the more successful and cost-effective your marketing, distribution, fulfillment, product engineering, manufacturing, and even financing efforts will be.

Questions abound about customers and the marketplace. Who makes it up? What do they want? What are their priorities? What pleases them? What turns them off? How often do they do business with you, and how much? How often do they do business with competitors, and how much? What are the points of market sensitivity? Who's managing the relationship? How well? CRM is much more than market research. It provides comprehensive, proactive, in-depth marketing-process management. But to illustrate our privacy–confidentiality–anonymity conundrum, let's stick with customer demographics and individual behavior.

In order to know as much as possible about your customers, you have to collect, store, manipulate, analyze, compare, and sometimes trade information. This information may be a crown jewel to your competitors and may require careful protection and management of your property rights whenever you share it with third parties. Is *confidentiality* an issue? You bet, and you're protecting your rights as owner and user.

However, this same information is about organizations and people you depend on for business. They should have some say about what information you keep, how you collect it, what conclusions you draw from it and whom you share it with. Even if *privacy* law and industry codes are vague, contradictory, or insufficient, your own pragmatic sense for keeping customers happy, to say nothing of sense of fair play, should kick in here.

Are customer privacy and your need for business confidentiality in conflict? Maybe. Maybe not. It depends on what business you're in and what you're doing with the information. Do you supply pharmaceuticals, financial services, tax advice, or toys? The confidentiality–privacy balance is different in each case. But the dilemma is not solved simply by access management software, and there is no single repository for guidance. Privacy law worldwide, as we shall see shortly, is not a single-minded, universally accepted code that is easy to understand or apply. In fact, in some areas, it's still a conflicted mess, and we've been at it for over 20 years. (I do mean "we." I've assisted in drafting privacy legislation for several countries, including the United States. It's not easy.)

Further to the point, this is an area where sticking to the letter of the law, or even the refined spirit, may not create the comfort level you want with your customers. For example, it may not be *illegal* to sell your customer lists to outside organizations without your customers specifically knowing about *each* sale. Many e-tail businesses simply subscribe to the generic "we may sell your information unless you specifically tell us otherwise" approach. In short, they attempt to put the privacy burden back on the data subject to perform some overt prohibition. That may play in B2C (although I have serious reservations), but is that the way B2B relationships should be built? I doubt it.

Besides, if you ran your business strictly according to law and nothing else, your more adept and market-sensitive competitors would eat you alive. The personality of your customers and the market personality you want to project are the prime movers here. In fact, you could easily torpedo all the advantages a CRM system provides by antagonizing major clients.

The issues of reciprocity require more finely tuned and attentive care for privacy, both personal and institutional. It's not just a one-file, one-record issue. When many forms of data can be accessed, composite personal or institutional profiles can be crafted from multiple shared profiles. (Law enforcement does it all the time.) Can I be identified by matching a confidential file's contents with a nonconfidential file? Patient identification during anonymous tests often surfaces this way. It's an overall application and file management procedure, not just access management.

So, what happened to *anonymity*? Anonymity enters the access management picture from a somewhat different direction. *Anonymity is defined as the quality of being unknown or obscure.* We all know about the nefarious sides of anonymity—the anonymous phone call, letter, or registration at a hotel (not always nefarious). But there are many times when anonymity is beneficial or mandatory—voting, sensitive research, double-blind testing, some auction bidding. Will the price of a vacant property stay the same regardless of whether Joe's Pizza or Bill Gates is interested? Yeah, right.

When is anonymity desirable and when is it not? When should it be an unconditional requirement for doing business? Once, again, it depends. The technical tools for establishing and maintaining anonymity (many are encryption variants) will be discussed in Part III. As more business activities take on auction-like characteristics, revealing identity before, during, or even after a transaction might result in a conflict or independence issue. But, as the demand for personalized service in general expands, expect additional demands for selective anonymity options from your customers, partners, and, in some rare cases, even your vendors. Better yet, try to anticipate those demands and turn them into a tactical advantage.

PROCESS INTEGRITY

There are at least four ways of looking at this objective:

1. Ensuring that the process, application, or function does only what it's supposed to do (no more, no less) and does it correctly and within process specifications. You could apply the term *quality* here and you'd be pretty close. We also come into the realm of demonstrability and auditability. They are not exactly the same. *Demonstrability* in this case calls for showing rigorously how the process is designed and works, what it does and produces, how it is secured, what connections and interfaces it employs, and a significant sample of all inputs and outputs including exception handling. *Auditability* means I can track a given set of transactions (audit trail) through the process and verify that what is happening at each critical processing point to the specific data in use is correct.

2. Ensuring that the process cannot be altered, copied, or destroyed except by authorized parties under authorized conditions.

3. Ensuring that the design, development, deployment, and maintenance functions maintain the integrity of the process as it is further modified, integrated, or distributed over time.

4. Protecting the process from external influences such as service denials that would affect its timely and complete performance.

The B2B structures we are discussing—extranets, NetExchanges, and NetMarkets—obviously add several orders of complexity to some of the business processes involved and also create more potential process volatility as the nature, structure, and population of the network changes. In other words, this isn't something you do once and forget. Integrity must be built into the architecture, design, deployment, and maintenance program as a formal and specific target.

The integrity expectations need to be expressed in complete and unambiguous language. By the way, it would also help if those expectations were appropriate and practical. Too many organizations that develop integrity fervor look for a blanket metric to use in all circumstances. At the highest level, perhaps that works. But integrity standards, like just about everything else we're discussing for our transitional hybrids, must be tailored and adapted to the need. Can you overkill on integrity? Yes! But since it doesn't happen all that often, don't try to use it as an excuse.

As we discuss the B2B sides and the functions of the Ps in more detail in later chapters, we'll keep revisiting process integrity.

CONTENT QUALITY AND INTEGRITY

The objective of content quality and integrity can easily get lost in the B2B design and development shuffle. Don't let it. It's a big deal that can cost you dearly if you don't pay attention to it. We've already shown how a variety of sources and services will be involved not only in the original establishment but in the ongoing management and processing of the network's information.

The very nature of B2B makes it inevitable that information content will come from and go to a variety of sources and endpoints. Some, if not most, of those sources, endpoints, and the processes that support them may belong to independent but cooperating partners. Here we go again with reciprocity and demonstrability.

While your provisions for process integrity, if applied network-wide (that can be a tall order in itself), may partially support the data quality and integrity requirements of the ongoing process, what happens when original or new versions of information are introduced by an outside source? (Remember, you may probably be someone else's outside source.) We have found that while developers will pay attention to the quality of test data, that first cutover can still be a nightmare if the startup production data is corrupted, misdefined, or incomplete.

But, remember, too, that in B2B, it is not uncommon for servicers and partners to frequently upload or download completely new databases—catalogs, customer lists, directories—refreshing previous partial updates to produce the evergreen database. This means that content quality and integrity is an ongoing issue, separate from but highly related to process integrity. As you'll see in Part III, data inspection and cleansing techniques take on much greater importance in B2B. By the way, data cleansing is a technical/business task.

NONREPUDIATION

This clumsy-sounding term has special importance in interactive, high-speed transaction systems, especially between external partners. A more graceful word, *deniability,* has unfortunately taken on a political, Mission Impossible, Teflon, or espionage tinge—it essentially means "go ahead and do it, but I'll deny ever knowing about it." Or, "Make sure you give me an out when it comes to accountability."

Nonrepudiation means that the execution and responsibility for a business transaction cannot be denied. In order to further explain nonrepudiation, we should explain repudiation as it is used in e-contexts:

Repudiation means to deny or seriously call into question the

- existence
- nature
- participants
- content
- mode
- timing
- circumstances
- authorization of a transaction, message, or other form of communication

Nonrepudiation says in response, "I have a combination of authenticated participant identification; proof of transaction and data integrity; time stamping; and audit trail to prove that a specific authorized transaction took place as stated, when stated, and between the stated parties. It happened as we say it did. It got there and was received and approved as such. There are no valid substitutes, competing "documents," or ambiguities, and we can prove it."

This gets critical, not just in cases of potential fraud or dishonesty but when errors occur in an application—a thousand carloads or a thousand units? It can be critical from a time standpoint—Did you meet the deadline? It can be critical from an authorization standpoint—We have the digital signature of an officer authorized to execute this transaction. And of course, it also works for establishing a legal record.

It also suggests that nonrepudiation requirements are primarily a business process call. Technologists can independently and confidently provide some of the basics such as logging and access management on the assumption that these services will be needed for a variety of objectives. But before committing to additional technology functions such as time stamping specifically for nonrepudiation, you should determine the business needs and the degree to which your current or planned security activities satisfy them already. Conversely, if you do see a new requirement, find out if the additional functions also serve other security and control purposes.

Applicable e-Trust Technologies and Procedures

We're just providing a list here. Don't go running for dictionaries or glossaries. Most of these technologies are multipurpose. The potentially strange terms like Kerberos, PKI, VPNs, SSL, and electronic vaults are explained throughout Part III. There is quite an available arsenal for nonrepudiation:

- Access management including tokens, smartcards, Kerberos, digital signature and PKI, biometrics, and one-time passwords
- Role-based access management
- Authorization management including Kerberos, digital signatures, and PKI
- Content encryption or digital envelopes for integrity
- Data-quality procedures for error detection
- Round-trip acknowledgement processes
- Time stamping and comparison of entry, receipt, and response
- System, network, and application logging recording and reconciliation
- Trusted path management such as VPNs, SSL
- Electronic vault storage
- Redundant records retention
- Backup and recovery
- Application-based sequencing, tagging, and watermarking, if applicable
- Third-party reviews

All of these taken together may be nonrepudiation overkill for a "vanilla" transaction or message system. Here again, nonrepudiation results from several trust processes and technologies being brought together.

Organizing and Developing a Nonrepudiation Program

Some of the following steps can be done in parallel. Ideally, this program should be developed by a joint business–technology team with assists from other staffs such as legal, contracts, marketing, purchasing, and HR:

1. Map the subcomponents of transaction repudiation as stated above against the major business processes to be supported by the network or B2B process.

2. Determine where some or all of these forms of repudiation can do sufficient harm to be worth investment of additional time and effort in nonrepudiation.

3. Prioritize the results according to value, frequency, impact, and need for immediate action. Examples:

   a. Is irrefutable time and sequence recording important? How often and where? It could be crucial in an auction process, but less so in others.

   b. Are there transactions that are absolutely unacceptable unless content integrity can be rigorously demonstrated? Are they widely enough spread to warrant a global, rigorous content-integrity program requiring encryption or matching multiple copies? Can we concentrate on one or two areas?

   c. Is it necessary to rigorously prove origin, authorization, path, destination and acceptance, and to rigorously eliminate all spurious origin or authorization?

   Notice how we keep using terms like *rigorous* and *irrefutable*. These value judgments will help decide how much is enough. Not all evidence has to stand up in court in order to provide sufficient results.

4. Determine what external forces may affect your requirements—regulation and law, contractual obligations, service for business partners, audit, public image, and so on.

5. Determine what other internal forces may also have an impact—company policies, labor contracts, and so on.

6. Map the various applicable procedural and technology processes that already exist to determine the degree to which you have solutions or alternatives at hand. Nonrepudiation is not all technology.

7. Determine what, if any, technologies and procedural changes will be necessary to support your net requirements, and when they will be needed.

8. Determine whether and where baseline, mandatory, infrastructural implementation for a given remedial step is required and where discretionary, application, or situation-specific deployment is sufficient.

9. Map the resulting requirements across business processes and technology environments (current and foreseeable future).

10. Enter into a technology design, performance, cost, and deployment evaluation to select possible solutions.

11. Enter the selected solutions into the appropriate procurement, deployment, support, and evaluation processes already established in your enterprise.

12. Establish a set of nonrepudiation objectives and requirements on your participating external business partners, service providers, and suppliers and get their agreement to their responsibilities and commitment for compliance.

13. Develop a measurement program not only to determine the cost effectiveness of the steps taken but whether any significant constraints or inhibitions in processing have resulted.

Why have we spent so much time on this topic? Because it's an issue made larger by B2B. The financial community has lived with this for all time, but the more interoperative and collaborative any business environment becomes, the more it will arise. Besides, some people and organizations are dishonest or stupid. In this period of knee-jerk litigation, it's a necessity.

FREEDOM FROM DENIAL OF SERVICE

Now here we have the all-time classic situation of an e-Trust objective looking for a functional and organizational home and ending up living everywhere. Unfortunately, in some cases, it ends up homeless. Let's look at some of the events and characteristics that can disrupt or reduce B2B service below satisfactory limits.

"Hold in your headlong flight, O consultant! What do you mean by 'B2B service?'"

You're not going to let me get away with anything, are you? But once again, you are spot on. Service is in the eye of those being served. So in a true sense, we're talking about the entire B2B buyer–seller (or exchange) experience from stem to stern. That view is very important in the context of e-Trust. Let's make it a wide-angle view.

Network outages or slowdowns are the obvious B2B whipping boy here, but they are just the tip of the iceberg. They are caused by everything from physical destruction, viruses, and overload attacks to mis-set switches or failure to anticipate and provide for peak loads. Capacity issues are the network availability culprit far more frequently than an attack or a cable-seeking backhoe. So is human or technology-assisted human error.

Software failures (system or application) are more subtle because they may still give some appearances of operating properly. That is, you may not detect the failure until you begin to encounter faulty results. Is this a denial of service issue? Perhaps not in the precise sense, but put it in the following context. Suppose your phone service was connected and active. Suppose no matter what you did, however, it kept connecting you to wrong numbers. Suppose you were being charged $20 a minute and no one could fix your account. How long would you continue to use the system? Yes, I know, it's a quality problem but the two are or should be closely related in your considerations.

Now comes the inevitable discussion about quality versus robustness or stability versus security. I submit that, from a business management standpoint and from a customer service and trust view, the debate is irrelevant. Certainly, there are important differences in technical and process responsibility and how you solve the problem. I've spent too many small hours of the morning troubleshooting systems and applications not to know that. I've also watched the final matches of the finger-pointing Olympics (a useless sport).

Start with the fundamental approach that you are dealing with a service, trust, and image issue that needs to be fixed. Make it clear that who picks up the tab and whose reputation is sullied are subjects for post-restoration discussion. By the way, these remarks are not directed strictly to the CEOs in the audience. This same frame of mind needs to be instilled in all B2B management. The stakes can get too high, the process too complex, and the players too numerous for "that's not my table" style management.

Again, there are overlaps. Clearly, software failures can come about in a variety of ways. Poor design, poor maintenance, poor deployment, attacks, ripple-effect crashes, accidental or deliberate corruption, and other variations on the theme can all have the same effect: a dissatisfied user whose trust in you is slipping.

Finally, there are the "force majeur" categories—the power outage, strike, flood, fire, epidemic, snow storms, war, and everything else that makes life a thrill. We are not going to launch off into a long discussion on preparedness, alternative processes, and recovery activities. There are hundreds of detailed publications on the subject, as well as major websites (just type "disaster recovery" in your Web search engine). What is important is how an organization's reputation (read user trust) can be enhanced by the way in which it deals with these events. All the advertising in the world is not going to favorably influence an electric utility consumer who waited 10 days for service restoration after a storm.

If all this sounds like self-evident motherhood, let me put forth a bit of experience here. Backup and restoration investments don't come cheaply. Sometimes they involve a complete replication (or more) of the primary environment. They can be complicated to build, test, and operate. Any number of issues can arise. I have seen several organizations sigh with relief when they successfully cut over to their backup facilities, only to discover later that they couldn't switch back to the primary again.

In this respect, aside from the inherent complexity, the major problem with new B2B management is heightened expectation of success and insufficient respect for failure. We hear over and over again: "Full (any?) backup and recovery is a second-stage activity, after we have a revenue stream going." You know the answer to that one as well as I. No service equals no revenue, unanticipated costs, and lost reputations. What's more difficult and costly? Getting a new customer or retrieving a lost one? Worse yet, you may not know you've lost them.

When an organization is fighting (literally) to get a complex environment on the air and is late, over budget, and not fully functional, backup and recovery is a problem they'd rather not think about. The problem with many B2B offerings is that in spite of the hybrid conditions, gradual cutover of a specific function or process isn't always an option. Strap on your chute and jump. To mix metaphors, you can bleed to death in the event of a failure if you don't have sufficient detection, protection, and reaction mechanisms at your disposal. Don't get killed if you have to use the ejection seat.

AUDITABILITY AND ACCOUNTABILITY

We mentioned auditability earlier under process integrity and accountability in nonrepudiation. As I said, these functions overlap. If your short-term memory is as faulty as mine, think of auditability as the ability to track and verify how a transaction or process behaves and what it produces against a standard of expected and desired results.

Accountability slips in from a slightly different direction. Here we're trying to place responsibility (there's that word again) and ensure identification, authentication, and authorization.

They are often lumped together, and I did it here to make a point. Actually, they are somewhat different. Auditors and security specialists are concerned with both, and they both begin with the letter A. More than enough reason for grouping them together. Snide remarks aside, the tools required to satisfy both objectives are a bit different, as well. Identity management ranks high in accountability circles. Sensors, monitoring, checks and balances, and reporting are the popular tools of the auditability trade.

I don't think at this stage that it's necessary to launch yet another sermon on the increased complexity, high speed, volatility, and high value of B2B processes and transactions. Nor is it necessary to beat the drum further about the wide range of entities, users, and processes involved in the environment. That's B2B. The major goal of most B2B (as well as B2C) environments is to provide stable, high-speed, easy to use, trustworthy service. Yes, I know, and make a profit while you're at it.

These objectives are NOT discretionary. They are an integral part of B2B. How you achieve them and what priorities you put on them is a set of decisions you must make in the context of your overall business strategy. But remember, don't give them enough attention and resources, and your business strategy will fail. "Maybe not today, maybe not tomorrow, but soon and". . . well, you've seen *Casablanca*.

In the next few chapters, we're going to reexamine many of these e-Trust objectives and associated characteristics—first in the context of special industry considerations and then as they apply to the four sides we discussed earlier—sell, buy, inside-common and infrastructure—and then once more in the context of the Ps.

8

Industry e-Trust Characteristics

Now we're going to turn our attention to some of the unique e-Trust characteristics of selected industries that are certainly different from each other but still have much in common in their B2B and Beyond aspects: healthcare, financial services (banking, insurance, securities), energy, distribution, and manufacturing. We covered some of the issues associated with transportation/hospitality in Chapter 3.

WHAT ABOUT THE OTHER GUYS?

Simply in the interest of brevity, we've excluded some other major economic and social sectors from our discussion. For example, telecommunications, agriculture, entertainment, real estate/property management, education, federal, state and local government, religions, institutions, and other nonprofit entities. This is not to say that these arenas do not display significant e-Business potential and e-Trust characteristics. Many of them are currently major users (or providers) of networked systems.

- Telecommunications providers have gone from a group of national monoliths to a spectrum of large multinationals on one end and small niche providers on the other. The same can be said of equipment and infrastructure suppliers. And yet, the whole purpose behind the telecommunications industry is to provide interconnected paths for all that demanding traffic. Interconnectivity within and between systems is crucial and must be managed over the very same networks that are supplying the service. High levels of communal trust in both the provision and management of telecom networks is a must.

- Bought a house or building lately? Real estate and property management nets are interesting animals. They have one foot in B2C and one in B2B. But in an industry that's as competitive as this one, mutual trust does not come easily and has hobbled some aspects of property management coopetition.
- Law enforcement, licensing, and tax collection have all taken on major networked personalities.
- Research networks (for profit and nonprofit) are beehives of collaboration.
- Education nets are huge and controversial at any scholastic level.
- Fund raising, job placement, advocacy, and religious groups are both B2B and B2C. Each has its own priorities and problems.
- Agribusinesses, especially those dealing in perishables, are classic examples of advanced collaborative distribution and price-setting mechanisms.
- Digital music and motion pictures are covered in our discussions on intellectual property rights.

Of course, one of the common traits of future B2B environments will be their cross-industry composition— some industries, especially financial services, make an appearance in just about every instance. But those mega B2Bs—NetExchanges, NetMarkets—will also have vertical industry networks within them or closely connected.

To do true justice to even the reduced list named in our opening paragraph would take a small army of specialist authors and would create a library wing of text or, in e-terms, terabytes galore. So to help you fit this volume in your briefcase or in the memory of your e-book, we'll just highlight a few illustrative situations resulting from or re-quiring e-Trust consideration.

I know, one more restriction and I'll have this chapter down to a cou-ple of pages. No such luck. This is one of the longest chapters in the book. You may be tempted to jump to your own industry or go only to those ex-amples that are of immediate interest to you and bypass the others. You are, of course, captain of your own ship. But in that list of industries, what you don't do for a living, you probably use. They're all important to all of us. Let's take a look at some of their e-Trust personalities and quirks.

HEALTHCARE

These next several pages on healthcare clearly have a U.S. flavor. Because of its size, scope, and complexity, to say nothing of the interactions between the private and public sectors, professional and business communities, and an enormous number of pressure groups, U.S. healthcare is a conundrum of major proportions. However, other countries' medical infrastructures, socialized or not, private or government managed, state of the art or developing, share common information protection and trust characteristics and requirements. In addition, there is much to be said for a steady increase in worldwide cooperation in all aspects of healthcare. So, while the specifics may not entirely resonate with international readers, we hope the general principles will still have value.

Healthcare! Here is the industry that, viewed from any angle, should be the poster child for trusted B2B megastructure communities. It has everything in the way of requirements:

- An immense user and provider base
- True "life and death" characteristics
- An extremely high and sensitive profile
- Regulations galore
- No lack of market
- Major financial and operational issues
- A community of increasing specialization
- A huge assortment of tightly linked companion business, professional, and other environments; many of these will develop or already have information megastructures of their own (in no specific order):
  - Professional certification and attestation
  - Professional associations
  - Nursing, therapy, paramedical activities
  - Pharmaceuticals
  - Prosthetics and appliances
  - Physical infrastructure, furnishing, and equipment
  - Property management
  - Fund raising
  - High-tech instrumentation and software
  - Telecommunications

- Research and library services
- Education and professional training
- Religion
- Government and professional regulation
- Public health support
- Law enforcement
- Insurance
- Employers and unions
- The military
- Legal and financial services
- Nutrition and diet
- Emergency service and disaster response
- Preventive and epidemiological functions
- All the other ones we left out

In the United States especially, significant regulatory initiatives are in place, affecting privacy, security, and standards for the electronic exchange of health information. New controls, such as the Health Care Financing Administration (HCFA—Medicare and Medicaid), formalize the policy and guidelines for the security and appropriate use of the Internet to transmit HCFA Privacy Act–protected and other sensitive HCFA information. (As of July 2001, HCFA was renamed The Centers for Medicare/Medicad Services, known as CMS.)

The Health Insurance Portability and Accountability Act (HIPAA) provides new regulations for the electronic exchange of health information among all covered entities (e.g., providers and payers). HIPAA was designed to assure health insurance portability, reduce healthcare fraud and abuse, guarantee security and privacy of health information, and enforce standards for the electronic transmission of health information. To enforce these regulations, two types of penalties have been defined: a general penalty for "failure to comply with requirements and standards," and penalties for "wrongful disclosure of individually identifiable health information." The penalty for the general noncompliance is $100 per violation, not to exceed $25,000 per violation per year. More severe penalties for security violations range from $50,000 to $250,000 per violation and up to 10 years prison time, depending on the nature of the violation.

We talk about these two in further detail in Chapter 12, "External Forces Affecting e-Trust," with other regulatory, public image, and socioeconomic considerations for e-Trust.

All the trust objectives outlined in Chapter 7 apply: confidentiality, privacy and anonymity, process integrity, content integrity, freedom from denial of service, auditability and accountability, and even nonrepudiation (controlled substances, prescriptions, status charts, procedures). Moreover, most, if not all, of the technologies and processes we present in Part III have significant value in healthcare.

This should be the B2B and Beyond to end all B2Bs. So how come it's not? We'll see shortly.

Time Out—Let's Regroup

But hold on a second, are we taking the right viewpoint on healthcare? Where's the focal point of all this? It's not really the provider or the insurers or the ancillary enterprises and organizations. *It's the individual! It's the patient, the care seeker, and those directly involved with him or her.* Healthcare is the archetype of all C2B2B2C2B2C environments, starting and ending with the C.

A well-coordinated, cooperative, network-assisted medical experience in its detail can make the travel experience we outlined back in Chapter 3 look like child's play. We were tempted to use medicine as our first example instead of the somewhat curtailed family outing we did use. Healthcare became too complex and daunting for an opening illustration. Either we would have oversimplified it and therefore done it and you a serious injustice or the chapter would have became a book in itself.

The same principle applies in the real healthcare world. Beware of simple problem definitions and solutions. Our transitional hybrid world will be with healthcare for some time to come. If you have ever been hospitalized, think back through the experience: The institutions, people, processes, and paperwork involved, the almost infinite opportunity for something to go wrong. The true "miracle of modern medicine" is that so much of it is successful. As we go forward, builders of healthcare networks, administrators, regulators, and legislators should join medical professionals in having the Hippocratic Oath emblazoned on their walls—at least the part that says, "Do no harm."

The Medical Record

Unless you have been uniquely blessed or were raised in the Amazon wilderness by polar bears, you have undergone professional medical experiences. You also know that during those experiences, a surrogate comes to life or returns from obscurity that is often more involved in the medical process than you are—*your medical record*. It takes on a life of its own, often far more complex than your comparatively humdrum existence, and goes places and sees people and undergoes processes that you probably would prefer not to know about. More decisions are made about it than about you. It grows and expands dramatically and amoeba-like, divides and develops branches and colonies and colorful strains. In sheer size and bulk, it outweighs and outmasses you several times over. The question is, Does it look like you? If you could see it in all of its manifestations, who would appear? Let's hope it's not the Picture of Dorian Gray (Oscar Wilde).

The other problem is that your medical surrogate is not one but legion. By the time you reach maturity, there are hundreds of medical records with your name in any number of traditional and not so traditional places. You don't know where some of them are. You probably wouldn't recognize yourself in some of them if you found them. And unless you run for public office and some enterprising reporter ferrets them out, you'll probably never see or hear from them again.

So let's just continue to ignore them, shall we? Not *my* records, thank you. Call me paranoid, but I'd like to have a little more knowledge and control than I currently have. In fact, I'll settle for the record holders having a little more knowledge and control. *The true Holy Grail of healthcare electronics is to get the medical record process under control.* Unless this linchpin can be firmly established, future healthcare B2B and all of its variants can easily disintegrate into high-speed, large-volume chaos. How can we avert this major meltdown?

The "Solution"

It's quite simple, really. Omniscient consultant to the rescue. Let's start out when an expectant mother first suspects she is expecting. As soon as the Baby2B's Mother2B begins her first session with her obstetrician, a record is established in a national (global?) database for the "child in development." Obviously, since at this first visit we don't know yet whether a boy, a girl, or a prospective basketball team is in the offing, we choose a single but dual-gender name for our example—Taylor. The database in which embryo Taylor's embryo record begins its life is maintained by a trusted third party paid out of the national budget under the control and guidance of the Department of Health and Human Services (HHS). The database(s) are kept in a series of securely protected virtual environments that are also Web-enabled to allow common access for all authorized and concerned parties. It is here that the medical records representing Taylor will grow as Taylor grows, change as Taylor changes, and very sad to say, die when Taylor dies—or maybe not. Very probably, her records will outlive her. *(Yes, I know. Hold on!)*

A partial national identification number is assigned to "Taylor in process," based primarily on the parent's identification, ethnic characteristics, and general demographics. The responsible physician, HMO or managed care process, medical insurance and so on are all entered into the record and the personal history begins and is supplemented with each visit, test, and medically related transaction. *(Be patient!! No pun intended.)*

At birth, the details, active participants, and circumstances of the event as well as the vital statistics of Taylor (girl) are added. Of course, not all babies come into the world with the prior assistance of obstetricians, so alternate record establishment procedures will also have to be developed for use at the time of birth. Her DNA sample, blood type, footprint and so on are taken and the characteristics recorded. In lieu of a birth certificate, an accessible record is established in the Health and Human Services database, and a full national identification number is issued and incorporated along with descriptive information into other federal (international?) databases such as Social Security, Internal Revenue, and Departments of State (passport), Education, and Justice. Of course, the Census Bureau will need all of her pertinent personal and demographic data, including her ethnic grouping and heritage.

Now, in addition to providing a unified medical record system, we have also taken care of many of those other time-consuming requirements needed to allow Taylor to go to school, apply for scholarships, collect an inheritance, work, travel worldwide, pay taxes, vote, and get a driver's license. Obviously, certain departments of the states and municipalities must also have authorized access. Of course, as she matures, her fingerprints, retina scan, voiceprint, and signature, electronic and manual, will have to be updated. Depending on election reform, her party affiliation and voting record may also be memorialized. *(Hang in there!)*

But we digress. This is a *medical* record we're talking about. We, of course, will require stringent national as well as international controls. The Tooth Fairy will have to register every time she swaps one of Taylor's baby teeth for some currency. Suppose, in her exuberant teens, Taylor breaks her leg on the slopes of St. Moritz. Her Swiss physician on the spot must enter her treatment and condition into the database directly or through an international medical-record clearing house. The database and its associated service structures must be capable of handling large graphics files (MRIs, CT and CAT scans, x-rays) and in some cases, recorded videos of treatment sessions and procedures to defend against malpractice suits, as well as to supply research and education material and historical backup for the more cryptic entries in her file. One plus—there'll be fewer illegible physicians' chicken scratches to contend with. Of course, her prescription history will be fully maintained, including allergies and reactions. *(Control yourself!)*

Dangerous work environments must be included (radioactive materials or carpal tunnel syndrome); recreational habits (auto racing, sky diving); substance use and abuse, and any travel to dangerous places. If she gets a communicable disease (let's hope not), recommendations for social restriction may be necessary. Her history of weight and height changes, blood contributions, and inoculations must also be tracked. The driver's license bureau; FAA, if she's going to be a pilot; and the State Department's Passport Agency at least will require her current eye and hair color, along with any disqualifying restrictions. *(Two more paragraphs to go!)*

And so it will go until that day 120 years in the future (extended life expectancy) when Taylor, having lived an exemplary life, either goes to her eternal reward (with an ethereal copy of her record in St. Peter's database) or is cryogenically preserved along with a copy of her medical history to assist some future generation in resuscitating her into a much braver, even newer world.

Throughout this entire process, we never once sent Taylor a bill; made her fill out an insurance report; questioned her treatment; called for second opinions; referred her to specialists; demanded co-payments, bounced between primary, secondary, and tertiary coverage; hit up against coverage limits and all the other swell stuff that makes healthcare such a delight to patient and provider alike. Maybe we should have called *this* "The Fable."

OK, civil liberties enthusiasts, please feel free to have an emotional outburst! You've earned it! And I share your sensitivity. But this is a grayscale world. Some of the processes we've described won't happen at all; some can be controlled to the advantage of the patient, practitioners, and society at large. Some may not be adequately controllable, and the social cost may just be too high. Some are just flat-out intrusive or oppressive. This is another arena with a potential for e-Trust win–win, but it won't come easily. Read on.

A Minor (?) Fly in the Ointment

It's somewhat ironic that this discussion of healthcare could possibly induce cardiac arrest in some readers who are avid civil liberty supporters.

Sorry. Even a cursory reading of the material above will demonstrate that this "solution" is rife with potential civil rights issues, privacy concerns, and Big Brother threats from both the private and public sectors. In 2001 at least, those in the U.S. who would feel comfortable with this scenario make up a very small minority. (I'm sure not comfortable.) However, it may not be ever thus. At some point, we may continue to sacrifice rights for convenience to a point where this scenario or close variant may be acceptable to the population at large. It is technologically feasible now, but the expense would be heart-stopping. More likely, we will slowly converge and evolve into progressively newer models with a fair amount of experiments and ideas going into the discard pile. The latest model's effectiveness and service to social justice will be a function of how we get there, how careful we are, who's in charge, and who is exerting influence.

A Brief Word on Controlled Anonymity

Some medical record keeping, especially clinical trials, have an interesting twist. In addition to being confidential (restricted to those involved), they go further to controlled anonymity—(identity *linkage* restricted to a disinterested and trusted third party). Most trials are designed to be double blind. Neither the subjects nor the test teams can know who got what. But in the event of, say, unexpected side effects, we sure want to be able to reconstruct who got the placebo and who got the errant medication. This is not the same as complete anonymity, such as one would want in voting or other civil liberties situations. And this controlled anonymity has to be maintained for years (centuries?). There are encryption-related services and anonymity mechanisms on the market that will aid and abet that. We talk about anonymity again in Chapter 10 when we address auctions.

It's Always About You, Isn't It?

Lest I leave you with the impression that all medical record keeping is patient-centric, let's rapidly move to other forms of records that are also crucial:

- Physician qualification and certification
- Referral processes and agreements
- Laboratory procedures and performance
- Equipment maintenance and certification
- Pharmaceutical and controlled-substance management
- Infrastructure management

- Nursing and other employee management
- Blood and other vital substance control
- Billing, insurance, and finance (repeat this one six times)
- Legal and regulatory records
- Law enforcement procedures
- Research, procedural, and diagnostic materials
- Fund raising and promotional programs
- Public and media relations
- Disaster management and response procedures . . . and more

So, Omniscient Consultant, What Do *You* Recommend?

No need to be snide. Where *does* this leave us? I hate to repeat it, but it leaves us with transitional hybrids. Today, there are at least three major orders of business in the U.S. healthcare information arena that need to be addressed posthaste. They are related, and they are complex. Reducing them to the following few paragraphs hardly does justice to the immense tasks associated with each:

1. *Rationalizing the information and transactional tangles that exist among all the different parties and functions (or at least, for starters, among the major parties).* Are all medical records a mess? Of course not. We'd be doing a terrible disservice to the healthcare community if we were to imply that. Nor are we implying that there is nothing going on to improve the situation. The professions are working in this area, as is government. HIPAA and HCFA are regulatory steps in the right direction but this objective requires far more than formal regulation and compliance. It takes aggressive industry cooperation and attention. Technology can be a major assist here, but there's a massive amount of procedural, financial, and competitive noise that needs to be filtered out of today's medical system before we leap into the globally interconnected future. If not, electronics could make it worse by amplifying some of the negative impacts.
2. *While we seek safe modes of wide range medical interconnection, we must simultaneously build a more robust and flexible electronic infrastructure in support of the care process at the individual points of supply.* These include doctor's offices, laboratories,

hospitals, clinics, and pharmacies. Harmonizing, converting, and significantly reducing the paper trail, institution by institution, may sound torturous, but it is a necessary condition to any overall rationalization of the healthcare process.

There's a critical, related problem, dealing with attitude and allocation of time. As a professional service practitioner myself, I am sorry to admit that some of the worst examples of archaic information processes can be found in the legal, accounting, and medical professions. (Yes, and some consultancies, too.) Professionals seem to find something demeaning in paying attention to support infrastructures. "We're too busy saving lives, pursuing justice, preventing bankruptcy to bother with that kind of techie stuff." There is truth to this certainly, but there is also a perception that professionals should not suffer constraints of any sort.

I have a little trouble with physicians who wander around all day with a clunky stethoscope around their necks but who are not able to deal with the inconvenience of a badge for secure room or computer terminal access. Obviously, the stethoscope is more than a tool. It is a distinguishing sign of the medical professional. (Maybe if the badges were subtly and functionally decorative and attached to the stethoscope, they might play better.)

Plus, there's the question of competitive edge. I know of one situation where there are three multimillion-dollar MRI facilities within less than a square mile of each other, but little infrastructural computing support in any of the same sites. There may be sufficient traffic for all three MRIs, but the MRI is also a sexy and visible symbol of modern medical care at its finest. The computer network and transactional support systems are mundane, to say the least. Can you imagine getting a notice in the mail today that says,

Dr. X is proud to announce her state of the art, highly secure, well-controlled local area network that will improve patients' record keeping, speed up payment and insurance processing, and provide faster prescription renewal service and appointment handling, as well as provide her and her staff with immediate Internet access to a vast range of online medical databases. Your personal medical information is fully encrypted and backed up, and access is permitted only to authorized individuals who can provide a password and pass a retina scan.

No, neither can I. But if you think about it, patient confidence, trust, peace of mind, and satisfaction could all skyrocket from just such a notice.

This is not an example of expensive administrivia to be simply dumped on the medical assistants and technicians. Physicians themselves, especially the self-employed variety, have a major responsibility not only to maintain their own professional capabilities but to stay ahead of their patients' knowledge levels. Electronics is playing a more important role in that process every day.

Doctors are beginning to worry in print and on the air about the *knowledgeable patient* (the one who goes to the Internet to study up on symptoms, possible disorders, treatments, reactions, and medicines before ever deciding to seek professional aid). An increasing number of patients begin interviews with, "I saw something on the Internet about this and I was wondering . . . ." or "How come you didn't recommend Superpanacea?" The concern is not just professional ego or worry about increased litigation (although in Japan, many physicians will not even tell you what's wrong with you).

With rising medical costs, scarcity of medical insurance, difficulty in scheduling visits, little or no choice about which doctor treats you, and an expanding universe of over-the-counter medications, there is a real possibility that a rising number of individuals will resort to self-diagnosis and inappropriate self-treatment. A PC and a one-year Internet connection probably costs less than a complete physical. This is a different but very cogent form of e-Trust. To be crass, if I think I know more about the latest fuel injectors than my mechanic, I may not trust my Ferrari (in my dreams) to him. On the other hand, I'd be stupid to try and fix it myself if I had any respect for the car. But not everyone considers his body to be a Ferrari. Mine looks and acts like a 1956 DeSoto. That, I might try to fix, if it weren't for my more sensible wife.

Computer-based research and transactional infrastructure and methods need to be taught more comprehensively in medical, law, and business schools and need to be even more critical items on the agendas of the professional associations. The newer generations of physicians (and lawyers, accountants, and consultants) are moving in this direction, but it needs to percolate upward and outward to the existing professional base. It's an attitude adjustment. Just like other industries, it's a quality, service, and trust issue.

I am also aware that the average medical practitioner is operating on very narrow margins and tight budgets. Not all technology and service offerings are priced to impoverish you. Quite the contrary, it's been a buyer's market for quite a while and is likely to remain so. Plus, we're talking transition, transition, transition! There are many services out there, Internet and not, that can provide cost-effective and trusted approaches toward enhanced use of electronics. By building cooperative critical mass, these advantages can be more rapidly and cheaply propagated throughout the medical community. The problem today is that many of the clumsy downsides of managed care often overwhelm the significant and important benefits. If managed care or a successor approach is to thrive and improve its image, it will have to evolve into a more sophisticated and modifiable suite of services and with a tailored variety of support for the physician and patient. Electronics is key to supporting that expectation.

3. *The quality of medical records is widely variable.* We spoke a bit earlier and will pick up again in Part III on the subject of data reconciliation and cleansing. Frankly, in healthcare, this can be an awesome, frightening, and repellent process. *But it needs to be done.* First of all, the number of records is astronomical. Too many medical records are in poorer shape than the persons they represent, and as specialization increases, they are becoming more diverse, incomplete, and conflicting. Records pass from practice to practice, facility to facility, with all the usual wear, tear, and lack of security and control. The fax, for all of its benefits, just exacerbates the problem. Malpractice suits can often result directly from poor or incomplete records.

How many of you readers have had an annoying incident, hopefully not crucial or life threatening, caused by mixed up or faulty medical records? I know I've had a few more blood tests than I really needed because of record handling. But, short of a global plague or a nuclear incident that almost eliminates the world population and the need for extensive future recording, there is no way other than a concerted effort on the part of the industry to improve the picture and reduce the burden and threats of data overload. Federal regulation may supply part of the motivation, but the healthcare industry has this as a major ailment that they must, slowly perhaps, but persistently, eradicate.

The scary solution we cited above may be more science fiction than fact, but an effective and controllable version can be progressively parsed, decomposed, designed, and constructed in such a fashion that adequate safeguards, prohibitions, and protection can be built in before the fact and at each stage of development. Human rights and increased human welfare are not antithetical. But it will take a lot of serious thought, ethical and legal expertise, procedural invention, hard work, good will, and technology to get to and maintain the optimal balance. We need it. When we reach Part III, think further about the requirements and the possible applications of security process and technology to this arena.

FINANCIAL SERVICES

If we were to use protective measures as a yardstick, we might conclude that we take much better care of our money than we do of ourselves. The financial services industry (FSI) has occupied the "private sector point position" in the e-Business protection parade for quite some time. This is especially true of banking/credit cards, but brokerage and insurance are also moving up there. In fact, with the exception of some military and intelligence environments and the occasional research facility (certainly not all), banking/credit cards is assuredly the most security conscious environment in the world. Brokerage is not too far behind in its exchange infrastructures, and insurance is a respectable third. Each one, of course, has different requirements.

It's important to note that these sterling characteristics belong to what we will call early-phase e-Business. Banks, credit card companies, and securities exchanges have been whipping around global electronic transactions for quite a few years. This is not to take any credit away from FSI today, but we must point out that this industry is undergoing one of its most comprehensive and dramatic sea changes since the biblical money changers first came on the scene. Here is a classic example of the world's financial market *functions* increasing in number, sophistication, variety, and depth while the *entities* and *institutions* involved in the process simultaneously contract, morph, and expand in different directions and modes. New instruments and services abound. Some are comprehensible to only a very small number of specialists. Try explaining derivatives to the average investor. Try explaining them to me.

Any first-year high school student in 1980 could have given you a reasonably accurate answer to the question, "What is a bank?" Today it's improbable that the Board of Governors of the U.S. Federal Reserve could come up with a consistent answer that would satisfy all of them and the industry. The press has more than once tolled the death knell for banks as institutions. The once relatively clear lines of demarcation between fiduciary, brokerage, investment, trading, guarantor, credit, and insurance institutions are faded and scrambled. Regulatory clarity is also becoming blurred.

What is Citigroup? What is Lloyds? What is Deutsche Bank? What is a central bank? What is American Express, Merrill Lynch, VISA, Mastercard, Barclays, Fidelity, Schwab, e-Trade, Nomura, MMC, GMAC, GE Capital? What will they be tomorrow? How will they coordinate with and support the NetExchanges and NetMarkets of the future? Will they be the netmarkets of the future?

In the following pages, we will address trust issues surrounding financial function with illustrations of today's or the near future's networks. Once again, remember our warning in the earlier discussion on transintermediation. The entities will change, new functions will arise; old ones will change or die. Financial function—credit, clearing house, arbitrage, cash management, brokerage, auctions, insurance and guarantees, and all the other thousands of variants—will move around the institutional galaxy. It would be convenient if we could completely ignore the institutions and just settle on the special e-Trust needs of functional financial areas. Unfortunately, the motive power and management are in the enterprises. That's where the direction, initiative, resource, and governance comes from. We'll take a look at several current examples of B2B—bank, brokerage, and insurance—and extrapolate to the next possible steps.

Banking/Credit Cards

We all use these financial services daily in our personal and business lives. I'm not going to drag out an explanation of how an ATM works or the wonders of electronic funds transfer or global clearing houses. Clearly, these systems have an extremely high requirement for security and e-Trust. Instead, let's concentrate on the integrated roles that banking and credit institutions play in the management and operation of other industries and how networking is making them the omnipresent third (fourth, fifth . . .) party in just about every B2B environment. Almost by definition, B2B demands an integrated presence from a banking or credit institution in most, if not all, buy/sell processes. Unless you're into barter, there's a "bank" in there somewhere. Among other things, this presents a somewhat different configuration of interest than we've been talking about up till now in the buy side/sell side arenas.

At one level, there is direct interaction among the buyers and sellers in whatever mode of commerce they are engaged—direct, auction, reverse auction. But each is also invoking their "bank" or credit guarantor as part of the transaction. These "banks," in turn, are communicating with each other to arrange and consummate whatever funds transfer or credit-related activity is required. ("What's new?") This. The terrible three rear their heads once again—speed, volume, complexity. Coupled with that is an increased role of the financial institution as gating factor. If a bank is going to be involved real time in a transaction, they must have the capacity to deal with the load and turnaround demands. But not just one bank, all the banks involved in the transaction. Remember our comments on apparent bandwidth. It's somewhat analogous to standing at a checkout counter waiting for the store to contact your credit-card company for an OK.

"Aha," you say, "that's a B2C example. Not all B2B transactions will require immediate intervention and participation by the bankers. We're operating on mutual recognition and a private level of e-Trust. (That's OK, Tex. I don't have to see your money. I know you're good for it.) Our own credit departments will keep us aware of who the deadbeats are." Well, yes, I agree, but it's not that simple. We've been preaching that the benefits of B2B derive from direct interaction by all the players necessary to a transaction. The intention is to electronically complete (*completely* complete) the process with as few returns to the table as possible—preferably none. It will be a while until we get there (think hybrids). And I admit that, in some instances, such immediacy may not be necessary, or even desirable. But, by and large, that's what B2B is all about.

You may have seen a great TV commercial from IBM e-Business Services that depicts a Japanese executive group meeting about a serious problem: A specific part costs too much and is blowing the profit margin on the end product. They are stuck with their one and only supplier. Amid much frowning, one young member of the team looks at his Internet-connected laptop and, smiling, announces that the company can get the part from MitchCo at an ideal price. "Where is MitchCo?"

asks the chief honcho. "Texas," replies the bright young executive. "Texas?" echo all at the table, incredulously. Next scene: Mitch in coveralls at workstation, beaming and thanking, in Texas-accented Japanese, the Internet services that made this unexpected boon possible. "Domo Arigato!" Stretching credibility? A bit, but charge it up to marketing enthusiasm and the time limits of a 30-second commercial.

Query: Would a large, overseas corporation place a major order for a component that can make or break product profitability with a company whose name someone just saw on a website for the first time without first exercising a good deal of due diligence? I sure hope not. (See our discussion on WebTrust in Chapter 21, "e-Business Assurance." It would apply here.) Would banks also be part of that due diligence? I sure hope so. How many? Certainly more than one. Given the business urgency, would said multinational company want to wait for weeks or even days to get the transaction off the ground? One doubts it. Sometime during the period the quality and availability of the desired "Mitch's valve" is being checked, so, too, is Mitch's financial viability. Mitch, on the other hand is going to need credit for his investment in components, raw material, and who knows what else to meet this gigantic opportunity. Making those transaction periods shorter and shorter, nearing instantaneous, is part of the B2B value proposition. We have a way to go yet, but the trend is visible and positive.

Fortunately, as I said above, the banking/credit industry, broadly defined, has been making major investments in being part of the B2B solution, rather than the problem. Worldwide, they have been investing in reliable, fast, and complex support systems that will make that TV commercial and others like it a reality. In the banking industry, B2B doesn't just mean Bank2Bank. It means Banks2everyone. Need we point out the high level of security, reliability, and e-Trust required? ("You just did.")

Brokerage

As the brokerage industry moves further and further into online services, it is becoming the classic example of B2B2C. We used a stock exchange example to first explain the working of a netexchange or netmarket, and we won't go over that territory again. Instead, I want to bracket the exchange and look at the online broker B2C environment and then look at the processing powerhouses behind the New York, American, and Nasdaq exchanges.

Let's examine the securities industry in both a consumer and institutional context. The article from Reuters in Exhibit 8.1 speaks volumes on transitional situations and both user and supplier adaptation.

Ms. Richards' comments are a marvelous summation of the situation in most B2B2C environments. Clearly, the industry is interested in increasing and retaining customers, accelerating trading volume, reducing time and costs, and opening up opportunities for new offerings—but there's that service, quality, and trust issue again.

Now let's look under the hood of several major securities exchanges.

SIAC and Nasdaq

In the next several pages, I am going to give over space to both the Securities Industry Automation Corporation (SIAC) and Nasdaq. The Nasdaq name is a service mark and logo that had its origins in the National Association of Securities Dealers, Inc. It has gone on to become a global entity. (Full disclosure: Both have been Deloitte & Touche clients for specific services in the past.) The purpose of going directly to their websites is to give you a direct look at how they present themselves to the public. They are not clones.

While you are reading, consider the interactions that are explicit and implicit in the services being described. Notice the different structures of SIAC and Nasdaq. SIAC is a third-party support unit for several exchanges. Nasdaq's functions are more integrated. Since we offered securities exchanges as familiar models for netexchanges in general, we are now showing you that even here, the proverbial cat may lose its skin in more than one way. Most of all, consider the e-Trust characteristics we have been extolling—confidentiality, integrity, nonrepudiation, privacy, availability.

I'm not going to set about explaining what SIAC has already explained. (The "in other words" syndrome.) Suffice it to say the SIAC is a work in progress.

Although some online services such as e-Trade began life in the Internet age, SIAC, like Nasdaq and most other e-Trust environments we've been and will be describing, transitioned into its current state as new technology, new market demands, new services, new regulations, and new relationships arose—sometimes leading, sometimes responding, but always driven by a complex of technology and business facts of life. The last hand has not been played in either of these games. Not by a very long shot.

Exhibit 8.1

The following is extracted from a Reuters report by Peter Ramjug. dated January 25, 2001

U.S. Examiners Critical of Online Brokerages

A study by the U.S. Securities and Exchange Commission of brokerages offering online trading finds the services sometimes risk the privacy of investors' personal information and fail to ensure customer orders are executed at the best price.

The SEC, prompted by an explosion in Internet trading and rising customer complaints, did a top-to-bottom review of large, medium, and small firms.

Without naming firms or taking specific action, the SEC staff report said the online services should also examine the quality of information they give customers, the objectivity of their advertising, and the robustness of their computer systems.

'With respect to e-mails, the staff observed many instances of confidential information being sent without any security measures, including account numbers, passwords, social security numbers, or details of trades placed,' the report said.

SEC examiners found 'many brokerages' were not meeting their best execution obligations because they sent their orders to their own clearing houses and either did not conduct independent reviews of execution quality or did inadequate reviews.

There are currently more than 200 broker-dealers providing online trading services to over 7.8 million retail investors, according to figures cited by the SEC. Those investors are making more than 800,000 trades a day.

Many of the firms examined were traditional brokerage firms that have added Internet trading to their services, although some were formed to provide Internet services to investors.

The SEC received more than 4,000 complaints from online investors in the 12 months ended Sept. 30, 2000. That compared to 259 complaints in the comparable period in 1997. The most common gripes by online investors included failures or delays in getting their orders processed and difficulty in accessing their accounts, the SEC said.

"Trading online is relatively new in the brokerage industry and I think with anything that's new it will take a bit of time for what we think of as best practices to become common practices," Lori Richards, who heads the SEC's Office of Compliance Inspections and Examinations, told Reuters.

Exhibit 8.2

SIAC Securities Industry Automation Corporation
The following is extracted from the SIAC Web site www.siac.com

*SIAC is the technological hub of the securities industry providing key systems support to:
   - New York and American Stock Exchanges (NYSE and Amex)
   - National Securities Clearing Corporation (NSCC) and its affiliates
   - National Market System
*Formed in 1972
*Joint subsidiary of the New York and American Stock Exchanges

MISSION
- SIAC's mission is to provide the highest quality, reliable and cost-effective systems to support the current and future business needs of the NYSE, Amex, NSCC and their subsidiaries. SIAC plans, develops, implements and manages a variety of automated information-handling and communications systems that support:
  — Order processing
  — Trading
  — Market data reporting
  — Trade comparison
  — Clearance and settlement
- SIAC provides automated routing and processing of orders to the Exchanges' Trading Floors and sends execution reports back to Member Firms

TRADING SYSTEMS
- Support every aspect of order processing, including
  — Order entry
  — Order management
  — Execution
  — Comparison and settlement
- Play key role in making a billion-share-day "just another trading day"

TRADE & QUOTE DATA SYSTEMS
- Systems developed and operated BY SIAC:
  — Consolidated Tape System (CTS)
  — Consolidated Quote System (CQS)
  — Options Price Reporting Authority (OPRA) systems

Exhibit 8.2 *(continued)*

These real-time systems collect and integrate trade and quote data from the NYSE, Amex, Nasdaq and the regional exchanges and consolidate it into individual last sale price and last quote data streams and distribute this information to all approved vendors for dissemination worldwide.

INTERMARKET TRADING SYSTEM (ITS)

ITS, developed by SIAC, enables trades in dually-listed securities to be executed across markets, based upon the best price. CTS, CQS, OPRA and ITS systems help define the National Market System mandated by Congress.

REGULATORY AND SURVEILLANCE

SIAC supports systems used by the NYSE, Amex and NSCC. As facilities manager for the Intermarket Surveillance Group, SIAC helps support the surveillance needs of all major U.S. securities exchanges as part of their efforts to help ensure fair and equitable securities markets.

CLEARING CORPORATIONS

SIAC supports NSCC and affiliated clearing corporations:
— Government Securities Clearing Corporation (GSCC)
— MBS Clearing Corporation (MBSCC)
— International Securities Clearing Corporation (ISCC)
— Emerging Markets Clearing Corporation (EMCC)

SECTOR, INC.

Sector, Inc., a wholly owned subsidiary of SIAC, provides a variety of communications and outsourcing services to organizations that require high-availability for critical operations in both data center and network operations.

This subsidiary consolidates SIAC's for-profit businesses into a single organization including SIAC's former Communications Division, known as Sector, which for more than 25 years has been providing a full suite of products and services, designed primarily for the financial services industry.

Sector offers a variety of products to financial service firms. Several data center-related services are offered, aimed at organizations that need high-availability for critical operations in both data processing and network operations. Leveraging the centrality and neutrality of SIAC, and the extensive data transmission network already in place, Sector also distributes many financial industry data files.

INDUSTRY-RELATED ORGANIZATIONS

• Securities Industry Middleware Council (SIMC)—SIAC representatives serve on the Board; dedicated to improving the quality of middleware and infrastructure software available to the securities industry
• Securities Industry Association (SIA)—SIAC has a long history with the SIA, complementing collaborative projects with technical expertise and advanced technology

Note also that the SIAC was originally a wholly owned captive of the NYSE. The AMEX and clearing corporations evolved into the mix. Could SIAC expand to support other exchanges? Do they want to? Are they looking at it? You'll have to ask them.

So let's move on to Nasdaq, probably better known to most people as the high-tech stock exchange. I don't want you to pay attention to the securities traded on Nasdaq. Manage your portfolios on your own time. Observe, instead, the functions and interactions explicitly and implicitly stated in the following website presentation in Exhibit 8.3. You will notice that while the services are comparable, if you add the NYSE and AMEX to SIAC, the operating philosophies are far from identical. "So which is better?" Better for what? The point is that each is different. As we said earlier, not only are these B2B2C environments different from the past. They are different from each other even within the same industry.

You can see different philosophies at work here. You can also see, in SIAC's case, institutional history of a longer duration than Nasdaq. The structure of NYSE and AMEX, the owners of SIAC, obviously have shaped it. Both, however, share more in common than not. Both have a major stake in maintaining trust with a wide range of players and both are global in scope. Both are putting massive investments into service,

Exhibit 8.3

The following is extracted from the Nasdaq Web site, nasdaq.com

About Nasdaq—The Market of Choice

Growth, liquidity, depth of market—and the world's most powerful, forward-looking technologies. These are just some of the reasons why The Nasdaq Stock Market^{SM} is the market of choice for leading companies worldwide.

Since its introduction as the world's first electronic stock market, Nasdaq has been at the forefront of innovation. Now Nasdaq is the fastest growing major stock market in the world—and home to over half of the companies traded on the primary U.S. markets.

Inclusive Market Model

Key to Nasdaq's success is its inclusive market model. On Nasdaq, trading is executed through a sophisticated computer and telecommunications network—a network that transmits critical investment data at lightning speed to more than 350,000 computer screens around the globe.

With no geographic boundaries, Nasdaq's network allows a virtually unlimited number of market participants to trade in companies' stocks. And companies benefit—enjoying greater access to investors, increased visibility in the market, and an environment that facilitates immediate and continuous trading.

Exhibit 8.3 *(continued)*

nasdaq.com

nasdaq.com is one of the most popular financial sites on the Web. Averaging more than seven million page views per day, nasdaq.com offers unprecedented visibility to listed companies. Investors can log on to nasdaq.com and see how Nasdaq, Dow Jones, and the S&P 500 are performing, scan the latest news and fund commentary and get quotes for stocks, mutual funds, and options on major U.S. markets.

Nasdaq MarketSite^{SM}

Located in the heart of New York's Times Square, Nasdaq's MarketSite Tower soars seven stories high and is the largest video screen in the world. CNBC, CNNfn, Bloomberg, CBS MarketWatch—these and other financial news media broadcast live throughout the day from the MarketSite's Broadcast Studio, putting Nasdaq listed companies front and center before millions of investors.

Unparalleled Service

Companies can expect unparalleled service when they list on Nasdaq. Each Nasdaq company has a single point of contact: their Nasdaq Director, who serves as a link to an extensive portfolio of services. Directors provide day-to-day assistance and can offer valuable insight on investor relations, market and industry issues.

Executive Programs

Nasdaq-listed company executives are invited to participate in a variety of programs designed to present top managers with timely information and networking opportunities. Nasdaq programs include a wide range of topics—such as industry sector specific seminars and investor relations forums—that provide companies with the tools they need to be public.

Nasdaq Online^{SM}

Designed for senior executives at Nasdaq listed companies, Nasdaq Online is a one-of-a-kind strategic planning tool. It provides market data on all US-traded companies and real-time quotes for Nasdaq stocks. Plus, there's key information on institutional ownership, research coverage, performance ratios and more. All data are continually updated and available in a single, integrated source. And Nasdaq Online is free to listed companies.

Global Vision

Nasdaq is building the world's first truly global stock market—digital and Internet-accessible, open to anyone anywhere in the world, 24 hours a day. Nasdaq has already broken new ground in Japan, Europe, Hong Kong and Canada. With additional plans for Asia, Latin America, and the Middle East. By reaching out around the globe, Nasdaq is creating new links to additional capital and an even broader pool of investors.

quality, and security. They are not alone in the securities arena, of course. Name a country or region. The United Kingdom, France, Germany, Austria, Australia, Canada, South Africa, Japan, the Baltic, Euro-Asia, New Zealand, India, Pakistan, Hong Kong, Singapore, and a paragraph or two of more names. How will these exchanges configure links to gain more leverage in the securities marketplaces? How will the netmarkets of securities exchanges take further form? How much will they trust each other?

INSURANCE

The insurance industry has a bipolar concern about e-Trust. It is both supplier and user.

The Insurance Industry as Supplier

When you think about it, the first and most obvious concern should be for the industry's business policy holders and the potential liabilities they will incur as a result of their use of networks. As systems, networks, and protective measures become more complex, expensive, and volatile, many corporate risk managers have been casting wistful (and wishful) looks toward their insurers, hoping they can take up some of the slack in their own protective armory. "Don't worry, we're insured."

The industry's management and underwriters have been doing some serious head scratching to determine what offerings they can bring to market that will support their customers' often ill-defined but nonetheless real risks as they move into the e-world. And, oh yes, not bankrupt the insurer with one claim. Could a major network outage have the same impact on the insurance industry as, say, a flood, earthquake, or hurricane? Under the wrong conditions, perhaps. What about widespread e-fraud? Is it any different from—what, snail fraud? Privacy, fraud, and other legal and regulatory concerns are rising as more Internet-related incidents appear in the press.

The major difficulty for the underwriter is that, unlike physical and natural disasters, *virtual* catastrophes, even those with physical consequences, represent largely uncharted terrain. There is little or no history and few realistic impact value points. How do you write a policy that provides meaningful and desirable coverage for the e-market without exceeding your own risk limits? Or requiring premiums that make taking the risk more tolerable to the insured than the expense of coverage? Or writing so many exclusions and terms and conditions as to make the coverage inconsequential?

How do you sell and service such coverage without super techno-savvy agents, underwriters, and claims managers? Should you set up a program of preventive assistance for the customer? Will that approach kill the prospective margin of the program or increase its attractiveness? Should you offer a premium rate scale that takes cognizance of the insureds' protective mechanisms? How do you distinguish a customer who's coverage-worthy from one who's not?

Are there standards for e-protection that are sufficiently well understood, effective, and applicable to enable you to make compliance a condition for coverage? (Not yet.) Several years ago, I was involved in one of the first attempts to tie insurance coverage to the use of digital certificates. It was developed for a secure message service. A somewhat clumsy but workable plan was developed that had levels of coverage commensurate with the type and scope of certificate process in use and compliance with different levels of certificate strength. It used the certificate security standards in effect at the time. They and the insurance program built on them were not easy to explain. It was also difficult to establish enough value in the eyes of the potential message service user to make it a significant market differentiator for them. I never saw a claim made against the system, and the premium was hidden in the pricing of the different levels of message handling. It was a start, but it also proved to me that the subject is far more complex than it may seem on the surface.

Finally, consider the nature of the entities to be insured. What is an extranet, exchange, or netmarket as an insurable object? Do you write coverage for each member separately and severally? Is participation an "everyone or no one" proposition? Do you offer group rates? Obviously, this is not the first time the industry has been faced with consortia or associations as clients. They represent a major segment of just about any liability portfolio. But these consortia will have varying levels of membership, responsibility, and assets at stake, and different needs for coverage. Does a participating content provider need the same coverage as a primary service provider? What's the content? (To say nothing of different players having different vulnerabilities and a maze of different consequential damage scenarios.)

Message to insurers: Be careful (but you already know that.) Message to potential insureds: Don't hold your breath. Coverage is coming, but slowly.

The Insurance Industry as e-User

Always an information-centric industry, insurance and its associated financial business processes today and in the future will rely even more heavily on network-based; fixed and mobile; departmental; and large, concentrated back-end systems. Although the Internet will no doubt take on a major position in insurance industry usage, there is a large, deeply seated and long-standing investment in conventional systems and other network designs that will endure for quite a while (transitional hybrids). Clearly from a technology and application standpoint, one size does not fit all. And, of course, the same is true of protective methods required.

In addition, the industry's offerings and market channels are diverse, dynamic, and often involve third-party suppliers and other external relationships (agencies, re-insurers, claims services, affiliates). They, too, must be recognized as requiring significant protective attention.

Policy holders and service clients in general are becoming accustomed to rapid, one-stop transaction support and are less and less tolerant of delay, inaccuracy, and inability to handle unusual or troublesome situations. They are less faithful to specific carriers and more likely to switch allegiances based on poor experience. As we've said, quality, trust, security, and control play an increasing role in customer satisfaction.

The insurance marketplace is global, cyclical in some sectors, volatile in many, and highly competitive in all but a very few specialty areas. Being first to market with a new service or key enhancement is becoming increasingly important. However, in this era of narrower margins, increased litigation, and larger settlements, cost control plays an important role in maintaining corporate profitability. Security cost-effectiveness is crucial.

Plus, like all aspects of the financial services marketplace, the insurance-related sector is decomposing, re-forming, re-consolidating, and redirecting. Very often, it's driven by electronics both as an enabler and as creator of business demand. As an example, visit the Marsh & McLennan Companies Website and see how many different business streams they are now swimming in. They are hardly an isolated case. Just as we asked above, "What is a bank?" we can just as easily ask, "What is an insurance company or an insurance-related company?" In many respects, the only thing holding these diverse business services to a fast-fading set of industry classifications and structures is a regulatory structure and not much else. And you know what is happening to regulation in the financial services industry.

But, for sake of illustration, let's take a more conventional (?) insurance company, as in Exhibit 8.4. It doesn't matter what lines the company offers. Let's see what it might look like in a relatively straightforward B2B configuration (early e-Business circa 1998– now).

We'll use this schematic again later in this chapter. Don't take it too literally. It is simply designed to break down business processes into semi-

Exhibit 8.4   Conventional Insurance B2B

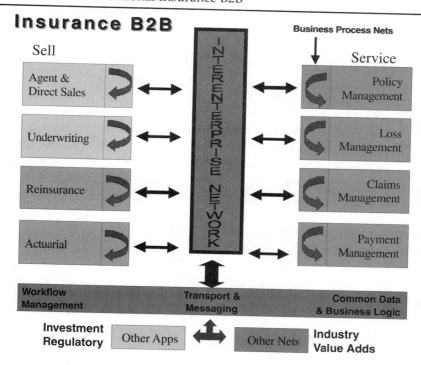

independent components. The key point to observe is that in a B2B environment, each of the business processes shown in the diagram can and often will be supported by one or more separate networks, which, in turn, may have a cascading support mechanism. (Wheels within wheels, nets within nets.) The fact that they are connected is less important than the types of traffic, the traffic patterns, and the business relationships those connections represent. Even more important is the degree to which the combined nets are involved in rapid turn-around interactive processing.

Let us assume for a moment that an insurance client is negotiating a policy with its agent (which could be an interactive website, but we won't push it that far.) Let us further assume that the intention at the end of the session is to issue a binder with an effective date of NOW. Let us further assume that it is a comprehensive coverage policy for a construction firm to include a large number of subcontractors. Let's put the project site in the Middle East. Let's also assume that while the client has been with the insurance company for a long time, it has a less than stellar premium payment history. Finally, given the circumstances and conditions, the insurance company is certainly going to want to spread the risk over a number of other players.

Now look at Exhibit 8.4 again and you can imagine a flurry of activity up and down, around and round and back and forth as the online-supported negotiations proceed. Now let's push it and assume that every single party to the transaction is a separate business entity. Does that stretch credibility too far? Not in future B2B. But scale it back to two or three if that makes you more comfortable. Even at this restrictive level—with, say, transactions and information from sales, reinsurance, and parts of claims management, underwriting, and actuarial coming from outside entities, the relationships and transaction traffic get pretty complex. But this *restrictive* level is a representation of the here and now for many insurance companies—and a modest version, at that.

Is the insurance industry operationally an area for e-Trust activism? We certainly believe so. As we've said and will say over and over again ("Oh, please!"), keep your eyes on the functions, not the business entities. One of the greatest contributions and threats that network-based processing has given the world of business is freedom of organizational structure. Terms like *institutional models* are being replaced with *information flow and transaction models*. To refresh your memory, you might want to go back and look at the Evolving Enterprise Exhibit 1.2 in Chapter 1. Then apply the categories to each industry we discuss. Some of those hybrids look more like the future than the past.

ENERGY

Now here's a cluster (or considering the daily price, availability, and regulatory conflicts, perhaps *family* is a better term) of related companies and institutions that will be more than just interesting to watch. It's vital. We are all affected by the energy suppliers, directly or indirectly, every day in just about everything we do. I'm not going to clutter up these pages with lists or tables of examples. This one you can do for yourselves. Just stop right now, and for 60 seconds, consider all the things you do or have done to you in a typical 24-hour period. As you run down the list, ask the simple question: Are the energy industries involved? Ready? Go! I'll be right back. I want to get something from the refrigerator.

Time! If you couldn't come up with at least 40 examples, you're leading a primitive life or you're taking your energy needs and usage for granted. I could say, "Imagine your world if energy distribution stopped." But then you wouldn't be able to read this book, assuming someone had written it out on papyrus. Those of us in the information technology business tend to run on about information being the prime mover of our civilization. I submit that in the 21st century, energy is giving information a very serious run for primacy, and may win.

Think for a moment of what proportion of your expense outlays goes for energy in one form or another. In spite of rising prices in all industry sectors, the United States has been living in an energy cost fools' paradise for years, compared to most other nations. Consider how much tax revenue comes from the energy sector. A major part of our interstate road system would have never been or would have crumpled away without that tax stream. Consider what happens to air fares or vehicles costs because of energy considerations. Finally, think about how energy figures in our quality of life—from ecological disasters and pollution on one extreme to being able to live, work, travel, learn, worship, heal, and entertain ourselves comfortably under the most variable and hostile conditions.

But serious as it is, dependence on energy is only part of the story. (A big part if you lived in California in 2001 or in any developing or war-torn country just about any time.) What is even more fascinating, at least to me, is the transition of the energy industry from a group of large, uneventful oil and natural gas companies (with minor Mideast exceptions) and Plain-Jane utilities to an arena that is now witnessing and will continue to witness some of the most dramatic and innovative changes we will see in B2B2C. ("Stodgy old energy? You're kidding. It only took eight chapters for him to completely take leave of his senses. I was getting suspicious with that fable stuff.") Bear with me, and I shall illustrate my point.

A Little History

Some of us are old enough to remember the Great Northeast Blackout—no dates, please—that literally stopped a major portion of the United States in its tracks. Major financial, government, manufacturing, and communications centers literally dropped off the screen. After this outage, I had the privilege to work with the developers of the New York State Power Pool as they set about building the distribution and control facilities of the "grid to end all power outages." IBM built some very sophisticated (for the time) hardware and software to meet the extreme demands of this new venture. Large power suppliers were linked throughout the entire Eastern Seaboard, across the border to Canada and with ties further west. A pyramid of control centers capped by the Power Pool's facility outside Albany, New York, monitored, switched, balanced, and reacted to the vagaries of supply and demand. This, of course, was during the period of extensive utility rate regulation, so the concentration was on distribution and supply, not making and balancing a market.

With all due respect to the thinkers and doers that made the Power Pool a reality, today's requirements and attempted solutions make it look like a first-year high school science project, effective though it was and still is. Throughout my professional lifetime, I have had the opportunity to work with many utilities, natural gas and petroleum suppliers, and electric power consortia throughout the United States and overseas. It's only in the past few years, as deregulation opens up new potential for the utilities and market demand puts new opportunities in front of the global oil and gas suppliers, that innovative (and in some cases retro) approaches are surfacing.

When Thomas Edison first launched electric power for public use in the form of lighting, he foresaw neighborhood generation plants— possibly even household electric generation. For economy of scale, distribution fairness, and a variety of other reasons, the centralized generation and distribution model in the form of regulated monopolies took hold instead. Today, Edison's model is being dusted off for possible application in a different usage context. Does it make more sense to further separate distribution from generation? Should individual entrepreneurs be allowed to offer their megawatts over community lines? Does co-generation work? Will the same model play with natural gas? What about solar power? What about wind? Can we use them individually and look to the electric power grids for backup and supplements? Is the concept of microgeneration coupled with microgrids feasible and desirable? How about a loosely coupled power distribution network of individual generation and distribution sites designed on the cooperative Internet model, managed, in turn, over the information version of the Internet, or a restricted, high-performance variant? Perhaps this will be Internet 3? Play with that one for a while. Talk about hybrids.

Is the California Independent Service Operator (CAL-ISO) power exchange that was developed to service the California market under deregulation a failure, or was this excellent extrapolation of the Power Pool concept undermined by poorly understood market and regulatory realities? CAL-ISO is a marvelous example of two tightly coupled functions interacting in real time—a commodity exchange in which power is literally traded as a commodity both on a spot market and a forward price basis. The megawatts are delivered via a companion computerized power distribution system. Both of these are related but must also be kept separate for security and control reasons. Security, control, and trust—in heavy volume and complex and high-speed situations. The terrible three ride again.

At the individual utility level, there has been an active program of network usage for planning, directing, and implementing grid and local power line maintenance, new installations, updates, and other customer services. One ice storm can illustrate how effective the power company's infrastructural control is. Can these functions be mapped onto the microgrids we described above? Will grid and power-line maintenance evolve into a separate, independent service? Is that what some utility companies are today?

You're Down Two Quarts

What about petroleum? While the electric and natural gas markets seem to be fractionalizing, oil giants are getting bigger and more global in their reach. Comparatively, they are "old economy." All are capital intensive. But even though physical assets dominate, these enterprises are information driven. Each marketplace and infrastructure is following its own path to optimization. Is this a conflict, or have we reached a point in the energy market where a variety of models can coexist, each optimized for specific purposes? Look at ExxonMobil, Royal Dutch Shell, TOTAL FINA ELF, or BP. Each is a merger of former rivals. Exploring, discovering, recovering, refining, modifying, selling, and distributing their products is a global activity.

Consider Enron, achieving its formidable growth by acting as an information, transaction, risk management, commodities broker, and transportation and storage provider/manager. It does no exploration, extraction, ownership, or distribution, but is heavy in Internet and communications exploitation. Or Unocal Corporation, which transmuted from an integrated oil and gas company to an independent exploration and production company by divesting its refining/wholesaling/retailing business. This change in 1997, along with rapid advances in seismic data collection and other high-tech tools over the last decade, has put enormous emphasis on sifting massive amounts of exploratory data, evaluating choices and priorities, and targeting likely cost-effective sources and markets for development.

Consider a different industry example: A tanker filled with crude oil makes its way across a major ocean while, through satellites overhead and cables below, ownership, value, and destination of the fuel in its tanks is changing not once but perhaps many times. We're going to talk about mobile and virtual warehousing further in our discussion of the distribution and manufacturing industries. (Can the imagination go too far? Of course. We need to keep logistical realities front and center.) But consider geological survey work using encrypted wireless links to rush data back for in-depth analysis and using the results to further direct the search in real time. Nor are remote unmanned surveys the things of science fiction, especially under water or ice or in inhospitable conditions. They are real.

So, What's the Story?

Today's school solution for energy is whatever best satisfies the market and provides the best returns. Expect conflict, redundancy, and inefficiency but also expect some innovative breakthroughs. Is nuclear power about to be resurrected? Will industrial and commercial power usage be satisfied by a different set of sources than home usage? Are there analogies for power in some of the changes in the telecommunications industry? It's still being sorted out, and a totally definitive process may never emerge.

However, one thing is clear. No matter what configurations for market management and distribution emerge, the B2B2C network structure is there for energy, in spades. The principles of e-Trust apply, and all of the concerns for confidentiality, data and message integrity, availability, and nonrepudiation need addressing.

Let's move to distribution and then conclude the chapter with a brief look at manufacturing. We'll pick manufacturing right back up again in the following chapter (9) on ERP.

DISTRIBUTION

Distribution is a complex industry. "What's so complex? You get stuff. You store stuff. You deliver stuff." Well, let's make a comparison to the airline industry, which is usually regarded as complex. You get people. You store people (often much longer than they want to be stored). You deliver people. The timely, accurate, safe, and reliable movement and storage of goods is every bit as complex, and it has a few additional issues. Except for the people who usually sit next to or in front of me on airplanes, most human beings come in a standard size range, are reasonably intelligent, are vocal (a plus and a minus), and are self-propelled. Tell a warehouse manager or shipper that all their goods will have those characteristics and they'll go into ecstasy. They have to deal with fragility, size, shape, perishability, toxic substances, sensitivity to cold, heat, radiation, magnetics, batch, and of course, lot management.

Distribution has also been the subject of some magnificent flights of technological and operational fancy, especially when it comes to reduced storage. Let the vehicle be the storehouse. Warehouses in motion. The standard container size and shape is becoming common to ships, trucks, trains, and aircraft. Just keep it moving. Yet another case of disintermediation. To listen to some just-in-time (JIT) enthusiasts, future archeologists will look at clusters of slowly disintegrating cavernous structures and wonder at the primitiveness and ineptness of a civilization that built warehouses. "What possible purpose could they have served, Professor? We're not sure, Crutchley, but we believe it was tied to a complex religious cult that worshipped cargo."

Seriously, the JIT-related mobile warehouse concept is a good one and has already saved billions in storage costs and late deliveries. It has meant that large organizations can significantly scale back their unfinished goods and raw materials inventories and the tax and handling cost they represent. It has increased production line efficiency. It has changed ownership and redistributed costs and liabilities. It has changed some of the basic assumptions of supply chain management, usually for the better.

But, it is not the answer to every shipping and distribution requirement. Consolidation and breakdown are major functions that need to be performed at optimum times and locations. Partial shipments are the bane of every distributor's existence, to say nothing of returns. The best way to load a ship or aircraft or to assemble a train may not be the best way of organizing for optimum, one-stop receipt. Not all goods movement is cyclical or predictable. There's the nasty problem of customs.

Nor does mobile warehousing always perform well. The tie-ups at the Union Pacific–Southern Pacific switching facility in Houston several years ago put rail transport into a state of suspended animation. It also pointed out that if you are going to use railroad marshalling yards as your warehousing facilities, a few things need to be improved, both in the yards and out on the routes. A major storm or strike, and your smoothly running system may run a fever. And your information systems better be up to the load. So mobile warehousing is a good idea that is working well in some places and has significant promise for the future, but once again, it's hybrid time.

Let's examine the distribution industry and the e-world a bit further from several vantage points and use two brief examples from industry folklore.

The myth still persists that all FedEx traffic—cross town, cross country, cross globe—goes through their Tennessee hub. It doesn't. It hasn't for quite some time. FedEx, like just about any large shipper or distributor, has multiple hubs. As any airline, shipping, or network expert will tell you, a single switch point is also a single point of failure—a phenomenon to be avoided at all costs if you're in the 24×7×365 mode of operation. The truly effective tracking systems that FedEx, DHL, Airborne, UPS, and a number of other shippers have developed have revolutionized package management. Think of all the sensing, data recording, record maintenance, and messaging that supports that website we so blithely go to when we want to know where our new sweater is. Or to locate the progress of that unit we sent back for repair. But tracking is the trailing edge of the process. Receiving, routing, switching, storing, transporting, and delivery are very tangible and difficult processes. Visit any distribution center and see. Consider the very unfair but very descriptive phrase, "Going postal." It describes the frustrations of a demanding, complex, and pressurized group of jobs. Networks facilitate distribution functions. They do not, by themselves, determine them—not, at least, until all goods become virtual. Excuse me, while I download a pizza.

Consider the Amazon story. The original premise: Order online from Amazon and it, in turn, never touching or moving the book itself, will manage the shipment from publisher or publisher's distributor to your front door at a vastly reduced price through the wonders of the Internet. (Since Amazon will probably handle this book, I won't go too far into critical mode.) Amazon works. It hasn't made a profit as of this writing, but functionally, it works. But it does not rely on the virtual warehouse concept that was touted early in its existence. One of its serious profit problems has been the bricks, mortar, and staffing costs it has had to put into its own warehousing and distribution facilities. Publishers and their distributors just weren't enamored with the task of shipping individual books, even if it meant that the volume of sales would be favorably affected. Nor is the bookstore dead. People like bookstores, just like they enjoy malls. The bookstore has changed into a social center, reading room, and sales room. It's not clear how profitable that model is, either. Amazon and its other Web-based competitors are excellent sources for on-the-spot or impulse demands. (Oprah Winfrey recommends it.) I've switched over to the Net several times as I was writing this book to order a text on a related subject. I've also wandered all over the Internet in search of information. Any author who is not connected to and using the Internet (even for fiction) is writing with a serious impediment.

That discussion on Amazon brings us to generalized support of the retail industry. Everything we've spoken about in B2B shipping or individual C2B2C shipments gets more complex as we move further into the B2C side of distribution. With all the attention being given to

Web-based shopping, attracting and keeping customers, price competition, navigation, and advertising, it's easy but fatal to miss a point that many virtual virtuosos gloss over.

Unless you are selling information and bit streams, somebody has to receive store, move, and deliver product. The physical infrastructure behind the retail world, even the online retail world, is enormous. As we mentioned earlier, handling returns alone is a formidable task for e-tailers. Yes, brick and mortar retail stores are closing, but not necessarily as a direct result of online function. Many parts of the retail industry just plain overbuilt, and the first economic downturn did them in. In spite of my very strong bias for electrons, pixels, and bits, I submit that the trustworthiness, quality, and service of the retail, distribution, and transportation industries rest as much, if not more, on their physical infrastructures and the electronics they use to control them as it does on the websites and kiosks they use to attract sales. Nothing happens until somebody sells something. And nothing will happen a second time unless somebody delivers the first order correctly, on time, in good shape, and at a shipment cost that doesn't sour the whole deal.

Distribution is an industry in transition (that word again). It does not exist in a vacuum. Manufacturers, extractors, growers, and other suppliers are at one end of the equation, and intermediaries and users (often those same manufacturers) are on the other. Distributors are pushed, pulled, and pressured from a variety of sources, and their costs are a subject of great interest to all parties. (Somehow, we have gotten it into our naïve heads that Internet purchases should be both tax- and shipping-cost free. File that idea under "Fat Chance.")

Distribution has all the e-Trust issues—cooperation and collaboration, confidentiality, authentication and authorization, integrity, nonrepudiation, and even privacy. Also add availability. The robustness of the infrastructure is key. Distribution is e-Trust territory.

MANUFACTURING

We're going to cover this last industry in this chapter somewhat lightly. For one thing, we have used manufacturing examples in our discussions of the "sides" and B2B in general. For another, we're going to briefly co-examine B2B, e-Trust, and ERP in the next chapter using a manufacturing setting.

So, to give a quick and generic overview of a current and near future manufacturing B2B just as we did with insurance, let's drag out the diagram again, now in Exhibit 8.5.

Exhibit 8.5

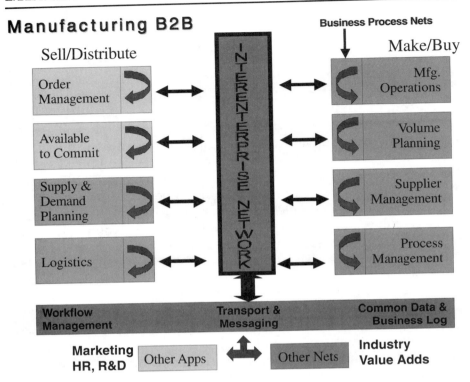

Something I should have mentioned the first time I used the diagram for Insurance—that vertical column innocently marked Interenterprise Network is probably a huge, sprawling, multihub, multitechnology, volatile, global set of connections, nodes, users, and traffic. It's the B2B equivalent of the Internet cloud.

This diagram started its life as a manufacturing B2B explanation but has been pressed into duty for a number of other industries as well (see our earlier discussion on insurance). As we demonstrated in the insurance discussion, the important aspects of Exhibit 8.5 are the potential for each subcomponent—order management, volume planning, supplier management, logistics—plus the others below the line—to be or become separate entities and separate networks, even large-scale B2B networks.

I am sure you are aware of some of the manufacturing NetExchanges and netmarkets emerging in the automotive, steel, chemical, pharmaceutical, and high-tech industries. (Did you ever open your PC and count the different logos and countries of origin on the parts and assemblies? Can you open your PC?) The extranets and exchanges take on a variety of constructs—some concentrate on optimizing parts and components procurement, such as ANX—the Automotive Network Exchange. Some follow the process from end to end. GM's Order to Delivery network starts with the gleam in the prospective buyers' eyes and puts their custom-specified dream car in their driveway two weeks or less later.

Look at just about every level of the manufacturing process. Whether you are controlling the relatively straightforward and repetitive process of bottling product under automated controls or building a custom HVAC unit from a unique bill of materials on a job shop floor, computer, network, sub-network, and sub-sub network interaction is increasing both inside and outside the enterprise.

This is B2B land, and much of the "sides" structure that we described earlier had its genesis in manufacturing environments. We're going to move on briefly to a discussion of ERP and B2B. Manufacturing will make a series of cameo appearances in that one as well.

NOTICE A TREND?

We hope by now, with these few illustrations, that we've put B2B, e-Trust, and the transitional hybrid into higher relief. As we mentioned at the opening of this chapter, each major industry is pursuing its own course and speed on its journey to and through B2B. Within each industry, individual mega and micronetworks will share common characteristics but differ in significant detail. Many entities will belong to several or more B2Bs. All will require a high level of reciprocal trust if the relationships are to be safe and effective. But, don't let that worry you. It's only the world economy we're talking about.

9

e-Trust and ERP

In this chapter, we'll resume our discussion on ERP and e-Trust that we began in Part I. Some people mistakenly believe that because ERP in its most comprehensive form is a highly integrated system, B2B connections are incompatible with it. "Get in the nest with the rest of us or go fly away. You can't be part of the flock if you perch on a neighboring branch." I hope to show that it ain't necessarily so. In fact, quite to the contrary, B2B and ERP can work well together. As you might expect, e-Trust is an important ingredient. In the next chapter we'll review a related set of topics, the sides—buy, sell, inside, and infrastructure. You should cover these two chapters as a unit, if you can.

WHAT IS AN ERP SYSTEM?

An Enterprise Resource Planning (ERP) system is a packaged application software system that enables a company to

- Automate and integrate the majority of its business processes (see Exhibit 9.1)
- Share common data and practices across the entire global enterprise
- Produce and access information in a real-time environment

Note that some business functions are currently more strongly supported than others. If you check the asterisks in Exhibit 9.1, you will see a close

Exhibit 9.1   ERP Integration

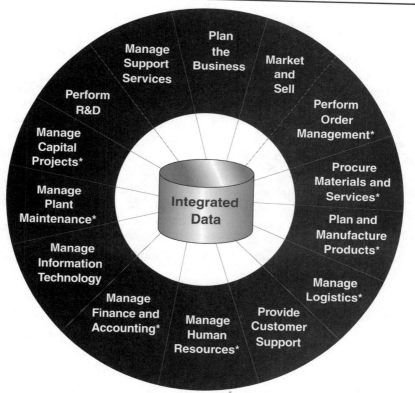

* Process Strongly Supported by ERP

connection to production. *Enterprise* doesn't mean pan-enterprise. Not all ERP systems are the same. We'll discuss that later in this chapter. For now, let's address the following Web question.

HOW WELL POISED ARE ERP AND THE WEB TO WORK TOGETHER?

Let's start out with a basic fact. ERP was not originally built with the idea of the Web as its primary support infrastructure or interface. ERP is sometimes referred to as back-end processing, and at its time of origin, the description was quite true. For example, SAP began life as a mainframe-dominated system, later provided a distributed systems form (minis on internal nets) with its Release 3 (R3), and then (with R4 and its Web derivative, MySAP) began movement toward Web support and integration. But important as they are, SAP is not the pattern for the entire ERP environment.

The term *supply chain integration* is often used synonymously with ERP. Here again, you get into difficult and dangerous ground by generalizing too broadly about ERP systems. You will also find that by taking the name *enterprise resource planning* too literally, you can get a warped view of its meaning. For example, does it only concern procurement and resource deployment? If you take a look at the processes asterisked in Exhibit 9.1, you'll see that's not true. Is it intended to be the answer to each and every enterprise need? I'm sure there are some marketing folks out there who would like you to believe that. But that, too, is not true. In order to get a clearer picture as to whether a Web-based B2B-ERP combination can serve your needs more profitably, you need to ask the question at the more specific product level, in the context of your unique need for and commitment to B2B and ERP and your business priorities. "Typical consultant answer!" Sorry, but anything else is misleading. Let's pick this back up again after we get a little more information out on the table.

EXAMPLES FROM CURRENT ENVIRONMENTS

At the moment we have coexistence moving toward integration. Some examples:

- A Web browser interface can allow customers and suppliers to inquire and enter data into the ERP system
- A single Web-based customer/supplier interface replaces a variety of individual application-based interfaces. Ease of use for the customer. Ease of maintenance for the system owner. The Web to customer/supplier site and interface may even be managed by a third party. The ERP to Web interface still rests with the system owner.
- Customer information for product configuration, current inventory level (available-to-promise), and pricing is available on the Web without building special transaction and query streams.
- 24-hour, 7-day-a-week access to the status of customer (order placed, products to order, shipping status, etc.)—the website runs asynchronously to the process systems unless absolute

real-time information is required. Some real time is more real than other real time.

- ERP portals enable end users to personalize and organize their computing environment.
- Business-to-business (B2B) maintenance, repair, operations (MRO) purchasing can be carried out over the Web.
- ERP will support and interface with Web-based sales catalogs

PROGRESS REPORT

OK, how well is this limited interoperation working so far? As you might have guessed, with some few exceptions the benefits of Web-enabled ERP packages have not yet demonstrated substantial dollar value to users. It's still early.

- Portals help end users personalize and organize their computing environments, but have been slow in facilitating full B2B interchange.
- The process of B2B MRO purchasing is efficient, but MRO purchasing rarely represents more than 20 percent of an enterprises purchasing function.
- Web-based selling has brought benefits (e.g., expanded market channels, increased customer base, and revenue growth), but the costs of maintaining the purchasing catalog is often greater than the savings gained in the purchasing process.

FUTURE CAPABILITIES

Moving forward, leading ERP vendors are focusing on using the Web for collaboration with trading partners to create Inter-Enterprise Communities (Virtual Enterprise), with capabilities such as:

- Multilevel supply chain available-to-promise (ATP)
- ERP vendors will offer "plug-in" packages of industry-specific functional depth, lower total cost of ownership, and superior, relationship-oriented services
- Business will behave as a "vertically integrated organization with partners"

Exhibit 9.2   ERP Security Functions

Security Function	Phase I Stand-alone service	Phase II Integrated Services	Phase III Integrated Supply-Chain Services
Point of Authentication	Application level	Centralized	Single sign-on
Point of Authorization	Application level	Application level	Single sign-on
Level of Authentication	User ID and password	Digital certificates	Public key infrastructure
Degree of User Monitoring	Minimal	Basic user monitoring	Intrusion detection statistical analysis

*Phase I—Stand-alone services, II—Integrated Services,
III—Integrated Supply Chain Services*

THE ROAD TO INTEGRATION AND E-TRUST

In Exhibit 9.2, we chose four security functions and have shown a progression of strength required as the Web–ERP integration gets deeper and more complex.

1. Point of authentication
2. Point of authorization
3. Level of authentication
4. Degree of user monitoring

Running across the columns, Phase I represents isolated Web functions on the same enterprise network, no doubt separated internally and possibly externally by a firewall array. For all intents and purposes, the Web and ERP are ignorant of each other's existence.

In the Phase II column, mutual awareness strikes. Carefully selected transactions, queries, and other activities are making arm's-length contact with ERP-related functions.

In Phase III, romance blooms, and many of the external functions that were provided by ERP through separate interfaces and networks (but not the Web) are *replaced* by directly coupled Web-based processes—from user to website directly to supply-chain functions.

As an example, let's look at Row 3, Level of authentication. Under Phase I, where the Web services are standalone, User ID and passwords may be more than adequate for authentication. In Phase II, with integrated services of the types we described as currently available, the direct substitution of digital signatures for passwords would add greater strength as an identity token itself, but would still use conventional modes of "password" management. Then in the tightly integrated environment of Phase III, where the impact of an unauthenticated user or process gaining access to a fully integrated system like ERP could ripple through the entire system, the extra management support that a public key infrastructure adds to the digital signature strengthens the authentication process further. See Chapter 18 for further explanation, distinctions, and definitions of digital certificates and PKI.

THEY'RE THE SAME BUT DIFFERENT

We are not going to walk you through a catalog of ERP systems. There are many. Let's take SAP, Oracle, and PeopleSoft, to name the most popular three. Each of these three came at enterprise integration from a different direction and birthplace (SAP from manufacturing, Oracle from financial and general ledger processes, and PeopleSoft from integrated HR), but they are all moving further into each other's points of origin and also venturing into some of those "unstarred" areas shown in Exhibit 9.1. Nor are such systems the exclusive province of the giants. J.D. Edwards has been providing comparable systems for the so-called middle market and doing it quite successfully. But, unless they can manage a richer set of interfaces and Web integration, such as the ones we suggested above, they will become constrained in their potential for growth.

Obviously, the greater the level of integration, the higher the level of e-Trust required. Vandals can do some damage by throwing rocks at my house, but once they're inside, we're talking massive destruction. In the next chapter, we will examine the so-called "sides." In one respect they represent a different cut at some of the same functions we've been discussing. The difference is they began life cognizant of and designed to take advantage of extranets, netexchanges, and netmarkets. Essentially, they are approaching the inner processing sanctums of the enterprise or B2B entity from the outside in. ERP is moving from the integrated inside outward. Whether they meet, collide, miss completely, or come within inches remains to be seen. As usual, just looking at the characteristics and design of the products will tell you much in a generic sense. But also as usual, the devil is in the details.

In any event, you can see that the trust requirements triggered by opening up ERP to the Web can be significant and complex. And yet, many extranets and exchanges are proposed around that very concept. That is, no doubt, one of the reasons we are in something of an absorption and digestion period in B2B, where we are figuring next steps and the levels of potential risk and complexity and, of course, the converse, levels of required e-Trust.

Please step this way. This car is leaving for Chapter 10. Watch your step—or, as they say in the London Underground, mind the gap.

10

A Little More on the "Sides," Please

No, we are not getting a haircut. At least, I'm not. I have no idea what you're doing while reading this. I assume you have perfected personal multitasking. If so, please go into single-task mode as soon as you can for this chapter. We're going to further explore the major components, functions, and characteristics that make e-Business what it is. After our relatively brief circuit of ERP land, let's take a somewhat longer look at the "sides" and their associated structures. Most of these same characteristics will be present in a more sophisticated extranet, as well as netmarkets and exchanges. Quite seriously, if you are tired or distracted, you may want to put off reading further. This chapter will take some concentration.

"SIDES" DEFINED, ONE MORE TIME

To prevent your scrambling back to Chapter 2, we've reproduced the definitions we presented there, only in shorter form. (We are still using the inside-common definition, not the inside and outside view we first discussed in that chapter.) There are four sides:

1. *Buy side*—The functions required to find, evaluate, "purchase," procure, receive, and take ownership of an item of property (tangible or intellectual), or a right to some service or status. The buy side has a strong genetic tie to the

151

industrial procurement process, but remember, we are talking about a wider range of goods and services, as well as B2B2C characteristics.

2. *Sell side*—Included in this function is a wide range of activities including website design and presentation, portal and service linkages, advertising, customer relationship management (CRM), market analysis, sales, fulfillment, service and returns, and a good healthy reach into supply chain and distribution management

3. *Inside–common*—The application gearbox between buyer and seller, which, depending on the number and nature of the parties and transactions, may be very complex. Inside-common membership varies with industry. Here we might find all of the dynamic and static records transfer, reconciliation, record keeping, payment, financial settlement, some billing functions, and so on between entities. These are processes, applications, and functions that *support* several or many separate, distinct processes or applications. You will also hear the term *middleware* used instead of inside-common. They're not synonymous. *Middleware is a subset of inside-common.* It is software that *connects* two otherwise-separate applications. Middleware is used to describe separate products that serve as the glue between applications. Inside-common does not necessarily mean inside a single enterprise. It means inside the extranet, netexchange, or netmarket structure.

4. *Infrastructure*—The technological underpinnings that support items 1 through 3. The most obvious is a complex, interoperable network. But also consider, as a trust-related example, the directory service and encryption key management processes that may be necessary to support this process.

Many sell, buy, inside-common, and infrastructure functions can be, and are, supplied by third-party specialists.

EGAD, HOLMES, WHAT IS THAT THING?

"Steady, Watson. It might be dangerous or it could be one of the most benevolent creatures on our planet. Approach it carefully; it's still rather rare." Before we start our discussion of the specific personalities of the "sides," let's take this opportunity to demonstrate how deep and complex a netmarket could get, viewed from one participant com-

Exhibit 10.1   NetMarket—An Enterprise-Centric View

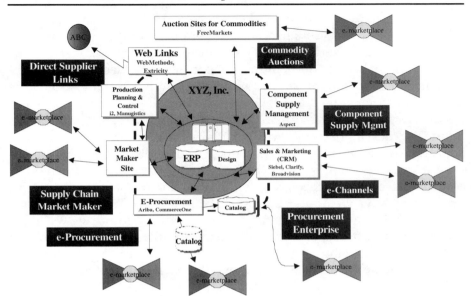

pany's standpoint. Take a slow and careful look at Exhibit 10.1. Does the animal exist? In its totality, seldom. In components and concept, yes. As we go on, keep thinking, "e-Trust."

This chart is not really as complex as it may look at first glance. I know—"That's what they all say." As usual, it's easier to think function than entity. We'll explain each box briefly. The diagram is lopsided. It's dominated by the buy side. In Exhibit 10.1, the large, dark boxes with white print identify business process environments. The white boxes in the inner ring describe functions or application groups. The names in the smaller fonts are typical systems or application solutions vendors for each area (by no means exhaustive nor necessarily recommended by D&T). The bow ties are other potential external e-markets for the services required. Quite a few aren't there? The arrows are arrows but notice they are all bi-directional. Interactivity and interoperation are at work.

ARE YOU READY FOR TODAY'S DISSECTION, CLASS? GOOD!

Our specimen is a manufacturer. Some label changes and a few redirected arrows, and you could have a financial services, distribution, energy, or healthcare environment. We'll start at the center and then progress counterclockwise around Exhibit 10.1.

LET'S GET RIGHT TO THE CENTER OF THINGS

Let's plunge right in at the heart. Here's our individual enterprise, XYZ, which no doubt considers itself the center of the universe. In our next chapter we refer to such enterprises as the powerhouses or stars. However, XYZ may be only one star in a galaxy and not necessarily as bright as some of its companion stars. But this is a simple diagram, so we'll let most of the other enterprises take care of themselves. You may have noticed where ERP and design are. Inside the enterprise, at least from an ownership and management responsibility standpoint. Could it be outsourced? More likely it would be insourced—with a third party running it inside the enterprise. Clearly our enterprise would have other connections and tentacles into other arenas. The treasurer's and CFO's offices may have a complex investment and credit netmarket that they work with. HR and legal may have their own. Periodically, we'll ask you to pause and think through the e-Trust implications of the subject we're discussing. This is such a moment. E-Trust must map to the environment, including all connections and interactions.

HOW TO REACH A SUPPLIER AND BUY SOME STUFF WHEN YOU DO

Most of the clock face from two counter-clockwise to four (component supply to procurement enterprise), represents variations on the theme of procurement. There is no implication of relative importance, or even that all of these business processes and specific functions would actually be in the mix for any given enterprise. It will vary by industry. (We're looking at manufacturing.) Obviously, they may come into play over different time periods, with varying speeds and priorities and be web enabled as needed to fit the overall business strategy.

COMPONENT SUPPLY MANAGEMENT

Let's start at the two o'clock position and go counter-clockwise. Component Management has a strong link to ERP. The classic bill of materials or its 21st-century electronic counterpart is in there driving the process. Only here, of course, XYZ has developed a composite components requirements view from all of their end products.

How many Defense-Department-approved machine screws ($250 apiece) do they need to support the entire manufacturing process for the next 90 days? (Or if they're into JIT management, for the next 24 hours.) What about using MitchCo for valves? Notice, however, that the requirements planning then links and progresses to the actual procurement process. Out they go to the relevant e-marketplaces. Or do they open their doors and let the marketplace in? When they approach those e-market bowties, what model are they using? Auction? Reverse auction? Are they anonymous or identified? Are they buying on the spot market or are they looking for forward pricing? Are they open to all comers like Mitch or do they operate strictly from pre-selected vendor lists.

Stop and think through how each of those choices will affect control and security. Identification, authentication, message integrity, nonrepudiation. Would digital signatures work here? Do they want them? Also consider all the entities involved that require some level of e-Trust.

COMMODITY AUCTIONS

From sheet metal to exotic elements, the commodity arena covers just that. Raw materials and raw services. However, extend your thinking. XYZ may be a buying player in the energy market on an ongoing basis. They could also be a supplier to the energy market. They could participate in spot markets on industrial diamonds or bid forward prices on semiconductor memory chips. "Semiconductors? That's a component, not a commodity." Yes and no. Unspecialized memory or processor chips are being treated in the market as commodities. As different elements take on common commodity structures and pricing models, this area and its rules of operation will become more inclusive. The lines of demarcation will continue to change. What *is* a commodity but some thing or service with sufficient common character and market demand that it can span large market segments.

The auction, Dutch auction, reverse auction, and related rules will prevail. Electronic auctions, by definition, are competitive, split-second, and not always polite. If you consider the e-Trust elements we mentioned earlier, nonrepudiation, confidentiality, probably privacy, certainly both process and data integrity, and lots of availability are necessary. Accountability and audit trail are musts. The phrase, "Let's review the bidding," has nothing to do with card games in this context.

Do we need identity management in an auction? Absolutely, but with an interesting twist. In certain circumstances, bidders and sellers may require anonymity before and during the process, and even thereafter. (Secret Agent 7.5, what has been XYZ's titanium bidding patterns over the past four years?) There are several mechanisms on the marketplace, including products from an organization aptly called Zero Knowledge Systems, that will make trace-back extremely difficult for all but a very, very trusted third party, and sometimes not even them.

HEY, DOESN'T ANYONE AROUND HERE BUY AND SELL THE PLAIN, OLD-FASHIONED WAY? BUYER AND SELLER DIRECT!

Of course, amid all the relative exotica, this is still the way most business gets done. At eleven o'clock on our chart, you'll see direct supplier links and a box marked Web links. This is the network-based transaction adjusted for the Web, and not too much else different. When we get to e-procurement, things will shift a bit more. Depending on the nature of the transactions, these links may have different levels of protection. Here's where the extranet structure comes into its own—a closed community selectively opened to trusted outsiders. The products shown facilitate common linkage. EDI or other transaction protocols may prevail. We're not dismissing this segment. It's just that it's the most used and, therefore, the most familiar. If you're on the net at all, you've been there, done that.

PRODUCTION PLANNING AND CONTROL

At ten o'clock, there is a category that looks like it may either be inside or outside the XYZ center. That's intentional. Although most organizations are reluctant to farm out all of their production planning and certainly their control, some outside entities, especially in logistics management and JIT planning, have a significant piece of the action. Here is a classic case of the beginnings of integrated, cooperative, and highly interactive e-Business. It may be managed by third-party ASPs or a group of suppliers or some combination. You will also see Content Service Providers in here. Needless to say (but we'll say it anyway), the variations can be substantial. Here's where data and process integrity will have a large role to play, as well as authorization management. The requirements for robustness and availability will increase as the process becomes more integrated and interactive.

SUPPLY CHAIN MARKET MAKER

Nine o'clock. It's getting earlier. Remember our definition of Market Maker in Chapter 2? No? Oh, good, I'm not the only one whose memory isn't flawless. Here it is again: B2B market makers are third-party intermediaries whose primary purpose, in most cases, is to match corporate buyers and sellers. They typically take a fee, make a spread, or receive commissions for their services.

Now, this could be a very specialized niche environment dealing with a restrictive set of commodities, parts, professional services, storage, transportation, travel, or just about anything an enterprise might want to buy. Or it could be the beginnings of a new netexchange or netmarket. The major difference, if there is one, is the degree to which the market maker actually participates in the transactions and transfer. As you move further into the netexchange, our old friend transintermediation kicks in, bringing buyer and seller into more direct contact through the structure and mechanics of the exchange, but not necessarily through transaction intermediation.

Obviously, the special market knowledge, expertise, contacts, and ability to facilitate that the market maker brings to the table are going to influence how essential it continues to be to the buy–sell process. This, too, will vary widely from industry to industry, environment to environment. You're going to see lots of grayscale here, so once again check your agreed-upon terminology. It's one more recognition of how ambiguous this world is with little sign of improvement.

E-PROCUREMENT

Seven to six o'clock. Since it was only a few paragraphs above, we will assume you recall our description of Web-enabled direct supplier links. (I'm using my own feeble short-term memory as a metric here.) e-procurement jazzes up that process significantly. Here is where the full, interactive, ubiquitous, and powerful abilities of the Web come into full play. Remember, we mentioned that e-Business growth is directed toward immediate transaction closure, not just acknowledgement. We're trying to reach it here by setting up the links, common transactions, infrastructures, terms, conditions, agreements, and atmosphere to make it a reality. Notice the catalogs and e-marketplace bowties (plural). There is serious multiparty, multiresource interaction going on here. All the e-Trust characteristics we've been examining will play out in force. Because this entire book is primarily about this environment and its next logical successors, we're going to move on to the next and final procurement category without further ado.

PROCUREMENT ENTERPRISE

This final example (five to four o'clock) is more of an organizational than functional or technological variant. The processes are essentially the same as the preceding examples, but we have now created a standalone enterprise to make its way, live its life, grow in size and stature, fulfill its value proposition, exceed market expectations, and make its management, employees, and stakeholders rich beyond compare. The e-Trust considerations, especially in the relationship, legal, and possibly regulatory arenas, will have profound differences from what we've seen.

And so, as the sun sinks in the west and our ship raises anchor, we bid farewell to beautiful Buy side, knowing full well that in our minds and in reality we will return, over and over again, to its enchanting shores. Not goodbye, just au revoir.

One more look backward. Any e-Trust issues here? You betcha! We listed some of them above, but they, just like this whole scenario, will continue to evolve. That hardly exhausts the buy side, but it may have exhausted you. Take a deep breath. Call the steward for some restorative sustenance. Our next port of call is the Sell side!

THE SELL SIDE—HAVE I GOT A DEAL FOR YOU!!

Let's finish our rotation at three o'clock. (Any three o'clock—0300 or 1500. This diagram is time zone insensitive.) It's the one point on our dial that is sell-side oriented, and we are about to take a much closer look. Notice the term, e-channels, and the potential e-marketplaces for sales and marketing. XYZ may use agents, distributors, in-house sales, re-sellers, aggregators, and hundreds of other individual channels, either online, Web-based or not, or at the other end of a fax machine and a telephone call center.

The whole marketing-support function is there, too, covering advertising, business shows, test markets, research. They are all potential networks in themselves. Finally, notice the inner box with the term CRM—customer relationship management. This will occupy us in depth a little later. Suffice it to say that there are a lot of different business relationships, as well as technological connections represented by the three o'clock club. If the relationships and connections differ, can the trust mechanisms and agreements come out of a single cookie cutter? Probably not. Actually, the technology could be somewhat more common than the operating terms and conditions. Of course, as we've stressed before, Sell is just one side of a two-sided coin. Buy (someone else) is always on the other.

LET'S SELL SOMETHING

You can stop looking at the exhibit now, since you no doubt can reproduce it from memory.

Full disclosure time: I have spent most of my life in sales, marketing support, marketing, and related functions. I have a distinct bias for this area. I will try to keep it under control. However, in today's e-supported marketplaces, there are an immense number of computer-based tools to assist in marketing, marketing support, and good ole direct sales in all its complexities. We'll decompose them shortly. Your enterprise may not break down the Sell side exactly into those three categories, but the odds are that you do all of them and more—even if you're a not-for-profit organization. (Fund raising?)

Many of these sell-side tools and services are going online or have been exclusively designed for online use. Most of today's online examples use the Internet—more specifically, the Web. But we are not going to take a tool or entity view. Once again, for a million dollars: We're taking an (a) functional, (b) functional (c) functional, or (d) functional view? What is your answer? "Functional." Is that your final answer? "Yes!" Hooray for you. See the cashier after the show.

SELL SIDE AND THE WORLD OF CRM

Flaky description time again. As we implied briefly, if you take CRM literally, you can make it cover most of the sell side. No matter what you do, there's a customer in there somewhere, and, directly or indirectly, there's a relationship that requires management. A few writers, I believe incorrectly, narrow CRM strictly to the management of customer data. We'll take the broader view. (BTW, for the umpteenth time, make sure everyone is using the term the same way in discussions.)

No matter how many or how few of them you cram into a CRM definition, all sell functions are there in your B2B(2C) environment. So let's talk about them without too much regard for how they are packaged. Of course, we can't maintain this aloofness from packaging forever, because many e-Trust processes and characteristics will appear in the individual package or service underpinnings. They will also appear in the inside-common and infrastructure areas. (No, we haven't forgotten them.)

But for the sake of getting on with it ("Yes, do"), we'll begin our Sell side explanation, function by function. No diagram this time. One fright is enough. We'll take on marketing first, then marketing support, and finally the sales process. There is a method to my madness. By proceeding from marketing through market support to sales, we pass through a shifting set of protective and trust requirements. Marketing, as I'm describing it, is dominated by information gathering; mining, analysis, and evaluation; strategizing and prioritizing. Sales is primarily operational; it is customer, product, and service specific and situational. Get and keep the business. Strategic versus tactical. Marketing support is in the middle. As usual, we're talking gray scale.

Obviously, for each of these three categories there will be industry variations and enterprise diversity. Marketing and sales of commodities, raw materials, finished products, professional and nonprofessional services, entertainment, travel, and hospitality will balance their priorities differently. We'll look at each category, examine its generic trust characteristics, and sample some potential Web-related sell-side functions that will support its requirements. The individual sell-side functions may appear in one, two, or all three of our categories. Once again, think matrix. We're going to look at each category sequentially. Before we plunge into a little more detail in each classification, you may want to get some idea of what is in all three of the categories and how I have somewhat arbitrarily divided them. Just page ahead a bit and look at the heading that starts each category discussion—Marketing, Market Support, Sales.

Marketing

Under the rubric of global, regional, national, and local marketing, we include

- Strategy
- Market segmentation
- Planning
- Strategic intelligence gathering
- New product and service evaluation
- Research, test marketing, and focus groups
- Market response measurement and analysis
- Competitive analysis
- Corporate image planning
- Brand management and differentiation
- Geographic and cultural differentiation

- Packaging design and test
- Test market design
- Customer satisfaction analysis and test design
- Analysis of marketplace perception of quality and service
- Channel analysis, evaluation, and selection

Now for some good news. We are definitely not going to cover each function individually. We'll just comment generally on the overall e-Trust characteristics. This area is information and data-scrutiny intensive. Data acquisition, mining, statistical analysis, and correlation are important. Data cleansing, integrity, and reconciliation are a must. Certainly the confidentiality of both intellectual property and process is one of the major considerations. But these are or have been in the past relatively static. What's new?

Is marketing a potentially interactive arena? I believe so. Collaborative modeling and gaming is a strategic science that is moving further and further into marketing environments. Continuous survey and sampling on the one hand and market analysis and reporting on the other can and will add a greater level of real-time dynamism to this group of functions. As the business processes become more real-time and network based, monitoring, extracting, and analyzing for quick response is critical.

You may recall our mention of Unocal's and other petroleum giants' exploration and market negotiation for drilling rights being governed by sophisticated, continuous source analysis. This area straddles buy, sell, and overall corporate strategy. Notice a trend? If the information and analysis is valuable, nothing as ephemeral as sell- and buy-side distinctions should stand in the way of its use. But as the information and its associated processes get wider uses and audiences, not just within the enterprise but throughout an entire alliance family, their asset value increases and their need for protection and precision also rises. I doubt ExxonMobil, Shell, or BP would want their detailed strategic oil and gas field exploration and development plans plastered all over the Internet.

Channel analysis and evaluation has obvious intercompany sensitivity and needs to be kept out of the wrong hands. It goes beyond sales performance and margin. As we have seen in the tire and automotive industries most recently, customer complaints, responses to satisfaction surveys, and the like can have immense impact. Are they getting back?

This area of strategic planning and design, coupled with think tank analysis, is going on the Web big time. It's building e-Trust concerns as it goes.

Market Support

Market support includes:

- Advertising
- Business shows
- Association and alliance support
- Internal contests and incentives
- Image management and some forms of external relations
- Image crisis management
- Sales promotion and customer incentives
- Marketing facilities and programs
- Collateral materials and support
- Catalogs and other descriptive materials
- Multilingual, multicultural, and multicurrency program design
- Test market support and implementation
- Launches and market removals
- Competitive intelligence gathering
- Customer satisfaction enhancement programs
- Channel support
- Channel and employee recognition programs
- Website marketing and service content
- PR and related functions
- Lobbying (in some industries)

In many respects, this functional grouping has the most potential for wideband damage or success. Although a sales effort can make or break an individual customer relationship, a poorly executed or prematurely leaked launch or support program can kill a product or service in the marketplace, torpedoing a well-thought-out strategy and plan in the process.

I know of (and mention again later) a cosmetic company that had to pull back a new product line because a competitor got out a month or two ahead with an offering that was practically identical in name, packaging, and description. They didn't build the product from scratch based on competitive intelligence. It was already in the pipeline. But they renamed it, tweaked the packaging, and accelerated the launch to blunt the first company's offering. It worked.

No moral or ethical judgments, please. The story is actually far more complex than I'm making it out to be. However, the intelligence was not gathered through clandestine cloak-and-dagger routines. Most of it was the result of sloppy handling. It came from several sources—in house, ad agencies, distributors, and the media each getting necessary advance notice of the launch. The irony is that the same cosmetics house had its R&D arm protected like Fort Knox. Is this an e-Trust situation? Of course. But it's one that will only be helped a little by protective technology. It would be helped a lot by procedural, contractual, and relationship rework. It gets more critical as more B2B processes become commonplace. Quicker dissemination to a broader audience increases the probability of leakage, misinterpretation, or misuse.

When I worked for IBM, our priced offerings and packaged combinations, and hence our sales plans, were extremely complex. We had a class of salespeople we referred to as sales plan strategists. These guys and gals would analyze the death out of the incentive program and, as they should, sell the products and services with the most rewards. However, they did this often to the exclusion of everything else in the line, as they shouldn't. There were also the sales plan lawyers who would look for loopholes, conflicts, and arcane combinations to wring every last bit of incidental and unintended compensation out of each sale, decreasing the margin on the sale in the process.

Whose fault was it if the plan caused other than desired results? Those who crafted it, of course. That responsibility will land in different places in different companies. But the impact will land in the same place every time—the bottom line. Incentive and compensation programs both internally and with channels need to be carefully constructed, launched, monitored, administered, and adjudicated. Otherwise, with Internet speed you may have a marketing program going in the wrong direction or off the tracks faster than you can fix it.

Two more examples, and we'll pass on to the sales. Channel marketing support might be less robust and responsive than expected, or might expose the channel to unfair disadvantages among its own competitors. e-Trust to the rescue. Also, for image crisis management, marketing support may or may not be primary but it's sure going to be involved, if in nothing more than PR and media relations. e-Trust comes into play from a variety of directions, especially for the required levels of confidentiality. E-mail discipline or lack thereof can be a major determinant but only one of many.

Sales

Sales includes:

- Forecasting
- Quota and incentive management
- Account management
- Territory organization and structure
- Sales and service staff recognition
- Sales force and management evaluation
- Sales training and development
- Performance tracking
- Operational intelligence gathering
- Executive awareness and courtesy services
- Pursuit planning, management, and execution
- Association and alliance management
- Collaborative selling
- Local sponsorship and support programs
- Presentations and proposals
- Order capture and entry
- Call center management
- E-channel management
- Website functional management and evaluation
- Post-sale followup activities
- Tech support, service delivery, or oversight
- Contract development and administration
- Fulfillment oversight
- Billing processes (consolidated, regional, third party, pass through)

If marketing is data intensive, this area is transaction intensive. Here is where much of today's CRM activities concentrate, from call center and e-channel management to customer billing and handling. Let's look at global collaborative selling and pursuit. Keeping the various sales managers and personnel in sync, up to date, and correctly recognized and compensated for global and cooperative campaigns is tough enough. Running a coordinated sales campaign is even more complex. It is not uncommon at Deloitte & Touche for us to jointly prepare in real time a proposal, presentation, or work plan converging from five or six different practice offices spread around the globe. We don't do it by fax or carrier pigeon. Version control, data integrity, confidentiality, and availability are all crucial. (DeMaio's Law: The availability of a necessary technology is inversely proportional to the immediate need for it. That's probably not original. If you want to claim it, go ahead.) Are we dependent on our networks? You better believe it.

But even more important than keeping internal ducks lined up is maintaining well-controlled, high-quality, secure links with your customers, clients, partners, and external channels. Web technology by itself will not do that. As an exercise, pick a few corporate websites at random and evaluate them for effectiveness, even if their only purpose is institutional identification. If they are oriented toward corporate, not consumer, business interaction, check them out further. Although a particular site might not be specifically indicative of how well the enterprise uses operational technology for B2B selling, it probably tells you something about how they view the use of the Web.

Fulfillment, tech support, and customer service—the three-headed bane of B2C—present an equally ominous shadow or glowing opportunity in B2B. It's probably time to drag out the quality, service, trust combination for another round of cheerleading. Like everything else that is "e," you can lose them and customers at electronic speed. It takes longer to build up or rebuild relationships than to lose them, but electronics gives you a marvelous opportunity to strengthen and cement them, if used correctly. Trust is at the center of that relationship building.

INSIDE-COMMON AND INFRASTRUCTURE

I've put these together for comparison purposes. One way of distinguishing inside-common from infrastructure is that typically inside-common is application and business function-aware and infrastructure is not. "Now, what the heck does that mean?"

An operating system and its associated security and control functions typically will serve a data-mining operation exactly the same way it treats a cataloging process—maintaining fundamental process integrity and isolation, safely allocating memory and storage, preventing address and path overlap, keeping network connections operational, supporting access management, and so on. Keeping the basic engine room going but without knowing whether it's supporting a cruise ship or a tanker. The inside-common areas have closer affinity to the actual processes. They support, connect, and enhance specific functions and applications with common functions and applications that are designed for use by several specialized environments. A common corporate receivables or payables system is on one extreme, a standardized application interface is on the other. We roam around these areas extensively in Part III but there is one point I want to make here. There was a time—and still is—when most people who dealt with computing believed that security and controls were the exclusive province of these two environments. Those days, as we have said, are gone forever. They are fundamental, they are deeply involved, but they are now part of a much larger ensemble.

Speaking of which, the e-Business Repertory Theater is gathering outside. On to Chapter 11.

11

Meet the *Players:* Powerhouses, Participants, ISPs, ASPs, CPs, CSPs, Portals, Hardware and Software Providers

This is not a Sesame Street *exercise on the letter P. It just fell out that way, and I took advantage of it. As we've observed, e-Trust communities can have a wide variety of players and roles. In this chapter, we are going to examine the relative shapes, forms, sizes, and functions that B2B players can adopt and, of course, their e-Trust implications. Where we have already defined and explained, we will not repeat. Where new constructs arise, we will try not only to define and explain them but also to put them in B2B and e-Trust context. As usual, individual relationships, industries, and functions will differ from environment to environment, so don't take these generic descriptions as being literally true in each instance of use.*

We'll talk only briefly about the powerhouses—entities that dominate in any B2B environment—since we've been spending most of our time in previous chapters looking at B2B from their viewpoint. We'll spend a bit more time on what I call the participant role—the company that usually acts as supplier to the big kids. However, for example, in distribution, retail, and healthcare, the participant can be both on the

*receiving and sending ends of the goods and services transactions—a
participant to some, a powerhouse to others. Finally, we'll pick up
again on the roles that can be filled by one or more of the product or
service providers we discussed in Chapter 2.*

*After a brief overview, we'll examine the players from three trust
perspectives.*

1. *Trust services, if any, that they may provide*
2. *Trust characteristics they must demonstrate*
3. *Special situations that may enhance or diminish trust*

OVERVIEW

Once again, we urge you to resist the temptation to pigeonhole specific
players and companies into one and only one category. Clumsy as it
may be in many circumstances, the functional view serves us better
here than the entity view. Think in terms of roles, with the understanding that in B2B we have high-speed repertory theater—a few stars,
some character actors in supporting roles, many bit players, and lots of
action behind the scenes. Each cast member may take on different roles
to satisfy the needs of the scene currently being acted out. So, as they
say in playbills, let's meet the dramatis personae.

THE POWERHOUSES

These are the stars whose names appear on the B2B marquee: The (in-
sert name of large organization) extranet. The Automotive Network
Exchange (ANX), starring GM, Ford, and, as of this writing, Daim-
lerChrysler. The securities exchanges and markets. We, and just
about everyone else, have discussed them at length. In true star fashion, they dominate the scene. Therein may lie a problem for the rest
of the cast, for themselves as well, and for the overall health and trust
of the B2B.

Stars are used to having things their own way and seeing the
world from their own perspective—exclusively. "Why not? They're
probably keeping the whole repertory group afloat. Where would
Mitch of MitchCo be without the big names?" (We'll have Mitch back
for an encore shortly.) On the other hand, there are few true soloists left
in the market. "Are you kidding? Look at all those vertically integrated
behemoths that dominate the scene!"

All right, let's look at vertical integration for a moment. Almost by definition, that's an ensemble process. In many cases, the only things keeping it together are a logo, an "org" chart, and consolidated financial reporting. Viewed from a process perspective, with one or two very rare exceptions, most of these vertically integrated businesses did their integration by merger and acquisition, and the absorption has only gone so far. In a sense, these earlier verticals are the progenitors of the B2B relationships we're describing now. As we said in Chapter 1, *What we are now testing is whether you can substitute e-Trust for direct ownership and control.* If so, business dynamics and economics will take on some remarkably new aspects. If not, well, we got this far.

But how much further can we go and at what cost? There are some who believe, with some cogent evidence, that the Internet and all its capabilities has contributed mightily to the economic slump that's afflicting the 2001 economy. (By the time you read this, the slump may be all over, or it may be much worse.) I submit there was little wrong with the basic dot.com and e-Commerce approach. There was a lot wrong with the riotous millennial land grab, the get-rich-quick mentalities, and the belief that major shifts could be executed without painstaking preparation and gestation.

OH, HAVE ANOTHER GIGABYTE—THEY'RE NOT FATTENING

"But the market for e-devices and net-based consumer services is in a state of glut, and many potential customers are disillusioned." Does this apply to the e-Business environments we are describing? Not entirely. For one thing, the consumer purchase of PCs, cell phones, and the like is not a good index of B2B development. It's a strange phenomenon, but industry and commerce, for years the leaders in the use of computers, are now in "later adopter" mode. It's easy to see why.

Much of the horsepower upgrades, bells, whistles, and gee-whiz features that drove the consumer PC market for so many years have little applicability to business needs (with one glaring exception: graphics). Many of us can barely say hello in a business meeting without backing it up with a million-color, animated, swipe and dissolve, high-resolution, and always original graphic extravaganza. And I am as guilty or more so as the rest. It is now embedded in the culture and it's a terrible waste of time and expense. "It looks professional." It sometimes looks ridiculous. What ever happened to simple lists? "They're all over this book." Ouch, one point for your side.

HOWEVER

There is another aspect to this commerce vs consumer pattern of hardware/software demand that is crucial to B2B success. The software developers and hardware manufacturers whose technology genes and history show strong bias toward the individual user and small network (they are legion and not only the usual suspects) have only recently realized that there is more to building industrial strength networks and processing environments than scaling up their baseline product set. You can scale a Piper Cub all you want but you won't get a 747 or A-300. You'll get a clumsy and un-airworthy Piper Cub. Forgive an old mainframer and more recently, a mini-based client server enthusiast, but there are key and fundamental design, usage, mean-time-to failure, performance optimization, capacity, multi-function processes, and security characteristics demanded by the types of B2B environments we are describing that are still not there in many of the products being offered for today's high-stakes markets. We'll have more to say on this shortly.

Let's scurry back to the subject at hand. Technological adoption is not the gating factor in B2B development. The issue at stake is whether the players can successfully analyze and adjust their own structures, business processes, controls, and policies and find the combination that is the most economically viable. Does an enterprise have to own everything it uses in order to assure control? Given the rise of third-party processes, the answer seems to be "no." Or is ownership just taking on a more subtle guise? I don't own you but I really do. How far can we extend the concept of coopetition? A major determinant will be trust, and much of that will be e-Trust.

REACH OUT AND FLOOD SOMEONE

One absolute necessity is for the powerhouse stars to put more effort into true outreach to the rest of the cast. By "true outreach," I mean more than a blitzkrieg of process engineers, financial planners, lawyers, auditors, security specialists, and technologists parachuting in, pushing and probing, and then dumping tons of standards, requirements, procedures, constraints, terms and conditions, and a long list of sanctions for nonperformance on participants and servicers. "Quickly, Sergeant, on to our next target."

True outreach means a powerhouse coming to an in-depth understanding of how the other entity operates and determining how a B2B relationship will impact them and thus impact you. In what ways can the stars modify their own behavior for the good of the relationship and ultimately for the whole production? "We haven't got time for that. We deal with thousands of vendors and partners. If they don't perform, we take them off our list. There's always someone else willing to jump in."

Sure, and I'm not suggesting that every relationship needs this "true outreach" approach. But switching partners is not without its cost to the stars. Maintaining and improving good relationships has some very real and very positive bottom line impacts. What has always puzzled me about the analysis and value propositions that show up around acquisitions and spin-offs is how little time is spent looking at how the actual marketplace operations of the new entities will be affected. And, as is often the case, how they will continue to interoperate.

And in B2B, we are talking about far more than traditional buyer/seller relationships, important as they are. We are talking about common and shared processes, liabilities, strategies, and performance. As we mentioned earlier, it's more than EDI. The powerhouses have trust obligations to their partners.

I remember a particularly nasty situation where an external, independent agent discovered that his territory performance, prospects, and deal strategies were getting into the hands of his competitors from—guess who? Not deliberately. Just slovenly data organization and security. The whole independent agency system, not just this one entity, was suitably aroused. Especially since they themselves were made to jump through hoops to make sure that the different stars they served never saw each other's data. The repairs and mitigation cost the powerhouse more than the original design for protection would have. The overall trust level sank. Even stars can't succeed without their agents.

To further illustrate the point, let us switch our attention to the supporting cast. Ladies and Gentleman, the e-Trust Theater proudly presents Mitch (of MitchCo) in a stirring performance of that all time hit. . . .

"THE PARTICIPANTS"

When we last left Mitch, he was patting his monitor and saying in exquisite Texan, "Domo arigato" to his website and his Japanese benefactors. The IBM commercial ended there, but life is longer than 30 seconds. As the curtain rises, Mitch sits pondering and then begins humming a few choruses of "This Could Be The Start Of Something Big."

As we mentioned in our look at financial services in Chapter 8, he is certainly going to need some financial assistance and support not only in scaling up production to fill the immense order he just received (Mitch does not believe in large inventories; that's one way he stays price competitive), but also in getting through the due diligence his Japanese star will no doubt launch before dealing with this stranger (we hope).

Now comes the first interesting turn in the unfolding plot. Will Mitch and his star seek an ongoing, formal, and hopefully profitable relationship, or is this a one-shot deal? If this was an online game or a reality TV show, we could all vote. Many factors enter into the resolution. What is the star's ongoing need? Is this end product that depends on Mitch and his valves one of the star's major offerings or an annoying, necessary, and hopefully profitable niche item? (You know, the kind the government orders hundreds of each year but they are the only user. Just enough to lock you in. Not enough to be profitable.)

For the sake of heightened drama and getting this exercise over with, let's assume this is the premier product in the star powerhouse's lineup. Let's further assume that its market life and performance is measured in terms of many annual reports. Let us assume even further that new products are on the design screens calling for Mitch's valve or—and this is important—other products and expertise Mitch may be able to offer. Thus, the frowns and smiles around the conference table. In other words, Mitch is singing the right song. This could be the start of something big.

But once the early euphoria subsides, our hero realizes that there could be a dark side to this relationship. Making sales through a website is one thing. Being latched into the global procurement system of a giant enterprise is another. Will he be scooped up at night and dumped unceremoniously in a DMZ? Will he be welcomed to the other side of the firewall? When he gets there, what will happen? Will he have to learn a new language? (Not necessarily Japanese—it could be EDI or SAP.) Will he have to invest in new software packages and hardware? What about security? Are they opening the doors to him, or is he opening his doors to them? Will their auditors and watchdogs add Texas to their visitation list? Will his price and delivery structure be plastered on a common catalog system for all, including his competitors, to see and profit by? How well protected is he against attacks, viruses, hackers, and the like coming from their network sites to his. If someone doesn't like the big Japanese conglomerate, will Mitch also feel the hacker's blast? Will he have to adapt to Japanese laws on a variety of intellectual property and confidentiality concerns? I suspect I've made my point by now.

So, let us draw the curtains on Mitch with the sincere hope that the something big he has started doesn't turn out to be a big pain. Am I trying to sink the integrated supplier concept? Absolutely not! I am saying that establishing trusted relationships is not an easy or one-shot stunt to pull off. If the stakes are high enough, it is worth the preliminaries to make the business and technological linkage as trustworthy as possible. In the long run, the economies are there. I am also reminding the powerhouse stars that when an elephant and a dog play with each other, most miscues are going to affect the dog more than the elephant. But, if the miscues are frequent enough or fatal, the elephant may lose a valued playmate in the process.

SERVICE PROVIDERS

Even with only the slightest knowledge of the theater, screen, or TV, you must know that there is a class of actor (both genders) who makes a significant living playing character roles. The heavy, the field marshall, the drunk, the glamour puss, the judge, the mother superior. Service providers are like that (not heavies or drunks). They usually play one or a small number of related roles in B2B.

You may recall that all service providers share at least one common purpose—providing access to a network connection, service, user base, or information resource. Whether it is simply opening the door to Internet access, supplying sophisticated navigation and linkages, resolving information and service searches, or processing entire applications or transactions, they act as support mechanisms for the network users. However, as they expand their market offerings, broaden their customer base and become more deeply bonded to their clients' operations, it becomes increasingly difficult to distinguish whether a content or service provider is supporting or replacing an organization's business processes.

Does it matter? It can, especially in terms of control, governance, and liability. It also begins to matter when that same service is supplying industry competitors with similar support. In short, they may become what the intelligence community calls a *covert channel* between businesses or institutions and may expose participants to accidental or deliberate compromise of their proprietary operations.

"But this is hardly new. Professional service groups and service bureaus such as ADP and EDS have been serving industry competitors for years." True! It's a matter of scale and speed. The differences in the e-environment appear in the scope, complexity, and number of net-based services a given entity may use and the relatively casual way in which those business relationships are often established and maintained. Sign on and go!!

A SHORT TOUR OF THE WORLD OF ASPs

The value proposition for an ASP is simple. *Why design, develop, maintain, and incur all the staffing and infrastructure expense of running your own applications and related data when we can do it for you, on the Web, more cost effectively, and with a higher degree of specialized expertise? Don't buy application software. We'll buy or develop it ourselves and maintain it, fight with the vendors, worry about interface issues, regulations, standards, and all that jazz. We'll sign on your partners and provide easy bridges for application-based B2B traffic among you. We make our money through standardized approaches, economies of scale, low Internet transmission costs, and numbers of subscribers. You run your business. We'll run your applications.*

Sounds attractive, and in many cases it can be. However, the years 2000–2001 saw a fallout in the ASP market that was only overshadowed by the death march of the dot.coms. An article in the March 5, 2001, issue of *Business Week* cites "market researchers as expecting 60% of the 500 or so ASPs to fail within the next year." Even major application software houses that have ventured into the direct application support and management business have stubbed their toes. However, there is a strong feeling among many software developers that unless they do supply services, their market for direct software sales will erode without a compensating source of revenue. Nevertheless, it's a different type of offering. Building software and providing vital application services are not the same thing. I have personal experience with several software developers who found this out the hard way.

WHEN'S THE FUNERAL?

(A couple are sitting in front of a TV watching a matinee idol in an old movie. She: "Isn't he dead? He: "No." She: "Well, who is?")

Is the ASP defunct or fatally wounded as a concept? Is the value proposition terminally flawed? Are ASPs as a group on the way out? I believe the answer to all of those questions is no. Those who are strong, agile, well managed, well financed with a high-quality, well-priced, broadly marketable or necessary niche service should do well in the long run, provided they can execute well. ("How profound, O omniscient consultant!" Yes, I admit you can say that about any enterprise. Welcome to Economics 101.)

But there is another message in the current ASP situation that is reflected in that same *Business Week* article. One of the major inhibitors for potential customers of ASPs is lack of trust. (I am not making this up or taking material out of context.) Not just technological trust. That's probably a relatively lower level of concern. Operational and business trust. Trust in the ASP's ongoing viability; in their industry and business experience; in their willingness to provide tailored service and quick response to special customer needs; in the knowledge and due diligence that must be exercised by the ASP to keep their customers compliant with applicable regulations like privacy and transaction integrity; in their sensitivity to dealing with competitive and arm's length relationships among their customers; in their security and control measures. In short, in all the stuff that you control when you run your own applications.

At a recent conference of security experts I attended, the single biggest worry about using ASPs was loss of control (perhaps not unexpected with security experts). But these folks and others cited in the article were reflecting or repeating their own management's concerns. In trying to restructure their operations and rebuild their markets, many ASPs need to reestablish e-Trust or perhaps establish it for the first time.

TABLE OF CONTENTS

Let us now take up the matter of content service providers (CSP). A using organization may only require incidental use or subscriptions to a CSP's subject matter repositories for research purposes. On the opposite extreme, a CSP may provide an entire catalog service on which the sales or procurement of an enterprise totally depends. What are the issues? Content quality and reliability are important in all instances. But improperly used or carelessly monitored by all of the players, the online catalog management scenario can also abet a number of abuses ranging from price fixing, collusion, and unfair practices to industrial espionage.

For example, this is a world where second-by-second price updates are technologically and operationally feasible. Sophisticated search techniques make both market pattern detection and instant reactive price adjustment easy. "All right, a pricing strategy based primarily on the other guy's last listed price may be fine for gas stations but. . . In B2B?" Try any commodity spot market. Auctions are on the rise, and CSPs support auctions. Of course, not all catalog services list prices directly. Some just list availability and provide links to the selling website. Either way, comparing the old 20-pound printed document, fiche array, or even CD-ROM catalog to an online CSP service is like comparing a turtle to a hummingbird.

THE PORTAL

The portal is really a marketplace or shopping mall where a variety of services and other delights are presented for the "employment and enjoyment of the distinguished business user." I am not talking about consumer portals, although many of my remarks would apply as well. This is B2B (and 2C). Some portals are closed—that is, all services are provided and managed by the portal itself. This would have described a typical department store, until they, too, started housing franchises. Most portals are open and, with disclaimers galore, provide access to a wide range of services and servicers, often oriented toward particular industries. One of the problems is with those disclaimers. Especially the ones tucked on Web screens in 8-point font, or in the last appendix of the service contract. By all means, consider and use portals when they make sense. In some cases, you may have no choice. But watch those disclaimers and perform your due diligence. This is an "eyes wide open" environment.

GOING ONCE, GOING TWICE, SOLD TO THE MULTINATIONAL IN THE FEATHERED HAT!

Consider also how auction sites can create a frenetic bid-response pace, to say nothing of a heightened competitive psychology. "Suddenly everything went blank, and I ended up paying a year's salary for a genuine ten-foot-long replica of the Battle of Hastings, signed by the original participants." The auction atmosphere doesn't end with individual collectors. Just look at some of the bidding wars enterprises engage in everyday. In price wars, auction frenzies, and supersonic trading, we all tend in the heat of battle to become as stupid and careless as our stupidest competitor. Just because we have the technological ability to jump off the deep end doesn't mean we should.

These are not areas for the same old controls or terms and conditions. Too many of our traditional application controls are reactive, slow, and built for single-stream transactions or transaction batches. To have an appropriate effect in e-land, they must be anticipatory, online, flexible, appropriately placed, and built for interactive multitransaction streams.

STOP PICKING ON US!

"Isn't this really a generic "e-problem?" Why single out the service providers?" For the same reason we should always look more carefully at functions we only indirectly control. We have less leverage, less ongoing knowledge, more motivation to compromise, and very often, slower discovery of problems. Granted that an enterprise that manages its own catalog system has the same or in some cases, greater potential for experiencing some of the abuses we cited. There is also much to be said for the state of the art controls, skills, and experience many third parties bring to their processing.

But any organization that uses a third party or parties to supply industrial strength, comprehensive, Web-based, critical services had better perform a great deal of study and evaluation on the service, its technologies, the service's own subcontractors and suppliers, its vulnerabilities, and its willingness and ability to take on and resolve liability. Further, you should examine these services in combination if they interlock to provide composite support such as catalog and product ratings. Finally, examine your own ability and experience in working with services. You could be part of the problem, if there is one.

Hardware and Software Providers

A little more full disclosure here. I worked for the IBM Corporation from 1956 to 1987 and quite literally grew up with the mainframe, the early operating systems, programming languages, networks, and devices. The Fable was based on real experience. No, this is not a trip down nostalgia lane. Nor would I trade my laptop for any of the museum pieces I worked on. (One mainframe I worked on, an IBM 7074, is in a museum. For those of you concerned about aging, discovering that fact can be a moment of grim reality.) But there was one thing for which I do have strong nostalgia—the sense of responsibility and responsiveness that IBM and other mainframers and mini hardware and software suppliers had toward their commercial clients. We didn't build everything right the first time. I can remember running the gauntlet at a number of user group and individual customer meetings about our hardware and software products.

But we made and kept integrity, reliability, security and control guarantees, and commitments about our operating systems and related products. We did it with heavy investment in a well-controlled, heavily staffed, and rapid response system. I grant that the user base was infinitesimal by today's standards; prices and margins on these products were totally different; and competitive pressure was nothing like today's market. Nor was there a consumer market to contend with. But, the needs of the commercial marketplace in 2001 and beyond (B2B or not) are pushing the envelope in all these regards and, frankly, the vendor response is not yet sufficient to warrant trust.

There's an interesting strategic side effect to the subsidence of consumer demand and the contemporaneous failure of many dot.coms. It's the same side effect that is causing software developers especially to start eyeing the service provider sector that we mentioned above. Suddenly, the commercial sector is where it's at. Fortune 1000—here we come. Many manufacturers and developers now advertise how they run their own businesses on their own products. If all the world was a gigantic, single-vendor software house or PC assembler with captive built-in tech support, that might be a little more impressive. But map many of the B2B environments we're describing against even the giant software or hardware developers and you'll find a depth, breadth, and variety of demand that goes well beyond any product, function, and trust requirement than any technology house has got internally. To say nothing about a major inventory of heritage systems that are still part of the average B2B scene. Remember hybrids?

In short, it may be something of a blessing that B2B takes longer than we may have thought. It may give the industry—suppliers and users—time to recalibrate. If not, B2B is going to be slower and more painful than it needs to be and the whole economics of e-Business will be the worse for it.

BACK TO e-TRUST

Service providers, like our character actors, come in many shapes, sizes, and roles. Let's define and evaluate the issues we mentioned in the introduction:

1. Trust services, if any, that they may provide
2. Trust characteristics they must demonstrate
3. Special situations that may enhance or diminish trust

Trust Services

The most obvious are the "pure play" trust providers. Digital certificate or registration authorities are two classic examples. (See Chapter 18, on encryption.) In fact, we refer to them as *trusted third parties* (TTP). They are the outsource alternative to building and maintaining an entire Public Key Infrastructure (PKI) certificate management system yourself. Network monitoring is becoming a popular function for outsourcing. Do you write and maintain your own anti-virus programs? Even firewall design, maintenance, and update are available from external providers. On the assurance side (see Chapter 21), a number of services online and off are available. D&T supplies some of them. Some parts of backup, recovery, and crisis management have been outsourced for years. So, information protection and e-Trust is no longer necessarily an inside job.

Trust Characteristics

Besides the expected levels of integrity, confidentiality, availability, and nonrepudiation that are implicit (but not always present) in any B2B exchange, the service providers occupy a special trust category. e-Trust is built into their whole reason for existence—to supply services more cost-effectively than if the users had to provide them themselves. Included in that cost-effectiveness is an expected level of trust commensurate to the relationship. But what is that level?

Let us take that a few steps further. It is incumbent on the service and the service recipient to make explicit their respective e-Trust positions. Just what are the trust obligations of an ISP to its customers? What specifically does the user want? Is $24 \times 7 \times 365$ availability one of them? Be prepared to pay handsomely for that assurance. How about encrypted transmissions? In an e-mail service, how many repositories are there, and how well are they protected? Can a foreign government exercise surveillance over the provider's traffic and repositories? Is a subpoena necessary? Will you know if one is served? What does it mean if you delete a message, entry, or service request? Is it gone forever, or is it stored in any number of backup locations? For that matter, what backup recovery commitments are required and what are supplied?

In an auction, what are the rules and how are they enforced? Is anonymity, if required, guaranteed? How and with what sanctions? Does the service take any responsibility for fulfillment and payment? The B2C online auction houses provide surprisingly little protection in any of these regards. It's not quite *caveat emptor,* but it's not trusted agent either.

Does a content provider stand behind the integrity and accuracy of the material being supplied? Are consequent damage compensations possible? Unlikely! What are the liabilities if a catalog or rating service makes a mistake? What recourse do you have? If the service is supporting competitors, how well are the information and service processes isolated? Are these services insured? By whom, against what, and for what amounts?

The list can go on and on. "I was afraid it would." Sorry. The purpose behind this "yet another list of questions" is to get you to pay more attention to the need for them—whether you are user or supplier. Too frequently, mature businesses, that certainly should know better, enter into such trust relationships without ever checking to the depth that the process requires. Each comes to the connection armed with a set of assumptions that are driven by exactly opposite motives (taking each other at inter-face value). The user wants total protection against all hazards for no extra cost. The supplier wants a liability-free relationship offered as part of a standard contract. Both are illusions. But in the eagerness to set up the service and move into the B2B process, they are often overlooked and only explored when an incident makes it necessary.

This sounds like a full employment program for corporate lawyers. Well, they should be involved in creating the final instruments of agreement. But, to be blunt, many corporate lawyers do not yet fully understand the implications of such arrangements. They should.

Special Situations that May Enhance or Diminish Trust

Licensing and certification come to mind immediately as an enhancement. This is an infant environment, and it is seldom clear who is or should be the licensing agent. (Don't worry. Not another catalog of questions coming up.) Once again, be careful to find out what the specific certification really means. For example, in Chapter 21 we address the WebTrust process provided by members of the AICPA-CICA, primarily in B2C situations. Here not just the security of the process but the business viability and practices of the supplier are checked according to good accounting practice. Is there a commensurate need in B2B? I think so. Whether the seal of approval comes from an outside authority or within your own organization, look for one or help to create one.

Does a content supplier provide the same guarantees to its online users as it does to its hard copy subscribers? If there is a variance, what and why? Also, it is crucial to find out if you are indeed dealing directly and exclusively with the service you have contracted with. For example, many small or not so small service organizations farm out their technical support call-center to an outside organization. These can vary from a simple answering service to a fully staffed expert group.

What portal or ISP supports your service entity? How good is it? Remember, the ways service groups can and do cut cost is through using outsourcing themselves, usually in the less apparent but necessarily less vital areas of customer service. The nature of the Internet is such that cascading transfers of service are commonplace. The next time you bring up a corporate website, see if you can determine if other parties are in on supporting the business portion of the connection. It's tough to tell, but the odds are heavily in favor of multiple parties. We heartily recommend a list of questions for a service supplier that starts with: Who provides your _____ functions? "We do our own," may or may not be the desired response, depending on the process involved. Many "home-made" foods taste terrible. Find out who's involved and then, unfortunately, if that secondary or tertiary service is key, you may have to do second-, third-, and possibly more-level checks. Is all this necessary? It depends entirely on your level of dependence and the consequence of supplier failure.

Finally, there is such a thing as a service supplier being too popular. Popular services make great hacker targets and may also suffer overloads. This applies especially to portals, ISPs, and ASPs. It's not always practiced, but it's good business to seek an alternate or backup source. In the case of ISPs and portals especially, consider splitting the service over several vendors from day one.

I hope our admittedly brief and incomplete introduction to the cast of the e-Trust theater has been helpful. You're in there somewhere, if you're involved in B2B, and not as a passive audience. Everyone's an actor. You may play several roles. One major role is to take all possible, rational steps to make sure the B2B process has a happy ending, if there is an ending. No room for farce or tragedy here.

12

External Forces Affecting e-Trust

This chapter deals with issues that B2B and Beyond enthusiasts ignore at some peril. Some of you, inspired by the spirit of "getting on with it," may, frankly and for that very reason, lack the patience and perspective of "realpolitik" required to work within the often frustrating, and in some cases destructive, constraints thrown in your path by some of these external forces. Having said that, I am not suggesting that all of these forces and issues we're about to discuss have been developed by bureaucrats or radical opponents of global business and technology simply to be as obstructive as possible. As others perhaps see even more clearly than we "net-o-philes" do, this is big-time stuff we're talking about. In planning and developing global networks of the types we've been describing, we are perhaps slowly, but certainly significantly and forever, changing not just how your company or industry does business. We're changing how the world does business (and lives and grows and prospers and comports and governs itself). I don't believe that is overly dramatic.

In many cases, it is not technology or even business problems but the social, political, and economic issues that will slow the rate of growth, alter the course, and create and sustain the need for retaining transitional hybrids beyond our expectations. The B2B and Beyond community is not going to achieve worldwide transformation and success on a timetable developed in isolation. Here, too, for better or worse, you are not alone.

This chapter is not intended to discourage you or to be a catalog of socioeconomic gloom and doom. It is intended to cover the waterfront of issues that you and your B2B companions should check for coverage and impact. Not all will apply equally, but if none of these resonate with you, you're not involved in B2B and Beyond.

A QUICK ILLUSTRATION OF A MISLEADING MINDSET

Let's assume you're a B2B enthusiast (a big assumption). In the midst of our own technomania, it's easy to become convinced that the entire world is unanimous in its approval of and avid desire for vast, global networks that bind us in 24 × 7 × 365 commercial interaction. It ain't necessarily so.

Recently, at a conference in Helsinki, I was challenged by several of my Finnish colleagues to explain why a small country like Finland could be so far ahead of the rest of the world in the use of cellular phones and wireless Web connections and why the tech-crazy United States lagged so far behind, relatively speaking. The answer is simple, really.

Getting 5.2 million Finns

- with an extremely high literacy rate,
- 93 percent of whom speak a common language,
- well over half of whom speak a second language, usually English, fluently, and
- who live in a country that is 338,000 sq.kms. but is 79 percent forest and lakes,

to accept a technology that is

- easily assimilated into their daily lives,
- provided and promoted by Nokia, one of the world's largest telecommunications equipment suppliers and a very major Finnish employer, and
- heavily supported by the Finnish government and telecom infrastructure

is no big deal, especially when so many citizens are involved in producing or supporting the technology and process.

I won't bore you with a defense citing U.S. or North American geography or demographics or the nature of the deregulated telecom environment or the fact that Finland has roughly the population of Tennessee. What is important is my Finnish friends were committing the same error that all of us in the technologically advanced business communities do when we try to project our model on the rest of the world and wonder why the dullards don't immediately and fully embrace it.

There is a vocal school of thought, not necessarily restricted to fringe activists, that sees global networking as a very powerful and insidious form of colonialism. In North America and the European continent, we speak of a digital divide separating the social, economic, and cultural haves from the have-nots. That same concept has also been projected on a worldwide scale by some well-known authorities, and with some justification.

What has this got to do with e-Trust? I hope you see it already. In a world environment that is already sensitive to the downsides of technology and does not always see global networking as the level playing field we believe it can and should be, we need to be extremely careful not to provide additional ammunition for projecting e-Business as a survival of the fittest, winner take all, land grab. E-Trust is more than a clandestine handshake between consenting parties. It is an open and accurate image of sensitivity, honesty, and above-board operation projected to the world and justified by the facts.

IT'S NOT JUST BANDWIDTH

Let's be clear. Networks and innovative business processes and organizations are *necessary* but they are *not sufficient* conditions for the growth and acceptance of B2B and Beyond. Our acknowledgement and appropriate response to national, regional, technological, social, legal, political, and religious concerns will make, break, or at least seriously alter or defer the arrival of electronic bliss (whatever that is).

If, at first glance, this list seems more appropriate to a B2C venture than B2B, read it again in the context of a large service entity trying to establish itself with business customers in the Middle East. These factors are interdependent. Together, they set the pace and character of e-Business expansion. If one aspect, say technology, no matter how viable, outruns the others, it may stay in limbo for an inordinate amount of time. Equally, there's not much point stirring the social or political pot unless the technology and economics make sense. Even if the economics look good and the technology is available, negative social reaction may throw a monkey wrench in the virtual (net)works.

PUBLIC OPINION—NATIONAL AND GLOBAL

When it comes to e-Business or even information technology, not everyone, even a true believer, shares the same vision, desire, or priorities.

"Nothin' wrong with expanding networks, I suppose, but if public funds, rights-of-way, building towers and satellite launches and hordes of antennas are needed, let's build roads, hospitals, schools, and airports first." Is that an attitude restricted to third-world countries and the backwaters of the United States, Canada, and Australia? Try again.

You'll find differing priorities and antagonism a lot closer to home (wherever home may be). Ask anyone who went to the November 1999 World Trade Organization Meeting in Seattle. Did those riots do serious damage? Yes, and I don't mean just to storefronts, parked cars, or hotel lobbies. An atmosphere of hostility, hypernationalism, eco-fanaticism, anti-technology, and shrill voices shouting from the peaks of the "moral high ground" can create a corresponding tentativeness, confusion, and counter-hostility in many global enterprises contemplating expansion, networking, exchanges, and e-Business.

Public opinion is volatile. It can swiftly swell or decompress, be loud or submerged, turn on a dime, change color, tone, and volume, and do irreparable damage. "OK, omniscient consultant (OC), stop beating up the obvious. What do you recommend?"

FIRST, GET OUR OWN STORY AND CONFIDENCE IN SHAPE

And I don't mean creating spin. *Spin* implies lack of belief in your own position. (Although one organization's external relations officer can be a "spin doctor" to some other group.) Let us assume that you are somewhere in the high neutral to supportive part of the B2B2C spectrum. How do you feel about the social and economic impact of what you're planning?

If we're having trouble convincingly explaining the benefits of B2B2C to ourselves, then how do we persuade others? At least in part by being honestly responsive to their concerns, fears, and priorities. Notice—I did not say "valid" concerns, fears, and priorities. We need to tone down our own judgmental attitudes and look behind the stereotypes to understand what is causing the issues. Some viewpoints may indeed be irrational or cynically self-serving by any objective scale. Unfortunately, they are still real and must be addressed. But most have merit. In some cases, once we see it from their viewpoint, we may agree they're right.

USE GEOGRAPHERS TO UNDERSTAND THE LANDSCAPE

Forgive me, but the average network designer is not always an astute practitioner of the economic, political, and social arts. For that matter, many Type A results-oriented business managers don't score high in the finesse department and often even fail to see the point of exercising diplomacy or recognizing the other guy's viewpoint. Of course, these are the very people whose skills and energies you want spearheading your project, but there are times when you shouldn't let them out alone.

Believe it or not, lawyers are not always the best choice for establishing proper social and economic perspective, either. I speak especially of the "win at all costs" variety or their polar opposites who believe completed legal staff work is giving you 20 reasons not to do something instead of finding a legal path to attain your goals. (Is this leading up to a pitch for consultants? Not necessarily, but you should take a look at your talent pool and determine who is best suited to work this part of the street. It's usually a group effort, especially if you are in a global environment.)

Remember, by definition, in B2B and Beyond your enterprise is not alone. And quite seriously, the problem, if any, may not be with you and your team. The other guys may be the social or economic dumbbells or kamikazes. How much do you and your partners trust each other to have the right level of understanding, experience, priorities, and willingness to cooperate both outside and inside the "club?" Depending on your industry, your specific business processes, scope, and a hundred other conditions, you may have to play the socioeconomic cards very carefully. Can the virtual equivalent of a major oil spill happen in a connected business infrastructure? Need you ask?

BECOME PC—NOT "POLITICALLY CORRECT"— PRAGMATICALLY COOPERATIVE!

It's a bit disingenuous to take an 19th-century "join our parade or get on the sidewalk" approach to well over half the world's population and then write them up in your business plan as sources of future expansion. Yet, many global network value propositions read exactly that way.

For a phenomenon like e-Business to catch on and continue to grow, there are a number of "soft" considerations you must take into account and respond to. No, we are not encouraging you to forcefully and emotionally embrace the early IBM motto "World Peace through World Trade" if you are not so disposed. (It's actually a pretty good idea.) Nor are we trying to discourage you from timely execution of your plans for B2B and Beyond. Quite the contrary, we are trying to make sure all your good efforts don't land on the rocks for lack of some basic local national and international, social, or economic sensitivity.

Image and trust are important in e-Business, not only with your business partners but with the environments in which your networks will operate. What are some of the things to take into account?

LITIGIOUSNESS

Everyone has their pet theories as to why society in general and especially in the United States is seeking the law courts more and more frequently to resolve their issues and disputes. I won't bore you with mine. While the root causes need to be dealt with or we will fall victim to "Every House is a Bleak House," the fact remains that litigation or blackmailing threats of litigation have taken hold. B2B and Beyond is a tempting target.

There is a hypothesis that major lawsuits are initiated not so much on the merits of the case or the impact of the damage but on the population of "deep pocket" participants who can be named as defendants. In some of the network environments we are talking about, it would not be surprising to see the entire global Fortune 1000 on the defendants list.

Not only that, but again by definition, global B2B2C networks will operate in an enormous number of different judicial venues and under a bewildering array of laws and regulations; many of which may be conflicting or mutually exclusive.

Global or multiregional nets can be scary to the uninitiated. They're favorite targets of the media although strangely the media is in the vanguard of building and exploiting networks. (Go figure.) They can be the archetypical symbol of big business throwing its weight around. Remember, Goliath did not have much of an image in the biblical press. Juries generally do not like "big." Some judges like to leave a historic legacy as the "Giant Killer." In short, get used to the idea that in the eyes of many, no matter what you do, you're going to look ugly, simply because you're big and you're using technology and processes that are not well understood and could therefore be threatening.

You also know, I'm sure, that an incident in one environment can be extrapolated by the press, public, and advocacy groups to any other group that looks remotely similar. Sometimes, it's justified. Have you ever watched an entire industry act like lemmings? In a price or market share war, the IQ of the entire industry can descend to the level of the stupidest player. Networking and blurred corporate identities can exacerbate the impact of one dope. "They're all the same, those big B2B's. Exploiters and oppressors."

"All right, so what do you suggest, OC? Stealth networks? Transmit subliminally? Use lots of dogs and cute animals in our advertising? Give all our profits to charity?

My, you're getting touchy! Actually, none of the above. The best advice I can give is "anticipate" and "be prepared." Put B2B external relations on a higher priority than it probably occupies, resist posturing, get some in-house and external expertise on the topics we're covering, and actively pursue the development of far more realistic approaches to regulation. We'll talk further about *safe harbors* under privacy. They are not panaceas. They can help. Get your own governments and social agencies on your side, even if you're convinced that other governments are hostile. You may be right.

Explain, explain, explain up front in terms that are meaningful to your specific audiences. Will it play in Dubuque, in London, Paris, Brussels, and Berlin, in Beijing, in Kuala Lumpur, in Ottawa, Mexico City, Sydney, Sao Paolo, Capetown, Oslo? Will it play in the Muslim, Buddhist, Hindu, Jewish, and Christian communities? Will it play with most major ethnic and racial groups? Will it play equally with women and men?

Do they see positive advantages and sources of hope, or just another form of interference, deterioration of their rights, and oppression? Are you playing into the hands of rabble rousers and demagogues, or are you taking the proverbial wind out of their sails? Can one version of your message cover that entire audience and spectrum of views and beliefs? Definitely not! Speak to each audience separately but consistently. Don't get caught talking out of both sides of your public relations mouth.

"But all this is going to cost money and possibly slow down the program." Yes. It's a cost of doing global B2B. But remember, in most cases, it's a shared cost across the network, and it's also a measure of how committed your partners are to the cause. You'll make some remarkable discoveries about them as well as yourselves in the process. Compare the up-front costs and efforts with having to dismantle or alter a major segment of the program after it's online, or paying all sorts of compensatory as well as punitive damages.

We are not naïvely suggesting that you can build a PR and legal "impervious force field." Some litigation and public damage is inevitable in the B2B spectrum. Accept that, prepare for it, and keep your expectations in check. You will still sustain some hits. But you will also live to fight another day. Wish I'd said that.

INTELLECTUAL PROPERTY RIGHTS

Now here is a classic example of the situations I was just talking about. Mention intellectual property in any general discussion, and you will immediately get back "Big Music—the rapacious recording companies," "Big Entertainment—the self-centered motion picture, print, and television industries," "Big Software—making it necessary for struggling countries and small enterprises to become pirates in order to survive." "Big Technology—stealing the rights of the small entrepreneur and inventor." "Big Pharmaceuticals—wringing every penny out of their patents and licenses." "Big Manufacturing—hiding product deficiencies" "Big Medicine and yes, Big Professional Services Firms."

In the past 20 years, there has been a slow but inexorable shift in our understanding and attitude about intellectual property. At first we kept trying to force-fit information into existing tangible property law and ethics. But the jig was up the first time we realized that you can steal intellectual property and still leave the original in the hands of the owner; that you can sell lists over and over and over again; that the value of a motion picture far exceeds the film or tape it's recorded on. That had been a customs and insurance issue for generations—how to value a film? I had an industrial film library destroyed in the 1970s. We were compensated for the value of the raw stock footage—period.

Privacy puts the whole concept of data ownership in high relief. Want to start an argument? Ask any doctor or medical administrator who it is that really owns your medical record. Should a doctor be able to transfer your records without your consent as part of selling or combining his or her practice? What are your rights as data subject, if any? We touched on privacy, confidentiality, and anonymity conceptually in Chapter 7 and will do so several times more in the "Making It Happen" discussions of Part III. In the next few paragraphs, we are going to discuss privacy in the context of regulation.

INFORMATION PRIVACY—THE REGULATORY SCENE

This is a long discussion because it's complex and, frankly, messy. We've tried to streamline it a bit and to give you Internet reference points if you or your staff wish to pursue it further. Bits of it descend into legalese and bureaucratese, but we're trying to use some primary sources here, not just interpretation. Hang in there.

If you had to characterize the intent behind information privacy protection regulation in one phrase, *it is to ensure that the personal data subject's rights are appropriately established, fairly represented, and preserved in all relevant situations.* It essentially creates a legally sanctioned and binding contract between the data subject and the data collectors, creators, owners, or users and those representing or dealing with them. Anyone for e-Trust? That contract can be enforced, if and as necessary, by an arm of the government with jurisdiction in the matter.

Having established that baseline, things then fuzz up pretty rapidly. The term *personal data* itself is interpreted differently in different world, national, state, local, and industry regulatory jurisdictions. There is some unanimity on the most common forms of individual personal data that should be protected, such as religion, race, sexual orientation, and political affiliation. Also important are other factors that could result in discrimination, embarrassment, or damage such as medical histories, arrest (not conviction) records, and ethnic origins. Most laws take special notice of children and those incapable of directly pursuing their rights.

But the specifics vary widely. There are also derivative privacy regulations that pack just as much authority as mainline legislation. Fair labor practices, consumer protection, banking and financial services controls, equal opportunity initiatives, healthcare, Social Security, election laws, and an almost infinite number of case law judgments all add different-colored tiles to a confusing mosaic. Please bear in mind that privacy protection extends far beyond specific privacy legislation and regulation. Your B2B2C privacy program should encompass all of the relevant guidance and strictures that will apply to all of the network participants. That can be a tall order if the extranet, netexchange, or netmarket is multiindustry and multifunctional, in addition to being multinational. We'll revisit some of these "derivative" privacy protection regulations in several other comments on external forces. For the moment, let's go back to mainline privacy regulation.

Oddly, there has been less historical unanimity on what constitutes a person. "Come again!?" It's true. Although it has been the subject of many reinterpretations and renegotiations, early privacy laws in Europe, especially, extended the concept of privacy to the legal person (company, institution, organization, government) as well as the individual person. As you might imagine, this approach created some consternation. The general U.S. consensus was that organizations had considerably more resources and protective options at their disposal than individuals— ranging from contract law to copyrights, patents, and the like—and that the extension of legal protection was superfluous and burdensome. Businesses in most countries also live under full disclosure and subpoena requirements that change the list of subjects that need protection. There is still a residue of the legal person in some laws and regulations but at this point it is generally agreed that a person is you and me.

By the way, there's still no full agreement on what this area should be called. You'll hear both data protection (Europe) and privacy protection (United States). There is a difference of intent and priorities implicit in those different names and, in the early years, the differences were far more explicit. Both names have ambiguities. Data protection is often confused with intellectual property rights. Privacy as a concept also encompasses illegal entry, spying, paparazzi and nosy landlords. In Europe, *data security* means safekeeping of all forms of data, personal and otherwise. In the United States, unfortunately, it can mean almost anything.

I'm dragging out a little of the history here in order to reveal some of today's privacy (data) protection's genetic code and regulatory forbears, and also to show off. I helped write and debate some of the U.S. and international language, terms, and conditions in a few of the early regulations such as the OECD—Organization for Economic Cooperation and Development guidelines in the late 1970s and early 1980s. Notice please, during this formative period, the Internet did not exist. Much less did B2B2C. Some of the existing legislation still reflects that difference in viewpoint.

Back then, transborder data flows emerged as a key privacy concern, especially since few countries had consistent laws on protection. What happens when information leaves one country and goes to another? Will it be protected the same way? Must a copy of everything shipped out remain in the country of origin? Often as not, transborder data flows referred to packing up hard-copy data files and physically shipping them to another country as it did to electronic transmission. (Some leased lines and terminals but no e-mail, FTP, or Web sites yet.)

Is this history relevant? In a way, yes, because legislation and regulation are often slow to catch up. If privacy laws in some countries sound a bit irrational or outdated, they probably are. Of course, much has happened since. Many changes, especially those concerning some but certainly not all aspects of the Internet, have been recognized and at least partially dealt with. Others are still on hold or being debated. Many laws have gone from specific direction to general statements of policy, leaving current interpretation to the responsible parties. Most major countries have some form of regulation. More has been done through compromise and operational agreements. Let's trace some of the typical forms, characteristics, and directions privacy regulation is taking on today.

MAJOR PRIVACY REGULATION ASPECTS

Sector versus General

In the United States, as we have indicated, much privacy legislation is directed toward particular industry sectors—financial services, consumer credit, healthcare—and is monitored and enforced by a variety of entities, often those involved in the overall regulation of the industry involved. Although this fragments the privacy protection landscape and makes it difficult to "one-stop shop" for your own regulatory guidance, it does make it possible to tailor privacy regulation to the individual needs of each industry. It also gives the industries a greater say in what goes into the regulation and how it is interpreted and enforced. Some U.S. examples are

- *GLB*—Gramm–Leach–Bliley Act—a U.S. law passed in 1999 (regulations were completed 12/20/00)
  - Establishes security as a valid subject for regulatory control and audit
  - Applies to all companies that "appear financial in nature" (No, we are not yet sure what that includes and excludes)
  - Given to a variety of agencies to enforce—usually the specific regulator of the sub industry (brokerage, credit cards, savings banks, insurance)

  Title V of GLB requires that financial institutions as vaguely defined above do the following:
  - Protect consumer data from technical, physical, and administrative threats
  - Write a privacy policy according to GLB guidelines
  - Disclose this privacy policy to each "customer" at specific intervals
  - Obtain consumer authorization prior to information sharing with "third parties"
  - Give consumers the ability to opt out of information sharing
  - Track third-party use of information (chain of privacy)
  - Strictly limit use of consumer information

  Each company was required to have a Board-of-Directors approved plan by July 2001. GLB grants to states the ability to enact stricter regulations. Many states have written or are writing strong supplements to this law.
- *COPPA*—Children's Online Privacy Protection Act requires verifiable parental consent before personally identifiable information from or about children under 13 can be used on the

Internet. Unfortunately, it is out of balance in not covering the same information offline (like the telephone). It concentrates on the medium, not the content. It has another provision that is causing consternation both in the United States and abroad. It claims jurisdiction over non-U.S. sites through the logic that Internet country of origin has little or nothing to do with the impact of the site in the United States. Hence, we must defend against all Internet offenses. The logic may or may not be flawed but our diplomatic consistency has been badly upset. The United States has insisted strongly in any number of international environments that it will not have its sovereignty impinged upon by foreign laws or regulations. COPPA is enforced by the Federal Trade Commission.

- *HIPAA*—Health Insurance Portability and Accountability Act and HCFA—Healthcare Financing Administration. We discuss these two in more detail further on in this chapter, as well as earlier in Chapter 8. Privacy and security for medical records and related activities such as pharmaceutical trials, billing, suits, and conflict resolution are covered by these two bodies of regulation. There are more than 1,500 pages of provisions and instructions in HIPAA alone. Most enforcement and interpretive responsibilities in these arenas rest with the Department of Health and Human Services.

- *FCRA*—Fair Credit Reporting Act—This one covers the nature and circumstances surrounding construction, collection, and dissemination of individual credit reports and the rights of data subjects. Again, the Federal Trade Commission has the enforcement ball.

- *EEO*—Equal Employment Opportunities—(To a lesser degree, *ADA*—Americans with Disabilities Act—may also apply.) This set of regulations has much to say about what information can be asked, gathered, kept, and transferred about employees and employment candidates. There are also supplementary state and local regulations involved.

    You will find some data collection rules in *OSHA*—the Occupational Safety and Health Act—and a much longer list of privacy-related regulations in many other venues.

To put it another way, if you gave a few college interns the task of tracking down specific forms of privacy regulation or policy provisions in each of the umpteen purviews of the federal executive, legislative, and judicial branches, their hit ratio would be extremely high. Their results at the state and local level would be more erratic. Not all, but most industries are affected. No, we didn't do the exercise ourselves, At least, not yet.

One of the obvious issues in the U.S. model is finding coherence and consistency. In Europe and most of the rest of the world, the converse is true. Data protection regulation is generic and crosses most industries and environments. But while it's easier to apprehend (but not necessarily to comprehend), it is more difficult to fine tune. There is a strong effort afoot in Europe and in some other countries to harmonize country legislation. This had its origins in the Council of Europe, which does not include the United States; the OECD, which does; and the European Union, with its 1998 directive on data protection. You can see the implications for a global B2B. Either way, you have homework to do.

Self-Policing vs. Proactive Government Inspection

Here again, the line of demarcation is between the United States and other countries, or perhaps more accurately, between large and small countries. In the United States, there are few if any privacy protection police actively searching for violations, except in the case of children online and some forms of financial transactions. HIPAA procedures are not yet developed enough to tell if proactive enforcement will result. Because of the sheer volume of information assets and flow, the United States relies on a combination of industry self-regulation and policing and response to complaints. Some European and Asiatic countries (e.g., Singapore) have taken the proactive "registration and/or inspection" approach. The responsible bureau is usually funded by registration fees and fines. Hmmm. This approach never anticipated the high-speed creation and dissemination of data that the Internet brings. Detailed inspection of individual files was never a serious procedural contender, and now, most organizations can comply by submitting generic high-level descriptions of the types of personal data they collect, maintain, and transfer.

Safe Harbor Principles

As part of a joint effort between business and the U.S. government to deal with the specific issue of protecting European data stored in U.S.-based and controlled databases, the concept of a *safe harbor* was jointly developed by business and the U.S. Department of Commerce. It is a voluntary process involving a code of conduct and principles. An enterprise can either use the services of a qualifying third party or develop their own policies and procedures in compliance with the principles. The process is uni-directional on the assumption that most European laws under the directive cover both foreign (U.S.) and domestic data within their borders. For further information see the Department of Commerce Web site, http://www.export.gov/safeharbor/. It's too soon to tell how well this safe harbor arrangement will work. At the moment, it is meeting with lukewarm response from U.S.-based organizations and therefore is not making much of an impression on EU authorities. Nevertheless we included it here for your examination. If personal data as defined in Europe is part of your services and offerings, it may be very much in your interest to pursue this or other joint business-government initiatives as you move closer to global B2B.

Other Very Important Agreements

As you may have already concluded, International Privacy Protection is not a slam-dunk subject. We are not trying to overstate it or prolong the conversation. By giving you minimum citations and directing you to appropriate sources, we hope to make this discussion pointed but also helpful in starting a privacy management program.

Many countries outside the European Union are building their privacy legislation around the OECD guidelines and its first cousin, the Council of Europe Convention 108 rather than the European Directive. While they are close in spirit, the Directive and Convention differ primarily where you'd expect—self-regulation versus proactive government intervention. Be careful in using that last statement. There are many other differences of varying significance, and each signatory country is free to put its own interpretation and national spirit in their own legislation. (Not all countries are OECD members; e.g., China, Russia.)

For example, Japan follows a voluntary program but provides a set of guidelines under the JIS, Japanese Industrial Standards. The standards bear a recognizable affinity to the OECD guidelines. They have recently created a "mark" or seal process to indicate that a given enterprise is complying with the standards. This seal is granted by JIPDEC, the Japanese Information Processing Development Center.

The OECD Guidelines, the Council of Europe Convention 108, and the Table of National Privacy Protection Instruments can be seen in their entirety on the OECD's website for information security, http://www.oecd.org/dsti/sti/it/secur/index.htm.

If you are concerned with these issues on a global basis, this site can be a significant help in sorting out the landscape and in giving you additional government and private-sector references. Use it in combination with the Department of Commerce site noted earlier.

CUSTOMS AND TAXATION

Right now, Internet-based commerce is still in a honeymoon stage as far as customs and taxation are concerned. There is a general period of restraint being exercised by most authorities at every level—local, state, provincial, national, regional, and global. Here is a transitional hybrid situation that cannot last. Too much national and regional revenue, self-determination, and control are bound up in the process. Although the discussions have centered on collecting or not collecting sales, usage, or value-added taxes on goods sold over the Internet, the issue is much broader and much more fundamental. Some people question, with a certain justice, that much of the privacy registration demanded by European authorities is in fact built to facilitate future tax and customs measures on intellectual property.

As services and intellectual property take up more space on the global economic pie-chart, things are getting far more complex. To be truthful, this is one area where your omniscient consultant definitely isn't. (Although our firm has some superb tax experts and authorities who can help in depth.)

If, for example, you are reading a hard copy of this book, there was probably a sales tax liability recognized somewhere, even if, depending on how you bought the book, the tax may not have actually been collected. Take this same text in e-book form and download it from a website in one piece or in segments. Listen to the audio version from a tape, MP3 disk, or a CD you downloaded from a website and burned on your own CD-Writer. Watch the TV series on the Public Broadcasting System. Wait for the Broadway musical (reality check, reality check). You see what I mean. Our tax and customs structures are still not sophisticated enough to deal with the same intellectual property value in different modes.

Can I tax professional advice? Sure, if the tax system calls for it. But if the advice is posted on an Internet site, does that change anything? Is it an interactive chat session among several parties? A one-on-one exchange? Is it a subscription site? Is it a subscription site based in Russia or New Zealand? How do you valuate the service? In what currency—from the origin point, from the destination, or in some arbitrary intermediary, such as the dollar or euro?

How do you control tax-free havens for intellectual property services housed in the Cayman Islands or afloat in international waters? I confess I don't know, and I'll leave it to my tax and international relations colleagues to step in. (But not in this book.)

The major point of this brief excursion is to ensure that you're watching this one (as if you wouldn't), not just in the conventional modes but in the newer service and intellectual property modes. If you return to Chapter 3 in an odd moment, try to figure out the tax implications to all the players in the Trip from Hell. The tax-free and customs forebearance honeymoon will not last much longer, and when all the in-laws start demanding a piece of the action, things could get nasty.

RELATED LEGAL AND REGULATORY AREAS

We are just going to fly over several key areas of legislation and regulation (mostly U.S.) that have evolved recently as a result of electronic transactions. They also exemplify some new frameworks that are evolving. Tons of materials have been written on each of the subjects we're addressing. Simply hand the subject over to several Internet search engines and watch the references fly. The important point is, regardless of how sector- or industry-specialized these regulations may seem, there is probably some content that affects your enterprise.

Healthcare

We discussed healthcare in Chapter 8. Let's expand our view by revisiting two of the most influential regulations and structures affecting electronically supported healthcare delivery in the United States: HIPAA (Health Insurance Portability and Accountability Act of 1996) and HCFA (Healthcare Financing Administration). *All healthcare organizations doing business in the United States that maintain or transmit electronic health information must comply.* If you would care to list off all the possible players affected in a major or minor way by these rules, it's easier to ask who is excluded. For all practical purposes, HIPAA/HCFA affects all beneficiaries, providers, insurers and other clients, customers, and partners. The partners can be an interesting list, especially as you track along the tentacles of healthcare networks. Nor is it possible to say with safety that these provisions will remain isolated to the United States. Healthcare increasingly takes on global characteristics.

As far as scope is concerned, HCFA involves all areas of healthcare—costs, access, quality, service delivery, financing, and payment approaches.

The provisions are far reaching and evolving. But several things are clear. Patient confidentiality, and, by indirection, professional privacy, is a number-one consideration. Data and transaction integrity are crucial, especially in those areas affecting diagnosis and treatment. Accountability and auditability, both financial and professional, are key.

Consider the broad arena of healthcare—including not just direct participants but second-level parties such as employers, pharmaceutical and other health-related suppliers, and network infrastructures. As the rules and the associated regulatory functions swing further into action, there will no doubt be many interpretations and judgments that will extend the reach of HIPAA/HCFA. Regardless of the nature of your enterprise or partnerships, it would be wise to have access to expertise in these areas.

Electronic Signatures

U.S. Public law 106-229, The Electronic Signatures in Global and National Commerce Act, went into effect in October 2000, with the electronic records provisions slated for March 2001. This legislation, with several major exceptions such as wills, court orders, eviction notices, utility suspension, product recalls, and documents related to hazardous materials, puts electronically signed documents on an equal legal footing with paper transactions. Obviously, such legal recognition is critical to getting the fullest value out of e-Business environments. However, you will search in vain for specific guidance in this legislation. It enables the use of, but does not specify the techniques for, electronic signatures.

You should be aware that as far as this law is concerned, electronic signatures are not restricted to encrypted digital signatures. There are a number of other techniques, for instance, that can electronically scan, capture, and indelibly watermark the written configuration of the signature or, by using a special electronic pen, record the unique "ballistics" of the individual's signing process (pressure, speed, continuity, etc.). So far, these are not excluded because consenting partners are free to choose their own procedures and requirements for electronic contracts, agreements, and records. No doubt, case law and contract law will further narrow the landscape. Here is another area where many international directives, laws, and agreements are already in place or are soon coming. The United States is late in arriving to this regulatory party.

Consumer Protection

We mentioned the Fair Credit Reporting Act earlier, but the area of consumer protection extends miles beyond the validity and use of credit reports. It may be tempting to say that as a B2B, most of these concerns only have secondary impact on you. You may well be right, but once again, once you connect to other entities, you connect to their connections as well, unless you have specifically and adequately erected a commerce barrier—a thing you most decidedly will not want to do in the interest of business growth. Are we implying that you can suffer from guilt by association? Perhaps, but more important is the impact if one of your partners' partners somewhere in the supply or transaction chain becomes a fragile or harmful link, breaking or weakening the e-Trust alliance.

Consumer protection comes in so many forms that it constitutes a library in itself. We may have told you more than you wanted to know about privacy in one reading. We are not going to repeat the process on this subject. However, there is one aspect we should address.

ARE NETEXCHANGES AND NETMARKETS ANTICOMPETITIVE?

How will the U.S. Federal Trade Commission and its overseas equivalents react to the new relationships being established through netexchanges and netmarkets? Is the consumer and the smaller business owner being sacrificed on an electronic grid? Are there possibilities for collusion, monopolies, cartels, and other forms of competitive strangulation? Yes! Does that mean it will necessarily happen? No! But its does require a level of sensitivity and understanding on the part of all the players to stay ahead of the process. In simple numbers, accidental violations will be far more likely than deliberate flouting of the law. Most of us are stupid far more frequently than we are evil. But to further complicate the state of affairs, new situations, markets, and relationships unexplored and unanticipated by regulators and lawmakers are going to face us daily. By the way, this concern does not just apply to the big global enterprises. Every player in a B2B relationship can and will be affected.

There is a companion danger, however. I've been personally involved in several large-scale and sticky anti-trust situations. In each case, as time, evidence gathering, and depositions dragged on, the "defendants"—by trying to out-think the regulators and the courts—began to see their own instances of violations in every nook and cranny. Near paralysis set in as every venture, policy, price change, offering, and relationship was scrutinized to its atomic level. Second-guessing and course changes abounded, and the marketplace began to get the distinct and semi-accurate impression that we had completely lost our way and even our senses. There are literally hundreds of liability and risk reasons that can be used to support staying out of B2B and Beyond. Unfortunately, most of them also involve stunting the growth and future success of your enterprise.

B2B and Beyond has serious but not insurmountable implications for the preservation of future competition. Think not as an enterprise but as a global environment, exchange or market. When I moved to Cincinnati, someone gave me a sign that said, "We don't care how they did it in New York." That's funny, but you can't take that attitude toward any new business arrangements, services, relationships, pricing, and fulfillment schemes. With B2B, you have to think globally.

EMPLOYMENT

The next two subsections are related but distinct. Under *virtual labor*, we'll comment briefly on the issues of employing services and individuals through the Internet, especially on a global basis. *Employee relations* speaks to managing and responding to a pool of workers operating under a variety of employer–employee modes.

Virtual Labor

If you recall the modified *Business Week* chart on the Evolving Enterprise we showed in Chapter 1, there were several strategic transitions that makes the idea of "virtual labor" compelling. By the way, in this context, "virtual labor" is very real. It's just not physically on your site or in many cases directly on your payroll. We spoke of hierarchical organizations transitioning to Web–network–exchange patterns. We mentioned flexible style replacing structured style. We said structure itself would migrate from *self-sufficient* to *interdependent*. We noted that many operations would move from *vertical* integration to *virtual* integration. And we said that many free agents would join the conventional employee base under a number of contractual and possibly noncontractual forms.

Notice that predicted evolution of workers from "employees" to a mix of "employees/free agents." You're probably there already. How many individual or corporate contractors does your enterprise use today? If you don't know, you have lots of company. Which way is the trend going? What is the turnover rate? Who engages these resources, and how? I'll bet it's not just your HR department. Do you have a standard contract? If you wanted a complete inventory of all outside contractors who are serving you right now, could you get it? Could you get a two-year history? Could you get a two-year projection?

Concentrate for a moment on your information processes. Your own environment may be reasonably well covered in terms of dealing with internal exposures from contractors (although don't bet on it), but how about liabilities to outside partners caused by or abetted by your contractors? Don't stop simply at the legal aspects. Consider your reputation and working relationship with your business partners. Can contract personnel affect the trust you enjoy in B2B? Need you ask?

Hello, HR department, are you listening? Of course you are. In many cases, you're the guys coming up with these new modes of obtaining labor, advice, and management. But you're not alone. In many organizations, anyone with a budget had the freedom to hire short-term outside help. Some of these "short-termers" went from budget year to budget year. I am not talking about formal consultant or third-party agreements. I'm talking about "I know a guy who builds websites in his spare time and maybe he can clean ours up for us. He's my sister's roommates' brother in-law." Is there anything wrong with this? In the spirit and principle of free enterprise, certainly not. In form and regulatory compliance, possibly a lot.

Too many organizations have been zinged for evading benefit payments, employing illegal aliens, violating union contracts, minimum wages and work conditions standards (especially using overseas resources), and a host of other practices. These sanctions frequently result from situations that at least started out being innocent (naïve?) and well intentioned. Often, these sort of arrangements result from hard-pressed, innovative project leaders trying to meet extreme performance and timeline expectations. Fortunately, that condition never arises in the development and operation of B2B and Beyond. Right!

Just about every group I have worked with in the last few years admitted that they could not say with strong confidence that they could identify every person working on their behalf at any given time. From moonlighting graduate students to work-at-home data entry clerks, from home-based telephone service support to by-the-hour coders, from on-call system and device maintenance to round-the-clock monitoring—the types and number of available support resources is exploding. Here, too, we're transitioning, and here, too, what your partners do can affect you.

We're going to come at this from a different angle in our discussions on identity management, where we give some practical suggestions about how you can control access by people working for you outside the normal

HR pattern (if there is one). For the moment, don't ignore this. (Yes, I know, I've said that about every item we've covered. But in William Shatner's timeless words for Priceline.com, "This is big, really big.")

Employee Relations

Here we are addressing your on-the-payroll employees. I was going to say *conventional*, but that word is losing all meaning in the worlds we're describing. A number of traditional employer–employee practices and relationships are getting blurred as we progress further into network land. Let's just list a few.

Telecommuting

This one has all sorts of cute side issues, from health hazards (carpal tunnel?) and worker's compensation when working at home to time and expense reporting and the cost of equipment, supplies, and services. A short imaginary dialogue.

> *Me:* "If I'm using my own computer and possibly my own Internet connection, what right, if any, do you have to tell me what else I can do with those resources on my own time?"
>
> *You:* "But you may pick up a virus, or your kids may destroy company data or proprietary software. You may be operating without properly licensed software."
>
> *Me:* "OK, install a separate system and link in my home and control it, or give me a prepackaged laptop. By the way, this is California, and I'm paying an immense amount for electricity to power your system."
>
> *You:* "But that's a lot of extra cost, and this is for your convenience."
>
> *Me:* "Sure, and the fact that you've been able to release four floors of office space and equipment doesn't enter into the benefits picture, does it?"

I think that's enough of the B2B Drama Guild. You get the picture. There will have to be trade offs. By the way, many security specialists and auditors dislike telecommuting as a company practice because it weakens control (except, of course, in their own case).

The Intrusion of Mobile Computing and Communicating

One of the wonderful advantages of cell phones, pagers, laptops, e-books, and all forms of PDAs—wired and wireless—is that we now have a whole new menu of ways to kill, maim, or seriously injure ourselves and others, especially behind the wheel of a car. Or get ourselves thrown off airplanes or annoy people in restaurants, waiting rooms, public transportation, concerts, and theaters. All in the interest of being available and on top of business every waking moment. (I'm going to make a confession here, and I'd prefer we keep it among ourselves. There are times I deliberately turn my cell phone OFF even when I am not in a moving airplane. Not just put it on vibrate—all the way OFF.) If captains of industry or masters of the universe fear missing a quarter-point rise in their portfolio, that's up to them. But....

Are we imposing a virtual 24/7 on-call and on-deadline work-week for an increasing number of our employees? Is B2B going to make it worse? Are they going to be happy about it? We hold some truths to be self-evident. We consultants get used to this regime up to a point. We're nomads, and we cross time zones like most people cross the street. I wake up each morning to a ritual mantra: "Where am I? What time is it here? What time is it at home? What hotel am I in? What kind of rental car am I driving, and where the hell did I park it?"

There are real personal and operational hazards associated with the interconnected world. Not the least of which is intrusion. We all rebel at being called by a telemarketer at dinner. How about being called by a business associate? How about being called in the middle of the night because he or she can't count time zones or frankly, doesn't care? There are definite contributors to burn-out here, and we're placing larger and larger numbers of people in their impact zone. It may be the price of the interconnected world but don't be surprised by the HR side effects, and do rein in abuses committed in the interest of "business efficiency." Now I've held off long enough. On to the all-time favorite in the Internet Discussion Topic Hall of Fame.

Use of On-the-Job Computers for Personal Purposes

"So what's to discuss? It's stealing company time and resources. The answer is 'No way, no how, no time.' Next subject."

Let's not be quite so categorical, shall we? First tell me whether telecommuting has taken some of the air out of the "never in the office" balloon. Then let's explore whether we are infringing on many of our employees' private time with porous work hours and 24/7 work on demand.

I recently attended a Monday morning security conference at which a hardliner was comparing "personal use" to stealing office supplies, padding expenses, or submitting phony invoices. Never one to avoid an argument (or maybe I was just bored silly), I asked him when he had last processed his e-mail, and how often he did so over the weekend. Answer: "6 A.M. that day and several times on Saturday and

Sunday." Did he usually report travel time? "No." Does he work on airplanes? "Yes!" Does he read reports or work in his hotel room, at home, or possibly even in bed? "Yes! but," he retorted, "I am not paid by the hour. I'm a professional." So restrictions on personal use should only apply to hourly employees, since your time is not a condition of employment? "But, there's the cost of the equipment and network links." Granted, but do you have any idea how much additional overhead is incurred by personal use, and is some of it balanced by the employee's use of his or her own resources in the company's interest?

Needless to say he was not convinced. You may not be, either. Nor am I, up to a point. If everyone went pleasure surfing, e-shopping, or game playing for extended periods while at work, the enterprise would fall apart. E-mailing your mother and entire family in Taiwan loads of large video, picture, and audio files of each time your new baby burps can mount up when multiplied by the entire population.

"So what do you recommend, OC?" This. Do address the issue. But get the nos, nevers, and threats of dismemberment out of the policies and procedures. Calm the rhetoric, if there is any, and start using words like *appropriate* and *reasonable*. "But that can be misinterpreted by individual managers." Yes, just like any other rules you establish that gives them latitude and allows them to use their judgment. It will probably cost less in the long run, compared to the Task Force for Drafting Rules for Personal Use of Computers and the enforcement arm it established. It might also improve the atmosphere and tell your managers you trust them to make mature decisions. Don't leave it in limbo. There may be security threats and virus attacks and all other types of untoward incidents that occur from a totally laissez-faire attitude. But which is more effective? An unenforceable, draconian approach that may precipitate other HR problems, or one that appeals to the maturity and business sense of your employees? I guess it depends on management and the employees. Don't get sloppy. Be sensible.

"OH, BOY! THANKS FOR SHARING ALL OF THOSE! I REALLY NEEDED IT"

At this point, some of you may be tempted to go back to bed, pull the covers over your head, and wait for the Good B2B2C Fairy to come, wave a magic wand, and sort it all out. Worse, yet, you may just want to stay in bed, period, and miss the parade altogether. Sorry! This is new, and we're all groping. The virtual enterprise is just arriving on the scene. But are we ready? How much does your legal department, industrial relations group, public and stockholder relations units, international trade experts, internal audit and security specialists know about these areas?

Do you and your partners have a concerted and harmonious plan and organization (it can be virtual—not nonexistent) to anticipate and deal with these issues? Are your plans properly oriented to a B2B network environment, or are they vintage 1980 wine in 21st-century bottles?

For example, we'll talk further about data classification and identity management in general in Chapter 15. You are going to discover that in a serious B2B network, the rules and assumptions underpinning these activities will have to be revisited by a group jointly representing the major players. And no, you cannot simply wave a generic standard and have everyone pledge compliance. It's more specific to the players than that. Nor does it always work to say, "I'm the big kid. We'll play by my rules." Your rules may result in partner inefficiencies, resistance, and, in some cases, failure because they were developed around a different scale, culture, business process, or level of technical sophistication.

ATTITUDE ADJUSTMENT, YET AGAIN

Most organizations are just at the most rudimentary stages of participating in a truly complex e-Trust community. Why? Well, for one thing, most current business protective policies, procedures, and technology still use the moat as their model. Create a barrier (firewall?) and hunker down behind it. Protect yourself and let the other guy worry. True e-Business, especially B2B2C, forces you outside the barrier and onto the field for some major aspects of the process. Third parties, who may be in coopetition with you, may be handling parts of your vital business transaction flow. *And you may be supporting theirs.*

Does this mean you throw off all the protection you've built up over the years; drain, fill, and pave over the moat; send the alligators to a retirement swamp; tear down the walls, and go out and merrily play in the traffic? Of course not! But it does mean a readjustment of protective viewpoint and scope from your enterprise to the communities in which you participate. It also means strong consideration of your responsibilities and liabilities in preventing damage to your partners.

It's going to take some time for this new attitude to catch on. Some organizations may never adapt. The important point to remember about the e-universe is that your organization is going to be a member of many intersecting or totally separate processing galaxies. The metaphor is not chosen lightly. In the universe there are many galaxies that pass through other galaxies while still rotating in their own plane. Many stars do the same thing. They have also been known to collide or pull other stars out of their paths. OK, back to Earth! Most organizations will be members of several, if not many, virtual communities and the trust characteristics may not be the same.

This is hardly an earth-shattering insight. Your organization belongs to many communities today. The point to consider is whether interactive e-Business can be supported by your current rules of behavior or whether your ways of doing business must be recast to account for all of the e-characteristics (and more) that we've mentioned above. The odds are heavily in favor of developing some new or seriously updated trust models. How?

PART

III

Making e-Trust Happen

Part III concludes this book. Hovering just above ground level, we'll talk about B2B technology, identity management (identification, authentication, authorization), accountability, monitoring, and dealing with attacks and outages. We'll also discuss at some length the different trust policies, procedures, architectures, designs, technologies, and approaches available to the B2B enterprises. We'll consider the pros and cons of each and provide some detailed advice on getting started with the newer security and control approaches such as public key infrastructure and digital signatures. We'll spend time on trust assessment and evaluation. And we'll talk about organization. We'll concentrate on what's different from the conventional and traditional.

However, Part III is not primarily for techies and practitioners. They know some of this stuff already. Part III is designed to give the nontechnical business executive a better and (practically) painless understanding of all that network and security jazz. You may emerge as a far more imposing figure in your discussions with the technocrats. Never again will they kick grains of silicon in your face. Your significant other will see you in a whole new light. And, provided you don't make a bore of yourself, you may get invited to more and a better class of cocktail parties. You may want to take a short breather, however, and ask the flight attendant for another drink. See you in Chapter 13.

13

An Overview of Key B2B Technologies

This chapter is going to take little extra concentration on your part, especially if you are not technically inclined. This is NOT a direct discussion of trust technologies. That comes later in Part III. To set the stage for discussing trust processes and technologies, we want you to have an appreciation for the wider range and variety of technologies that make up the e-Business arsenal. We're going to concentrate on equipment and software that would usually apply to more than one type of B2B environment, although some of the items we'll talk about may sound specialized. There are many more than you think. Stick with us. You may get a few answers to stuff you haven't understood, and you'll discover that e-Business technology doesn't simply begin and end with the Internet. However, having said that, to kick things off, let's spend a little more time looking at the Internet.

INTERNET BASICS: DECENTRALIZED STRUCTURE, COOPERATIVE HANDLING

As you probably intuitively know, the basic character of Internet design that differentiates it from prior hierarchical, centralized, "legacy" network models is *collegial cooperation* between processing nodes, service suppliers, and users. In plain English, the Internet has no head to speak of. However, characterization of the Internet as pure, single-level socialism is a vast oversimplification. Even in the Internet, "all animals are equal but some animals are more equal than others." (See *Animal Farm*, by George Orwell.)

Because of its distributed nature and multipath design, the Internet was envisioned from day one by its military sponsors (ARPANET) as a rugged and resilient environment that could carry on in spite of localized outages or service loss. Individual data packets carrying destination identifiers are sent out and automatically transferred along available, alternative paths till they arrive at their target. Internet traffic management is a bit like airline baggage handling, only with a much higher success rate. The intermediate Internet node (or switching point) follows an approach of "examine the message's destination and if it's not for you, kindly pass it on." The data packet will get an available path. It may not always be the fastest, most efficient, or shortest distance path but it will be the one available. So how come you can't always get where you want to go on the Internet?

GRRRRRRR!

Today, when you cannot connect to a destination service or site, it's generally because the site itself is not up or is overloaded. You probably got far enough to find out the gate was closed. The Internet as *such* wasn't down, the desired site was. That's not much consolation if you can't get there from here, but it is important, nonetheless. It's tough to knock out the entire Internet, or even major segments.

Unfortunately, if that site you wanted is your Internet Service Provider (ISP) that connects you to the Internet or your portal (e.g. AOL, Yahoo) that provides connection plus other services; or your favorite search engine (Alta Vista, Lycos), your Internet travels are going to be seriously curtailed. Understand, then, that the overall Internet is highly redundant and is designed for dynamic rerouting. But if your points of takeoff or ultimate destination are shut down, all the clever rerouting in the world still isn't going to get you there. This situation is further complicated by the fact that there are a relative handful of sites that constitute the Internet backbone. Not all Internet hubs are the same. Think of the hubs in an airline system. If one or more of these backbone sites go down, traffic can still be rerouted, but the resulting service level will be reduced and, for your purposes, may be unacceptable.

ROUTING, ROUTING, ROUTING

Today, Internet super portals like AOL or Yahoo may give the impression of turning us back to proprietary centralization. If you can't get there, you may be dead in the water—not because of Internet architecture but because you have chosen to be dependent on that portal for a significant number of services. The ISP, whether a simple connection facility or a multiservice portal like AOL, is indeed a major point of prospective failure. But even in that event, you may be able to circumvent it if you know how to navigate. Many businesses use multiple ISPs for just this reason.

Of course, you must also make sure all of your physical connections are not going through the same phone or cable switching system. A lost switching center or telephone company point of presence (POP) will kill all of your communications unless you have planned for alternate paths and redundancies.

PEER-TO-PEER

There are also new Internet peer-to-peer technologies, such as Gnutella (remember the Napster flap?), that quite literally allow you to set up your hard drive to share directly with mine and vice versa, bypassing websites and portals altogether in the actual transfer. The websites are reference, not transfer points. Once you establish the initial relationship, you're on your own. The popularity of Napster was a result of the strong desire of young and clever users to share recorded music without paying, being monitored, or controlled. "If they can stop me or charge me at the website or portal, let's bypass the website and share PC to PC, direct." Essentially, you register on a website as a sharing member of a community, keep your system up, and allow direct access to certain parts of your hard drive. A user asks the service site for the locations of a specific file name, usually a song but it could be anything, and the website in its role of community directory for the song's availability, gives the addresses. Then it's up to the searcher to find your specific open PC, drive, and the desired file name and download a copy. From then on, searchers can directly look for and negotiate with that specific PC (or other device) for further content.

Is this any different than downloading from a website? Not in a general technological sense. But in an intellectual property sense, it's very difficult to establish control or accountability. What you have is a very loosely conducted swap meet. Once an unencrypted copy of the file is in the hands of a participant, there is no way to monitor or control further exchange throughout the community. The referencing website doesn't have the material itself or a log of traffic, only a list of possible locations. Therefore, it is only a secondary point of content control. You could try to shut down the site or make it pay, which is what the recording industry essentially did to Napster through the courts. The sites claimed they were directing traffic, not actually exchanging intellectual property. But as any intellectual property owner knows, once an item is on one site, it will proliferate broadly and at electronic speed. The answer to this one lies more in ethics, law, social attitudes, and intelligent pricing techniques.

However, let's not toss peer-to-peer connections into the dimly lit back alleys of the Internet. It can be abused, of course, but properly controlled, there are some quite useful applications, such as areas of collaborative development without the need for a middleman. Whichever way the entertainment issues sort themselves out, direct, peer-to-peer connection will be around for better or worse. However, instituting cost-effective controls and version management in peer-to-peer environments will not be easy. The use of mutually trusted websites is the preferred mode of collaborative operation.

Regardless of how many evolutionary changes take place, this open and collegial characteristic is firmly implanted in the Internet's genes. *Most of the trust issues surrounding the Internet as a base for B2B activities boil down to how to establish appropriate and effective controls and trustworthy cooperation in a basically open, interdependent environment.*

The point of this little discourse on Internet architecture is that it is flexible, dynamic, and changing. The Internet is still very much a work in progress and there may be future Internet-like architectures that are fundamentally different. But for the major part of our discussions, we'll stick with "as-is" rather than a far in the future "to-be." If an e-Business technology or approach is in serious play, we'll talk about it. If it's a fuzzy gleam in some futurist's eye, we may note it and move on.

VARIABLE PATH TRANSMISSION

So, open Internet design and redundancy, if not thwarted, can provide strength and resilience. A second aspect of this design can enhance confidentiality and integrity, but it has also caused some serious rethinking and redesign of basic security approaches. As we noted above, physical and virtual Internet transmission paths to a single, given destination may vary with each instance of use. Alternative paths can be invoked *within* the message transmission. Under TCP/IP (Transmission Control Protocol/Internet Protocol) messages are decomposed into semi-independent packets and may follow independent paths to a common destination. This makes over-the-line interception (tapping) difficult. Where would you hook up the tap? However, it also makes it difficult to create fixed, *physically* protected paths. (We'll talk about Virtual Private Networks later.) Most Internet interceptions occur at or immediately near the end points or intermediate nodes (servers, switches, routers) using computer attack and penetration techniques. Protecting the end points and switch points becomes critical. The external line tap as such has moved inside. Now the major reason why bad guys still climb poles or towers is to disrupt, not intercept.

THE OTHER SIDE OF ANONYMITY

Another major Internet characteristic that affects trust is personal anonymity. Unfortunately, the bad guys seem to benefit more than the good guys on this one. The supreme irony of the Internet is that, amid massive complaints about personal privacy issues on the Web, unidentified attackers can still carry out many frauds and attacks with substantial chance of anonymity and well-covered tracks. A domain name, URL, or IP address is not a particularly reliable personal identifier, and even IP addresses can be faked or camouflaged. You can trace IP addresses to a device but beyond that point, identification is often based on circumstantial evidence. For business transactions, we need new and better techniques for strong identification and authentication. There are some in existence, and we'll describe them a bit later.

VARIABLE ISSUES—VARIABLE SOLUTIONS

Before going further, let's re-establish a basic e-Trust dictum: *A single, protective solution, regardless of how sophisticated, is not going to handle all the trust issues that can occur in such a wide range of technologies, usage patterns, and content types.*

There are technical solutions that address most e-Trust problems, of course. Most require some form of encryption. We'll discuss them in subsequent chapters. But there is one thing that is fundamental to Internet trust. Like the Internet itself, Internet trust is a cooperative effort requiring a combination of protective measures, technology, contracts, personal integrity, law, and regulation. The days of buying "set-it and forget it" security are gone. Like the processes and infrastructures they affect, security, trust, and protection are getting more and more complicated.

OTHER E-BUSINESS TECHNOLOGIES

There are many. New ones arise almost every day, and they don't develop in sync. There are a number of good technological ideas gathering dust, waiting for other infrastructural or supplemental advances to support or enhance them. Some will wait forever or disappear. Others, such as encryption, will advance from wallflower to belle of the ball status when the time is right. If you don't already, we want you to fully understand and appreciate that the Internet and related technologies required to fully support B2B (and B2C) are complex, interdependent, and oftentimes conflicting. They are not being developed by an all-knowing central intelligence, but by a highly competitive marketplace with all the hype, false starts, misaligned design, and premature release that you would expect. In this arena, timing is as important as creativity in achieving success. This especially applies to trust, control, and security mechanisms. They usually trail in the development parade. Anyway, let's start with bandwidth.

BANDWIDTH—THE INTERNET'S EL DORADO

What's so important about bandwidth? For that matter, what does it mean? Bandwidth is another one of those useful engineering terms that has been coopted and distorted by business, the press, and management pundits into a cool but vague buzzword signifying any type of capacity, speed, personal capability, corporate resources, strength, lasting power, and so on. Let's not go there.

Simply put, as it relates to network technology, bandwidth is a relative measure of network data capacity and speed. It involves the movement of bits and bytes. How much information can I push through a pipe, and how swiftly? Fast is good. Faster is better. High volume is good. Rapid turnaround is good. Immediate availability is good. Waiting is bad. Crashes and restarts are very bad. Strictly speaking, bandwidth refers to transmission functions only. In many discussions, however, it has been expanded to cover the wider range of total transaction throughput. You can examine it from different viewpoints: time to send, time to receive, time to turn around a response, time to find, time to come up or shut down, resistance to overload, and congestion. Anyone who saw or read about the infamous 1999 Victoria's Secret online fashion show (an electronic mob scene) or the initial results of AOL's flat-rate pricing (an information brownout) has seen bandwidth constraint in action.

How much does bandwidth cost? Will it scale with demand? More appropriately, will it anticipate demand and permit hungry new technologies and processes to prosper? For example, true and immediate conversational interactivity on the Internet is still restricted to a relatively small, simple, and low-demand set of environments. But there is a growing base of real-time text chat, audio/video interaction, teleconferencing, and community services that will be taking an increasing role in B2B interaction.

"PERCEIVED" BANDWIDTH

Notice, please, that "perceived" bandwidth (the user sees it most graphically as response time and upload/download rates) is not just a function of the base speed of the medium. High-speed fiber optics, cable services, or telephone DSL (digital subscriber lines) may initially mask a lot of other performance sins and suboptimization, but it won't cover them forever. Perceived bandwidth also depends on the capacity and agility of the end points and intermediate nodes, routing and network complexity, robustness, interoperability and compatibility, responsive back-end processes, efficient browsers and Web servers, low or no-loss data compression, and intelligent network, infrastructure, and process management.

Plus, acceptable perceived bandwidth is a moving target. If you think otherwise, just consider your own tolerance for personal computer response times. No matter how fast the processor chip or how swift the operating system (yes, I know, an oxymoron), we are never satisfied. It always has been and always will be an "eternity" for a PC to boot up no matter how much shorter that time actually is or how much function is being initiated. Waiting, by definition, is intolerable, even if on an objective scale the wait is getting shorter. The enemy of interactivity is wait time. In case you didn't notice it, security and controls can affect wait time, usually (but not always) negatively. More on this later.

A related security factor comes into play here. The new cable and DSL technologies come close to providing on-demand response. Warning—in order to provide instant availability, the usual mode for these connections is "always on." Those of you who own satellite TV know that most people leave the set top box on all the time. They usually turn off the TVs and VCRs. Similarly, if you also leave your computer on with an "always on" data connection and do not have an active and effective firewall, you've left your front door open. Many of the new virus attacks take advantage of this. Even a firewall is not invincible. While some experts claim that turning computers on and off shortens their life, leaving your system on in an "always on" connection may shorten the life of your data and software.

DIRECTORIES, DIRECTORIES, SEARCH ENGINES, SEARCH ENGINES

You ignore this area at your peril. Network navigation, identification management, verification of existence, conflict resolution, relationship maintenance, and a host of other business necessities depend on a robust, interoperable, accurate, and trustworthy directory system. The mere statements—"look it up, search, or surf the Web"—imply a powerful combination of lookup, analysis, and search assistance. Search engines and their associated databases are the logical brain trust (big processors, bigger storage) behind the public Web. However, in complex e-Business extranets, netexchanges, and netmarkets, as well as intranets, directories are the life blood of the transaction system.

We cover directories in greater detail later, but we want to make one point very emphatically now. Directories serve many processing and transmission purposes. One of them is the linkage of identification, authentication, and authorization information with user-presented credentials. If you are considering a new security system, especially encryption-based Public Key Infrastructure (Chapter 18), start by getting your directories properly designed and implemented. Otherwise, you're building on sand.

INTERACTIVITY AND PERSONALIZATION

Today, the Internet, especially the Web, still has more in common with broadcast than with true interactivity. Although the chat room is a great attraction to a substantial but hardly dominant population of Internet users, most website surfing and usage is still equivalent to progressively fine tuning an immense spectrum of broadcasting sources, until we find the information we want. A search engine is essentially a complex tuner. If the information exists and is available, I'll eventually find it in that global jukebox. *In most cases, the repository is stocked in anticipation of and asynchronous to the demand.* Most subject matter websites anticipate demand and thus can procure and provide material in advance. The problem is they may not always satisfy the need in a timely fashion—or at all. They who anticipate (guess) best satisfy the most users.

An intermediate stage is what we'll call personalized broadcast (narrowcasting). By providing a static profile, users can give the information service guidance on how to supply, organize, and direct information that is more likely to be of value to them. A more ambitious approach is dynamic or learned personalization, where the users' prior history with the information service and perhaps other cooperating services is used to continuously update and modify the profile(s). Each of these techniques is a significant improvement in matching demand to supply—raising the hit ratio—but they have a hefty price tag. The requisite technology is sophisticated and not yet fully developed, the data sources must be quality controlled, and most important—there is a privacy issue here that just won't quit. In the sell and buy sides, remember CRM? The great conundrum is, how much of yourself (personal or business entity) are you willing to reveal to receive a desired service? We'll have lots more to say about this and related issues.

But some B2B and B2C applications require new material and decisions created on demand. That needs mutual, synchronous interactivity and/or collaboration. Yes, a lot of it may still be based on recompiling or combining existing material. Static and dynamic personalization are here to stay. But some cases are more complex and demand immediate additional processing to respond.

AN ONLINE SEMI-AUTOMATED B2B BUYER-SELLER INTERCHANGE:

Buyer: Do you have ten widgets in inventory?

Seller: *(Inventory application looks up available to commit file)* No!

Buyer: When will you have ten widgets in inventory?

Seller: *(Inventory application looks up available to promise file)* Three weeks.

Buyer: Will you make ten widgets for me tomorrow if I pay a 15% premium?

Seller: *(Inventory application calls for help. This one takes additional file searching, decision making, priority checks, customer relations checks, raw material and shop floor availability checks, premium-cost calculations, and possibly even legal checks to produce the answer.)* Only if you take them in blue. We ran out of red paint.

Buyer: Suppose I send you some red paint by tonight?

Seller: *(More checks on ability to switch the paint facility for ten widgets, how to get the paint on time, additional cost. Is it still worth it?)* Only if you take a hundred widgets.

Yes, you supply chain and manufacturing experts, we know the example is fictional, simple minded, and has at least a dozen omissions and mistakes. We're just trying to make a point for the unfamiliar that truly interactive B2B can get complex pretty quickly.

As an exercise, please develop complete and detailed controls and audit trail processes for the above interchange. Just kidding . . . but consider how much under the surface activity is going on. Today, this sample interchange couldn't possibly be totally automatic except in a few of the most sophisticated systems under development. Too much judgment, weighing of alternatives, and intermediate decision making still would make human intervention—assisted human intervention—a requirement. If for no other reason than having someone to blame if the transaction goes awry. But that's the direction e-Business is going. It's another form of *transintermediation*.

Process intervention: The plaintive cry, "Can I *please* speak to a human being?" (instead of, "Press 6 to be summarily disconnected") should be a warning siren as we design extranets, netexchanges, and netmarkets. Maintaining process intervention capability becomes more and more critical as the process itself becomes more complex. Eventually, the intervention system will be highly automated. On the Internet, nobody knows you're a piece of software and not a dog.

The next time you are rerouted by an airline with a mechanical failure or weather en route, if you can maintain your temper, try to objectively imagine what is going on behind the airline operations scenes. Does interactivity and bandwidth count in rerouting and/or finding accommodations for 300 passengers? You bet. Is high-speed back-end processing required? Of course. Does control and audit count? Well, why do you always have that nagging feeling that the new flight you've been assigned doesn't exist, or that someone else already has your seat? Will you still get your frequent flyer miles? Actually, it's a miracle airline systems don't collapse more frequently than they do.

INTERACTIVITY IS NOT THE ANSWER TO EVERY PRAYER

Most e-mail uses store and forward design, as well as an intermediary post office system. Pure, interactive e-mail would be a disaster. Suppose you're not there. It's the same as having a telephone without an auto-answering process.

Download and upload is basic electronic package interchange (see also FTP). It can approach interactivity. Things only begin to get truly interactive with chat functions and true, real-time, online transaction handling. Collaboration expands on interactivity in the sense that we are not just communicating but are together dynamically producing something—a document, assembling a shipment of goods, a work of art, a completed process. In collaboration and interactivity, the participants have a sense of mutual awareness. Both sides are active. Conversely, pulling material from a website or bulletin board implies that one side, usually the source of the information, is passive.

DATA STREAMING

Another form of information flow needs to be added to the equation. When they are transmitted for direct and immediate interactive use, high-density content such as music, video, and large format pictures are not assembled in exactly the same sense as messages or transactions. In this instance, the term *streaming* is used quite literally. Open the spigot and here it comes. Interrupt or slow the stream and the potential for image or sound corruption or distortion is very high. Those of you who have satellite TV systems have no doubt seen "pixelated" images breaking into squares of color because of signal interference or interruption. It's not an identical analogy but it's close.

Streaming data for immediate, real-time use is not the same as downloading that same music, picture, or text for storage and subsequent use. In the download for storage process, interruptions, repeat transmissions, and speed variation won't matter as long as the product finally arrives complete, intact, and ready for eventual use.

An increasing number of B2C and B2B applications will involve both download and streaming. Control considerations and constraints can be dissimilar. Suppose, in order to prevent piracy, you wish to apply encryption to that intellectual property. Encrypting and decrypting a downloaded versus a real time data stream is different. In the former case, the additional calculation and content overhead from encryption probably has negligible consequences. Encryption can be performed any time prior to transmission. The file may travel a bit more slowly than it might otherwise but it gets there and can be decrypted and usable, if you have the right key. Decryption can be performed any time prior to actual end use, which may be immediately on receipt or delayed.

In real-time streaming, encryption can occur any time before transmission, but decryption must be immediate for real-time access. The additional content or processing overhead imposed by encryption cannot be allowed to affect the stream rate. Otherwise it will throw the whole process off. Again, think of satellite TV and your set top box. The same is true of any mathematical data compression that is carried out to reduce the size of the transmission.

UBIQUITY THROUGH WIRELESS

Another major development that is further expanding or perhaps transforming the Internet is freedom from physical connection. Cutting the cord. The cell phone in its digital form was the first step toward widespread development of other wireless digital services. Here again, bandwidth rears its head. But it's a more complex form of bandwidth because multiple services are involved. RF (radio frequency) transmission combined with ground line and satellite linkages.

As today's users know, consumer wireless is in its adolescence. Cell phone owners, analog and digital alike, all share the frustrations of dead zones, intermittent signals, and distortion. Incompatible digital cellular standards don't help much. There are two major digital wireless standards in use. They both involve dividing content into sub-units so that multiple, simultaneous calls can be accommodated. However, they do it differently. And as you might expect, a near religious war rages between their respective adherents.

One approach, Code Division Multiple Access (CDMA), evolved from military use and manages multiple calls by pre-assigning a different and almost-random key to encode the transmission. At the beginning of the call, this key is sent to the receiving station, which then searches the incoming multiplexed traffic flow for that specific key (and any others it may be servicing) and only picks out, accepts, demodulates, and decodes a call unit bearing that key.

The other approach, Time Division Multiple Access (TDMA), divides the channel into time slots and allocates individual conversation bursts to each time slot, permitting multiplexing. Both systems have enough advantages and disadvantages to support an extended debate. Pick a topic— station cost, compatibility with analog, speed, bandwidth efficiency, interference, applications, location constraints, scalability, security. Yes, unfortunately, security processes differ in the two technologies.

At the moment, TDMA has a major beachhead established in spite of the fact that CDMA is the standard of choice among most U.S. cellular carriers. TDMA is the de facto standard in Europe and most of the Far East and is the basis for the European Global System for Mobile communications (GSM). As of this writing, North Americans require a GSM-compatible phone system if they want to use it on both sides of the Atlantic. Only one or two vendors supply them in the United States.

SO WHAT IS THIRD-GENERATION (3G) WIRELESS?

Third generation is the generic term used for the next generation of mobile communications systems. 3G systems are intended to enhance the services—such as voice, text, and data—predominantly available today. The technology concepts for 3G systems and services are currently under development based on today's GSM standard, but they are evolved, extended, and enhanced to include an additional radio air interface, better suited for high-speed and multimedia data services. This system is intended to enable users of current second-generation GSM wireless networks to migrate to the new 3G services, with minimal disruption. But 3G is not yet ready for prime time.

By early 2001, 3G and its backers had encountered a number of significant economic and technology issues that must be solved before it becomes a viable, much less dominant, communication mode. For example, because 3G operates at higher frequencies, it will require a greater number of relay stations and antennas to cover the same territory. And since it is a different mode, significant investment in new equipment and franchises are also required. Some early participants are becoming more tentative and watchful of the market. 3G or something like it is needed for future wireless expansion, but don't throw away your current processes just yet.

A QUICK COMMENT ON STANDARDS

Think back over the last 20 years at the technology standards disputes that have raged in the consumer electronics marketplace—BetaMax vs VHS; incompatible color-TV standards; MDAT cassettes; CD-ROMs; DVD; HDTV and encryption. Standards are seldom simply about technology. They are about protecting investments, markets, and corporate survival; they are about geopolitical dominance; they are about nationalist and, sometimes, military advantage. Sometimes they are about personal ego.

We will discuss security and related standards a little later. They are vital to Internet-based trust. But by definition, the standards process trails technology development. In today's atmosphere of rapid and highly volatile development, standards can only be depended upon to frame the issues and deal with them after major investment has been made by competing parties. The old saying, "driving by your rear-view mirror" applies. This is not the fault of the standards process. "Art is long and life is short." Very little of today's technology would be in the market if aggressive business organizations and the military had not pushed it forward before standards could be totally agreed upon. The results of a standards war can be wasteful and frustrating but the alternative of waiting for agreement before investment is usually worse or, in many cases, just not possible. (See Chapter 19.)

ADVANCES IN PORTABLE DEVICES

The value of digital wireless will expand beyond providing better, cleaner phone service to broader service capabilities only if portable digital devices keep pace. Several types of portable devices are converging on the wireless target, but each has its own dominant genes. Multifunction phones are first and foremost communications devices with added digital bells and whistles. Communicating personal digital assistants are

Palm Pilots that can communicate. They are now frequently Web-enabled. Enhanced pagers are just that, enhanced pagers. Electronic books are enhanced pocket display devices. It may well be that much of the required technology will come from the electronic game industry.

There is a chicken-and-egg debate going on over the development of full-function Web browsing capability in a pocket-size device. Which comes first, the Web device or the browser? There are also practical limits to reducing the hand-held device's keyboard, tracking device, and screen size. The average Web page is a very busy place. Think of an AltaVista or Yahoo screen being displayed on a Palm Pilot. Instant eye test! Will websites have to be redesigned to be practical in a hand-held environment? Absolutely. Will current browser design cut it? Probably not. An editing and filtration system will be required at the server level to scale down the Web page to the essentials for PDA reception. Do we need full Web function on a PDA? Not clear. At the end of the day, simple text and graphics may suffice.

Ah, you say, "This technology cries out for voice activation and command." However, those of you who fly or are in offices with cubicles, imagine the noise level if everyone is talking to their computers simultaneously and continuously. Consider the proposed jumbo Airbus with 600+ people talking to their e-mail together. (Yes, I know it's an exaggeration, but it will make today's cell phone racket seem like serenity.) How about privacy and security, when everyone is talking to and listening to their computer? Are earphones and subvocalization pickups the answer? Maybe. Is a laptop with a screen, keyboard, and wireless modem going to be the surviving form factor? Don't count it out. Smaller is not always better, unless it also has other desirable functions going for it.

Expect this area to have a number of false starts and disappointments before it takes off solidly. There is and will continue to be a long period of hybridization. Be careful of business applications that depend solely or heavily on hand-held devices. They will have a long maturation cycle. Among the obvious concerns such as battery life, screen size, pointers, keyboard, or keyboard substitutes, look for security and control as issues.

By the way, the smaller they are, the easier they are to lose or steal. Small devices loaded with personal or business information can be a significant loss. Unless and until we can keep all information except basic access management off the device in some great Internet repository in the sky (did somebody say bandwidth and trust?), the PDA, like the laptop but worse, can be a dangerous device if insufficiently protected.

THE WIRELESS LAN

Not all wireless communication needs to be long distance, or even connected to a phone company. There are many applications for very-short-distance digital wireless devices and protocols—shop floor, in-office, conference centers, at home, at school. They can be used to communicate with service devices such as ATMs, ticket handlers, toll-booths, and soda machines (true). We are referring here to nonvoice applications mixed with voice. Imagine an aircraft mechanic wedged in the tail section of an airliner wanting to bring up a print of the unit he's working on. He reaches for his Blackberry Super Plus or similar device and connects to the local maintenance database. Diagrams are displayed on demand. (Not quite yet, but coming.)

Are these necessary? Well, yes, even the soda machine. Among their very real advantages is the relief that these devices will bring to the long-distance wireless bandwidth because their range is localized, their power requirements are lower, and they can be used inside a protective cordon. Don't just think of them as localized cellular phones or PDAs. See them as extended and truly portable LAN workstations. By the way, protection has not yet been fully worked out, but there will no doubt be some forms of encryption involved.

ADVANCES IN PRESENTATION AND DATA HANDLING TECHNOLOGIES

The Web format that we are all familiar with is based on the concept of hypertext. Hypertext, as we mentioned earlier, is essentially a linkage process that allows you to dynamically reference and transfer to specific content and other content sites from your current position in a document or transaction. It also enables you to navigate back to a starting or intermediate point. Browsing and surfing are appropriate terms. Hypertext Transfer Protocol (HTTP) and Hypertext Markup Language (HTML) are the two basic Web-enabling technologies.

HTML allows links to be inserted into text or graphics that will, in turn, be interpreted by HTTP as a new jump destination (possibly on a totally different website). After that jump, you can return or head off in yet another direction or quit. In short, HTML is indicating possible destinations and by clicking on the individual Web link, you're activating HTTP to get you there through Internet addressing. If you are a surfer, you go through that exercise all the time, but you're probably far more conscious of the logical progression of information retrieval than the fact that in the process, you may be traveling electronically from website to website, location to location, country to country.

Writing in HTML was quite a chore when it first came on the scene, but since that time it has become easier through high-level languages like Java and specifications like CGI, the Common Gateway Interface. There are also Web-page formatting kits that make it relatively easy to create a site if you don't mind looking like everyone else.

But HTML has its limits, especially in the areas of customizing hypertext tags. Tags are used to instruct the markup language (and by indirection HTTP) on how to format a specific Web-based document. Included in that formatting are such elements as data definition, transmission modes, validation, and interpretation of data by the receiving application, browser, or server and between organizations.

Handheld Device Markup Language (HDML) is used to format content for Web-enabled mobile phones and similar devices and is compatible with its own transport protocol, Handheld Device Transport Protocol. HDML is popular in North America. As usual, more than one standard is in play. Wireless Markup Language (WML), an XML language, is used with the European (Nokia) Wireless Application Protocol (WAP) and is gaining in popularity. Confused? So is the rest of the world.

XML—A MISMATCH RESOLVED—HOPEFULLY

HTML and HDML were designed for navigating the Web through the browser and for presenting screens and content. But suppose you want to trigger and manage a transaction? Or talk to an existing computer application? Take my word for it. HTML can be a pretty clumsy or impossible way of communicating with SAP, Oracle, MS Excel, Quicken or the millions of privately developed applications that are out there. Nor can you use it to easily write new transaction-based applications. (And no, Java is not a total panacea either.) This is a large magnitude problem for many of our loftier ambitions for compatible web-based processing. Most of today's computer applications can't understand HTML even if it is trying to say something besides how to present a screen or jump to a new URL.

Extensible Markup Language (XML) to the rescue. XML as the name suggests provides a much wider range of formatting and conversion options, making the Web a much more compatible user interface for all of those PC, server, and mainframe applications. It also facilitates the integration of Web-based data repositories into business systems.

It is more than just another formatting language. XML and its supporting protocols provide the much needed bridges to application land. Some argue with much justice that XML is more of a data manipulation language than a presentation language. It is a very necessary component for our B2B2C ambitions.

However, like many of the technologies we are discussing, a conservative approach to adopting XML or making commitments based on XML is strongly advised. It is new, it is complex, AND to be truly valuable, it must be widely available and implemented consistently. So far, consistent design and implementation from vendor to vendor has not been its strong suit. Inconsistent "designer" versions are appearing. Nor is it yet ready for some of the large scale, industrial strength punishment predicted for it.

XML also presents security and control issues. In the broadest sense, XML provides the ability to access and share a much wider universe of resources. Will it also fully support and facilitate the control functions required to manage that sharing? That's not clear yet.

By all means, give XML a high priority in your web transition plans. But treat it for the evolving model it is and ask plenty of specific questions about the versions you are contemplating. It is too critical a component to do otherwise.

BROWSERS AND SERVERS

Obviously, the major Web interfaces are the Web servers and the browsers. The browser fundamentally locates and displays Web pages. First it was text, then graphics, and now—with appropriate plug-in code—they also present multimedia. As we noted earlier, the desktop/laptop browser is commonplace and reasonably mature. However, the browser technology for hand-held devices such as phones and PDAs, wireless or otherwise, Web appliances, and special devices for point-of-sale or information kiosks is still coming on stream.

You don't just pick up a PC version of a Web browser and dump it in a hand-held device. As hand-held devices become more popular and functional demands on them increase (not just text but graphics; not just graphics but animated active color graphics; not just animated active color graphics but three-dimensional animated active color graphics; and, oh yes, toss in earphone stereo sound and streaming video), the browser will become an even more critical success factor. Just remember that while there's a server on the other end doing many wonderful things, it doesn't have to squeeze function into some of the spaces that a browser must. Remember the old statement about Fred Astaire and Ginger Rogers. He was truly one of the world's greatest dancers of all times but when they partnered, she had to do most of the same things in high heels, a big swirling dress, and backward. Remember that the next time someone tells you about all the wonderful server-based function that's available. The browser and its host device also have to be able to handle most of it.

ENCRYPTION

Encryption has had a long and tortuous journey in coming into its own. We've devoted several chapters around encryption and its applications, so we'll simply note for the moment that as networking, data storage and usage, application processing, and end user presentation continue on their interactive road to loosely connected, semi-independent environments, it becomes more difficult to use physical or pathway controls alone. There are too many variables. Encryption permits the protection of independent data elements, variable paths, and, through digital certificates and similar token forms, can provide strong authentication between specific parties. In a sense, the Internet demands encryption in a way legacy networks never did.

ELECTRONIC AND DIGITAL SIGNATURES

Be careful of these two terms. They don't mean the same thing. In mid-2000, the U.S. government made electronic signatures legal for a wide range of business and personal usage. There are some exceptions, like medical transactions, product recalls, and the like, but generally, the legal doors have been opened for electronic replacement technologies to share the certification space reserved for centuries for written signatures on hard copies. The U.S. law deliberately does not specify a technology, or even specific technology requirements. Several are in use today. The most likely leader is the digital signature, based on unique encrypted keys, that can be attached to a variety of data elements, transactions, and interactions. We cover this area in depth in Chapter 18 on PKI (Public Key Infrastructure) and encryption, and we looked at it in Chapter 12.

If you consider the nature of B2B and B2C interactions, there is a strong need for identity management—participant identification and authentication; authorization management; content protection; privacy protection; and nonrepudiation (proof of transaction integrity, timeliness and agreement/commitment by the concerned parties). Digital signatures serve these purposes rather well. There are administrative, operational, and technological costs but at the moment they seem to be the best alternative for most, but not absolutely every, security environment.

SMART CARDS AND TOKENS

Here is another family of technologies that has been trying to scale the marketplace walls for quite some time. As you probably know, tokens and smart cards with their embedded chips vary in form factor. The smart card looks like the conventional credit card. A token may take on other shapes and sizes as well, like keys, tiny calculators, even charms. They communicate with a reader and their basic purpose is to store and provide on demand, information that will enable transactions. The most generally recognized application for the smart card in North America is as a bank debit card. More about this in a moment.

The time-honored security rubric for strong identification calls optimally for three factors:

1. Something you know—a passphrase or PIN
2. Something you are—a biometric characteristic (fingerprint, hand geometry, iris shape, voice print)
3. Something you have—a badge, passcard, token, or smart card

(Occasionally, location is included as a fourth factor.)

Together, they can provide a high level of assurance of personal identification. Even singly or in pairs, they can be effective security mechanisms. Here, the token and smart card have captured some significant territory.

Smart cards come in two basic types: memory and logic. The memory card uses its chip as an extension of the magnetic stripe on conventional cards, storing information for the reader to pick up and transmit to a processor. On the logic card, a processor joins the memory functions on board the card. When it is activated by the reader and its power supply, it shares in carrying out the actual transaction. The logic card can personalize transactions and add to the security of the process.

The smart card has a much more vigorous life in Europe, partially because it was mandated by state-owned organizations such as the telephone services. In North America, the debit card as a concept has never been popular for two reasons: our check-handling system is quite good, and people do not like the idea of giving up float in their balances.

So here we sit with a conundrum. The smart card can be an excellent adjunct to online security but probably not as a security-only pure play. We all complain about how many ID, credit, and affinity cards we carry around now. Adding more of them strictly for identification usually doesn't sell.

What is required is a concerted effort on the part of industry partners to abandon the competitive exclusion provided by the single-function, single-supplier card and move toward multipurpose cards. It's going to be a tough sell. Will the airlines combine their cards? Probably only after more mega mergers. How about Visa, Amex, Discovery, and MasterCard? Not too likely, with the current market's attitude.

However, it's this same change of attitude that will determine the success of the netexchange and netmarket concept. Before you say it's strictly a B2C problem, look at the travel industry, more specifically the business travel industry. I have more than a dozen unique cards from airlines, hotels, auto rentals, and restaurants plus traditional credit cards in my wallet for the sole purpose of supporting my travel as a consultant. In Chapter 3, we presented a couple of advanced illustrative scenarios around travel. Think about going through them with your current population of cards. You probably do. Fun, huh?

SCAN YOUR WAY TO SUCCESS AND SATISFACTION

Here is a family of devices that have far more potential uses in B2B than they are given credit for. Actually, optical scanning technology has gone through a wonderful transition from its early days. Today, desktop scanners are super accurate, high resolution, and dirt cheap. But if sophisticated graphics and rapid document conversion were the only uses for scanning technologies they'd be helpful and productive but not *that* important. But of course, optical desktop scanners aren't the only devices in the arsenal. Nor is optics the only scan medium, as we'll see.

UPCS

What is the lowly, ubiquitous, and usually ignored UPC (universal product code—you know, the bar code) doing in a discussion on B2B? Nothing much, except acting as a major link between the virtual and the real. What connects all the B2B and B2C bits and bytes whizzing back and forth across the ether with the tangible raw materials, work in process, goods, containers, rail cars, and packages whizzing through factory floors, warehouses, transfer centers, and physical transport links? Right! UPC. And while everything and its dog has UPC identification, the bar code and all of the sensor technology that goes with it is seldom examined in its entirety in B2B discussions. Point-of-sale terminals have been with us it seems for an eternity. But they only initiate or terminate the buy–sell process.

If maintaining control and trust in the "click and mortar" world is a dynamic and interactive process, then the ability to continuously and accurately identify, authenticate, track, direct, and redirect real, tangible goods and property is critical to many e-Business segments. How well does the UPC serve these purposes? It's cheap, ubiquitous, standardized, and relatively easy to create and scan. Not bad for many applications, but UPC and similar codes have several major shortcomings.

For one thing, they are totally passive. Once encoded, the bar can be scanned an infinite number of times but has to be re-encoded physically to update information within the code itself. That's not an insurmountable obstacle for today's systems, where status and projected paths are all contained in the control systems.

But envision far more complex systems where multiple control activities from a variety of sources (say, manufacturer to shipper to distributor to retailer to tax authority to local delivery to service organization) all want to electronically determine not just the article's identity but its current status, age, location, destination, condition, cost, price, warranty status, tax status, and so on. The single focal point for this information needs to be a well-protected, updatable, high-capacity, embeddable device in or on the object that may also be detected remotely (for safety) and from a distance (for ease of use). UPC can't do all that.

Moreover, because the code is physical and visible, it is subject to all the problems of obliteration, alteration, and positioning. Lining up scanners and code bars is becoming less of an issue with improvements in laser technologies, but a laser still only sees what is there to scan.

UPC codes are removable. Often rather easily. This can also be a drawback, as can the fact that on many objects, they are unsightly.

RADIO FREQUENCY IDS (RFIDS)

Under development and making their way into the market are a group of devices that fall in the generic category of radio frequency ID. The general technique has been around for quite a while. You recognize it as that stupid alarm tag they forget to remove before you leave the department store. That technology is really very primitive and the tag just responds to a simple signal querying status. Are you in magnetic state one or two? Or even more simply—are you there, or have you been removed? A very welcome advance is the roadpass ID used in an increasing number of tollgates across the world. These devices can be individually identified, but again most of the updating and checking is done within the system, not on the device itself.

RFID expands on this concept by producing a very robust device about the size of a rice grain that can be embedded in or attached to the article or container. It is electrically passive and does not require its own power supply. It has a significant digital storage capacity and can be coded, queried, and updated by appropriate sensors and communications techniques. It does not actively broadcast but responds to queries. It can respond to remote queries from significant distances. It solves most, if not all, of the UPC shortcomings but has a few of its own, such as the usual problems of digital radio transmission. It can't be used in high-interference environments, for example. It can be encrypted to protect it from unauthorized scans and alteration. It can last the life of the object and continue to be updated for such data as current service status, current owner, and location if it is maintained within an ongoing system.

In addition to the usual UPC replacement and enhancement, there are some more dramatic and controversial applications for RFID. Non-removable or tamper-proof license "plates" embedded in the vehicle. Did we say above that UPCs are on everything and its dog? One developer has RFIDs embedded under his dogs' pelts so they can be located when they stray. Can kids be far behind? Hospital patient IDs? Criminal justice systems and corrections departments are, of course, interested, as are the military. This will no doubt bring social, civil rights, and to an extent, economic concerns to center stage, and rightly so.

However, it is clear that these devices have a significant role to play in B2B, B2C, and B2B2C. As noted above, they have the major advantage of providing several avenues to expand and enhance e-Trust. Any auditor or resource manager will tell you that physical inventories are one of the most arduous, mistake ridden, and time-consuming activities ever known, especially if the inventory is mobile or dynamic. Although statistical sampling techniques have made many of these jobs more cost-effective for valuation purposes, control of specific objects or groups remains painful. Devices like RFIDs may make controls easier and more accurate across a wide spectrum of applications.

GLOBAL POSITIONING SYSTEM (GPS)

If you are trying to keep track of materials, vehicles, and beings, it helps to have a commonly accepted mode of determining and specifying location. GPS, currently a military and navigational necessity, is emerging from its upscale automobile accessory status to a level of more generalized commercial and personal application. If we are going to ask "where are you?" with increasing frequency, we must have an accurate way of all agreeing on just "where" is. GPS, with sophisticated network and presentation interfaces, has an important e-Business value and is part of its increasing arsenal of control and trust techniques.

CERTIFIABLY RELIABLE TIME AND TIME STAMPING

As more nodes, networks, processes, applications, and end users join in the $24 \times 7 \times 365$ global e-Business process, time synchronization, sequencing, and stamping become critical. If network nodes go out of synch or must restart, they need a common, trusted time reference to get back in step. If orders are being entered in sequence, that sequencing process must be trustworthy. If transaction nonrepudiation is required, time stamping is part of the equation. If accountability is to be maintained, trusted time is part of the accounting process. If on-time performance is critical, super accurate time measurement is also critical. There are several new devices and services in existence to answer these and related requirements. You'll be hearing more about them.

THERE AND BACK AGAIN

This chapter was probably more detailed than you'd expected. Before we go on, let's just pause a second and recap. Though it may have seemed so, this was not intended as an exercise in naming all of the world's technologies. For example, we completely ignored optics and biotech. Although, who knows about photon or gene-based processors? If we can stop and restart light in its tracks, we can create light speed switches (literally) and computing devices. If we can alter DNA dynamically, can a genetic processor or storage device be far behind?

Nor was it an attempt to create an overwhelming "gee whiz" attitude about e-Business. B2B is complex but it's alive, reasonably well, and in many sectors, it's thriving. We were just trying to illustrate that e-Business is not business as usual. If earlier chapters and this technology review didn't make that clear, we hope our discussions in the next chapters will. e-Business means much more than putting up a flashy website and waiting for the e-money to come pouring in. But you knew that. We hope you have a better appreciation for the technical options, prerequisites, and constraints that need to be addressed in order to become and, more important, stay successful in these environments.

14

Secure e-Business Architecture and Design

We are not going to make secure e-Business architects out of you unless, of course, you have a passionate desire to be one. If so, go read a different book. We are, however, going to give you some insights into our approach to architecting secure, trustworthy, B2B systems. The definitions and Exhibit 14.1 fell out of my fevered brain in the late 1980s with very strong collaboration from my esteemed colleague, Bill Murray. It appeared in my first book, Information Protection and Other Unnatural Acts, in 1992, well before the dawn of B2B as we think we know it. It has since been used in any number of articles, proposals, presentations, and graffiti. There is an unconfirmed report of a close approximation being found in an Incan Temple, left by visitors from another planet. I include it here for three reasons: (1) blatant sentimentality; (2) the expectation that it will be engraved on my tombstone; (3) it still works. Notice, please, that while the definitions speak to architecture and strategy, the diagram speaks to the overall information security process and how architecture fits. Fear not, we have more diagrams on later pages that are more specific and of much more recent genesis.

DEFINITIONS

Architecture: The parts of system, application, or business process design dealing with appearance, function, performance, location, and

Exhibit 14.1   Architecture Based Information Protection Process

interface. How do things work together? (Architecture has both technology and administrative content.)

Strategy: High-level plans for achieving specific goals and objectives.

Perhaps the most important aspect of that edge-worn diagram is the placement and directions of the arrows. They indicate a highly interactive and iterative process that has no real ending. Architecture and its associated functions and processes live as long as the business processes live.

Having used those definitions for a virtual lifetime, it has also become blatantly apparent that "architecture" is a lousy descriptor for what we are about. Actually, there's nothing *all* that wrong with it. It just carries a lot of misleading baggage. So let's "purify" our thinking here.

Most traditional architectural constructs deal with static designs— buildings, vehicles, ships, aircraft, works of art. Some folks can't make the leap to applying architecture to dynamic systems. We're talking about dynamic, nay, volatile systems in our B2B environments, so our architecture is in an evergreen state. Pope Sixtus IV della Rovere kept asking Michelangelo about the ceiling of his namesake, Sistine Chapel. "When is it going to be finished?" If the great artist and sculptor had been a systems architect, the appropriate but irreverent reply to His Holiness would have been, "Never! Stop bothering me!"

That first point often leads management to despair and designers to the convenient assumption that all is tentative and therefore their commitments are only approximations, at best. Wrong! System architectures can and should be locked down to achieve specific levels of design closure. "Here's the 2002 model." And they should be ruthlessly enforced. What the dynamic nature of the process is really saying is: "There's a next version, and probably another after that." The strategy drives the evolution of the architecture.

Locking down a design is the bane of all process developers. But it is crucial in trust situations. It works both ways. Shoving an extra bit of last-minute function into the already overcrowded phone booth is often done for the sake of product or service enhancement. It may also blow quality out of the water. Conversely, dropping a function at the last minute because it's more difficult than projected, or more expensive, or hasn't successfully completed testing is dirty pool if the user base has been told to expect and rely on it. No, I do not advocate shipping untested code, although it often seems to be an industry standard. I advocate keeping commitments.

Here is yet another variation of e-Trust. The product or service promised must be the product or service delivered, very preferably on time and completely tested at the agreed upon price. This is absolutely crucial in a world of interdependent systems, applications, and functions—in other words, the e-world. If vendor X doesn't deliver all the function expected at the interface so vendor Y and a lot of other guys can pick up the baton in the transaction integrity and confidentiality relay race, guess who loses? No one wants to have to say, "Your directory structure is supposed to be standards compliant. How come it misses here, here, and here?"

THE ARCHITECTURE OF THE SECURE e-WORLD

For openers, let's explain why we've shifted from trust to security. (You did notice, didn't you?) The reason is simply manageable scope. If you remember all the components we said belonged to e-Trust, the diagram structure we'd have to display and the interplay we'd have to describe would force the publisher to classify this book as a philosophical work on cosmology or a scientific treatise on quantum mechanics. We wouldn't want it to lose its status as light entertainment, would we? We'll start with an overview of Exhibit 14.2, and then move on to examine its component views—functional, life cycle, solutions, and integration. Again, the diagram is not complete.

Notice that the *business strategy* for the B2B environment frames in everything. We have omitted other components of the business strategy from the diagram. They include such areas as marketing and revenue generation, R&D, financing, expense management, HR, resource planning,

Exhibit 14.2   Security Strategy Architecture

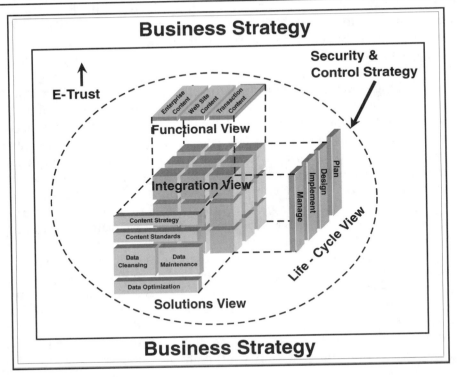

and supply chain. The inner *e-Trust strategy* frame includes law, regulation, contracts and relationships, practices, ethics, and the always crucial quality and service objectives. For our discussion on *architecture,* we'll concentrate on the elements encircled by the *security and control strategy.*

WE ARE NOT ALONE

Many architectures and substrategies are required to satisfy our business strategy. They include business process, application, infrastructure, network, data management and, of course, security and control architecture. All of them are important to our discussion of security and control, because no architecture stands independently. This is especially true of security and control because, while it may include many dedicated security processes—encryption, identification, and authentication—it also is heavily involved in the security characteristics of the other architectures. How does an application handle authorization? What are the integrity characteristics of the operating system? How robust is the network?

So we believe that individual security and control architectures must be developed in the context of their companion designs. Security and control architectures:

- Must be adaptive
- Derive from . . .
- Depend on . . .
- And integrate with . . .

data, network, application, systems architectures, and strategies.

All are driven by business process requirements and priorities. All require synchronized strategies.

Unless a security and control architecture is strategically dovetailed with its peers and provides a collaborative and adaptable environment, it will be ignored or badly twisted out of shape. Further, there is a constant argument as to which comes first—standards or architecture. I firmly believe that you should develop architecture to fit the individual needs of the business and then determine what roles standards will play in solidifying and supporting your design. There are too many organizations that decide they will be X.989898 compliant before fully evaluating the appropriateness of standard X.989898.

But you may retort, "Standards are critical in B2B. How else will we achieve commonality and synchronization?" Of course, but the adoption of standards for their own sake or simply because they are industry good practice, without due diligence on their true applicability and impact, is foolish. There is such a thing as selective compliance. It is practiced all the time. Selective compliance is easiest when your adoption of the standard is voluntary. But when you are selectively compliant, you are obligated to ensure that all interested parties are aware of and understand what you are doing. Of course, if you are being licensed or certified to a standard, selectivity can be more difficult. But even there, permitted variances are not uncommon.

WHAT ARE THE OBJECTIVES OF AN OVERALL B2B ARCHITECTURE?

The main objectives are:

- flexibility
- interoperability
- availability
- performance
- manageability
- integrity

Exhibit 14.3   Different Views of Security Architecture

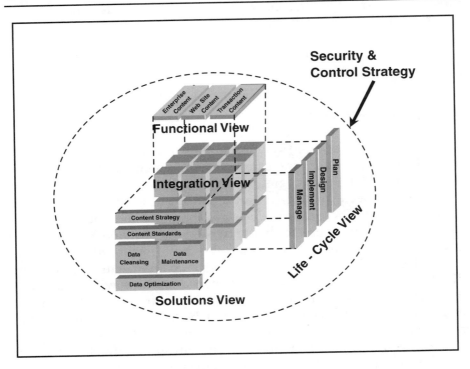

- scalability
- reliability
- security and control
- trust

After our prior discussions, I don't think it's necessary to define and parse each one of these elements. So let's zoom in on Exhibit 14.3 a bit and focus on the different views of the security architecture—functional, life cycle, solutions, and integration.

FUNCTIONAL ARCHITECTURAL VIEW

The functional or content-related view examines the security and control characteristics from a business function aspect. *Enterprise content* refers to the general business processes and data that traditionally were not exposed to external access but now, as a result of B2B design and activity, become open to third parties. Consider any outsource, ASP, CSP, or partner relationship. In the world of advanced B2B, what was an arm's length, transaction-driven process (such as EDI) now takes on a more integrated approach, providing third parties direct access to online files, processes, and facilities (not necessarily over the Web and generally in controlled extranet relationships).

For example, a third-party logistics manager or a managed healthcare organization may directly share in many of the databases and processes used by the manufacturer or health provider. Because of the newness and serious consequences of such arrangements, this is the functional area that requires the most scrutiny and management—not just through the use of protective mechanisms but at a business level—through terms and conditions; mutual acceptance of liabilities; confidentiality, nondisclosure and privacy agreements; regulatory compliance; and a complete mechanism for assessing and reconstructing processes. All of these "business" agreements will be reflected in application, data, network, data management, and specific security function design with a composite security and control architecture emerging from the collection.

The *Web view* obviously speaks to the functions and transactions that will be offered to the external world through Internet connection. The security tools, surveillance functions, and protective activities that we have discussed and will discuss again in succeeding chapters will speak to some of the specific requirements and peculiarities of various levels of Web-based services and interactivity. The important thing to remember is that these functions are not totally separated from enterprise content. Indeed, as the Web is further exploited, the lines of demarcation may become non-existent in certain business functions. Before taking out your eraser, carefully walk through all the implications. Establishing a viable interface is just the beginning. The interplay of queries, transactions, data movement and mining, and a variety of other functions, even if intentionally authorized by B2B agreement, may produce some unintentional side effects. Clearly, isolation and DMZs are the order of the day, but remember, the shoe may be on the other foot. You may be sharing via the Web on an ASP's site. Who else is there, and how well are you and they protected?

The *transaction view* is the traditional arm's-length process that has characterized online relationships for years. Three aspects should catch your attention:

1. The fundamental security and control in the transaction process itself.

2. The impacts, if any, of shared access on the traditional transaction stream, and vice versa. Can a transaction be deliberately or accidentally corrupted as a result of the new boarders? Again, isolation and file mirroring are key components.

3. The transition of the traditional transaction stream to Web-based status. (There may be an occasional reverse mode as some process is taken off the Web for any number of business or technical reasons. Let's hope there are not too many.) Many enterprises have publicly stated that they want to ultimately reach a point of total migration to the Web. What are the security and control implications of these shifts? Will there be hybrids? Need you ask?

Consider again our discussion of XML. It is a primary link between Web and transaction. It is also a serious link in the security chain.

While we have separated the three functional domains in Exhibit 14.4, the fact is that your architectural efforts in this view may concentrate more on the interface *between* than on the activities *within*. Just don't stop at the interface.

This, like all of the security architecture views we are examining, will be a complex joint effort. I get concerned with any security architecture project that is delegated exclusively to the information security specialists for development. It has nothing to do with their skills or experience, which can be prodigious. It has everything to do with scope and responsibility. This is task force and project office country. Either or both should be proactive contributors, not just approval stamps. Many of the most serious security conflicts, overlaps, gaps, and disconnects are discovered in the architectural phase through detailed walkthroughs by the business function, application, network, and data management groups. It's often tough to get them involved. But they need to be.

Exhibit 14.4   Functional View

Functional View

Enterprise Content   Web Site Content   Transaction Content

That provides a transition to our second detailed view, the *life cycle* (see Exhibit 14.1). Occasionally, we get push-back on including this one as an architectural construct. "Isn't it more strategy and process than architecture?" Yes, but very few credible project-management timelines are developed without having a design in hand. When we look at the *solution* and *integration* views, this interlock will become even more apparent. Conversely, the availability and maturity of third-party products and services, resource constraints, and functional interdependencies may all send the architects back to the drawing boards for a second or third shot. Many multifaceted projects, especially those with complex vendor participation, kick off the initial design stages with Plans B and C, as well as the primary. If you're pushing the state of the vendors' art or your own competence, or both, design alternatives can be critical to success.

LIFE-CYCLE ARCHITECTURE VIEW

The *life-cycle architecture view* looks at the design components and process steps required to bring the security-related functions into full operation. Each view is designed in concert with the other architectures. It is important to develop preliminary versions of how each of the other architectural views will be planned, designed, implemented, and managed as they emerge, as well as an overall approach to the complete project. "Hold on! That's a lot of life-cycle planning." Not all that much. What I am suggesting is that while building the early stages of the functional and solutions views, also build the early stages of comparable life-cycle views for those components. Why? So you can see in as much early detail what mismatches there are in solutions and functional processes, and get them on the critical path for solution.

There's that phrase—*critical path*. Is this an exercise in critical path design? You bet. With the wide array of objects, processes, interdependencies, venues, process layers, cost, participants, venues, and constraints, use of critical path or an equivalent is a must. As we develop the integration view, the life cycle views are also integrated.

Once again, bear in mind that you, assuming you are the central player in this architectural exercise, are not the only player. The potential for using ASPs, third-party software, and security function suppliers, to name only a few, kicks in very early in the architectural process. There is a cartoon of a pair of mathematicians staring at a set of equations on a whiteboard. In the lower left-hand corner, one expression in the set is, "And then a miracle occurs." Before blithely filling in the blanks on your

Exhibit 14.5   Life Cycle View

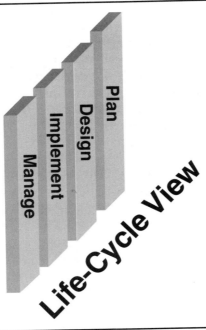

design structures and timelines with "3rd-party supplier," check carefully and early that your trust is worth giving.

ANOTHER WAY OF LOOKING AT THE LIFE CYCLE

Take a look at Exhibit 14.6. While the first three phases look straight line, there is a great deal of iteration, especially between Phases 2 and 3. Phase 4 is an ongoing operational environment. Remember once again that you will be designing and implementing these functions across multiple environments, either simultaneously, if danger is your food and drink, or on a staged basis. Expect to have several or many of these plans in play but not necessarily at the same stage at the same time in any complex environment. Don't forget, you also need a master plan of plans.

Tucked away in the bottom of Phase 2, there is that interesting box labeled *technology and product alternatives*. This will include not only the specific security products you have as possible choices, but also the security characteristics of the system, network, middleware, application

Exhibit 14.6   Modified Life Cycle Plan

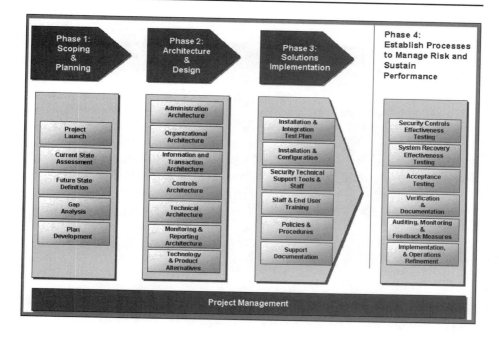

products, and in-house development you may be doing. This will further extend to any third-party services you are examining, either as ASPs or trusted third parties.

The next two views, *solutions and integration,* will flesh out the nature and types of services and offerings that go into those technology and product alternatives.

SOLUTIONS ARCHITECTURE VIEW

Exhibit 14.7 presents the various security and control solutions that will interact with the applications, network, middleware, other infrastructure, and data management services that make up the overall business architecture. Remember, please, that they do not represent the totality of the security function in the architecture. They are the *separable* functions that may be supplied by an ASP, trusted third party, hardware or software vendor, or the do-it-yourself store. Of equal importance are the complementary functions that must be embedded inside the network

Exhibit 14.7   Solutions View

Solutions View

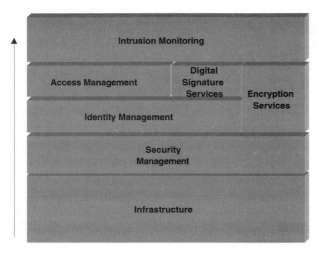

Solutions Areas

- Infrastructure
- Security Management
- Identity Management
- Access Management
- Intrusion Monitoring
- Encryption Services
- Digital Signatures

and other functions. These are the processes that call, use, and exploit an external service, such as encryption. Finally, there is our old friend, the *interface*. Vendors do not always supply full interface capability for *both* sides of the link. It can be a shock to discover that batteries and the last five feet of the bridge are not supplied. You may also find that you have to tweak what is provided. Be extremely sensitive to interface issues. They, more often than actual function, are the rocks on the tracks that will derail your architecture and your life-cycle planning.

Most of the areas described in the diagram are covered throughout the rest of Section III, and we will only name but not explain them here. The first two, infrastructure and security management, need a little more (but not too much more) explanation.

Infrastructure security involves the security characteristics of platforms and networks (UNIX in all its variations, LINUX, the Windows family, the IBM and Novell family, the MAC family). Each has its own design traits (and quirks) that can strongly influence, support, and sometimes negate the value of the other security functions. *Security management* refers to overall system monitoring, reporting, and response to other security anomalies and incidents besides intrusion detection (a separate function).

Exhibit 14.8   Integration View

Integration View

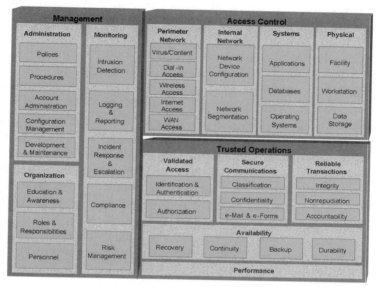

INTEGRATION ARCHITECTURE VIEW

Take a look at Exhibit 14.8. This is the big box of little boxes that were in the center of Exhibits 14.2 and 14.3. This is the view that puts all the function together. However, it does not replace the other views. It concentrates instead on how well each element works with all of its peers inside the larger venues of *management, access control,* and *trusted operations.* "Trusted," in this case, means products and services rigorously tested and demonstrated to be secure in themselves, as well as providing security services. If you want to attack and take over a system, one excellent way is to first take over or thwart the security system. These functions are the heavy-duty defense mechanisms.

Next we must concentrate on the interoperability of management, access control, and trusted operations. Also, consider that these functions extend to and support all of the other business strategy architecture components. Remember that this is B2B we're talking about. All of these models apply just as well to a single system environment, but they get really interesting (and complex) when the architecture is mapped across a global, multiindustry network. Be kind to your architects.

Theirs is a critical task. (I have just antagonized a very broad spectrum of developers, coders, managers, and support groups, all of whom believe, with some real justice in each case, that they are the indispensable ingredient in the recipe. I apologize to all and sundry.)

Notice, please, that the diagram contains a large number of management and procedural functions as well as technology. We made the point at the beginning of this chapter that strategy and architecture are a mix of both—although some architects refuse to cede this point. In B2B, you can't ignore it, especially in hybrid situations. Frequently procedure and management have to bridge the (temporary, we hope) disconnects or mismatches in technology or, as in the case of data and transaction cleansing, act as a filter to reduce technical mishaps.

Also notice, modestly stripped across the bottom, the performance factor. As we've mentioned many times before, performance is more than the speed of the individual parts—it is the direct result of how well all the parts interact.

For example, as I am writing this book, the central processor on my laptop gets long and frequent periods of well-deserved rest because my unimpressive memory, thinking, and keyboard speeds are the gating factors in the process. This book would take just as long on a computer with twice the internal speed, except for one thing—graphics. Watching complex graphics generating and regenerating themselves on a screen can make any writer take the "no diagrams" pledge. So suddenly our assumption about the uselessness of a faster engine in a document-producing application has developed a large "it depends" factor.

The purpose of this humble literary analogy is to suggest that assumptions about optimizing performance are very situational and are often trade-offs. Unfortunately, optimizing performance, especially in so-called "overhead" processes like many security and control activities, is as much art as it is science.

TESTING, ANALYSIS, DEPLOYMENT, OPTIMIZATION, AND CHANGE MANAGEMENT

These are the final topics on our architectural tour. Some traditionalists may argue that they are part of the baseline, ongoing IT processes, and are just assumed to exist in most architectural activities. It's precisely because of this attitude that I have raised them here. Put each one of these in a B2B context and you've got some serious process design to do. Who is responsible for test? Do we need separation of duties across the B2B relationships? Should you test and I look over your shoulder, or should we get a third party to do quality assurance? The same question applies to *analysis?* Whose metrics do we use? Do we all agree on them? If we do, who wields the yardstick?

Obviously *roll-outs* and *deployment* are tied directly to how the functions are structured, as well as the business units and sites involved. Once again, design affects deployment. For example, has a digital certificate system (PKI or not) been so constructed that it has to be rolled out in one swoop, or can it be phased in? What prerequisite functions have to be fully operational? Does the certificate program depend on a new directory system?

Optimization is best reflected in those dual-direction arrows we showed in Exhibit 14.1. Total success seldom comes with the first deployment. Not only are fixes required, but improvements may become obvious and appropriate.

Finally, *change management and version control,* never easy tasks, are magnified by the B2B relationship. Synchronizing and assuring the deployment of updates after they have been successfully tested across a multienterprise network is critical. As we have all found out, shipping an update doesn't mean it will be installed. I don't know *how many* sites are running on back level, or even no-longer-supported versions of platforms or applications. The most common reason: "We finally got it to work. Don't touch it." Then when an intolerable vulnerability is discovered (an almost everyday occurrence with today's extensive range of platforms and applications), it's the passing parade of procuring, installing, testing, and confirming a long daisy chain of prerequisite upgrades and modifications, or going for a totally new version of the product. Either alternative, performed under pressure, can be chaotic.

What has this to do with architecture and design? It's in the architecture and design that the progression, sequence, and timing of activating product function is determined. All the bells and whistles prescribed by the enterprise design team for the *steady state* version are seldom fully deployed on day one. The change management and version control process begins, and the beat goes on.

This concludes our expedition to Mt. Architecture. I hope we didn't lose anyone in the climbing party. Before we leave, let's fix broken ropes and empty climbing shoes. Unlike mountain climbing, getting back down is very simple. Just turn the page to Chapter 15.

15

Identity Management

Unless your life is one supreme ego trip, you know that the primary reason for a system of identity is to establish links to others—other individuals, other entities, and other processes—and conversely, for them to establish links to you. The more precise, timely, and unique the identifier, the more likely the linkage will be established correctly—not necessarily beneficially, but correctly.

Although self-awareness is an important, many say distinguishing, characteristic of our humanity, it's not going to occupy us very long in this chapter. We've all run into Rene Descartes' famous, "I think, therefore I am." A friend's dog has a sweater that reads, "I stink, therefore I am." We'll leave those considerations to the philosophers and veterinarians.

We're going to concentrate on that numeral 2 in B2B. B2B doesn't just imply, it loudly proclaims, "linkages." What makes it a subject worth discussing is the criticality, complexity, variation, size, and volatility of the linkages that B2B and Beyond brings to the table. Are the tried and true technologies, policies, and procedures that we have relied upon for identity management over the past 40 years up to the task? Not without a good shot of steroids.

LET'S TAKE A WIDER-ANGLE VIEW

Many discussions on business identity management begin and end with examinations on how to satisfactorily answer the questions, "Who are you, and what are you allowed to do?" But as networks expand, automatic functions increase, and outside pressures mount, we have to raise another set of questions: "What is that signal, and what does it mean?" Awareness first! Then comes recognition! "I see or hear something. What's out there? Should I let it come in?" Is this an alarm, anomaly, threat, attack, or just another transaction in business as usual? "Do I know what I don't know?" Profound, Huh?

In everyday life, far more demands for recognition come from things, events, and processes than from other individuals. That strange sound in the transmission, the changing temperature, that flashing light, that funny smell, that drip of water. Think back to that technological catalog we ran you through in Chapter 13. How many of those technologies throw off some form of critical signal we have to recognize and accept (e.g., time signal, UPC code, network disconnect, or GPS ping)? Conversely, how many of them have to recognize reciprocal signals from us to proceed? By the way, who are "we"? The other guy or process wants to know. Think back to the business structures and processes we described throughout Part II. How many of them are critically tied to complete and unambiguous recognition, identification, acceptance, and authorization? Most.

In short, everyone in the trust game needs to understand and act on the fact that while "friend or foe, go–no go" is still the foundation of our access management, we have to be far more sophisticated in our awareness and detection abilities—sensing, gathering, discriminating, and recording "outside stimuli" before going on to identification, authentication, and authorization. Access management implies that you are aware of what you're managing. There's a significant danger in B2B networks of things like denial of service attacks or embedded viruses sneaking in under the radar.

"NOW, JUST A SECOND! YOU'RE CONFUSED."

Some of you will no doubt argue that I'm confusing system and network management with identity management. I'm not confusing them. I know they're (semi) distinct. I'm trying to point out their growing interdependence, made even more striking by the size and nature of the nets we're talking about. Don't expect your identity systems to be any better than the "senses and sensors" that are supporting them. More to the point, make sure that as your organization develops and deploys more sophisticated and widespread identity management that your systems and network management capabilities are keeping pace and going in the same direction. We've already spoken about many of the characteristics of sensing and monitoring in our discussion on Architecture in the previous chapter.

We'll bring up the issue again in Chapter 21 when we discuss attack and penetration as part of e-Business assurance.

iMAAP™

So now let's get down to something we in Deloitte & Touche call iMAAP™—identity management, authentication, authorization, and protection. No, we do not believe we invented and trademarked identity management. iMAAP™ is an approach to identity management that we have specially designed and tuned for the ERP and B2B and Beyond environments. It is not a software package. It's a method for growing, extending, modifying, terminating, if necessary, but definitely integrating your existing identity management processes into an expanded, cohesive, and coherent structure that can be applied to your entire B2B environment. And it does it safely, cost-effectively, and productively.

iMAAP™ has its genesis and roots in our work with ERP technology, internal controls, business application function, and information protection. It has as its primary goal the *integration* of the management, authentication, authorization of your networks, business applications, and systems infrastructure. It has been expanded and refined to serve the B2B environment by extending the traditional identity arena not just to employees and (some) contractors but to the much broader universe of your customers, partners, suppliers, and stakeholders.

CHANGING THE CENTER OF GRAVITY

iMAAP™ also changes the point of focus from within the individual centers of process to the shared environment of the B2B network. That change is extremely important because you and your networked partners are now sharing, directly or indirectly, in the overall management and protection of the net(s). Remember our description in Chapter 6 of reciprocity—the willingness of all the players to extend protection, not only to all the other players but also to the network-based environment itself—the common cause. We also recognize, however, that developing a brand new, super-identity management system from scratch that standardizes and replaces all existing approaches and technologies is probably not in the cards, at least during the early transitional phases. There will probably always be some procedural and technical variations caused by economic, organizational, or technological drivers (or just plain orneriness. It does happen). We usually begin a networked system by first managing interconnection, move on to interoperation, and proceed to integration. The difference is that the approach takes cognizance of the network from day one and matures as the network matures.

SO WHAT'S DIFFERENT NOW?

Let's review the bidding. Today, identities are often (1) unique for each system supported; (2) supported by multiple administration processes; (3) with varying levels of efficiency; (4) with varying levels of strength.

Identities can become (1) common throughout environments; (2) supported by one administration process; (3) with a consistent level of efficiency; and (4) with the appropriate level of strength.

We mentioned earlier in the book that generic identity management consists of:

- Identification—Who or what are you?
- Authentication (verification)—Prove it?
- Authorization—OK, now we'll tell you whether you can go somewhere or do something, but only if and when you try. No advanced roadmaps extended to users or bad guys, just to administrators and managers.
- Protection—not only for the enterprise processes but for the protective system itself. Compromise the defenses, and you own the place.

Most major organizations have one or more traditional access control processes in place on their current systems and networks. Some are pretty sophisticated. Others . . . well. For years, security and controls specialists and software vendors have been listening to and trying to respond to the siren songs of single sign-on; single-use authenticators; single points of administration; and coordinated sources of identification, authentication, and sign-off. We address each in turn.

Single Sign-on

One and only one act of identification and authentication by the user is required for each log-in. The access management system, network, and applications will all proceed from that point to interact under the covers and as often as necessary using that one verified ID to determine where that logged-in entity can go and what he, she, or it (a process) can do throughout the session. Less work, confusion, and irritation for users.

But wait! There's more. Suffice it to say that any identity management mechanism that is going to successfully control tomorrow's B2B and Beyond must be capable of recognizing aliases. Does your UserID match your e-mail ID and your employee ID and your ID for the Super-Exchange and your ATM ID, and on and on? Probably not. Then can I establish an automatic alias system that safely provides for John Doe aka J.Doe aka DoeJohn aka Hotwheels to be recognized as the one, the only, and the original John Doe? Yes I can, but it can cost in administrative effort and complexity. Often, it is worth every penny.

Single-use Authenticators

The longer an authenticator (password, digital signature, fingerprint, retina or iris scan, voice print) is in repetitive use, the more vulnerable to compromise it becomes. Single-use technologies are oriented toward changing the representation of the authenticator to the system each time it occurs. The device produces a different authenticating character set from the same scan each time you activate it. You key in your ID but you don't key in a password. The device, usually a smart card or token, generates one for you, changing it each time.

Whoa, how does the system, network, and application stay in sync? I'm out here merrily changing my authenticator every time I log in, but how does the system know what I'm doing, and how do we keep it secure? Is that really true-blue me with a newly generated authenticator, or is it a hacker using my UserID and playing with passwords until one works? There are several highly proprietary technologies based on synchronized time or mathematically deduced relationships that can make it happen. Just search on the Internet for terms like *security token, security smart card,* or *single-use passwords* and you'll encounter a number of solutions and suppliers.

Single Points of Administration

This requirement has grown in importance and has frequently moved into the number-one priority position as networks expand in size, population, complexity, and move to 24 × 7 × 365 service. When and where do you introduce a new identity into the network? In how many places? How do you keep the process in sync? What about updates, purging? How do you change authentication rules when a new level of authority is granted to a process or individual? How fast can you take someone or some process completely off the system? Whom do you notify? Is

there some way to control the entire process from one virtual administration point (e.g., a controlled website) while granting rapid access and
turnaround? By the way, how do you control the administrators? Access control administration is very often the largest recurring cost in security systems. This is further aggravated in systems where there is
rapid turnover in participants and processes.

Part of the cost depends on the number of times an individual has
to change a password, forgets a password, or compromises an authenticator, and how many levels of management sign-offs are required for
the change. Times can vary from weeks to seconds and neither is an indicator of the strength or efficiency of the respective systems.

Coordinated Sources of Identification, Authentication, and Sign-Off

Now we're getting even further into issues that are more heavily ac-
cented by extranets, exchanges, and netmarkets. User identification,
authentication, and authorization requests will be coming from a variety of sources to that (hopefully) single point of administration:

- Customers and clients through your marketing systems
- Employees through your HR program
- Partners, contractors, and licensees through purchasing or
  contracts administration
- Stakeholders through investment relations
- Suppliers through ERP or similar processes
- Service suppliers like legal, medical, accounting, and auditing
  through their respective units or purchasing or both
- Tech support and third-party suppliers directly through
  network, system, or application administration
- Financial institutions through the CFO and treasury functions
- Regulators, wherever they want to come from

What will those requests look like? What about the procedures that guarantee them? Does a request for a contract employee to be entered into the
B2B system imply that they have been vetted by the appropriate individuals in their own entity, or simply that their names appear in a corporate
directory or are being subcontracted from somewhere else? What liabilities does the requesting entity take on in the subject's behalf? (Some business partners or clients don't care who I am personally. They just want to
know that I'm a partner or director at Deloitte & Touche with appropriate

guarantees from the Firm.) Sometimes, appropriate individual personal credentials are key. Am I a certified practitioner in the art of alchemy? Whom did I study with? How much gold have I created from lead? Were there credible witnesses? Part of the B2B reciprocity agreement must deal with common or at least compatible identity management. There's another reason for beating this to death here. We want you to appreciate the functions required and the problems to be solved when we reach our discussion on encryption, digital signatures, and PKI in Chapter 18.

THE USER'S VIEW

Let's reverse the viewpoint and look at the access targets for a few moments. Here I am. A user. All dressed up, recognized, and authenticated. I want to start a transaction. Now what? Where do I go, and what happens when I get there? How does the target react? The reason this may seem like the repeated material may be tied to your prior experiences with mainframes, if you had any. For years we had treated access management as a unified process, all controlled by a single operating system and access management scheme serving a whole family of applications and resources under its comprehensive and solicitous roof. It's not that way anymore.

- Identification and authentication may take place in different places. I'm identified on my PC and then authenticated by the PC and then by a supporting server if I'm on line.
- Authorization is controlled by the specific applications or a surrogate operating on their behalf.
- Administration (centralized or not) works with all of them.
- Directory systems keep everyone from getting lost. (More on directories shortly and in Chapter 17 on changing network design.)

Access management has been dis-integrated and distributed around the entire network complex, Yes, even ones with single administration points. Why? Well, for openers, to maintain flexibility and make it easier for a new application, player, or environment to join the game.

Why is *authorization* often separated from identification and authentication? If we keep the authorization criteria, structures, and system within the application or a surrogate, it can deal more readily with identities coming from a variety of sources and establish an application-centric audit trail. Who's been here, and what did they do?

There's a second and often more important reason: speed and efficiency. Those of you old enough to remember the early days of Disneyland will recall the ticket books with different classes of ride—A through E. The book itself had a number and date on it. I could stay in the park until closing, but the tickets let me on the individual rides. If you had an E ticket available, you could go on the super-exciting stuff. If all you had left were As, you were stuck with the little kids. The important thing was that by buying the right mix of tickets on entry, you didn't have to go back over and over again to the main gate. Net result: Fewer bottlenecks, smoother traffic, more efficient use of the rides, and proportionally targeted ticketing. Little kids bought more As. Big kids bought more Es.

Now, of course, Disney and many other theme and amusement parks use a single, undifferentiated pass to all attractions because it's all included under one larger price. It cuts down on overhead dramatically. No ticket takers. Faster movement. Besides, there are marketing downsides to differential pricing for amusements in the same park. Is a C attraction not as entertaining as an E?

B2B networks very seldom can tolerate such undifferentiated authorization. There are some places and processes that must be reserved for the big kids—the ones with the special D and E tickets. The ticket book analogy has an additional application for widespread networked processing. Assuming we still want to differentiate, as long as all the "rides" were a short distance from the ticket seller and traffic was reasonable and similar, single-point ticket selling (identification and authentication) and ticket taking (authorization) would work up to a point. But at the intense transaction rates and volume, widespread global targets, variable paths, and highly differentiated processes and participants, single points degenerate into unmanageable bottlenecks.

You can still establish, update, and distribute the users' credentials from a centralized source. For the sake of consistency, quality, and security, you should make every effort to do so. But that administration is a separate transaction stream. When it comes to a busy day at the park, we want the credentials to be immediately available with the transaction and locally accepted or rejected by the only process that matters at the moment—the one you're trying to use. If there's a mismatch, get out of line and go back to administration, but don't hold up the other players. Time and volume are of the essence. So let's drop the theme park analogy and turn to a version of the real thing.

KERBEROS

(Some of the following material will be revisited briefly in Chapter 18. We've chosen to put it here to compare it against other forms of access management.)

Named after the (mythical?) three headed dog that guards the gates of the underworld, Kerberos is a trusted authentication software system that, through the use of shared secrets or keys (tickets), establishes a "trusted" end-to-end path or connection for use by two parties or processes. It was developed originally at MIT but has since been modified and incorporated into several operating systems such as MS Windows 2000, as well as application support systems. It can be used in circumstances where it is otherwise impossible to rigorously establish mutual trust, such as dial-up, remote, or Internet connections. Communication through Kerberos-authenticated sessions can eliminate the threat that passwords, data, or software traversing open networks in the clear can be viewed and/or captured. It is important to note that while Kerberos authenticates but does not authorize users, applications can make authorization decisions based on Kerberos authentication.

HOW DOES KERBEROS WORK?

As we've noted repeatedly, the new levels of connectivity, efficiency, and effectiveness provided by today's open networks can unfortunately create major security threats. An unsecured network is vulnerable to break-ins at anytime, by anyone, and increasingly from anywhere. Legitimate users and attackers alike can now access vast repositories of corporate information. When neither the end points nor the path can be trusted, Kerberos acts as a third-party intermediary and, through specialized encryption, "vouches" for the session and its members.

Once the user is authenticated to the workstation or server, the Kerberos security protocol presents credentials in a way that avoids ever sending readable passwords across vulnerable network links. Sensitive information can therefore be protected from being viewed, intercepted, or changed. The span of protection can also include a variety of hardware, operating systems, and software in a multivendor network. Verification of user identity is assured, while impostor "spoofing" of network addresses is detected and eliminated.

Kerberos can be deployed in environments that require protection from not only active hacker attack but passive attacks as well. Kerberos can eliminate the risk that an intruder connected to a given network can readily receive all or some of the data intended for another. Kerberos can also eliminate the risk that information being sent across the Net appears to have come from somewhere else.

The primary component of Kerberos is a master database that maintains a list of each of its clients and their private keys. A client in this instance is a query or process triggered by an individual or another process. These private keys are known only to Kerberos and the client/owners. Because it knows these keys, Kerberos can act as a trusted intermediary and create messages (validation tickets) that convince one client that another is really who it claims to be. In other words, while neither process may know or trust each other directly, both trust Kerberos because of the key structure each has given to the system. To prove the validity of the relationship, Kerberos encrypts information about one client with the other client's key. If that second client can then decrypt the message using its own key, it will accept that the information in the message is valid (because only Kerberos could have encrypted it); otherwise, it will reject the message or request as being invalid or from an unauthorized source.

Key Distribution Center (KDC)

In order for the two parties or processes to communicate in a trusted manner, they must share a secret. This secret is known to Kerberos as a *key*. These keys are shared with the key distribution center (KDC) so the KDC may mediate communications between the parties/processes through the use of encrypted digital tokens known as *tickets*.

Tickets

Tickets are issued by the KDC to request services on behalf of the authenticated user. Tickets generally contain credentials such as the user's name, time of issuance, length of time the ticket will be valid, the name of the requested application or "service," and a randomly generated session key. A ticket can only be "opened" for use by the user by providing a valid password. Once opened, the ticket is passed along to the server. The server can trust that the ticket provider is the intended and authenticated user and, upon appropriate authorization, grant the request for service.

Other Things Worth Noting

- *Kerberos provides inter system and inter application authentication, not authorization.* It provides for mutual authentication and secure communications between principals on an open network by manufacturing secret keys for any requestor and providing a mechanism for these secret keys to be safely propagated through the network. Kerberos assumes you have been identified and authenticated at your point of entry by any of a number of entry authentication modes. Kerberos does not, per se, provide for authorization or accounting, although applications that wish to can use their secret keys to perform those functions securely.

- *Misconceptions about Kerberos:*
  - *Kerberos implementation is costly.* It's not. Several third-party vendors also provide their own versions of Kerberos that contain improvements or extensions.
  - *Kerberos solutions may not be used outside the United States.* That's not an issue any longer.
  - *Kerberos and PKI are the same thing.* No, see Chapter 18.
  - *PKI will eventually replace all Kerberos usage.* That's not clear at this stage.

- Unlike other methods of user authentication, *Kerberos provides mutual authentication.* Not only is the user authenticated to the service, but the service is also authenticated to the user. In open networks such as the ones we are discussing, neither party may be known to the other.

- *Kerberos, when combined with other security mechanisms such as smart cards and one-time passwords, can achieve other information protection objectives such as single sign-on.*

DIRECTORY SERVICE FUNCTIONS

Here is another technology grouping that deserves coverage in several different chapters. We've mentioned it already in Chapter 14 in our discussion about architecture and design. We'll talk about some of the mechanics of directory services in Chapter 17. Right now, we just want to briefly mention an extremely important concept that can make or break e-Trust in any B2B environment.

It doesn't matter how well specified and defined objects (data, processes, technical functions) are in a network. They won't do you any good if you can't find and get to them. Networks live and die by their directories. A poorly organized directory system can slow a high-speed network to a halt. Unrecognized or faulty relationships (pointers) can send you off on wild goose chases. Unprotected directories are a very serious trust exposure. Identity management not only involves tying identification and authentication to the object or individual it represents. It must also facilitate rapid targeting, easy update, scalability, and portability.

For the purposes of closing our discussion here, let's just point out that identity management has the establishment of linkages as its number one objective. Objects are identified and authenticated through naming and access-management techniques. Linkages are mapped, revealed, and facilitated through directories and search engines. Data are organized through database functions. Networks provide the paths and plumbing. Unless they all work well together and provide mutual support and protection, B2B won't work.

In the next chapter, we're going to look further at two activities related to data quality and data protection. They further extend some of the material we've talked about here.

16

Data Quality and
Data Classification

We've gotten so tied up in process and connections and identification and transactions that we may seem to be ignoring the fuel and end products of all this effort—information. Protecting information while still making it easily accessible is not quite a contradiction in terms, but it's also not that easy. Neither is making sure the data are acceptable for use—a concern that has added poignancy as we rely more and more on the generosity of our friends in supplying us with data. Data, Here's looking at you, kid!

DATA QUALITY AND INTEGRITY

If you examine the basic principles of B2B interdependence, one of the most critical questions each partner has to address is, Can I trust the information you're giving me? Can you demonstrate to my satisfaction that I can trust what you're sending me? Conversely, can you trust my data? Can I do this on an ongoing basis, or do I have to subject each batch or transaction to individual scrutiny and evaluation? What are our respective liabilities and responsibilities if our information goes sour?

What criteria are we going to use to give our mutual "Data Trustworthiness Seal of Approval" to each other? Be careful here, the mutuality may apply to not just pairs but a large number of enterprises. Who is going to determine and, if necessary, arbitrate that? What do we do in the event of failure? Who has the responsibility to fix the problem? Is this something we agreed to? And of course, those basic questions: What will it cost? Who pays? Who has the liability?

Data quality and integrity (DQI) are related but not exactly the same. Data quality speaks to the accuracy and required precision of the information, its completeness, timeliness, appropriateness, and usability. Is this the latest and complete demographic information on Zone C? What is its margin of statistical error? Are all pertinent fields in the records filled in and within relevant parameters? Is it in a form that we can readily use in our customer relationship management system? Can we trust it, use it, and make good business decisions on it?

Data integrity speaks to another aspect that has a close bearing on quality. Have the data been corrupted in any way as to render them unusable or untrustworthy? The data management program drops random records on alternate cycles. Someone has unleashed a virus on the system, and what was once there no longer is. The network crashed in the middle of a streaming transmission.

You could argue with certain justice that the effects are the same. Either way, the information is unusable. So what's the point of the distinctions?

The protective and corrective mechanisms are different. Data quality is ensured primarily but not exclusively by sampling data entry, data conversion, and application-processing controls. These can include the lowly but time-honored hash total, field content range checks, dual mode entry, sequence checking, field relationship and sanity testing, historical validation, authorization and so on, depending on the value and impact of the information.

Most, but not all, data integrity issues are dealt with at the middleware and infrastructure level. This includes virus protection, line conditioning, media tests, firewall and routing checks, access management, time stamps, and encryption in content, digital envelope, or digital signature form.

DQI management must answer three significant questions:

1. Is the original baseline data you (I) have supplied trustworthy?
2. Are the additions and modifications equally trustworthy?
3. Does the process for developing and maintaining these databases and files meet our mutually agreed upon criteria? (Of course, this assumes you have developed mutually agreed upon criteria.)

There are a number of tools and techniques—ranging from brute force field checking to statistical analysis—to enhance dynamic and static quality management. The important point is that you implement appropriate procedures and guidelines to make it happen.

Let's explore those same three DQI processes now and ask the classic B2B question: Who has the responsibility? Why, the data supplier and infrastructure manager, of course. And in an extranet, netexchange, and netmarket they are . . . ? Not that easy to define. CPs and CSPs are obvious, but as the information is further refined, augmented, and modified by each succeeding application using it, the culprit(s), if any, are harder to locate. Do we have an adequate audit trail, validation, and version controls, interface checks, and other techniques? Could we reproduce the transaction flow?

TESTING! TESTING! 1, 2, 3

What about test beds and test data development? Why do application bugs show up two years later? Often because the testing regime was not sufficiently inclusive and rigorous. "Hey, they gave me the data and the expected results. It's not my fault." In B2B *they* may be a member of your own organization, a contractor, third-party supplier or processor, one of your partners, or a Web-based user with a flair for unusual combinations.

Anyone who has ever programmed an application knows how maddening unexpected test results can be. Unexpected production results are a bit more serious. These questions are not unanswerable. The answers, however, will be conditioned by the circumstances of use. (Don't touch that data. You don't know where it's been." Mom wasn't always wrong.)

CONTENT QUALITY—EXAMPLES

To address content quality issues, B2B e-Business environments will need to determine responsibility and agree on the procedures in at least three areas:

1. Data quality—Who is going to analyze and assess the initial state of data quality? How? What data? How will it be corrected and revalidated?
2. Data conversions—What conversions are planned (content, format, protocol, merges, re-sorting)? One time, or ongoing? Are controls being developed to convert data after its initial quality has been established?

3. Data monitoring—Will continuous interfacing and data maintenance require a data monitoring program? If so, how?

Infrastructure and middleware integrity and monitoring are covered in Chapters 14, 17, 18, and 21.

WHO IS RESPONSIBLE FOR WHAT?

Exhibit 16.1 separates the DQI responsibilities of an exchange and participants. These divisions of labor are not hard and fast, but they could help you get started on some negotiations, and negotiation is necessary.

ENCRYPTION AND WATERMARKING

Let's round out our discussion with a very brief discussion of two technologies that can assist in certain DQI situations: encryption and watermarking. We devote a chapter and more to encryption, so I will make just one passing remark. Encryption techniques will not create and maintain integrity. They will tell you when the data have been altered deliberately or accidentally corrupted. How? You can't successfully decrypt an altered or incomplete encrypted message. We'll see why in Chapter 18. A digital signature and time stamp will establish a high

Exhibit 16.1   Content Quality—What Should Be Done

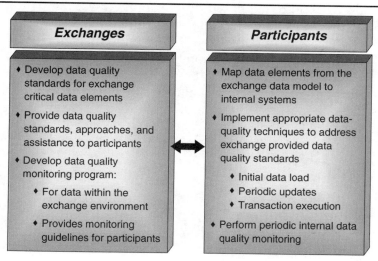

level of authenticity, and the time stamp can be integrated into the encrypted message along with sender's public key.

Watermarks are the electronic equivalent of the marks you see on some paper currencies and on company stationery when you hold it up to the light. They are not holographs. They are not the little photographers, artists, or computer-generation-program IDs that you see on many graphics.

Watermarks are used especially with digitized graphics to establish and maintain ownership rights and copyrights. It's more difficult to do with digitized streams like music or video. They are usually invisible to all but the process or individual that made the mark. The culprit cannot be sure they are there or not. There are some very sophisticated techniques that alter individual pixels in a complex and repeated pattern to create the mark and can still be detected after compression, format conversion, cropping, and image alteration.

DATA CLASSIFICATION

The development, maintenance, and administration of an *interoperable* information classification system requires careful planning and design—both from a technological and procedural standpoint. The larger and more diverse the user population and the broader the spectrum of information involved, the more carefully the program should be designed, developed, and *tested.*

Don't develop security classification in a vacuum or strictly along "best practices" lines. Similarly, don't apply regulatory, certification, and standards requirements blindly. Examine laws, regulations, and standards for protection and interoperability in the context of the e-Business entity's requirements and determine their degree of applicability and their compliance options.

Is there an optimum design? It must be a balance between the need for protection and the operational value/utility of the information. Security classification must reflect the nature, culture, priorities, and operating constraints of the individual organization(s) for which it is being developed. Obviously, not all organizations have identical characteristics or modes of operations.

It must also provide room for dealing with low-level or noncritical information resources. There is a strong tendency, especially among high-trust organizations such as the military, law enforcement, and some medical areas—to place and keep too many information resources in the most restrictive categories. The theory is that it is better to err on the restrictive side. This approach can often result in depriving or delaying access to needed information by justified users.

An overly protected and inflexible information system that inhibits appropriate business decisions and timely transactions can be more of a business threat than most of the potential attacks against it.

IMPLICATIONS FOR INFORMATION PROTECTION

All of these elements should reflect in the B2B's information security policy structure and classification schemes. Information security should protect and enhance process, product, and service quality without inhibiting the companies' marketplace agility or significantly affecting the cost of operation. Most important, it should reflect the B2B's continued philosophy on risk management and uphold its reputation in the marketplace and the world.

With the rapidity with which business opportunities and new technologies present themselves, the Information Security process must be flexible and capable of handling multiple approaches to providing confidentiality, integrity, continuity, and nonrepudiation while achieving common risk-management objectives. It must do this both within the B2B and within the broader environments of cooperative network exchanges and netmarkets that we will see in the future.

This means that the B2B's information security policy must be carefully crafted to give maximum guidance with minimum micromanaging specificity. It must have longevity but permit alteration and addition of new procedures, guidelines, and technologies at the operational level without requiring completely revamping the policy and classification structures. The policy must serve the needs of the IS, internal audit, HR, and security organizations, but first and foremost, it must serve the needs of the business units and senior management.

The B2B wishes to ensure that its information protection program grows and adapts as new information-related opportunities or risks arise. Therefore, the program should be built not simply to reflect good industry and professional practice, important as they are, but to support the unique culture, image, and operational characteristics that make the B2B what it is. Risk management requires a careful monitoring of the effects of a security program. It can neither stifle nor choke with bureaucratic inhibitions, nor can it roll over and play dead in the face of aggressive pursuit of new markets or cost reductions.

Although information technology is a crucial factor in the B2B's continued growth and very existence, the information security policy should not be dedicated exclusively to technology. It should enable the use of technology to provide security function but still concentrate on the fact that information security is a business and, therefore, a people responsibility.

Finally, in this age of partnerships, alliances, demonstrability, and external scrutiny, the information security policy and associated guidelines should be presentable to the external world as a clear and comprehensive statement of where the B2B stands, what it expects of those who work with you, and what it will provide.

SECURITY POLICIES AND DATA CLASSIFICATION

(In the following text, partially extracted and adapted from our methodologies, we use the term B2B to apply to a wide range of different network-based relationships—extranets, netexchanges, netmarkets, and, for that matter, any electronic interaction between business entities.)

Deloitte & Touche believes that the development and deployment processes are as, or even more, important to the success of an information protection program as the actual information security and classification guideline documents, themselves. Most policy documents that are simply extracted or copied from books without adequate tailoring and preliminary "socializing" meet resistance and often are half-heartedly and inadequately implemented.

We've learned from long and varied experience how political and controversial such policies can be, especially in diverse and information-intensive organizations such as B2Bs. So, we devote extensive attention to the preliminary fact-finding and opinion-seeking processes among the business and support units that will be most affected. If we carefully orchestrate and involve the B2B management, such "up front" work can go a long way toward enhancing ownership, acceptance, adoption, and integration of the policy within the organization, as well as ensuring that it has the unique cultural B2B look, feel, and approach.

Information security policies aren't popular. Information protection is not a natural act on most people's parts. Most information security policies are developed by either information security or internal audit staff and are therefore looked upon by most business, IT, IS, and other support personnel and managers as metrics for getting into trouble. Many organizations try to counteract this effect by conducting major awareness programs after the fact with speeches by senior management or responsible staff. These usually take the form of long lists of responsibilities and directives, and often have exactly the opposite effect.

Although we don't believe that information protection should be sugarcoated, we do believe it can be made more acceptable if the people of the B2B see the *direct* applicability to their jobs and functions and understand that their immediate management has not just accepted but has participated in the policy's development. They should also understand that although the basic principles and objectives embodied in the policy are fundamental with a long life expectancy, the individual practices, guidelines, and procedures will be flexibly developed to support the policy in each business and technology context.

We recommend the use of test "focus groups" in the development of classification schemes. Many organizations tend to overclassify, to create more categories than are necessary, to promote assets and processes to more stringent security categories than they require, and to impose expensive or prohibitive technologies universally when they should be used specifically. We recommend the conduct of several focus groups made up of managers and staff who will be using the guidelines. We ask them to come prepared to examine how the guidelines would work in their environments and extract from their comments changes in structure, language, and often basic process, as required. This also enhances the sense of ownership.

We also concentrate on delivery, deployment, and packaging. Examine how best to propagate the policy and its associated guidelines throughout all the players within the B2B. Adapt a summary version for public use. Unfortunately, too many security policies end up being "credenza ware" in thickly bound volumes or "virtual credenza ware" in inaccessible online files. Ease of use and accessibility of specific work-process-related guidance is key. The policy should be organized in its delivered form to be useful to the end user. A separate version organized by overall topic for use and administration by security and audit professionals is also necessary. The possibility of Web-based delivery or integration of specific processes into general work guidelines should be examined.

As you might expect from all of our previous discussions, we follow a business rather than technology driven approach. New technologies, such as the Internet, mobile devices, collaborative processing, and others do indeed change the risks and corresponding security requirements. But, for example, the policy should not reflect the risks inherent in the Internet as much as the risks inherent in how the B2B uses the Internet. Generic approaches often result in security technology overkill or companywide implementation of technologies that are best suited to individual risk situations.

The control and risk management objectives of the B2B should be common and consistent across the organization. But, this does not necessarily translate into the single and universal use of a given set of security technologies. Many security technologies depend on other technology prerequisites (such as directories and common application interfaces) for their success. Timing and deploying these security technologies should be synchronized with the larger effort and not imposed prematurely or inappropriately by isolated security directives.

We concentrate on the policy process as well as simply creating a document. At the conclusion of developing a policy and classification scheme, you should have a means for future test, development, maintenance, and modification so that it continues to be appropriate for your future needs. Information protection is no longer a "set it and forget it" process.

The policy itself should be a basic, enabling, and authorizing document. It should set objectives, direction, and scope, provide the basis for action, establish review and conflict resolution procedures, and outline content for more specific guidelines, procedures, and standards.

CLASSIFICATION SCHEMES

Classification schemes should create a minimum number of categories of information sensitivity based on business and regulatory requirements. Each category should be distinct not only in the nature of the risks involved but also in the steps that must be taken to avert or mitigate these risks. The system should be designed to discourage expensive and inappropriate overclassification and should be adaptable to different process and technology environments. It should contain the definition and rationale for each category, the steps for selecting appropriate categories for each information object or process, and the protective steps required for that category. If the categories overlap or are ambiguous, they should be revised. A small number of exceptional, specific, eyes-only security categories may even further refine and restrict certain documents. Lawsuit and merger and acquisition content come to mind.

A NINE-STEP WORK PLAN FOR CLASSIFICATION

We believe from experience that classification is an iterative process involving the following nine steps:

1. Identify the appropriate concerned parties who will determine classification. In distributed and interoperating

environments, this is often more than one entity and may have to be done jointly. Even though I recommended it in my first book, the use of the terms *owner, custodian,* and so on can result in counterproductive disputes about authority, budgets, and hierarchy when the objective is to establish a working agreement on protection. Live and learn.

2. Establish preliminary classification categories according to need for confidentiality, integrity, nonrepudiation, and resistance to attack.

3. Describe the protective actions to be taken for each preliminary category (e.g., encryption, strong authentication, audit, and monitoring) in all the relevant environments (e.g., network, data storage, portable devices).

4. Test these actions for possible reduction of categories by determining whether the degree of difference is small enough to warrant combining categories. The smallest number of appropriate categories is a major objective in order to reduce overhead, maintain consistency, avoid conflict, and achieve clarity. Most industrial organizations today rarely exceed four categories, including *public.* Regulations and standards may require more, but the categories should be thoroughly examined before you accept them.

5. Actually walk through classifying and applying these actions to a test set of information resources, especially shared resources, with a team of affected business and technology managers. Evaluate the operational, administrative, and technology impacts versus the protection afforded.

6. Revise or refine categories, if necessary, based on the results of step 5.

7. Develop implementation plans for deploying classification across the target environments, with special attention to the impacts of sharing and timing.

8. Publish the criteria for developing and conducting training programs.

9. Since this is what the exercise is all about, apply the classification criteria.

Classification can be an extremely time-consuming and costly process if you don't keep it to a very pragmatic level. Attempting to be overly precise or exhausting all possible scenarios, however improbable, has ruined many classification-development programs. For this reason, it's crucial that members of the classification team include representatives from the organizations that will be using the information resources. It is also extremely important to maintain a pragmatic discipline in project management.

FINAL THOUGHT ON DQI—A PUZZLEMENT

As we said at the opening of this chapter, with all the time we spend on process and infrastructure design, the actual information itself—the primary subject, object, and purpose of the exercise—often gets less attention than it deserves. "Are you kidding? Do you know what our data management system costs us? Database design alone would buy a good-sized shopping center. What do you want?" I'm not talking about the structure, location, directory services, or architecture of the data systems, important as they are to the continued integrity and quality of the information. I'm asking if we know whether that beautifully categorized, readily accessible, logically organized data is any good? And if it isn't, where did it go astray, and how do we fix it? OK, I've resisted this for several pages: Garbage In, Garbage Out. Only in B2B, you can cooperatively and reciprocally build a major and complex garbage creation, pollution, and distribution system, if you don't plan and execute DQI correctly and classify and protect your information conscientiously.

Next stop, networks.

17

The Changing World of Networked Systems

If there are any members of the telecommunications cognoscenti in the audience, these next few pages may read like "Dick and Jane Meet Networks," as written by their little dog Spot. Sorry, but viewed from the deck of the good ship "Net User," awash with tidal waves of arcane techno-jargon and blown about by blustering "my way is the only way" pronouncements, I felt that a few minutes spent discussing some basic network characteristics might advance the cause of e-Trust a bit with the other passengers and crew. By all means, call the steward and order a drink to while away the time, if you choose.

WHAT'S A NETWORK FOR, ANYWAY?

Let's get that principle down immediately. *The primary purpose of a communications network is not to establish connections but to deliver traffic over those connections.* The value of any network must be judged, not by its components, protocols, or configuration, but by how well it accomplishes its individual purpose—delivering specific types of traffic to specific end points with appropriate ease, speed, unit-cost, accuracy, efficiency, reliability, security, and control. Self evident? Not from some of today's literature and hype surrounding network structures, architecture, components, and vendors. There is no single network or network technology that is ideal for all purposes. Although it is flexible, the Internet is no exception.

So while e-Business may seem to be absolutely and irrevocably wed to the Internet and even more specifically to the World Wide Web, do not close your eyes to using other technology alternatives simply in the interest of standardizing on a "one-image, one-protocol network." Also, don't be too eager to ditch some of the existing non-Internet links you have been using. In today's competitive market, their price performance index may get more and more favorable.

NETWORK COMPOSITION—A FUNCTIONAL VIEW

Without regard to any specific technology, you can view any network in the following six functional categories *(note to techies—I'm deliberately avoiding the seven ISO layers):*

1. Nodes
2. Paths
3. Media
4. Traffic
5. Directory structure and systems
6. User communities.

We'll address each of these in detail.

Nodes

Nodes are points on the net where the information flow originates, ends, changes direction, pauses, is relayed, enhanced, managed, monitored, filtered, or blocked. They include the following:

- End points—workstations, PDAs, laptops, telephones, pagers, e-books, or a massive computer-based system located at the point of message origination/termination.
- Switch points—points for redirecting traffic. For the airline fanatics, a hub.
- Relay points—en-route watering holes for refreshing the strength mode or composition of the message-bearing signal before it goes further on its journey. These are amplifiers, signal formers, microwave repeaters, or satellite ground stations. (Yes, I know, ground stations are usually also switches.)
- Transformation points—points where basic mode or form of the message is changed—from analog to digital, or optical to

electrical—or changing among more complex protocols. We'll look at it shortly from the message's viewpoint in our discussion of traffic.

Protocols define a common set of rules and signals that computers on the network use to communicate. They can affect the digital code (there are several); the message structure (blocks, packets, stream, single character); or the message format. The format can be unified, with a single header, message, and trailer, or it can be packetized, with individual packets that have their own ID, destination, sequence number, content, and check sum, that will be assembled into a single message as everyone arrives, possibly through several paths. Protocols can also affect protection, described later.

Traversing almost any global network, a message may go through several protocol conversions, depending on the age, location, origins, structure, and technology of the network segment it's passing through. Since there's still a lot of analog transmission out there and probably will be for some time, modems—analog/digital converters—are the most prevalent but by no means the only form of protocol converters. New modes such as wireless are introducing additional message protocols.

Functional nodes can also include the following:

- Concentration points—staging areas for multiplexing, composing, decomposing, compressing, or decompressing traffic in groups of the same type or heading for the same destination.
- Filtration points—Boundary markers and border crossings.
- Monitoring points—traffic identification, measurement, and recording.
- Store and forwarding points—temporary warehouses for traffic waiting to get to its final destination.
- Control points—Points for managing the network in whole or in part.
- Servers—Computers and *devices* that allocate *resources* for a network. These include file servers, print servers, security servers, and address servers.

Again, these are functional descriptions. Many of these processes can be and are combined in a single device or facility. The reason for this catalog is to point out that each functional node can, to a lesser or greater degree, have an impact on the network's stability, security, and control and thus affect the overall trustworthiness of the Net. If any of these node types

Exhibit 17.1   Network Configuration Formations

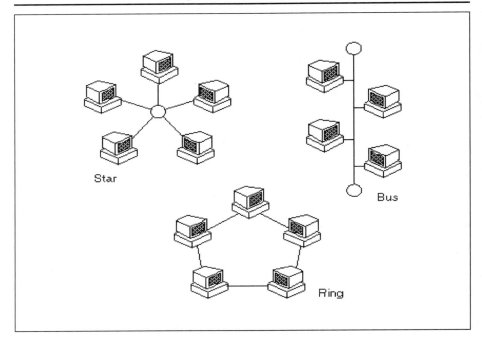

operate suboptimally, the whole Net can be affected. We'll discuss the security implications of several of them in more detail, shortly.

Paths

The routes over which the traffic flows are called *paths. When combined with nodes you have the geometric configuration or topology of the net.* (And like an airline route map, none of the actual routes may be a straight line or gentle curve.) Quite obviously, routing can be critical not only for performance but for quality, reliability, security, control, and availability. Redirection of traffic through dynamic alternate "pathing" is a major availability feature of the Internet, but it also means that you have less control of which paths you want used or shunned. Think of paths both virtually (New York to St. Louis, Plant 2 to HQ) and physical (ground station X to Satellite Y, telephone company point of presence to local in-building wire room). Exhibit 17.1 shows three of the most basic formations, which are the building blocks of network configurations.

Exhibit 17-2   Any to Any Topology

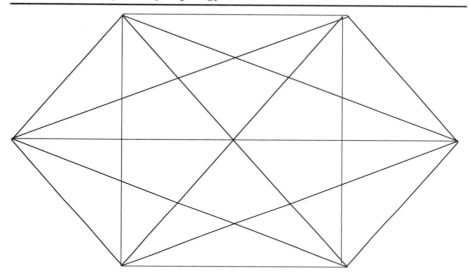

In all of these illustrations, all traffic originates and ends within the specific formation. In Exhibit 17.1, you may notice that while the star has a central control point and the bus has control points at either end, the ring has none. Actually, the ring is a cooperative "pass-along" configuration designed so that a failed node can be bypassed. Like LEGOs and Tinker Toys, you can combine these topologies, but there is more to combining than connections.

As we indicated above, certain topologies require certain protocols for control and transmission. So it's not anything goes—universal plug and play. Traffic may be subjected to protocol shifts as it moves about the net.

Exhibit 17.2 is the "any to any" topology. It can also be described as "peer-to-peer." By the way, the center point may or may not be a node. (For a really fun party game, sit everybody down—twelve or more is best—and then connect each one to each other individually, no hubs or relays, using lengths of string. Oh, you'll laugh for hours. Not really, but you'll make quite a tangled mess.) Each node is its own control point. Access is direct. No relaying. "What happens if a node is out of action?" You just can't get there; if you trace it, you'll see that relaying won't do you any good. Needless to say, this arrangement isn't very popular or cost effective.

Actually, the Internet is a configuration hybrid that can appear in a combination of most of the configurations shown in Exhibits 17.1 and even 17.2. The Internet uses a protocol called TCP/IP (Transmission

Control Protocol/Internet Protocol) to manage its configurations, traffic, data format, and a number of other functions.

Media

As you know, media is the plural of *medium* (a word you rarely see in reference to communications, because media travel in packs). This is not only true for press conferences. Networking media include optical cables, wire, and radio.

Traffic

We talked about protocols and media. Now let's look at them from the viewpoint of message attributes. Consider:

- Base technology—analog/digital, voice, data, video
- Format—packets, streams, strings, bursts
- Purpose—control signals or user information
- Size—single blips or monstrous video signals
- Industry—EDI or ABA or any number of other formats
- Security—scrambled, encrypted (they're not the same) or clear
- Sensitivity—critical military, medical, or law enforcement data, sensitive financial and business strategy materials, or just a bunch of surfers out for an afternoon goof

Directory Structures and Systems

To use a travel analogy, directory structures and systems are the road maps, "GPS," highway and street signs, addresses, floor numbers, and individual names that make up a B2B or any type of network. Imagine trying to navigate an environment like the Internet without a substantial and trustworthy guidance system. The design, placement, size, accuracy, robustness, and response time of directories can have more impact on your apparent bandwidth than most other performance factors.

Although they are usually viewed as operational mechanisms, they also act as major security and control components in any complex network. Not only do they help to direct traffic along paths to nodes; they also identify the characteristics of the nodes including some aspects of their security categories.

Consider the major effort in joining two (or more) major nets, such as we illustrated in the fable in Chapters 4 and 5.

- Arranging and then optimizing directory entries
- Placing them strategically at the appropriate logical intersections of the net
- Replicating them when and as necessary to enhance access and speed
- Developing and facilitating cost-effective insertion, update, and purging of the individual entries at every place they appear, as close to simultaneously as possible
- Ensuring accuracy, stability, confidentiality and integrity of the directories themselves in order to protect the destinations and objects they catalog. (Hackers love directories.)

These are significant tasks. Do not underestimate them in your plans.

User Communities

They are also a major functional component in any network. I deliberately put them last to conceptually separate them as far as I could from Item 1—end points. Too frequently, we combine the two and assume that the device describes the user, or vice versa. It ain't necessarily so. The behavior, attitude, location, and knowledge-level of the user becomes critical, especially as we go further into portable and wireless devices. You can no longer assume the user's characteristics from the device and supporting software they are employing.

Nevertheless, we've tried for years to pigeonhole users, their behavior, their reactions, and their priorities into technology-based categories—the laptop road warrior; the workstation data diva; the graphics geek. In the process, we have made assumptions about the security and control needs of these users based on the device they use instead of the uses to which they put the device. For example, which one of the devices has a greater need for on-board encryption? You might be tempted to say the laptop because of its portability, but my response is, Since I don't know for sure how any of them are being used, all of them.

Now obviously, in the design, development, and management of any communications network, all of these factors are going to co-mingle and be governed by trade-offs involving such issues as operating constraints, location, ownership contracts, regulation, costs, ease of use, maintenance and update, priorities, the user base, vendor reliability, and availability of services and technology.

Consider the telecommunications industry itself. Some of the complications we mentioned would be more controllable (or at least greatly mitigated) if there was a single global or even national supplier to charge with all these responsibilities—a PTT or an ATT (pre-breakup). "Them days are gone forever."

Who's in charge? I remember a cartoon of a car smashed into a tree and all the occupants standing around talking to a policeman. The caption read, "There was nobody driving, officer, we were all in the back seat." While telco competition may benefit the consumer and the economy in many ways, it sure doesn't make things simple. And as we point out in Chapter 19, don't expect standards communities to make up the difference and carry the load by themselves.

In short, as you dedicate more and more of your business to online processes, understand the complexity of the environment you're getting into and make prudent provisions. If you apply the yard (meter) stick of e-Trust, as we've been using it, to a network, you can also see that many more factors besides security and control enter into the development of a trusted network. If we're going to do e-Business in an atmosphere of trust, it should be supported by an infrastructure and message-handling process that is optimized for all of those trade-off issues.

"THANKS FOR THE TUTORIAL. IS THERE A POINT YOU WANTED TO MAKE?"

Yes, in fact there is. For years, we have concentrated our efforts on protecting and strengthening the network infrastructure itself, paying insufficient attention to the message. *Now as communications networks get more complex, we are only beginning to appreciate that the traffic itself needs more attention.* The nets are too heterogeneous, widespread, and dynamic to be the sole focus of protection. That's why we're spending so much time and effort on encryption and other message-related control functions. We're starting to send our traffic out into the streets wearing helmets and seat belts. But as usual, not everyone is wearing them.

"CAN WE SEE THAT AGAIN FROM A DIFFERENT ANGLE?"

Thanks. Exactly what I had in mind. Having examined the components of a network in very broad terms, let's do a short review of the changing requirements for security in networked environments. Is there really a need that didn't exist before for new security technologies and approaches? Yes.

Suppose we take a moment and compare a few characteristics of yesterday's and today's network-based information processing. If the differences can be summed up in a single phrase, it's *accelerated dynamics*. The structure and components of most major networks are in a constant state of flux—as are the applications, transactions, and users that traverse its pathways. This has a profound influence on the nature, location, scope, and effectiveness of protective mechanisms.

To enhance highway safety, where do you concentrate? Do you focus on the roadway, the vehicle, in-car distractions like radio, video, cell phones? The driver, the passenger, road signs, terrain, weather? Monitoring? Answer: All of them. Why even ask? Because the analogy applies almost perfectly to network safety and security. I won't bore you with a catalog of comparisons. But like the world's highway systems, data and voice networks and the traffic that flows over them are different, and our controls haven't caught up yet.

I will grant that the multiplicity of node types and the variations on technologies can cause a controls specialist to devote a lifetime to the infrastructure trying to determine the best places and ways to put firewalls, set up sensors, monitor protocol conversions, protect store and forward processes, shield and control servers, monitor logs and reports, and note where and how to use encryption. All this while the environment churns, truly changing not just engines but the whole aircraft while it's in flight.

Look at the Exhibit 17.3 approach and see if it helps explain why the old approaches won't do.

It illustrates some of the fundamental differences between traditional closed systems and open (often Internet-based) environments.

Exhibit 17.3   Open versus Closed Networks

	Legacy/Closed Network	Modern Open Network
User Environments	Known and Stable	Mobile/Variable
End Points	Established	Dynamic/Open
Network Structure	Established/Known	Dynamic/Open
Processing	Mainframe/Internally Distributed	Multisite/Multi-Enterprise
Data Objects	Linked to Defined Process	Often Independent

These differences do much to explain the significant upsurge in interest in encryption technologies. The formerly tight linkage between the medium and the message is softening and breaking up.

More messages/transactions in different forms are traveling across more borders over different technologies and being stored or displayed in different environments and reaching users who are not under your direct management. Increasingly, the message must rely on its own protective resources as well as those supplied by the infrastructure. Encryption makes a major contribution in that direction—aiding and abetting confidentiality, privacy, integrity, authentication, authorization, anonymity, nonrepudiation, and even recovery (see Chapter 18). Notice, please, the terms *aiding and abetting*, not *ensuring, guaranteeing*, and other such words that have little realistic use in these environments.

Encryption will not save a message from destruction. It will not keep it from going astray, although it will strongly mitigate the consequences. It will not protect it from corruption, but it will tell you that corruption has taken place. And while occasionally it can result in the right person not being able to gain access to authorized materials, it is very good at keeping the wrong people out.

Clearly, each network is unique, and most display a mix of the characteristics shown in Exhibit 17.3. But the trends toward openness and variability are pretty clear. The implications for security can be profound. Security embedded or "hard-wired" to the system and network infrastructure cannot carry the entire load alone in many of the more mobile and open environments, especially where dial-up is dominant. A more flexible mode that addresses the infrastructure, user, workstation, environment, and data objects is required.

As an example, envision the differences between

- A route salesperson who returns to the office workstation in the evening to enter the day's orders (online batch)
- That same worker now entering, on a laptop through a radio or dial-up phone link, those same orders as they are being taken at the customer's premises (dial-up interactive)
- Third-party operators taking orders at an 800-888 call center
- Those same orders being entered by the customer on a Website
- A combination of the above

Essentially, the application is still the same: order entry. But the process is dramatically different, ranging from batch entry to Web-based e-Commerce.

In the first case, the infrastructure, environment, process, and user are known, stable, and can be well controlled. The classic access control facility and/or security server generally carries the load.

In the second instance (interactive dial-up), the employee (we need to verify it's an employee) is still directly involved, but now we have the portable device and its on-board functions and data, the dial-up connections, the network, the points of entry to the enterprise, and the enterprise processes themselves to protect if we want to achieve the same level of control we had in the first instance. We may also be dealing with a one-at-a-time, interactive transaction stream.

The third instance (call center) combines voice and data entry, and it involves a third party as an additional point of quality and security risk. The network connections (there are several to consider) may be closed or open, public or private, password protected or not.

The fourth (Web-based) approach adds a string of unknowns and potential risks created by the customer's direct involvement and linkage through the Internet to the company's system.

Finally, the fifth (hybrid) scenario calls for significant compatibility adjustments on top of the other considerations. By the way, this scenario is not unlikely. A very dangerous assumption in promoting Web-based services is that you can readily discontinue the other service modes. It seldom happens.

Consider the changes to identification, authentication, and authorization targets and processes in each instance. Consider monitoring and the audit trail. Then consider the integrity and availability issues. Finally, the potential for repudiation begins to rear its ugly head. The differences are real and significant.

THE EVOLVING BUSINESS NETWORK

Remember that most network-based systems in operation today have evolved, or in many cases, accreted into their current state—adding infrastructures and applications on demand and using the technology available at the time. Darwin notwithstanding, some of the currently surviving networks are not necessarily the fittest. In most of the literature, we characterize networks as examples of a specific class—open–closed; intranet–extranet; LAN–WAN–Internet; protocol X–protocol Y. While these necessary and valuable distinctions can be used to describe physical and logical infrastructures, we must remember that when viewed from the business processes they support—supply chain, order entry, funds transfer, patient record processing—most "business process" nets are technological and structural hybrids.

The important point is that now security strategy and architecture decisions are being driven increasingly by specific business requirements, not just technology. This is especially true in the application of encryption-related techniques such as PKI. Looking again at our order entry example above, the application of consistent protective mechanisms for a hybrid order-entry scenario will undoubtedly require compatibility and interoperability across platform and network types unless the entire system is rebuilt to one specification. This seldom happens unless the enterprise is embarking on a massive reengineering effort and/or deploying major application suites like SAP or PeopleSoft.

To be effective, a protective mechanism must appropriately bind with the object and the environment requiring protection. In open networks, the connection, structure, and relationship of the components are more loosely defined and variable. Therefore, the protective mechanisms must be more granular, focused, and more directly linked to the object and/or process to be protected than was the case with legacy systems. Formerly, protection processes operated primarily at a "subterranean plumbing" level, surfacing only in password and authorization administration and logons. Now the castle moat is being supplemented with "no-go" zones, personal bodyguards posted at strategic spots, food tasters, and trusted messengers.

To finish off this chapter, we're going to turn back to infrastructure for a few moments. We're going to take two short side trips—at no extra charge—to examine a pair of network architecture features that have a bearing on B2B trust and have mysterious names: VPNs and DMZs (with their associated technologies.). They are by no means the only features in the arsenal, but they are often misunderstood. We'll try to help clarify them, or at least not make things worse.

VPNs

You may remember that we touched on VPNs in our charming and heartwarming fable in Chapter 4. But since you were surely too busy wiping the tears of laughter from your eyes and trying to regain your composure under the puzzled stares of those around you, I'll repeat them here. (I am not paid by the word.)

Virtual private networks are the Internet equivalents of a leased-line arrangement (with, as usual, some differences). They are set up by hardware/software combinations at each end (gateway) of the specific link to be protected and provide a transparent encrypted channel (tunnel) for transmitting and receiving data. The user, by calling up the appropriate Intranet URL, gets the immediate benefit of the VPN. Depending on the logon process of the system being used, an additional password may or may not be necessary but no further user action is required during the session. VPN protection normally does not extend past the gateways into the supporting systems and servers. It is called point-to-point protection. Protection from user workstation to user workstation requires additional support. This is called end-to-end protection. They are not the same.

Now, an interesting and somewhat disconcerting point for security specialists: VPNs were not originally established as security mechanisms. They were and are used as cost-effectiveness measures, getting more message volume through the same "physical pipeline" by subdividing the pipeline into channels—a variation on multiplexing. The difference is that each channel can be isolated and assigned to different entities and services. Each entity "owns" that channel. The composite effect is more users inside divided lanes going down the same highway, with less unused capacity. The encryption features allow you to take the concept out into the public highways (e.g., Internet) secure in the knowledge that your portion of the figurative pipeline is encrypted, even if the messages are not individually pre-encrypted. Do not assume that an organization offering VPNs is, by definition, supplying pathway encryption. Most do, but make them "cut the cards."

By the way, if you care, this is not the same as an "encryption wrapper" that is encryption uniquely applied to an individual message by someone other than the originator—e.g., a network server or switching center. Each wrapper may or may not be different, and the messages are not restricted to traveling on VPNs. With VPNs the channel itself is secure. With wrappers, the message is secure. In other words, someone has done the work for you within their area of service. The wrapper comes back off when the message crosses the border. So once again, you're covered gateway to gateway. The links between the gateway and you as user at the end point may or may not be secure. How many stages does a message go through between the user and the gateway? Depends on how the internal net is laid out. It could be quite a few. Can a gateway wrap a message already encrypted by the originator? Can you send a previously encrypted message over a VPN? Yes to both. In short, you can get 3 levels of encryption. Each will give you extra protection, and you should look for opportunities to take advantage of the combinations whenever you can.

DMZs, FIREWALLS, BASTIONS, AND BEARS. OH, MY!

DMZ—demilitarized zone—is one of those terms that doesn't exactly mean what the name suggests. Or, more accurately, most people misuse the term *DMZ* to denote a sort of no-man's land that all combatants avoid. In network land, a demilitarized zone is one that is actively controlled, patroled, and utilized. Lots of things happen there. It is an active part of your Internet services and internal defense strategy, not a dead spot.

A DMZ is used by a company *that wants to host its own Internet services* without suffering unauthorized access to its private network. It's difficult to think of many significant B2B relationships that would not involve some level of Internet hosting. However, the role of host is a condition for structuring a DMZ. The DMZ sits between the Internet and the internal network(s)' lines of defense, which is usually some combination of firewalls and bastion hosts. Typically, the DMZ contains devices accessible to Internet traffic, such as Web (HTTP) servers, file transfer (FTP) servers, e-mail servers (SMTP), and domain-name servers (DNS.)

You cannot buy a DMZ at an Internet store (or at least you shouldn't), nor should you blithely accept someone else's design as being appropriate for you. In fact, very few DMZ designs look identical. Why? Not because the technology isn't common but because the rules you want that technology to invoke will reflect the business relationships you and your partners want to maintain. If, for example, you anticipate opening up your baseline corporate identity website to all comers but want to restrict your research or transaction management sites to a select population (probably not the same populations), the profiles will be different for each. The rules for sending or accepting files or e-mails to certain internal destinations may also be different.

By the way, most discussions about DMZs, firewalls, bastions, and the like concentrate on keeping bad stuff out. There is a converse set of requirements to also consider seriously—keeping stuff inside and/or denying your own employees access to certain sites and facilities. "Let's not go there." I'm not just talking about porn sites or competitors' recruiters. No-go restrictions may result from anything from individual agreements to legally imposed consent decrees. The DMZ works and looks both ways.

WHAT'S A FIREWALL?
(Again, we go to webopedia.com for some support)

A system designed to prevent unauthorized access to or from a private network. Firewalls can be implemented in both hardware and software, or a combination of both. Firewalls are frequently used to prevent unauthorized Internet users from accessing private networks connected to the Internet, especially intranets. All messages entering or leaving the intranet pass through the firewall, which examines each message and blocks those that do not meet the specified security criteria.

We explained it before, but recall that the Web and most Internet services run on a packet-switched protocol called TCP/IP. TCP (Transmission Control Protocol) handles the connections between nodes. IP (Internet Protocol) handles the message decomposition into packets as well as the identification, assembly, address, order, and checking of the data packets going over the link, and provides the reverse services on the receiving end.

There are four main types of firewall techniques:

1. *Packet filter*—Looks at each *packet* entering or leaving the network and accepts or rejects it based on user-defined rules. Packet filtering is fairly effective and transparent to users, but it is difficult to configure. In addition, it is susceptible to IP spoofing, which is a technique used to gain unauthorized access to computers, whereby the intruder sends messages to a computer with an IP address indicating that the message is coming from a trusted port. To engage in IP spoofing, a *hacker* must first use a variety of techniques to find an IP address of a trusted port and then modify the *packet* headers so that it appears that the packets are coming from that port. Newer *routers* and *firewall* arrangements can offer protection against IP spoofing.

2. *Application gateway*—Applies security mechanisms to specific applications, such as FTP (File Transfer Protocol) servers (bulk data transfer). This is very effective, but can impose performance degradation.

3. *Circuit-level gateway*—Applies security mechanisms when a connection is established through TCP or UDP (User Datagram Protocol—a convenient broadcast technique for sending the same message to a large number of recipients). Once the connection has been made, packets can flow between the hosts without further checking.

4. *Proxy server*—Intercepts all messages entering and leaving the network. The proxy server as the name suggests effectively hides the true network addresses from the outsider substituting its own address out in the DMZ.

In practice, many firewalls use two or more of these techniques in concert.

A firewall is considered a first line of defense in protecting private information. For greater security (you guessed it), use encryption.

SO, WHAT'S A BASTION HOST?

A bastion host is a gateway standing independently between an inside network and an outside network. Used as a security measure, the bastion host (a computer) is designed to defend against attacks aimed at the inside network. It differs from a firewall by being a separate protective node unto itself whereas firewalls are "attached" as part of the individual node's technology. Putting it another way, a firewall is not usually considered to be a node.

Depending on a network's complexity and configuration, a single bastion host may stand guard by itself, or be part of a larger security system with different layers of protection. They are not always used.

NOW, ABOUT THOSE BEARS (OH, MY!)

To our professional knowledge, bears are seldom used as network protective devices.

A FEW MORE WORDS ON NETWORKS, AND THEN ON TO CHAPTER 18

We hope that we have demonstrated that although you can download a firewall software package for your home PC (and you should, especially if you have an "always-on" connection service like cable or DSL), the firewalls, bastions and DMZs used in big-time networking are not trivial. Nor are they "install and forget." Defining and maintaining firewalls are major, ongoing network design and management tasks. The firewall and DMZ are not designed solely around the technological characteristics of the Net. Quite the contrary, your overall network protection strategy must be driven by the business processes on the net. As I hope we've shown, although firewalls are important protective technology, they are certainly not the totality of B2B network protection. So, let's add another vegetable to the stew. We've been bringing encryption up over and over again. It's time for Chapter 18.

18

Encryption, PKI, and Digital Signatures

Those of us who've been around information protection for a while have seen an ongoing beauty pageant of technology contestants that smile and strut and promise new and total solutions but frequently don't make it past the first round of judging. Are encryption, digital signatures, and public-key infrastructure (PKI) just another trio of pretty faces destined to be Miss Congeniality, Miss Poise, and Miss Enthusiasm, or is there sufficient rationale to believe that they just might make it to the top step? There are some very good reasons for optimism in this case (actually, a majority of strong positive votes are already in for encryption), but we've been overly optimistic before.

So, let's examine encryption, digital signatures, and PKI as objectively as possible and see if we can come up with a consensus of sorts. To do that, we need to know more than just the design principles. Many a slick and sophisticated design has turned embarrassingly sour when implemented and put into demanding application and operational contexts. There are also the questions of economics, market readiness, and operational/technological prerequisites, all of which can send a brilliant idea back to the beauty parlor for more work.

LET'S START WITH ENCRYPTION

Basically, encryption is a process for making intelligible information unintelligible through the application of sophisticated mathematical conversion techniques. Obviously, to be useful the process must be reversible (decryption). There are three major components of the encryption–decryption process:

1. The information stream (the data) in clear and/or encrypted form.
2. The mathematical encryption process—the algorithm. Interestingly enough, most commercial algorithms are publicly available and are not secret. So, what turns a public process into a uniquely secret one?
3. The encryption key. The encryption key is a string of random data that is mathematically combined with the information (clear or encrypted) by the algorithm to produce the opposite version of the data (encrypted or clear). Remember that all data on computers are represented in binary number coding. Binary numbers can be operated upon by the same arithmetic functions as those that apply to decimal numbers. So by a combining process of complex arithmetic operations, the data and key are converted into an encrypted message form and decrypted using the same process and *same key* (with one critical exception we'll discuss shortly).

AN ILLUSTRATION OF ENCRYPTION

Encryption and decryption are best explained graphically. Let's do it.

Step 1

We start with an information stream (see Exhibit 18.1). It could be characters—a sentence, part number, e-mail message, or spreadsheet. Or it can also be a graphics picture, music, movie—anything that can be represented internally within a computer and over telecommunications lines as a string of binary bits. This, of course, is the way digital computers see everything all the time. So "Now is the time" converts to a digital stream of 1's and 0's—The exhibit is not an actual translation.

Step 2

In Exhibit 18.2 we call on the crypto engine, which may be a software program, hardware device, or a hybrid. It should be easily accessible and closely protected. The crypto engine performs a series of complex

Exhibit 18.1 Encryption Step 1

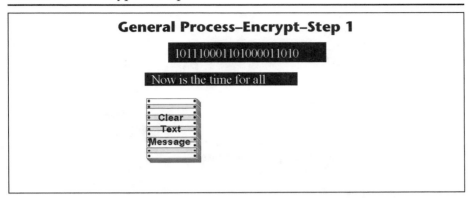

Exhibit 18.2 Encryption Step 2

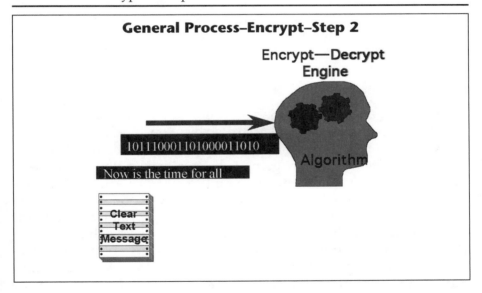

arithmetic processes to produce the encrypted result, but the engine's processes (algorithm) are always the same and most are publicly available, even standardized. "Huh?" Hang on until the next step. We prepare the clear text for submission to the engine, but first we need to address Step 3.

Exhibit 18.3   Encryption Step 3

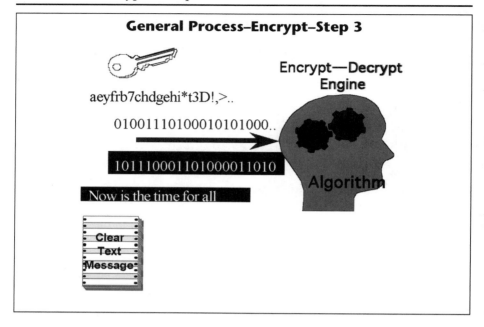

General Process–Encrypt–Step 3

aeyfrb7chdgehi*t3D!,>..

01001110100010101000..

10111000110100001 1010

Now is the time for all

Clear
Text
Message

Encrypt—Decrypt
Engine

Algorithm

Step 3

In Exhibit 18.3, we develop the encryption key. As we said above, the key is a random set of binary bits created by a separate *key generator*. It's the key that provides the uniqueness to this specific encryption. As you'll see in Step 4, they are going to be combined arithmetically with the binary digits that make up our clear text and create the end result—a binary form of the message. The complexity of the encryption engine's arithmetic just makes the process more convoluted and assists the key in making the end result more difficult to break. True randomness is extremely difficult to achieve, and the degree of protection afforded by an encryption system is at least partially measured by how random the sequence of binary digits are in the key. If a key was made up of all binary zeroes, for example, nothing would happen. All ones would produce an encrypted message that is very easy to crack. If a repetitive pattern appears in the key, this greatly reduces the effort required by an attacker trying to break the message.

Also, the same key will be used to later decrypt (with one major exception), so it is absolutely necessary to have the correct key to decrypt the encrypted message, No key, no clear text. Because keys can be used repeatedly (if not, you have a key management problem that won't quit), gaining unauthorized access to a key can compromise all the messages that have been encrypted under it. Is that a weakness? Yes, but hold on.

Step 4

So far, we haven't actually done anything other than get our components ready and lined up—clear text, key, and crypto engine. Now comes the actual encryption. The bits that make up the clear text are entered into the engine in blocks of a fixed size along with a comparably sized number of bits from the key. Using a complex but openly available algorithm, the two blocks are combined by binary arithmetic. If you don't know binary, don't worry. It only uses the digits 0 and 1, and all arithmetic functions are a variant of add or subtract ($0+0=0$; $1+0$ or $0+1=1$; and here comes the one that causes all the grief: $1+1=10$; don't say "ten," say "0 and carry the 1 forward." Wasn't that fun?). The process goes on until the entire message is combined with the key and encrypted result is generated. But messages, especially graphics and movies, can be huge. Does the key have to be of equal size, and random, too? No, when you run out of key, you just start again with the first digit and so on. However, you can see that the length of the random key can make an important difference. One of the important techniques of cryptology (breaking codes) is searching for repetition and patterns. The shorter the key and the longer the message, the more frequently the key will be repeated. Its pattern could show up in the encrypted message because it's being used over and over. The longer the key, the fewer repeat cycles, the better. By the way, there's a whole set of regulatory issues associated with key length that we'll touch on later. See Exhibit 18.4

Step 5

See Exhibit 18.5. Cipher feedback is one of several optional but frequently used processes that can make the encrypted result more complex. As the first digits of the encrypted result are developed from the first round of binary combination, they are fed back into the encryption process as a third binary string and combined with the key and the clear text. I oversimplified before. The algorithm isn't combining two digit streams. It's actually combining three. The purpose of this rather arcane activity is to ensure that if any change is made to the encrypted result,

Exhibit 18.4   Encryption Step 4

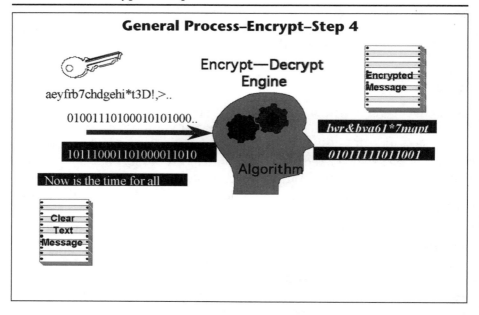

you still cannot decrypt it, even with the key. If I have the original message, the appropriate key, and the same algorithm, but I can't decrypt the encrypted message, the encrypted message has been corrupted. If you understand that, fine. If not, please accept it as fact. It's a helpful way to maintain encrypted message integrity or, more properly, to detect that the message is corrupted deliberately or through failure.

That concludes encryption. *Decryption* is illustrated in Exhibit 18.6. Provided it has remained uncorrupted, all we need to do is to push the encrypted message back through any engine with the same algorithm using the same key and the clear text will appear. Notice the cipher feedback.

The question sometimes comes up: If one pass through the encryption engine is good, how about running the message back through for a couple of more passes using the *same* key? The answer is, the effect is beneficial and strengthening, but not for the full value of the number of trips. Two-pass encryption using the same key is not twice as strong as single. It's in the math, and I'm not going to explain why even if I could. If you use *different* keys on each pass (double or triple encryption), the strength is significantly greater. In today's environment, such techniques may be necessary. Triple DES is used extensively today.

Exhibit 18.5   Encryption Step 5

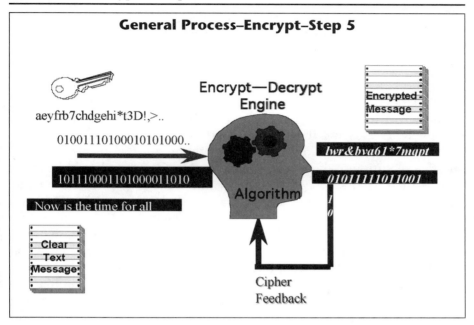

Exhibit 18.6   Decryption

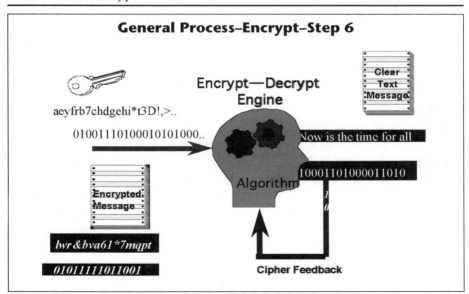

A SHORT DIGRESSION ON ALGORITHM STRENGTH AND CRACKING

We said earlier that most encryption algorithms available for commercial B2B use are known and published. Counterintuitive as that may seem, it is equivalent to knowing how the lock on a safe is constructed and whether it can easily be thwarted by some ingenious set of processes (shades of *Mission Impossible*). However, as is often the case, the only way to get inside may be trying every possible combination. To some extent, knowing the structure and design is helpful to you as attacker, since it may just keep you from wasting time trying clever mathematical solutions when you already know that the unsophisticated "brute force" approach of trying every key is the only means available.

Now, let's go back to the early days of the so-called DES (Data Encryption Standard) algorithm, which was developed by IBM in the late 1980's and presented to ANSI (American National Standards Institute) and the then Bureau of Standards (now NIST). It was adopted as a national and then international standard (ISO) and was promptly attacked as having a trap door that could be used by the U.S. intelligence community—an allegation never demonstrated or proved. I was one of an IBM team that negotiated the turnover of DES to the U.S. government and to ANSI. I still have a couple of dueling scars from that one.

Nevertheless, it was generally agreed that rumors of trap doors aside, the way to beat the DES was to try every possible key combination—brute force. On average, you'd hit it at the half-way point of your calculations. Given the state of the computing art then (single systems with relatively slow processors—we're talking the 80's now), brute force was a very long (years plus) process. You can see where this is going.

Time passed. Computers got faster and could be combined into task-sharing networks. Chips could be optimized for specific mathematical functions. Net result: at the end of the 1990s, brute force took a few days or even less. So-called triple DES (three passes, three different keys) filled and continues to fill the gap. But time is running out. Time for a new algorithm. At the end of this chapter, as a segue to our chapter on standards, we discuss the competition mounted by NIST to come up with the Advanced Encryption Standard (AES) on behalf of the global computing world. Just hold your breath for the next 15 minutes while we get back to some more encryption characteristics.

HOW DO YOU KEEP A KEY SAFE, AND FOR HOW LONG?

Why, the answer to that is perfectly obvious. You encrypt it with a different key. "But, splutter, splutter." Yes, I know, you launch a seemingly endless daisy chain or one of those infinite series of questions that three-year-olds love to ask. "But where did *that* chicken come from?" Eventually, the sequence (and it can be lengthy) gets back to something called a root key (Tolkien fans, "the ring to bind them all"). The root key must be protected physically, as well as logically. Compromise or destroy it, and the whole sequence can collapse like a house of cards. (It's not quite that easy, but it is possible.) In the case of compromise, an attacker can progress backward to successive keys. In the case of destruction, depending on how rigidly controlled and structured your protection schemes are, access to successor keys may be lost forever. There are ways around it, but we won't drag that one out here.

There are storage devices based on smart card technology, such as the Chryalis Luna card series that are used to protect keys. In our Secure e-Business Technology Center in Deerfield, Illinois, Deloitte and Touche keeps its own and client root keys and other primary keys on Luna Cards inside individually locked compartments in a further locked waterproof, fireproof safe in a radiation-free environment controlled by three-factor entry authentication and controlled authorization (ID badge, PIN, and iris scan). No one person has all the combinations and entry privileges. All this still does not meet U.S. Defense Department or intelligence community standards. (We do not normally maintain their rigid environment test and scan regime schedule. It's very expensive. If required by a client, we would.)

How long do you keep keys? It depends. One major determinant is what you're using encryption for.

MESSAGE AND FILE ENCRYPTION

Useful key life can span from one-time to "infinity." In a message or transaction system, we recommend that once the message is received, acknowledged, and decrypted at the authorized recipient's end point, destroy the key and switch to a new one. (It's a quick, automated process.) That way, even if the key was captured and compromised, only one message is in jeopardy. The attacker would have to go further up the key hierarchy to do more damage. If that seems a bit much, at least change keys at the end of each connection session, although in these days of always on, constant connect, that could be a long time.

Now, for something completely different—file encryption. While a message or transaction requires protection only over its brief journey, stored data may have a veeerry extended life. Here's one place where the elaborate safety and security measures we described above kick in. Key loss can be as devastating or worse than key compromise.

Am I scaring you away from using encryption? That's not the intent. The purpose is to show that it can be used at different levels and for different purposes and like all protective mechanisms should be seriously reviewed from all angles before adoption.

SYMMETRY AND ASSYMMETRY

Remember, on the first page of this chapter we said there was an exception to the rule about using the same key to encrypt and decrypt. Here we go. First, one more definition is required. The process we described above using the *same key* to decrypt and encrypt is called *symmetric* crypto. It has several advantages, including exceptional speed on computers. It has a serious drawback. In any population of communicating users (n), in order to have *individually unique* links between each pair of users the total number of keys required is $(n^2 - n)/2$. (Stop whining. It's the only formula in the whole book.) Try it with a small number. It gets big quickly. 4 individuals = 6 pairs = 6 keys. That's a sissy example. Use something bigger. 75 users = 2775. If the population of users gets large enough, the number of individual keys required to maintain individually unique pairing becomes unmanageable. This is one (but not the only) reason why crypto has not had a great reception in the commercial marketplace in the last 20 years.

The salvation of crypto for practical business use has been the application of a different class of cryptographic algorithms using *asymmetric* key pairs. The mathematics is complex and is not intuitively obvious, but the result is a *pair of linked keys or key halves that must be used together*. Either key half can be used to encrypt or decrypt, but the other half must then be used to perform the opposite function. Using the same half for both will get you nowhere. There's a major advantage to this.

Only one of the pair, the private key, must be kept secret by the key owner. The other half of the pair—the public key—can be openly distributed to anyone wishing to communicate with the key owner. A partial analogy is the cash depository in which a large number of customers have the same key for depositing through a one-way door but only the bank official has a key to open the door for extracting the cash. This technique vastly reduces the number of keys required for the same population to communicate safely and uniquely. For more information than you could possibly want on the process, search the Internet on "asymmetric key encryption," "public key encryption," or RSA.

ENTER PKI

If the public key is distributed openly, how do you know that it is valid and belongs with the appropriate secret key and the key owner? How do you manage the creation, use, and termination of these key pairs? That is the foundation of public-key infrastructure. Several definitions follow:

> The comprehensive system required to provide public-key encryption and digital signature services is known as the *public-key infrastructure* (PKI). The purpose of a public-key infrastructure is to manage keys and certificates.—*Entrust Inc.*

> A public-key infrastructure (PKI) consists of the programs, data formats, communications protocols, institutional policies, and procedures required for enterprise use of public-key cryptography—*Office of Information Technology, University of Minnesota*

> In its most simple form, a PKI is a system for publishing the public-key values used in public-key cryptography. There are two basic operations common to all PKIs:

> • Certification is the process of binding a public-key value to an individual organization or other entity, or even to some other piece of information such as a permission or credential.

> • Validation is the process of verifying that a certificate is still valid.

> How these two operations are implemented is the basic defining characteristic of all PKIs.—*Marc Branchaud*

THE DIGITAL CERTIFICATE AND CERTIFICATE AUTHORITIES

Obviously, from these definitions, a digital certificate is the focal point of the PKI process. What is it? In simplest terms, a digital certificate is a credential (in digital form) in which the public key of the individual is embedded along with other identifying data. That credential is encrypted (signed) by a trusted third party or certificate authority (CA) who has established the identity of the key owner (similar to but more rigorous than notarization). The "signing key" ties the certificate back to the CA and ultimately to the process that bound the certificate holder to his/her credentials and identity proof process. *Note:* The generation and use of certificates does not constitute the complete PKI process. There are other functions, as we shall see. Watch how the term PKI is

used. It should be employed only to describe the complete infrastructure. Just substituting a certificate for a password is a worthy step in the
right direction and worth doing. It's not PKI.

By "signing" the certificate, the CA establishes and takes liability
for the authenticity of the public key contained in the certificate and
the fact that it is bound to the named user. Now total strangers who
know and are known to a common, trusted CA can use encryption not
just to *conceal data* but also to *authenticate the other party.* If the public
and private key halves of my certificate don't work together, I am not
the recipient of valid certificates from the CA. In short, with a short exchange of certificate-based public keys and validation by the private
keys, I can authenticate your identity and you, mine. You can see the
value of the certificate as part of identity management. The certificate
(*cert* in infosec jargon) can substitute for the password as well as performing other encryption-related functions.

The continued *integrity* of the message is also ensured. If you
change it, once encrypted, it will not decrypt. You can't prevent an integrity attack. You will know if one happened. The message *cannot be
repudiated* because it has been encrypted using the sender's certificate.

WHO ARE CAs?

Some large institutions are their own CAs—especially banks (private
CAs). There are some independent services (public CAs) developing
and governments, using the licensing model as a take-off point, are
moving into this environment in the United States and abroad. It may
become a new security industry.

As you would expect, there has been a move to include more and
more information in the certificate, making it a multipurpose document. There is one major problem with this. Consider your driver's license, printed on special watermarked paper, showing your picture
and a few vital statistics, and encapsulated in plastic. If you wished to
maintain more volatile information on it, such as current make of car(s),
doctor's name and address, or next of kin, you'd have to get a new license for each change.

The same is true for a certificate. Back you go to the CA for a
new certificate each time you make a change. For a small and readily accessible population, this may be reasonable. However, PKI is
usually justified on the basis of large populations in open environments, often across multiple enterprises. The cost and administrative

logjam can build up with the addition of authorization updates, *if embedded in the certificate.* This is why relatively changeable authorization data (permissions) are seldom embedded in the certificate but rather attached. There are several certificate structures that allow attachments or permissions that can be changed independently of the certificate itself.

Let's review! The certificate is the heart of the PKI system. A given population of users who wish to intercommunicate selects or is required to use a specific CA to obtain a certificate. That certificate contains the public key half of an asymmetric key pair, as well as other indicative information about the target individual. This individual is referred to as the *distinguished name*—implying that there can be no ambiguities in certificate-based identification. All Smiths must be separately distinguished by ancillary data.

WHERE ARE CERTIFICATES USED?

Certificates are used primarily in open environments where closed network security techniques are inappropriate or insufficient for any or all of the following:

- Identification/authentication
- Confidentiality
- Message/transaction integrity
- Nonrepudiation

Not all PKI systems serve the same purposes or have the same protective priorities! This is very important to understand when you are trying to justify a PKI system for a specific business environment.

HOW DOES PKI SATISFY THOSE BUSINESS ENVIRONMENT NEEDS?

Market Expectation

As PKI becomes interoperable, scalable, and generally accepted, companies will begin to accept the wide use of encryption-related products. Large enterprises such as government, banks, and large commercial firms will develop trust models to easily incorporate PKI into everyday business use.

Current Reality

It isn't that easy! Thus far, a significant number of PKI projects have been curtailed, revised, or temporarily shelved for reevaluation. The reasons most often given are

- Immature technology
- Insufficient planning and preparation
- Underestimated scope
- Infrastructure and procedural costs
- Operational and technical incompatibilities
- Unclear cost-benefits

Apparent Conclusions About the Marketplace

PKI has compelling justifications for many enterprises but there are usually more variables and pitfalls than anticipated. Broadside implementation, while sometimes necessary, has not been as cost-effective. Pilots and test beds are strongly recommended. A properly designed CA/RA administrative function is always a critical success factor.

CERTIFICATES, CERTIFICATE AUTHORITIES (CA), AND REGISTRATION AUTHORITIES (RA)

How do these work, and how are they related? First let's look at the PKI certificate lifecycle itself. It's more involved than you may think. A digital certificate is a secure and trustworthy credential, and the process of its creation, use, and termination must be appropriately controlled.

Not all certificates are considered equally secure and trustworthy, and this itself is an active subject of standards and industry discussion. The strength of the cryptography supporting the certificate is actually only one discriminating factor. The degree to which the certificate complies with a given standard, X.509, for example, is another criterion for trustworthiness. The standards cover a wide range of requirements, including content, configuration, and process. Let's spend a moment on process. The following is hardly an exhaustive list, but it will give you some insight into some of the basic requirements:

1. Application—How do the certificate owners-to-be apply for a certificate? To whom do they apply? What supporting materials are required? Must a face-to-face interview be

conducted, or can a surrogate act for the subject? What sanctions are imposed for false, incomplete, or misleading statements? How is the application stored and protected?

2. Validation—How is the applicant's identity validated? By what instruments? By what agencies? For what period of time?

3. Issuance—Assuming the application meets the criteria and the validation is successful, how is the certificate actually issued? Are third parties involved? Is the certificate sent to the individual or, in the case of an organization, some officer of that organization? How is issuance recorded? How are those records maintained and protected?

4. Acceptance—How does the applicant indicate acceptance of the certificate? To whom? Is nonrepudiation of acceptance eliminated?

5. Use—What are the conditions of use? Environments, systems, applications?

6. Suspension or revocation—In the event of compromise or suspension, who must be notified? How? How soon after the event? How is the notice of revocation published?

7. Expiration and renewal—What are the terms, process, and authority?

WHO AND WHAT ARE THE PKI ENTITIES YOU MUST CONSIDER?

You must consider several PKI entities, including certification authority (CA) and registration authority (RA). Certification authority (CA) is a person or institution trusted by others to vouch for the authenticity of a public key. A CA can be any of the following:

- A principal (e.g., management, bank, credit card issuer)
- A secretary of a "club" (e.g., bank clearinghouse)
- A government agency or designee (e.g., notary public, DMV, or post office)
- An independent third party operating for a profit (e.g.,VeriSign)

A CA makes a decision on evidence or knowledge and after *due diligence*. It authorizes issuance of certificate and records the decision by signing a certificate with its private key.

Registration authority (RA) (the usual differentiator between certificate usage and PKI) has these characteristics:

- RA manages certificate life cycle, maintaining certificate directory and maintaining and publishing the Certificate Revocation List(s) (CRL).
- RA can thus be a critical choke point in PKI process and a critical liability point, especially as it relates to CRLs.
- An RA may or may not be a CA.

Other trusted third parties may serve as PKI entities. These may be service organizations that manage the PKI process, brokers who procure certificates from certificate suppliers, independent auditors, or consulting groups that evaluate the security of the PKI procedure. Also, individual subscribers or business subscribers may be involved. In many large organizations, two additional constructs are used:

- The responsible individual (RI)—The enterprise certificate administrator
- The responsible officer (RO)—The enterprise officer who legally assures the company's commitment to the certificate. In many business instances, it is actually more important to know that this certificate is backed by a viable organization that will accept liability than to be able to fully identify the actual certificate holder. In a business transaction, the fact that I can prove I am a director in Deloitte & Touche who is empowered to commit the Firm usually means more than who I am personally.

Types of CAs and RAs

CAs and RAs come in a variety of types. Some of the more common are:

- Full service public CA providing RA, certificate generation, issuance, and life-cycle management
- Branded public CA providing RA, certificate issuance, and life cycle management
- Private CAs using CA turn-key system solutions internally

There are also wide variations in trust structure models. This is driven by the business process and network architecture. Hierarchical Trust models (a classical hierarchy, which may involve multiple levels and a large number of individual domains) include

- VeriSign, Entrust
- X.509v3 certificates (See Chapter 19)
- One-to-one binding of certificate and public-key

The Web of Trust models (a variation on peer relationships between domains) include

- PGP
- Many-to-one binding of certificates and public key
- Constrained or Lattice of Trust structures

There are also hybrids of hierarchical and Web models, such as Xcert.

There are a large number of standards, guidelines, and practices that are applicable to PKI. This is both a blessing and a curse. The most common are listed in Chapter 19. Individual explanations can be gotten at several websites. For a comprehensive set of links, start at http://www.cert.dfn.de/eng/team/ske/pem-dok.html. This is one of the best PKI link sites available.

CA/RA Targets of Evaluation

In order to comprehensively assess the trustworthiness of the individual CA/RA and the associated processes, Deloitte & Touche has developed the following list of required evaluation targets.

System level (in support of the CA/RA process and certificate usage if applicable):

- System components comprising CA/RA environment
- Network devices
- Firewalls, routers, and switches
- Network servers
- IP addresses of all devices
- Client workstations
- Operating systems and application software
- Cryptographic devices
- Physical security, monitoring, and authentication capabilities

Data object level (in support of the CA/RA process and certificate usage):

- Data structures used
- Critical information flows
- Configuration management of critical data items
- Cryptographic data
- Sensitive software applications
- Audit records
- Subscriber and certificate data
- CRLs
- Standards compliance where appropriate

Application and operational level:

- Certificate Policy. Named set of rules governing certificate usage with common security requirements tailored to the operating environment within the enterprise
- Certificate Practices Statement (CPS): Detailed set of rules governing the Certificate Authority's Operations
- Technical and administrative security controls
- Audit
- Key management
- Liability, financial stability, due diligence
- CA contractual requirements and documents
- Subscriber enrollment and termination processes

THE CRL—CERTIFICATE REVOCATION LIST

Of all the administrative and control mechanisms required by a PKI, the CRL function can be one of the more complex and subtle activities. The CRL is an important index of the overall trustworthiness of the specific PKI environment. Normally it is considered part of the registration authorities' duties. Essentially, the CRL is the instrument for checking the continued validity of the certificates for which the RA has responsibility. If a certificate is compromised, if the holder is no longer authorized to use the certificate, or if there is a fault in the binding of the certificate to the holder, it must be revoked and taken out of circulation as rapidly as possible, and all parties in the trust relationship must be informed. The CRL is usually a highly controlled online database (it may take any number of graphic forms) at which subscribers and administrators may determine the currency of a target partner's certificate. This process can vary dramatically by:

- *Timing/frequency of update*—Be careful of the language here. Many RAs claim a 24-hour update. That means the CRL is refreshed every 24 hours. It does not necessarily mean that the total cycle time for a particular revocation to be posted is 24 hours. It may be longer.

- *Push–pull*—This refers to the way in which subscribers can get updates from the CRL. Most CRLs today require subscribers to pull the current update. A few private RAs (see below) employ a push methodology. There is a significant difference in cost and complexity and most important the line of demarcation between the RAs and the subscriber's responsibility and liability. For lessened liability alone, most RAs prefer the pull mode.

- *Up link/down link*—There are two transmissions in the CRL process: the link from the revoking agent to the CRL and the distribution by the CRL to the subscribing universe. Much work has been exerted by RAs to increase the efficiency of the latter process, but because it depends on the revoking agency, the uplink is often an Achilles' Heel. Obviously, the overall time is a combination of both processes, plus file update time.

- *Cross domain*—The world of certificates may involve multiple domains and hierarchies. Each domain has a need to know the validity status of all certificates that are used within its bounds. In some large extranet environments, this may involve multiple and multilayer RA and CRL structures. Think this one through very carefully and be aware that the relationships may change each time the network encompasses a new environment.

- *Integrity*—One major way to undermine the trustworthiness of a PKI environment is to compromise the integrity of the CRL process. If you cannot assure the continued validity of the certificate population, the whole system is at risk.

- *Archiving*—How long should individual CRLs be kept, and for what purposes?

- *Liabilities and commitments*—These should be clearly, unambiguously, and completely stated by all parties involved. In any case of message or transaction compromise traceable to faulty PKI process, the RA is invariably going to be involved. Make very sure you have a common understanding.

HOW WELL DOES PKI SATISFY TODAY'S OPEN SYSTEMS SECURITY NEEDS?

In a nutshell, PKI is an evolving process. It has the fundamental strength, granularity, and flexibility required to support the security requirements we outlined at the beginning of this chapter. In that respect it is the best available alternative. But wholesale adoption of PKI as the best, final, and global solution for security needs is naïve and dangerous. It should be examined selectively by business process or application to determine whether there is sufficient "value-added" to justify the direct and indirect cost associated with deployment. As suites such as RSA and others become more adaptive and rich interfaces to ERP systems like SAP become more commonplace, I believe PKI will be the security technology of choice for major, high-value processes. It will never be the only game in town. Uncomfortable or disillusioning as it may be, the security world will be a multisolution environment for quite a while.

WHAT'S INVOLVED IN ACTUALLY MAKING PKI A COST-EFFECTIVE REALITY?

The most common approach to launching PKI is a pilot environment. Get your feet wet. Map the due diligence and procedural requirements against the culture of your organization. Look at the volatility of the certificates you will issue. What is their life expectancy and need for modification? Check the interface issues. What is the prospective growth curve for certificate use? How many entities will be involved? Is cross-certification a necessity? Above all else, examine the authorization process requirements that must coexist with PKI. PKI is not a full-function access control process. Look into the standards and regulations that affect your industry. Are there export control issues associated with the PKI solution you are attempting to deploy? Is interoperability a major requirement? If so, how flexible is the design of the solutions you're considering?

The most popular approach to PKI today is the pilot project. This is not a "sandbox" or theoretical exercise. It usually involves putting an actual environment into play.

CA PILOT CONSIDERATIONS

- There are several ways of creating a pilot project. Type of Pilot:
  - Proof of concept—may be a test bed or an actual production environment.
  - Operational—a total but carefully scoped environment. Make sure you have a clear statement of expectations against which to measure functional and business results.
  - Interenterprise—avoid this as a startup if possible, but sometimes it is the real justification for adopting PKI. If so, spend considerable time and effort getting a set of procedures and objectives agreed upon by all of the partners involved. An objective third-party evaluation can be very helpful here.
- Examine standards alternatives and requirements carefully—especially in a regulated industry.
- Check product and package compatibility, interoperability, and scalability VERY CAREFULLY.
- Develop alternative compatible product scenarios. At this stage of market maturity, a Plan B is essential. Obviously not all products are universally interchangeable. Develop a backup suite and do some preliminary testing on it.
- Investigate outsourced support as an initial step into the environment. Although your company's philosophy may dictate an internally developed solution, the first round may be better deployed using outside resources.
- Decide what service levels are explicitly or implicitly required.
- Start internally with friendly environment. You need all the support you can get, especially from business process owners.
- Provide sufficient time and resources for procedural infrastructure development, including CA policy, CPS, and training.
- Don't promise more than you can deliver!

IS PKI AN EXCEPTIONAL APPROACH OR JUST ONE OF MANY ALTERNATIVES WORTH LOOKING AT?

The answer to that question depends largely on the security objectives of the organization. PKI is ideal (but potentially expensive) for extranets and environments where more traditional identification and authentication are insufficient. Tempting as it may be, resist the urge to find *the single solution.* Most network-based environments and the associated enterprises are too complex at this moment for one single global solution. Examine the potential for SSL, SMIME, Kerberos, PGP, single sign-on, and VPNs. If you can make the technical, operational, and cost-justification case for a single, PKI-based security approach, by all means do so. PKI is a powerful structure, but it is not a religious icon. Leave yourself room for tailored, multisolution environments.

SO WHAT'S A DIGITAL SIGNATURE?

Once again, it may seem like we're dragging out the obvious, but let's answer a more fundamental question first: *What's a signature?* The one you and I are most accustomed to is Webster's Dictionary's first entry: *"The name of one as written by oneself."* However, it's the second dictionary entry that resonates in the e-world: *"A distinctive mark, characteristic, modus operandi, or sound effect indicating identity."* If you think about it, it's the older of the two because it does not require the ability to read and write. "By gosh, I'd recognize those teeth marks anywhere. This was done by Growlf, my pet saber tooth tiger." An illiterate king could still convince armies to go out and get killed in his behalf by affixing his seal to an order written by a scribe. "Caramba, it's the mark of Zorro!" OK, that's enough. You get the point. We're talking about definition 2, and it permits us a wide variety of options when it comes to both electronic and digital signatures. Digital signatures are electronic. Not all electronic signatures (e.g., graphics facsimiles, ballistic facsimiles) fit the strict definition of a digital signature. A *digitized* signature is a scanned copy of a written signature. It is not the same as a digital signature.

Webopedia.com defines digital signature in this way:

> A digital code that can be attached to an electronically transmitted message that uniquely identifies the sender. Like a written signature, the purpose of a digital signature is to guarantee that the individual sending the message really is who he or she claims to be. Digital signatures are especially important for electronic commerce and are a key component of most authentication schemes. To be effective, digital signatures must be unforgeable. There are a number of different encryption techniques to guarantee this level of security.

Are digital signatures and digital certificates the same thing? No, though they are very closely related. All certificates can be used as digital signatures. Not all digital signatures are certificates. Perhaps the simplest distinction is that in creating a certificate, a third party, the CA, is involved in acting as a guarantor of the certificate and public key associated with it. Digital signatures can be used by individual parties without the need for a CA or other trustee by simply sending over a trusted link, including certified mail or courier, a copy of the digital signature to be trusted by the other party. (Never send it the first time with the actual document.) Both or many parties can keep these signatures on file securely for comparison when a signed message is sent. If the group gets too large or begins to contain members who are not known to everyone, a trusted third party may become necessary. By the way, the message content does not need to be encrypted if all we are trying to do is establish identity.

What are the downsides? The digital signature process works best where the parties are already known to and trusted by each other and want to assure the recipient that a specific document came from the trusted sender. The certificate, CA, and PKI system are used when neither party knows or trusts each other and requires a third party to act as intermediary.

If the population gets big enough, exchanging unique digital signatures, even among trusted parties, gets clumsy very rapidly for the same reasons that symmetric keys do. We assume that you will provide a different signature for each relationship pair. (That may sound odd at first reading, but remember, we're using symbols here and the symbols can and should vary within the sets of participants to control who can see what and to prevent forgery. You must have the right signature for our specific relationship.) You can see how the number will rapidly add up.

There are situations where a *comparatively* simple digital signature will serve just as well as its more complex cousin, the digital certificate. The business environment, the population, the type of network, and the materials in question will be the major deciding factors. See Chapter 12 for some of the legislative differences between electronic signatures and digital signatures and Chapter 19 for additional material on applicable standards.

A FEW BRIEF TRANSITIONAL COMMENTS ON ENCRYPTION STANDARDS

To aid and abet our transition to the next chapter on standards, let's move away from PKI, fascinating though it may be, and go back to the encryption process itself. Remember, we were talking about key lengths, cipher feedback, algorithm strength, and multiple iterations through the algorithm. You don't remember? Well, take my word for it, we did, and you were appropriately awestruck at the time.

Surely, you remember that as brute force attacks got more brutal and forceful, a newer algorithm, more impervious to brute force, was sought by NIST, acting as broker for the global commercial encryption user community. Good. Now I shall give you a short chronology of how the AES (Advanced Encryption Standard), which is just shedding its toddler clothes, came to be. This should simultaneously give you further insight into both the encryption and standards process.

- August 1998—NIST announces that 15 algorithm candidates have passed a first round of submission screening. The algorithms came from 12 countries. Some submitted more than one.
- March 1999—NIST holds a conference and presents the first round of test results for comment, discussion, and argument.
- Mid-year 1999—NIST has narrowed the field to five.
- April 2000—the five finalists are discussed at length and NIST gets much advice and counsel.
- October 2000—NIST announces the winner—a Belgian submission called Rijndael developed by Joan Daeme and Vincent Rijmen. (**RIJ**men a**Nd DAE**me a**L**gorithm) It is stronger and faster in several respects. The block size encrypted at one time is 128 bits. DES is 56. Bigger is better. DES as released for general use and export has a standard key length of 56 bits, although some private versions use longer keys. Rijndael is adjustable to use key lengths of 128, 192, or 256 bits. Longer is stronger.
- February 28, 2001—First draft of the FIPS submitted publicly for comment
  - With acceptance by NIST, Rijndael is in the process of being published as the official United States government encryption standard, a FIPS (Federal Information Processing Standard) for all government sensitive, but nonclassified data. Like many nations, the United States has more powerful, nonpublic algorithms it uses for defense and intelligence work.
  - There is a very strong likelihood that ANSI will then adopt the FIPS (Rijndael) for use in the private sector by ANSI members in the U.S. including but not restricted to the financial communities.

- Next stop after that is the ISO, where the ANSI standard is expected to become a global standard with a useful age of about 20 years. Of course, DES had a much longer life predicted for it, so the final word or algorithm has not been spoken. How long will Rijndael actually stay in service? You've got me.

How long until Rijndael is in common global use? Several years. The obvious question is one of cost effectiveness: whether, how, and how long to wring out the last drops of usefulness from DES, which is embedded in many devices and software implementations in use today before switching to the new algorithm.

By the way, I publicly apologize to my colleagues. I fully expected there to be more than one NIST winner, based strictly on international pressure and politics. I guess I'm getting cynical in my old age. However, the ISO adoption process is not complete. Could more than one international candidate be chosen? Who knows?

19

Process and Technology Standards

And now, an examination of standards, especially as they apply to B2B processes. This, too, will be a high-level overview. There is an assumption, especially among business managers, that the standards process will single-handedly, with strength and right, bring order to the technological and business process chaos that could result from B2B. "We'll comply with the industry standards, and that's all we need." Sorry! Much as we'd like to assign such omnipotence and clarity to the standards process, that's not the way it works, especially in cutting-edge situations. Often as not, standards trail rather than lead innovation and development. The standards process itself is rife with political, intellectual, and commercial conflict. Often, the guiding principle is, "By all means, let us standardize as long as we standardize on my version." Is the standards arena a totally objective and unimpeachable process? Does special interest have no place in standards development? Is the Easter Bunny real?

Am I being too cynical about the value of standards? Au contraire! I am a strong supporter of standards. I am only insisting that we be realistic in our expectations about what they can and cannot do, especially in uncharted waters.

In this chapter, we will review the general characteristics of standards; the processes for developing public standards; the difference in some national and international standards bodies; and then, we'll briefly look at some of the technology and business-related standards that could affect your move into B2B.

There is, of course, the other side of the standards process—the internal or intercorporate standard. In most respects, they resemble the public standard, differing only in the population involved and the authority invoked. We'll speak about them here, as well as in the next chapter on organization. So read on. We are not going to drag you through sections, subsections, paragraphs, and citations. We're going to give you an overview of the standards landscape and leave it to you to assign the task of sorting them all out to some up-and-coming star who needs a little more seasoning and grooming.

A STANDARD? I CAN'T DEFINE ONE, BUT I KNOW IT WHEN I SEE IT!

A somewhat circuitous definition of a standard from webopedia.com is: *A standard is a definition or format that has been accepted and approved by a recognized standards organization or is accepted as a de facto standard by the industry.* In other words, we (as authorities from whatever right, privilege, or responsibility) have agreed that this is the accepted definition, method, or structure to be used in creating a specific process, product, or object.

In the world of standards, especially technology, there are generally two classes of standard (Oh boy, I finally get to use my six years of Latin schooling):

1. De facto standard—For any given function, this is the design or approach most people are using, frequently due to manufacturer or designer dominance, broad licensing of patents, and tons of existing product survival of the fittest and even piracy. At some point, if the de facto shows signs of prolonged presence in the marketplace (not always true in technology), it becomes appropriate to establish it as the . . .
2. De jure standard—"Kneel, oh fair standard, I dub thee ISO 123456.33 Revision 2-2001." Official sanction and ongoing support is now provided for the standard by a recognized body or bodies.

WHAT ARE THEY USED FOR?

That is not a stupid question. A standard, in addition to describing a process or thing, is also used as a norm for measurement of compliance and thereby enhancing trust. Listen to the auditors and assessors perking up their ears.

For example, a standard tells you what it takes to send and receive television signals in a given country or what a plug and power receptacle should look like and what you must do to be in compliance with those requirements. Or how to describe and set up Web-interchange languages.

Standards processes can be costly because they require

- An authority and owner of the standard
- A measurement program
- An interpreter and arbiter (who may or may not be the specific owner)
- A submission process for approval
- A deviation or exception authorization process
- An enforcement process

If you don't have all that, you don't have a standards process, no matter what you call it. This is true of public and private standards.

"LET'S STANDARDIZE!" HAVE A CARE, THERE!

When should you develop standards in your own organization, and what characteristics should they have? The question applies equally to global, national, and industry standards.

- They should cover a critical subject of sufficient importance to warrant the effort.
- There should be a high cost associated with the consequences of nonstandardization. (Such as, nothing I brought with me works here.)
- They should have a wide effect on the relevant population. (If only three people are affected, let them fight it out in the parking lot.)
- There should be multiple, viable, possible options. (There isn't much point writing a standard for laws of gravity. There's only one . . . so far.)
- They should cover a long time span. (Don't write a standard for a process that is going to be obsolete or abandoned tomorrow.)

- They should be written to be broadly applicable. (Otherwise, you end up with a very large number of individual and possibly conflicting standards.)
- They should be enforceable. (Not much point, otherwise.)
- Finally and most important, don't overdo them. I believe about half the corporate or institutional standards floating around are really procedures or guidelines dressed up in formal clothes or have no right to exist at all. That, of course, is my opinion. We'll pick that point up again in the next chapter.

THE IMPORTANCE OF STRONG AND ACTIVE B2B AND INTERNET STANDARDS PROGRAMS

This paragraph probably fits in the category of "We hold these truths to be self-evident." The problem is that standards programs are high maintenance, especially in these subject areas. Last year, I briefly joined an Internet security technical standards group. I had not done such penance for several years. Due to time constraints, my participation (mostly online) was shamefully low, and I withdrew because of a nagging conscience. I make this unseemly confession, confident in the fact that I have plenty of company. During that brief period, about 10 to 15% of my substantial e-mail load came from that one source. This did not include going back to the group's website repeatedly. My point (also self-evident) is that even with the trappings and functions of modern technology, the standards process can be drawn out, detailed, and difficult.

Now that you have been enticed by such an attractive proposition, I'm going to ask, nay insist, that as executives of B2B (or B2B to-be) dependent organizations, you budget resources for standards participation and monitoring. Consider it part of your corporate fitness or, if you prefer, protection program. Do not relegate the task to the most junior, most dispensable, or most disliked members of your staff. Like it or not, this stuff is important to you and requires subject matter expertise, industry and market knowledge, a sense for the use and abuse of language, stamina, and a strong diplomatic streak.

"Aha," you cleverly reply, "Here is a classic case of exercising e-Trust. I'll trust someone else to do it for me." Representatives from a competitor, perhaps? From a regulatory body? Consumer advocates? Other countries or regions? Nice try, but let's not push trust too far. On the other hand, let's be realistic. You and your organization can't possibly cover the entire spectrum. A little later, I'm going to list but not explain in any serious detail some of the wide range of standards that affect B2B and Beyond. You're right! You can and should exercise e-Trust in the standards arena. Here is an opportunity for trusted partner cooperation and co-ordination. That will take some management, too. But that's what we do for a living, right?

HOW DOES A STANDARDS BODY OPERATE?

In a standardized manner, of course. Sorry, I couldn't resist. Assuming the standards body already has a defined mandate, the typical cycle is as follows:

1. Receive, filter, interpret, reject, or accept proposals for a new standard or modification.
2. Create or assign a category and responsible sub-committee.
3. Research, propose, create, and distribute drafts within the sub-committee.
4. Send progressive drafts to affected other sub-committees for their review. This process can be lengthy, complex, and acrimonious. Too many standards sub-committees and groups try to solve their issues or break an impasse by dumping the problem on another body. "It's on their side of the interface."
5. Prepare and distribute a preliminary "exposure" draft for general membership comment and response. This has a time limit for responses.
6. Receive replies and repeat steps 3, 4, and 5 as necessary. (I know. I should have used a flow chart.)
7. Take it public for review and comment. Here's where all the other affected standards bodies, third parties, nations, organizations, institutions, experts, media, advocates, and just plain interested people get a shot at it. Usually this process has a time limit built into it, too.
8. Back to step 6, as necessary. It will be.
9. Submit the final version for formal vote and hope you get acceptance. Otherwise, it's back to the drawing boards. (Consider Steven Wright's quip: "What did the guy who invented the drawing board go back to after his first failure?")

ALTERNATES OFTEN USED IN TECHNOLOGY

Many technology standards manifest themselves in actual design criteria, specifications, and even real product. (Many ad hoc standards become de jure in this fashion. Some cynics call this reverse standards engineering.) The question is raised. "Two thirds of the world does it this way. Isn't it time we acknowledge, refine, and formalize the fact?"

Or in a different situation, the realization crystallizes: "There's no product or technology out there that adequately meets the spirit or letter of an existing standard any longer. Let's update the standard by asking for competitive design submissions. Winner will be named the new standard."

Classic case: encryption. As computers got faster, functionally more powerful, more ubiquitous, and code crackers improved their art in using them, older algorithms lost their protective aura. They could be broken within days instead of eons. Time for an upgrade of devices and standards both. Voila—the advanced encryption standard. (See Chapter 18.)

In both of these cases, the development is usually in four, often iterative, stages.

1. Get the objectives and overall requirements settled (see 1 through 9 above). This is not as easy as it seems. Even if a single manufacturer's product is the de facto standard, it still may not satisfy all of the objectives required for de jure acceptance. In the other case, if we're seeking improvement on an existing de jure standard, what do we want? Anyway, assuming miraculous intervention as needed, once that's done, move to stage 2.

2. Request design submissions. This may result in changes in the basic standard content as the contestants query, argue, suggest, and otherwise prepare for entry.

3. Conduct a bake-off and declare the winner(s).

4. Sit back and listen to the howls of protest. (What did you expect? Adulation?)

INTERNATIONAL VERSUS DOMESTIC STANDARDS BODY

There is another important aspect to the global standards process that you have to understand if you're venturing into worldwide B2B. Standards bodies are very different in their composition, genesis, and source of authority. To state it briefly: In the United States, most standards arise from nongovernment sources. ANSI (The American National Standards Institute) is actually supported, managed, and staffed by industry membership. NIST—the National Institute for Standards and Technology—creates the standards to be used by most of the U.S. government itself. It is also frequently engaged in testing and reporting. It's predecessor name—the U.S. Bureau of Standards—gave the impression that all U.S. standards came from or were legitimized directly by the government. Not so. ANSI, the IEEE, IETF, and a host of others are independent entities.

However, in most other countries and economic regions throughout the world, the standards process usually is a direct or tethered arm of the government. Does this create status issues in international negotiations? You bet. Remember that technology and process standards can have major positive or negative impacts on a country's economy, prestige, and in some cases, defense. It may call for rebuilding infrastructure, or securing worldwide sales. Finland has leveraged the Nokia mobile phone not only through design, manufacturing, and sales, but through standards. Formal and market acceptance or rejection of the wireless application protocol (WAP) for Web support of hand-held phones is a major event for them (and others).

We briefly discussed the *Advanced Encryption Standard* (AES). Recall the length of the process and the players involved. That competition was considerably more than an arcane technology exercise. Big bucks, national defense, major industry, design, and device decisions rested on that call. Was nationalism an issue? What do you think?

WHAT ABOUT PROCEDURES AND GUIDELINES?

Not every end product of a standards group, private, corporate, or public, is a standard. Procedures and guidelines also populate this world. They are not simply second- or third-class standards that couldn't make the cut. Often, they deal with *how-to*, including how to comply with a standard. The standard states the requirements. The procedure or guideline indicates the process we will use. I believe the major distinction between the two is that procedures are usually mandatory and the guideline is advisory.

Deviations from standards should be possible, but they should be rather difficult to get. Even though procedures may be considered mandatory, they should have a relatively easier deviation approval process, at a lower level of the standards management process. Guidelines, being advisory, should be the most flexible in this regard.

Finally, let's look at some B2B and e-Trust relevant standards.

ISO 17799

When the International Standards Organization standard ISO 17799 is published and approved, it will be the most widely recognized security standard developed thus far. Its origins are the British security standard BS7799, last published in May 1999. It covers a wide range of security issues and control requirements. Good news–Bad news. It provides a common metric for use worldwide (if accepted worldwide). We will have fewer tail-chasing exercises to contend with on local levels. However, compliance is not going to be that easy and certification, when and if necessary, can be even more daunting unless the B2B players and environment have a coherent protection program in place or on the way.

The standard has ten major sections:

1. Business Continuity Planning—Counteracting interruptions to business activities and to critical business processes from the effects of major failures or disasters.

2. System Access Control—(1) Controlling access to information; (2) Preventing unauthorized access to information systems; (3) Protecting networked services; (4) Preventing unauthorized computer access; (5) Detecting unauthorized activities; (6) Providing information security when using mobile computing and related functions.

3. System Development and Maintenance—(1) Building security into operational systems; (2) Preventing loss, modification, or misuse of user data in application systems; (3) Protecting the confidentiality, authenticity, and integrity of information; (4) Conducting IT projects and support activities securely; (5) Maintaining the security of application system software and data.

4. Physical and Environmental Security—(1) Preventing unauthorized access, damage, and interference to business premises and information; (2) Preventing loss, damage, or compromise of assets and interruption to business activities; (3) Preventing compromise or theft of information and information processing facilities.

5. Compliance—(1) Avoiding and preventing breaches of any criminal or civil law, statutory, regulatory, or contractual obligations and of any security requirements; (2) Ensuring compliance of systems with organizational security policies and standards; (3) Maximizing the effectiveness of and minimizing interference to/from the system audit process.

6. Personnel Security—(Be careful here. This does not refer to protecting people. This refers to people-generated threats.) (1) Reducing risks of human error, theft, fraud, or misuse of facilities; (2) Ensuring that users are aware of information security threats and concerns and are equipped to support the corporate security policy in the course of their normal work; (3) Minimizing damage from security incidents and malfunctions.

7. Security Organization—(1) Managing information security within the entity; (2) Maintaining the security of information processing facilities and information assets accessed by third parties; (3) Maintaining the security of information under outsource conditions.

8. Computer and Network Management—(1) Ensuring the correct and secure operation of information processing facilities; (2) Minimizing the risk of systems failures; (3) Protecting the integrity of software and information; (4) Maintaining the integrity and availability of information processing and communication; (5) Safeguarding of information in networks and the protection of the supporting infrastructure; (6) Preventing damage to assets and interruptions to business activities; (7) Preventing loss, modification, or misuse of information exchanged between organizations.

9. Asset Classification and Control—Maintaining appropriate protection of corporate assets and providing information assets with appropriate levels of protection.

10. Security Policy—Providing management direction and support for information security.

That, with one or two small exceptions and variants, pretty much spells out all the elements of an enterprise and B2B security program. What's the likelihood of it being accepted into the halls of ISO standards? Not bad. How compulsory will it be? Ah, now, that depends on the individual member countries of the ISO. Remember ISO 9000? Some countries made that mandatory for contracting or doing business with them. Others treat it more as an advisory mechanism but do not insist on certification. Some ignore it.

My personal belief is that this standard or some variations and extractions from it will influence global B2B. It's not breathing at your door, yet but I would consider building any new security program out of ISO17799 compliant bricks.

FEDERAL STANDARDS

In other chapters, we've discussed HIPAA and GBL and encryption and telecommunication and SEC and Controller of the Currency standards, as well as others. There are many more we haven't mentioned, and don't worry, I'm not mentioning them here. In the last analysis, information-related standards cluster around data form and content; process, transmission, and infrastructure; data subjects, data owners, and data users. Business and professional standards cover much more comprehensive arenas and vary widely within industry sectors. e-Trust, as we've been using it, involves both. B2B may be intra- or intersectoral. Remember how we said financial services pop up all over the place.

Help! Is there a single arbiter of U.S. federal standards? Sadly, from a one-stop shopping standpoint, no. But this situation has an up-side. From a development, adjudication, enforcement, and improvement standpoint, I'll go for the sector-by-sector approach, every time. It gets messy, and conflicts may arise. Encryption technology has been caught in a four-way tug of war among Commerce, State, Justice, and Defense since the first codes went into the commercial domain. Who owns privacy concerns? Intellectual property? Infrastructure safety and robustness? Sorry, but this is one area where the enterprise and its related B2B entities are not going to be disintermediated. You're in the middle and out on the edges and every place in between. This is a fact of life that must be faced as another cost of progress.

How about other countries? Their standards bodies are usually less fragmented. In a cosmic sense you may be able to go to one standards agency, but it is just papering over, in most cases, directorate roulette. Bureaucracies abound, and it is naïve to assume that B2B will make them less complex. If anything, it will complicate matters.

EXAMPLES OF TECHNOLOGY-RELATED STANDARDS

What are some of the basic technical standards you can expect to encounter in B2B process and technology? They may not be directed toward e-Trust, security, or control directly but this is a world of allusive and elusive relationships. We listed a group under encryption and PKI in the previous chapter, and we won't repeat those. Some of these we have mentioned elsewhere, but in the interest of one-stop shopping, we'll define them again. None of these lists come near to being exhaustive (exhausting, perhaps). (Again, thanks to webopedia.com.)

Core Internet Standards and Protocols

- *American Standard Code for Information Interchange* (ASCII)—
  Pronounced *ask-ee,* ASCII is a code for representing English
  characters as numbers, with each letter assigned a number
  from 0 to 127. Most computers use ASCII codes to represent
  text, which makes it possible to transfer data from one
  computer to another.

- *Transmission Control Protocol/Internet Protocol* (TCP/IP)—The
  suite of communications protocols used to connect hosts on
  the Internet.

- *Telnet*—A terminal emulation program for TCP/IP networks
  such as the Internet. The Telnet program runs on your
  computer and connects your PC to a server on the network.
  You can then enter commands through the Telnet program and
  they will be executed as if you were entering them directly on
  the server console.

- *File Transfer Protocol* (FTP)—The protocol used on the Internet
  for sending files.

Browser and Data Language Standards and Protocols

- *Hypertext Transfer Protocol* (HTTP)—The underlying protocol
  used by the World Wide Web, HTTP defines how messages are
  formatted and transmitted, and what actions Web servers and
  browsers should take in response to various commands.

- HTTP is called a stateless protocol because each command is
  executed independently, without any knowledge of the
  commands that came before it. This is the main reason that it is
  difficult to implement websites that react intelligently to user
  input. This shortcoming of HTTP is being addressed in a
  number of new technologies, including ActiveX, Java,
  JavaScript, and cookies.

- *Hypertext Markup Language* (HTML)—The other main standard
  that controls how the World Wide Web works is HTML, which
  covers how Web pages are formatted and displayed.

- *Extensible Markup Language* (XML, and extensions)—Designed
  especially for Web documents, XML allows designers to create
  their own customized tags, enabling the definition, transmission,
  validation, and interpretation of data between applications and

between organizations. XML is critical for enabling business applications to directly operate over the Web.

Messaging Standards and Protocols

- *Simple Mail Transfer Protocol* (SMTP)—This is a protocol for sending e-mail messages between servers.
- *Post Office Protocol* (POP)—This is a protocol used to retrieve e-mail from a mail server. Most e-mail applications (sometimes called an e-mail client) use the POP protocol, although some can use the newer IMAP (Internet Message Access Protocol).
- *Multipurpose Internet Mail Extensions* (MIME)—a specification for formatting non-ASCII messages so that they can be sent over the Internet. Many e-mail clients now support MIME, which enables them to send and receive graphics, audio, and video files via the Internet mail system. In addition, MIME supports messages in character sets other than ASCII.

TRANSACTION STANDARDS OR PROTOCOLS

There are many transaction standards, and they are often industry specific. One example from Financial Services is Secure Electronic Transaction (SET), a new standard that will enable secure credit card transactions on the Internet. SET has been endorsed by virtually all the major players in the electronic commerce arena, including Microsoft, Netscape, Visa, and Mastercard.

By employing digital signatures, SET will enable merchants to verify that *buyers are who they claim to be. And it will protect buyers by providing a mechanism* for their credit card number to be transferred directly to the credit card issuer for verification and billing without the merchant being able to see the number.

OBJECT STANDARDS AND PROTOCOLS

An object is generally defined as any item that can be individually selected and manipulated. This can include shapes and pictures that appear on a display screen, as well as less tangible software entities. In object-oriented programming, for example, an object is a self-contained entity that consists of both data and procedures to manipulate the data.

Java is a high-level object-oriented programming language developed by Sun Microsystems, modified to take advantage of the World Wide Web. Java is similar to C++, but is simplified to eliminate language features that cause common programming errors. Java source code files are compiled into a format, which can then be executed by a Java interpreter. Compiled Java code can run on most computers because Java interpreters and runtime environments, known as Java Virtual Machines (VMs), exist for most operating systems, including UNIX, the Macintosh OS, and Windows. Small Java applications are called Java applets.

CORBA, short for Common Object Request Broker Architecture, is an architecture that enables pieces of programs, called objects, to communicate with one another regardless of what programming language they were written in or what operating system they're running on.

DIRECTORY STANDARDS AND PROTOCOLS

LDAP, short for Lightweight Directory Access Protocol, is a set of protocols for accessing information directories. LDAP is based on the X.500 data standard but is significantly simpler. And unlike X.500, LDAP supports TCP/IP, which is necessary for any type of Internet access. Because it's a simpler version of X.500, LDAP is sometimes called *X.500-lite*.

X.500 is an ISO and ITU (International Telecommunications Union) standard that defines how global directories should be structured. X.500 directories are *hierarchical* with different levels for each category of information, such as country, state, and city.

SECURITY STANDARDS AND PROTOCOLS

- IP Security (IPSEC) is a set of protocols being developed by the Internet Engineering Task Force (IETF) to support secure exchange of packets at the IP layer.

- Secure Sockets Layer, SSL, is a protocol developed by Netscape for transmitting private documents via the Internet. SSL works by using a private *key* to encrypt data that's transferred over the SSL connection. Both Netscape and Internet Explorer support SSL, and many websites use the protocol to obtain confidential user information, such as credit card numbers. By convention, Web pages that require an SSL connection start with https: instead of http:.

- S-HTTP is another protocol for transmitting data securely over the Web. Whereas SSL creates a secure connection between a client and a server, over which any amount of data can be sent securely, S-HTTP is designed to transmit individual messages securely. SSL and S-HTTP, therefore, can be seen as complementary rather than competing technologies. Both protocols have been approved by the IETF as a standard.

- S/MIME, short for Secure/MIME, is a newer version of the Multipurpose Internet Mail Extensions protocol that supports encryption of messages. S/MIME is based on *RSA's* public-key technology. S/MIME makes it possible for people to send secure e-mail messages to one another, even if they are using different e-mail clients.

- X.509—Public key infrastructure (PKIX), is a great example of things not necessarily being what they seem. X.509 is actually a large collection of standards, protocols, recommendations, and white papers covering the entire PKI environment. It is still very much under development, although an increasing number of pieces are coming in place. Unfortunately, vendors have implemented portions of X.509 in different ways. For example, both Netscape and Microsoft use X.509 certificates to implement SSL in their Web servers and browsers. But an X.509 certificate generated by Netscape may not be readable by Microsoft products, and vice versa. When told a product is X.509 compliant, you need far more information. Go further and ask how is it compliant, in what areas, and with what other products?

- The information above was partially extracted from the RSA Laboratories' website, www.rsasecurity.com. Here is a classic example of de facto standards at work and transitioning to de jure status. The public-key cryptography standards are specifications produced by RSA Laboratories in cooperation with secure systems developers worldwide for the purpose of accelerating the deployment of public-key cryptography. Since 1991, the PKCS documents have become widely referenced and implemented. Contributions from the PKCS series have become part of many formal and de facto standards, including ANSI X9 documents, PKIX, SET, S/MIME, and SSL.

APPLICATION STANDARDS AND PROTOCOLS

I'm going to let you off easy on this one by saying that vendors, third parties, and other suppliers, plus each industry group have a bunch. Far too many to list. (Joint sigh of relief by reader and author.)

"WERE YOU REALLY TRYING TO PUT ME TO SLEEP?"

No, frankly, I was trying to wake you up, if you needed it, to the incredible number and immense variety of standards that affect B2B and e-Trust. And to coin a brand-new phrase, we just scratched the surface. How much of this does your organization have to contend with? Most, if not all, at some level—either in understanding and selecting standards and protocols for their applicability and then using them as product or project requirements, or detecting some that could seriously affect your organization, network, or B2B entity. One thing you can't safely do in this arena is play ostrich.

There are, of course, your own enterprise standards, and on top of that, the standards governing the B2B relationship and the supporting infrastructure. We'll talk a bit more about them in the next chapter, "Organizing for e-Trust."

20

Organizing for e-Trust

Here is another chapter that could be a book in itself. It has a rather arrogant title, implying that there is one and only one method for organizing e-Trust functions for B2B and Beyond. Not true. Don't expect neat little "org charts" in the next few pages. There aren't any. Instead, we'd like once again to concentrate on the changes developing in conventional security and control organizations as a result of B2B structure(s) and the way e-Trust manifests itself. We'll give you a few thoughts on policies, guidelines, mission statements, and one or two new roles that are emerging. We're going to stress demonstrability and reciprocity yet again. (Cheer up! There are only a few chapters left. How many more times can I drag those two out again?) You may also think I am talking out of both sides of my mouth in a few places in this chapter. You know, the old "on the one hand, on the other hand" routine. It is not intentional, but it's sometimes unavoidable because one should organize to fit the environment, not the other way around. And B2B environments can be—altogether now—different! Very good. Tenors, a little more fortissimo next time. OK?

A STARTLING REALIZATION

As I was preparing to write this chapter, I had a minor epiphany. Don't worry. Two days of bed rest and I'm as good as new. It occurred to me that while we have alluded to, elliptically described, anecdotally presented, demonstrated, and otherwise beat around the bush, we have never, throughout this entire text, faced up four square to the question: *How is a B2B organized?*

What is the answer to this cosmic issue? I could be snide and say: "Any way it wants to." Oddly, with only a few restrictions, that reply comes pretty darn close. Let's come at it by eliminating some of the candidates that at first blush may seem most likely.

"A B2B is simply a larger version of its members—a macrocosm." No. You could probably say that about some netmarkets, but the B2B environments we've been describing are not simply clusters of functionally identical units connected to make a larger but otherwise identical unit. Many such nets exist, and they serve many excellent business and institutional purposes. I suppose, literally, they are basic B2Bs but their functional aspects are just repeated over and over at different levels of aggregation and the e-Trust aspects are fairly fundamental. Lots of connectivity and communication, but not much collaboration or integration.

However, those nets are often the first steps toward the more integrated B2B, where the essence is interoperative specialization. That's where the business economies, strengths, and growth potential of B2Bs come from. Each member brings what they do best to the party, and everyone profits from it. There is minimal duplication and maximum benefit. Utopian? Probably. But that's the ideal design point. Most B2Bs will land in the middle for the next few years.

"Hey, what's the problem? The B2B is the network." No again. The paths, nodes, and characteristics of the network support but do not define or even describe the nature or functions of the B2B. Many different business processes may share parts or all of the same network structure. Some parts of the net are one-trick ponies. One function, one connection. Others carry every type of traffic imaginable. The topology of the net is important to many key decisions, especially about e-Trust, but it does not fully define the B2B entity.

"Well, it's the sum of its different parts." Not entirely. In this case the whole is greater than the sum of its static parts and even different. The cooperative dynamics of B2B come from harmonious interaction. Just like an orchestra. One instrument can kill the effect. But it takes combined forces to provide the signature sound and magic and that combination has unique characteristics of its own. Let's not get too lyrical.

"Didn't you describe the Internet as 'anarchy by design' or an 'oligarchy'? " Nice try. Ten points for remembering. But the Internet is not the B2B, or vice versa.

"All right! Enough is enough! How do you organize a B2B? You organize it to optimize the business objectives of the alliance, and that can take on any number of different shapes or forms. The point of this tiresome exercise was to bring home an important point. *Don't try to organize for e-Trust until you can describe the objectives, members, relationships, nature, priorities, flows, functions, constraints, risks, and capabilities of the composite B2B.* From scratch? Hardly. But don't just assume that you'll get there by simply expanding and exploiting the trust, control, and security mechanisms and entities that exist among the parts and players. Borrow, adapt, tweak, but remember, we are talking about something that is—different.

INTEGRATE OR ISOLATE? CENTRALIZE OR DECENTRALIZE? COORDINATE!

Let me state for the record one more time, your Honor, that e-Trust and its friendly associates—controls and security—should be primarily organized around the business processes the B2B environment supports. Not the enterprises, the processes. "But business processes span individual organizations and centers of technology in B2B." Yes. "And people work for individual organizations." True, or third parties. "Aha, you're trying to get us to outsource our control and security functions, you scheming consultant." Nope. Sometimes that works, sometimes not. We're more than happy to take on such assignments if and when they make sense. What doesn't make sense is trying to unload trust responsibility and liability onto a third party. We can help, certainly, and we can mitigate the burden. However, no matter how much lighter we can make it and share it with you, that e-Trust monkey is still attached to *your* back.

But . . . who is *you*? Good question! Remember that many enterprises will be members of several B2B environments. In turn, an individual B2B may be linked to others (netmarkets). In each case, it depends on how you've organized the primary B2B identity, legal and business structure, ownership, operating responsibilities, processes and liabilities, and the relationships of the members. Don't fight the organization. Work with it: 99 chances out of 100 you're going to end up with some variant of a matrix structure mapped around business function and infrastructure.

YOU CONSULTANTS ARE AT IT AGAIN. MAKING WORK FOR YOURSELVES

Not necessarily. By all means, use what you have available from the different members and from industry practice as an opening model. If it works with some modification and extension, go for it. If it fits perfectly the first time, you have probably missed some requirements.

Remember, each level and process will probably have other e-Trust objectives, a different composite set, some overlapping, some not. But do some serious walkthroughs against the background of the B2B processes and modify as necessary.

WHY ARE WE DOING THIS AT ALL?

A few possible motivations:

- Quality
- Improved customer service
- Risk management
- Unit-cost / headcount reduction
- Global consistency / interoperability
- Enhance business justification for security and control
- Enhance responsiveness to business units
- Enhance third-party security management
- Streamline administration
- Agility for moving to future environments
- Accelerate and rationalize technology adoption
- Move as appropriate, from reactive to proactive
- Attain early, visible, significant benefits followed by progressive transition to fuller implementation

SOME THOUGHTS FOR GETTING STARTED

Work backward from functional models to trust models. For example, how is *Identification and Authentication* management to be handled? Will all the members agree to each one doing their own or is a centralized administration process in the cards? Does centralized administration mean all entities use a common database and associated facilities or is a full-blown central service group the way to go? Is a "trusted" third-party necessary to instill the appropriate level of trust? Initially? Over time? If you are going to use certificates and a full PKI implementation, the CA and RA functions must be accommodated. By the way, CAs and RAs are not always external third parties. In the financial services arena, for example, many banks and a few securities exchange functions do their own thing.

Authorization may not be organized the same way as authentication. That's a habit that has hung on from centralized mainframe days. Authorization is often application specific and again, certain applications may perform their functions both inside and outside the B2B network.

Although the B2B may be a closed community for the processes it manages, its members are still free to play in the outside world. For example, will a company use two purchasing systems, one for raw materials and products used in the integrated B2B supply chain and a totally different one for company infrastructure, supplies, et al.? It could go either way. But each B2B member will probably still have a significant amount of identification, authentication, and authorization that has nothing to do with the B2B itself. In other words, as a networked business architect, don't design for relinquishing function to the all-powerful central control unless it makes sense for the individual members. It usually won't. Harmonized and standardized process, format, protocols, and infrastructure, by all means. Total or even managing responsibility surrendered to master control? Be careful.

This is not an all-or-nothing consideration. Some things are better handled in exclusively centralized form. We mentioned the merits of a single CA and RA.

Now, let's switch over to the *emergency response*. This one should probably be a "central plus" cooperative system. You are certainly going to want some "eye in the sky" surveillance and response team supporting the entire B2B net. Network outages spread, have cascading effects, and require quick cooperative handling. SWAT teams at several levels with a tested response and repair mode are key. But an outage on an individual segment of a net may or may not be a subject for common response. If it's down for unscheduled maintenance (something broke), then setting up bypasses and load leveling through other segments of the net are necessary, and the appropriate combined network ops groups should be on the job. Now, suppose a virus, denial of service attack, social engineering, or hacker shows up in one location. The entire net needs to know—pronto!

What about *design, implementation, and deployment* of trust functions? These are usually best structured on a cooperative project office basis with lots and lots of liaison and attachment of specialists to the application and infrastructure design and development teams.

And the *assurance* functions? We take them on in the next chapter.

INTEGRATE–ISOLATE? CENTRALIZE–DECENTRALIZE? COORDINATE!

You have seen in previous chapters that many security and control functions support more than one trust objective. What this should suggest to you is that segmenting trust objectives or technologies into isolated programs can sometimes be counterproductive.

Wherever you can, the obvious answer is to separate responsibilities as necessary to get the job done but actively and comprehensively coordinate. Coordination is crucial in B2B, where many functions affecting an e-Trust program will probably be farmed out to other players, including third-party vendors.

POLICIES, STANDARDS, GUIDELINES, PROCEDURES, JOB DESCRIPTIONS, MISSION STATEMENTS

A fear often expressed about complex e-Trust programs is the prospect of spawning a major bureaucracy to support it. The concern can be real. There is no escaping the fact that you will be introducing one or several new administrative and technical processes into the mix or some part of it, and as a result, restricting some people's freedom of operation.

That's why early manager and user "buy-in" throughout the alliance is so important. A sense of authorship and proprietorship among those who must implement and modify the program to their own needs can do a great deal to defuse the bureaucratic image.

But even if you can't make the image go away completely, you can still take major steps to streamline things. There are two major culprits:

1. Organizational overkill (Why use one department when twelve will do?), turf wars, and organization chart roulette
2. Procedural overkill (How can we micro-manage a program into paralysis?)

We have spoken at some length about organization and standards. I'd like to revisit policies, standards, procedures, and guidelines here, exploring their characteristics and implications; outlining their use and misuse; and providing criteria for choosing the right vehicle.

LET'S TALK ABOUT AN e-TRUST POLICY

What is a policy? Oddly enough, there is a lot of room for disagreement here. I have seen *policy* manuals that take up yards of space on bookshelves. I have also seen policies cut into marble facades over doors. Although size itself doesn't define the policy, it gives a pretty good indicator about what the enterprise thinks it should be and do. *I believe a policy is a high-level statement of enterprise (netexchange, netmarket) beliefs, goals, and objectives, and the general means for their attainment for a specified subject area.* The last part of the definition, "and the general means for their attainment for a specified subject area," is what often causes overblown policies. The *general means* become "very specific and detailed means" and the *specified area* (in this case, e-Trust) becomes far more detailed, covering subjects like password management. I don't believe you can have a policy on passwords. Standards, guidelines, absolutely.

I further believe that the choice of vehicle should start from the bottom up. If the guideline will do it for you, stop right there. I have a special phobia about standards that aren't really standards. We'll discuss standards, guidelines, and procedures in more detail in short order. For the moment, let's stick with policies, specifically e-Trust policies.

WHAT ARE SOME BENEFITS OF HAVING AN e-TRUST POLICY?

In no order of priority and no pretense that the list is totally comprehensive, here goes. (For ease of notation, *enterprise* equals enterprise, extranet, netmarket, or netexchange):

1. It helps the enterprise develop a prioritized value for information.
2. It's an enabling platform for protection strategies, plans, and implementation.
3. It provides a clear and consistent internal statement for member management and employee guidance.
4. Along with standards, guidelines, and procedures, it provides a basic yardstick for review and assessment.
5. It provides a clear, consistent, and demonstrable statement for all interested parties (e.g., stockholders, customers, vendors, processing partners, regulators, auditors, the media, and the public).
6. It contributes to the effectiveness and direction of overall enterprise risk management.
7. Finally, it may assist in or be required for responding to legal and regulatory requirements.

WHY A FORMAL POLICY?

Many organizations get along with informal policies, passed along by word of mouth, custom, folklore, and the like. Why an explicit, written e-Trust policy? Some of these reasons you've heard before.

1. E-Trust is different enough to warrant a specific, explicit statement. Put another way, e-Trust is not an intuitively obvious process. In fact, parts of it run counter to our basic instincts.
2. There is a great deal of ethical ambiguity about privacy, confidentiality, and intellectual property.
3. There is also great deal of legal and regulatory ambiguity, indeed conflict.
4. An explicit policy may be mandated.
5. As a common base for management, an explicit policy is far superior to implicit, even if the explicit statement is generalized and puts heavy reliance on individual management judgment.
6. Only an explicit statement can be convincing in courts of law, in a customer contract, in vendor relations, in acquisitions, and in public relations.

WHAT ARE SOME OF THE CHARACTERISTICS OF A GOOD e-TRUST POLICY?

They are not much different from those required of any policy. A good e-Trust policy should be

- *Targeted*—Consider very carefully what modes, processes, entities, and information the e-Trust policy will cover. Is this a single e-Trust policy on all aspects of B2B interchange and partnership or just the information exchange? The decision can make quite a difference.
- *Simple and understandable*—The language should be written to be understood by the least knowledgeable individuals required to abide by it. If that comes out as "Dick and Jane meet e-Trust," so be it. Jargon, special organizational references, and so on should be minimized.
- *Applicable*—This is especially important if you have been borrowing or researching the policies of other enterprises. Simple question: Do the characteristics, requirements, and environments stated or implied in the policy actually describe

your case, especially a B2B environment? If not, get them out of there.

- *Feasible*—Can the average bear do what you're asking? This isn't the same as item 2. I may understand quite well that you want me to fly on my own power. The problem is, I can't.

- *Enforceable*—This has a kinship with feasibility, but it has a slightly different spin. If you state or imply that certain activities will be subject to sanctions and punishment or that certain individuals are charged with enforcing these rules, make sure they actually can be enforced.

- *Phased implementation*—Any new e-Trust policy, if it speaks to dates at all, should allow for gradual development of the desired situation and results. It should also facilitate revision and modification.

- *Positive guidance, not prohibition and punishment*—I find a practically unbroken stream of prohibitions a disheartening form of behavioral guidance. You are not trying to entrap, threaten, intimidate, or even inhibit individuals in performing their legitimate activities. You are trying to assist them in performing them safely and with appropriate integrity. A high violation count is a sure sign that your program isn't working. "Gotcha" has no place in e-Trust vocabulary, especially in a policy.

- *Avoid "all-or-nothing" statements*—Words like "ensure," "absolute," "total," "complete," "eliminate," and "guarantee" are terms that most organizations are reluctant to put in their contracts with others. Think twice about putting them in your e-Trust policy. They set objectives that you may neither desire nor be able to meet. They could also be used against you in a contractual sense if you publish your policy externally and then fail to reach the stated objectives. I can hear it now, "But, Mr. B2B, it states right here in your e-Trust policy that you *intend to ensure total protection for all* information assets developed by you or given over to your care and use. My client, and I'm sure the courts will agree with us, thinks that by permitting that virus to affect your files that contained our information, you have fallen far short of your fiduciary responsibilities and the goals and objectives you publicly proclaim in your policy document. Therefore we are seeking. . . ."

- *Enable the concept of risk acceptance, as well as risk avoidance.* There are certain risks that prudent business people and organizational administrators have to take. The alternative measures may be too costly, insufficiently effective, or flat-out impossible. Don't write a policy that speaks about eliminating risk. Use "reducing" or "mitigating." Make sure you don't undermine the position of management by making the prudent acceptance of certain risks no longer acceptable.

- *Make sure the level of content is appropriate to the vehicle.* We've discussed standards, procedures, and guidelines earlier. Each has a different purpose and different level of detail. They are differentiated, not so much by the nature of the content as the level of the content. A lengthy policy is a sure sign of the upward creep of standards and procedures.

What difference does it make? Plenty, if you subscribe to the idea that policy can only be issued by senior management and requires lengthy review and sign-off. Going to the Board or Executive Committee (there may be many in B2B) for every functional shift in an e-Trust program may become a bit much. They may not understand what you're doing, either. Insist that a policy should be a relatively short, high-level statement, providing clear, straightforward, enterprise-wide guidance, especially if it is going public or external.

Structurally, the policy should enable and should generally refer to the subject matter of standards, procedures, and guidelines without actually cataloging them. The standards, procedures, and guidelines should cite the enabling authority.

WHAT SHOULD A POLICY LOOK LIKE, SOUND LIKE, AND CONTAIN?

The actual format will probably be governed by whatever policy manual structures, if any, your enterprise group and partners use. Above all else, make it readable.

As to content, the following list applies not just to policies but to standards, procedures, and guidelines. A given topic will probably be covered in a sentence or two in a policy. It may be the subject of an entire standard, and there could be several procedures and guidelines to support the standard. Notice, please, I said "may" and "could," not "must" and "should."

A SHORT DIGRESSION (WHAT, ANOTHER ONE?)

I know we spoke about minimizing bureaucracy, and it sounds like I'm doing the opposite. Not really. I'm trying to make the case for giving the appropriate level of guidance to the audience for whom it's intended, without building a gigantic library of microinstructions and an administrative structure to go with it.

In some situations, a policy statement and a few guidelines may be all you need. In others, because of the far-flung diversity of the organization coupled with strong interdependency, there may be a need for more extensive guidance and instruction to keep everyone consistent and efficient. In the second circumstance, there also needs to be a very skeptical attitude toward policy—standard—guideline expansion. "Why do we need this?" should be the first question raised every time a new one is proposed or an old one revised upward in scope or content. You'll see in a few moments how I feel about the use of standards and the problems they can cause. End of digression.

CONTENT

Here's a suggested list of items and topics for "enabling mention" in a policy usually in no more than a sentence or two. They are also candidates for expansion through standards, guidelines, or procedures:

1. Introduction
   a. Purpose—What is this for?
   b. Definitions—What are we talking about?
   c. Authority—Who's the prime mover behind this?
2. Supporting background and rationale
   a. Why do we need this?
   b. How did we get here, and where are we going?
3. Scope
   a. Types of environments covered
   b. Types of information resources covered
   c. Organizational entities covered, including outside entities such as contractors, vendors, customers, and processing partners
   d. Types of issues addressed
   e. Exclusions (optional)
4. Supporting specialist organizations
5. Development / deployment
6. Access management

 7. Risk assessment

 8. Risk management

 9. Security and continuity strategies (preventive/reactive)

10. Architecture / requirements

11. Technical design / specification / standards

12. Administrative design / specification / standards

13. Media control, declassification, and destruction

14. Review and test

15. Enforcement and violation handling

16. Research

17. Education, training awareness, external relations

18. Policy (standard, etc.) revision and update process

You may wish to include other subjects. They may be standards, procedures, or guidelines content. Certain of the topics mentioned above may appear elsewhere, such as human resources, financial or technology policies, or procedures. Some of the topics may not seem relevant to an e-Trust policy, but before you drop them, think your decision through carefully.

Does policy have to be lengthy? Quite the contrary. We have created policies for clients that address that entire list in as few as five or six pages. Nor does every policy item require a separate supporting standard, procedure, or guideline. Many of those that do can be kept short. The simple point is that no single level works everywhere. The most important determining factor on depth of detail and length is the nature of the audience for whom the policy, standard, procedure, or guideline is being written.

A few other notes. Auditors use standards, procedures, and even guidelines as measurements of control effectiveness. Read your procedures and ask how an auditor would read and interpret them. There's no point in making things vague so the auditors won't have a source for finding specific violations. They'll just write you up for having vague standards and procedures. Trust me.

DOCTRINAL PURITY

This next comment may anger a few people. Slavish compliance with "best practices" and purity of process for its own sake has to be tempered by practical considerations, especially cost and resources. The doctrinally correct way, whatever that is, may not be the most practical way. On the other hand, the most practical way is also not the way that costs you the least or gets the monkey off your back. It is the way that accomplishes the objectives set out, in the most cost-effective manner. Some compromise is implicit in that process.

Don't ever release a policy, standard, procedure, or guideline without first testing it on a sample of those who have to live with it. Role play. Try to teach someone new how to carry out the process described, by following the procedures strictly as written. See what happens. Determine in advance how you're going to enforce it. If everybody ignores it, what will you do? Will you even know?

Policies, standards, procedures, and guidelines do not promote or enforce themselves. They rely on management to do that. Unless you have the affected (not just responsible) management on your side before you take standards and procedures out for implementation, you may be digging yourself a large and uncomfortable hole.

HOW ABOUT e-TRUST-RELATED MISSION STATEMENTS AND JOB DESCRIPTIONS?

There are two general groups for whom e-Trust-related mission statements and job descriptions are appropriate:

1. e-Trust specialist departments and individuals.
2. e-Trust content in nonspecialized missions and job descriptions. This is where the users, owners, and service suppliers would be covered, as well as e-Trust-related staffs such as human relations, general security, legal, external relations, MIS, and telecommunications. This last group may contribute to the e-Trust process directly as well as in the role of user, owner, or service supplier.

Mission statements serve three general purposes:

1. Organizational planning
2. Individual and group guidance
3. Measurement

They should be designed to serve all three goals. Assuming your organization places any credence at all in the use and value of mission statements and job descriptions, there are several characteristics you should seek to develop:

- Set priorities. Mission statements that are laundry lists of every possible responsibility are usually greeted with the disdain they deserve. If e-Trust functions are a part-time function (some will be), build your e-Trust requirements into the overall context of the job being performed by the current incumbents. If the job is full time and brand new, it is even more important to establish a sense of proportion about what is really important and what is not.
- Write mission statements and job descriptions with the steady state (ha!) environment as a target. Start-up tasks and special projects should be reserved for individual agreements and setting of periodic goals and objectives.
- Write the statements and descriptions in terms that can be measured, at least qualitatively, if not quantitatively, and as unambiguously as possible. This is for your benefit as well as the assignee's. People are much more secure and effective if they can determine for themselves whether they are doing a good job and can have a reasonable expectation that management, using the same yardstick, will arrive at the same conclusion.
- After you've developed your job descriptions, ask the incumbents or potential incumbents to play back their understanding and compare it to your intentions. You may often be surprised.
- Make sure the functions, relationships, and work to be performed can be carried out by the people and organizational structures to which they've been assigned. Take special cognizance of the skills, experience, job level, and pay scales of the individuals and the classes of responsibilities they would normally be expected to take on. Basic as this may sound, remember that the population of individuals you will be working with will normally be small and the number of tasks large. The temptation to get all the work assigned to someone can often produce some unrealistic mission statements and job descriptions.
- Once again, make sure the jobs and missions fit the culture of your organization. By all means, seek guidance from other enterprises and sources, but test each element described against your own requirements and priorities before you accept them.

One last word about bureaucracy before we change the topic a bit. In order to be as comprehensive as possible, I've presented a very wide spectrum of duties and activities associated with e-Trust in this chapter. In the process, the result may seem very bureaucratic, indeed.

Do you need them all? For a fully effective program, all of the functions should be present, but the degree to which you carry them out is strongly conditioned by your business needs. A large, information dependent enterprise with widely distributed information processing facilities, armies of users, scores of developers, and mission-critical applications is obviously in a totally different dimension from a small or intermediate business that wants to protect a couple of PCs.

MANAGEMENT

I am not going to catalog all the different types of B2B e-Trust management positions that are possible. I do want to mention two that are emerging.

B2B Chief Security Officer

This individual has the general responsibilities usually assigned to enterprise security officers—only at the B2B level. Like all the other structures we discussed, this title and its responsibilities have to be crafted and implemented very carefully so as not to impinge on individual enterprise management or leave gaps in coverage.

B2B Chief Privacy Officer (A new gun in town)

On the front page of the February 12, 2001, Business Day section of the *New York Times,* there appeared an interesting article, "First Line of Defense—Chief Privacy Officers Forge Evolving Corporate Roles." The article notes that there are at least 100 U.S. privacy chiefs as of the date of publication, including CPOs at IBM, AT&T, and Eastman Kodak.

In a sidebar, a former associate from my IBM days in privacy protection, Alan F. Westin, former professor at Columbia University and now a corporate consultant, recommends the following duties for a CPO (bracketed additions are mine):

- Set up a privacy committee.
- Study and assess privacy risks of all operations involving personal data.
- Develop a company [entity] privacy code.

- Interact with concerned regulators and consumers, and provide a contact point for consumers [and all data subjects]
- Create and oversee employee [and management] privacy training.
- Monitor privacy laws and regulations and the company's [entity's] compliance.
- Conduct privacy reviews of all new products and Internet services.

Do you need a CPO in your B2B environment? It will, of course, depend on the nature of your industries and the amount of sensitive information a data subject may wish to have protected.

Finally, to finish this chapter, let's ask this question: *Do you need a chief e-Trust officer?* I don't know the answer for your specific needs, but from everything we've discussed in this and previous chapters, I hope we've helped you come up with a sound rationale for creating one or not.

I hope we have given you some material to discuss with your staffs or management that will prime the pump on organization considerations. In the next chapter we discuss e-Trust assurance—a subject not to be treated lightly.

21

e-Business Assurance

Now, let's spend a little time on the "a" words—assurance, assessment, audit, attestation. They are not the exclusive province of accountants. Do not skip this chapter if you are a designer, business manager, or implementer. e-Trust is all about mutual assurance. As you enter B2B, you are also moving more deeply into collaborative reviews and self-assessments. In other words, you're not just the target any longer. You're the assessor, too. We believe that assurance is just that—a program to enhance confidence at every level and on every subject that can seriously affect the quality, service, cost, and trust of the B2B environment.

You will recall, I hope, the discussions we had in Chapter 6 about the different characteristics and requirements for e-Trust. High on the list of requirements were reciprocity and demonstrability. Most of our illustrations called for some assurance mechanism to enhance the comfort of B2B partners. All were serious business initiatives that need evaluation for cost-effectiveness and correctness. We looked at security and control technologies.

We also listed in Chapter 12 some of the external forces requiring cooperation, caution, and compliance. We've been raising the issue of complexity and shared process throughout our discussions. We've looked at standards, policies, and organizations. Finally, from an economic and social standpoint, B2B is serious stuff—often impacting not just the success but the survival of the entities involved. For all these reasons and probably a hundred more, assurance programs must be a major order of business.

A GENTLE DISCLAIMER

Assessment, audit, and attestation processes are all subject to stringent professional standards of form and language. Since this book is intended to provide a general overview for a wide audience, we have opted for ease of reading and comprehension. Our language and descriptions in this chapter will be accurate but, with a few exceptions, lacking in rigid precision and accounting words of art. Therefore, this chapter should not be regarded as the complete or definitive professional statements of Deloitte & Touche on the subjects discussed. We will be more than happy, on request, to supply you with specific, definitive, comprehensive, and scrupulously edited material that will satisfy those requirements.

WHAT'S INVOLVED?

We're going to examine assurance processes under B2B. *We're using the term "assurance" in this chapter to describe assessment programs and methods that create the required levels of confidence about the areas under consideration for the benefit of parties concerned.* Obviously, this level of confidence (assurance) will vary widely with the arena, governing rules, the object, and the audience.

We're taking a middle of the road approach that should be recognizable to audit and assessment professionals as well as security and control specialists but still resonate with any business or technical people who have participated in or been on the receiving end of these investigations, analyses, and reports. We'll cover the following in the context of B2B environments:

- Types of assurance
- Control objectives, standards, and other metrics
- Scope
- Responsibilities
- Review cycles, priorities, and frequency
- Methods, procedures, mechanisms, and performance standards
- Reporting

TYPES OF ASSURANCE

As usual, one size does not fit all. Assurance can vary in purpose, audience, subject matter, and the level of confidence required. For example, I'd want to know a bit more about the evidence used, methods employed, and professional credentials of someone who formally attested to a manufacturer's claims for the value of an expensive device than someone who told me a specific soup was delicious. I'd especially want to know all about those assurance processes if I was the one who, in turn, had to testify before Congress or on nationwide TV about the benefits and harmlessness of that device.

Attest, audit, and assessment are not the same, even though most of the world's population may think so, if they think about the subjects at all. We will use precise words of art here because there's an important set of concepts that often gets lost or mangled. It's important that we get them straight for our B2B explorations.

Attest

Dictionary definition: to confirm, corroborate, or verify

An attest engagement is defined in AICPA Statement on Standards for Attestation Engagements (SSAE) 10, *Attestation Standards: Revision and Recodification* (AT 101) as an engagement in which "a certified public accountant in the practice of public accounting (hereinafter referred to as a *practitioner*) is engaged to issue or does issue an examination, a review, or an agreed-upon procedures report on subject matter, or an assertion about subject matter, that is the responsibility of another party." Ordinarily, the objective of such an engagement is to provide assurance about the reliability of the subject matter or the assertion.

We often shorthand that statement as "providing an opinion." Let's take a look at that definition again. The confusion usually arises around the subject matter of the opinion. In a strict sense, what the practitioner is doing is *formally corroborating management's claims about its own condition*—no more, no less. Most attestations have been financial in nature, although there is nothing that prevents a qualified third party from formally attesting on other matters. But, in so doing, they are putting themselves in a position of potential liability. In the case of companies registered with the U.S. Securities and Exchange Commission, there is a formal and extensive set of required items that management must, by law, address in their financial statements and have attested by certified public accountants. This requirement varies from country to country. In the case of B2Bs, registration, jurisdiction, and levels of attestation can get complex. For example, whether an exchange or net-market as a separate entity would have to register, and where, would depend on its structure and form of incorporation.

Attest Is Not for Everyone or Every Situation

You can see where formal attestation is often a necessary component of B2B assurance. "So what's the big problem? Order up attestations for everyone, and let's stop fooling around with all this other stuff." Hold on, while we explain a few facts of life. Accounting firms have not survived and prospered by blithely corroborating any claims management cares to make. The claims must be within our scope of competence. Sufficient verifiable evidence must exist to support a thorough examination.

The procedures to be followed must either correspond to legal or regulatory requirements or fall into the category of "agreed upon procedures" in which management and the auditor agree on the objectives, scope, procedures, and purpose of the attestation.

The audit process itself must be conducted according to rigorous professional standards, and the results must be reviewed by several levels of partner–practitioners. Finally, the opinion issued will be very carefully structured, worded, and circumscribed to limit misinterpretation and unwarranted extrapolation. In other words, we're not kidding around here. In fact, while they're not very welcome, adverse opinions are not that uncommon. In extreme cases, audit firms have resigned from engagements and relationships.

So, while an attested opinion (a redundancy) from a qualified and professionally certified third party sounds like the thing to get, it can be costly, demanding on your resources, narrower than you desire, and, in many cases, overkill for the type of confidence you wish to develop. Although attestation may be the only alternative to satisfy legal, regulatory, or contractual requirements, it is not the only available approach. That is why we offer other forms of professional assurance. We'll get to them in a moment. But let's wrestle with another term that can be bothersome in more than one way. It, too, is often loosely used. I remember a group of college students who didn't understand a colleague's presentation about his profession for the first few minutes because they thought auditors were students who attended class for no credit.

Audit

Dictionary definition: to formally check or review

We are going to try to simplify the landscape a bit by simply defining audit as *the formal, professional process employed by competent practitioners to produce an attestation or other statements of assurance.* That definition is not rigorously precise or professionally sanctioned but is close enough for our purposes. It can apply to external as well as internal audits and a variety of other professional assessments as well.

SO WHAT OTHER KINDS OF ASSURANCE ARE THERE?

Quite an array, actually. For the B2B environment, with its broad range of "interested" parties, assurance can come in a variety of forms. We'll touch on several of them here.

Compilations of anecdotal or statistical information are one form of assurance tools. Analysis of targets exclusively for management's internal use is another. "How are we doing? Are we in compliance with regulation x or law y?" Results are not for external consumption, but management expects and is expected to make business and technical decisions based on those results. This is often the role of internal auditors, security specialists, quality, safety, HR, and a variety of other staffs inside the entity. However, external professional service firms are often brought in to assist or, if the area is beyond the current capabilities of the client, to design, manage, and conduct these reviews. A wide range of performance reviews also fit this category.

If you engage an external professional services group, make sure at the outset that the purpose and scope is clearly understood and agreed by all parties. We often have clients who wait until an internal assessment is completed. If they like the results, they want to publish them. We often have to disappoint them, unless the review was conducted according to attest standards. This process needs to be examined carefully in a B2B environment. Who is management? When does the distribution of a report go from internal to external? What is its purpose?

Third-party reviews are an important assessment tool, but the name can be confusing. It is an assessment or audit conducted on behalf of a service entity (ASP, CSP, portal, service bureau, netexchange, netmarket) to be presented to the auditors of its customers, partners and, occasionally stakeholders. Its purpose, frankly, is to keep a horde of different audit firms, each representing a specific customer, from deluging the service supplier with individual demands to conduct their own assessment. It may not eliminate the problem entirely, but at least it usually drastically reduces the number.

One professional firm, hired by the service entity, prepares and conducts an assessment of the service in question using rules and procedures accepted throughout the profession. The results of that assessment are then passed on to the auditors representing the customers and users. Although they are not obligated to (and occasionally will not) accept the results without further question or analysis, most audit firms will not insist on duplicating the steps already performed by the service auditor. Usually, if there is a challenge, it is for interpretation or coverage of additional matters.

You will hear the term SAS-70 misused in this context to cover all forms of servicer reviews. SAS-70 is actually a narrowly defined term used by the accounting community, implying certain professional standards. It frequently has attest status. Don't use the term unless you precisely mean it. Third-party reviews can take on a number of different shapes, sizes, and colors. The frustrating part of the expression in the B2B context is, Who's the third party? The servicer is a third party to its customers. The servicer's auditor is an objective third party to the customers' auditors. The customers' auditors are third parties to the servicer. Oh well.

Expert witnesses are called upon to appear in a hearing, litigation, or other dispute to give evidence but not to specifically attest to the claims of one or another party. The primary beneficiaries should be the parties making the judgment, not the litigants.

Technical test and evaluation. In 1998, I was responsible for developing the Deloitte & Touche Secure e-Business Technology Center. One, but certainly not its only, mission was to *perform research* and *conduct evaluations on security offerings* for vendors as well as potential users. As the marketplace becomes increasingly saturated with solutions and products, there is an increasing need for third parties to provide both internal and external evaluations and recommendations analogous to those performed by the Underwriter's Laboratories on the one extreme, Consumer Reports in the middle, and a variety of publications and critics on the other. Again, check the nature, purpose, object, and competence of the review and reviewers.

Special purpose tools, as the name suggests, can be any form of evaluation the parties concerned want it to be. We'll talk a bit more about them under the next characteristic—scope. Because B2B is such a complex and variable environment and because e-Trust is critical to its success, you can expect new and innovative assurance processes to enter the arena.

Risk Assessment

Risk assessment does not lend itself to attestation and is seldom projected as such. Essentially, a risk assessment looks at five things:

1. The potential threats to the entity and their likelihood of occurring. (A number of hostile countries have ICBMs. Some of them are aimed at me.)
2. The current vulnerability of the entity to those threats. (We have a fleet of missile submarines, but they are strictly retaliatory.)

3. The risks associated with the current situation. (We could get hurt.)

4. Possible mitigation strategies and their value in reducing vulnerability and risk. (SDI is outlandishly expensive and years away. How about a combination of diplomacy, economic incentives, a cultural exchange, and veiled threats of our own? No hostages, please.)

5. Risk management: Accept the risk as is; manage it down; insure against the financial consequences if you can get coverage; begin an active campaign of prayer and good works; or make the investment to eliminate the vulnerability. It's more difficult to eliminate the threat.

WebTrust, SysTrust, CA Trust, and Their Other Relations

WebTrust are a family of assessment offerings designed and developed jointly by the AICPA and CICA (the Canadian Institute of Chartered Accountants) specifically for use in Web-based environments. Initially developed for B2C entities such as e-Commerce websites, ISPs, ASPs, portals, and CSPs, it is currently being adapted or, more properly, thoroughly redesigned to fit the very different needs of the B2B community. WebTrust is intended to provide individual e-Commerce sites with the ability to publicly (on their Web page and elsewhere) declare that they have been examined by an AICPA/CICA firm and have met the requirements of the specific WebTrust seal they are displaying. Periodic reviews are required to keep possession of the seal which can be technologically removed by the AICPA/CICA in the event of disqualification.

The process covers:

1. Business practices and information privacy practices
2. Transaction integrity controls
3. Information protection controls

More information can be obtained at the organizations' websites.

RECOMMENDATIONS

Now that we've examined a long list of assurance types, let's zero in on the other, and usually more important, purpose for assessments, *professional recommendations for solution, mitigation, or improvement.* Although a report card for public display or internal consumption is indeed valuable, anyone who has been to a parent–teacher conference knows the next question always is, "What do you recommend?" Here, of course, is frequently the major value to a B2B initiative of both the audit and consulting sides of the professional services community. "Now that you've told me what you think of me, Consultant or Audit Person, based on your experience and the information available to you, tell me about best practices in our area. Show me some industry or technology benchmarks. Using appropriate care for their confidentiality, what are the other guys doing? Help me design an enhancement plan. Help me implement and manage it. Help me evaluate it after it's deployed." And so the cycle repeats itself.

In an attest situation, recommendations may fall into several categories—those that must be adopted immediately before an "unqualified" (no provisos) opinion can be issued; those that should be implemented in a timely fashion, and so-called "value added" comments. In other forms of assessment, recommendations can provide advice on improvement, mitigation, or suggestions for the future. We are not going to catalog all the forms that recommendations can take. Suffice it to say that although we covered the topic in two paragraphs, it is a key component of the assurance process. Assurance procedures are designed to help and improve, not condemn miscreants to the firing squad.

SCOPE

The most obvious difference between financial audits and B2B assessments are the entities and relationships they cover. Financial audits deal with specific entities registered with the U.S. Securities and Exchange Commission. A similar rubric applies in most other developed countries. Even if a B2B relationship (netmarket, netexchange) is structured and governed as a separately registered company, there will be gaps in the coverage. As we note a bit later, the assurance scope of a B2B is more than representations of its individual parts.

Before we go on to examine the various waterfronts and depths that our B2B assessments should cover, there's another topic associated with the financial audit that makes the scope of its report and comments different and not as useful for our purposes.

Financial audits, as you may suspect, cover all the topics that are required to attest that management's claims are a fair representation of the enterprise's financial condition, and that they have been developed and presented in accordance with generally accepted accounting principles. But the attest team, in developing its opinion, does not concentrate on each topic at the same depth each year. They cycle (see below). For one cycle the revenue stream may be the primary object for detailed study, the next, the expense stream. One-time topics that affect the financial state of the organization, such as new obligations, mergers, or acquisitions, will be treated as they occur or affect the financial condition.

Even though the audit is paid for by the company under examination, the audit firm, in order to maintain its third-party objectivity, determines its own scope and cycles. How confident would you be as a stockholder if the audit opinion covered only those items selected by management? However, as part of the assessment process, the audit team may examine related areas that it believes are, or should be, of interest to management. Needless to say, to keep the assessment process leading to the opinion within bounds from an expense and resource standpoint, and to produce timely results, careful scoping is necessary.

The Matter of Materiality

Another consideration also affects the scope of the auditor's formal comments: *the financial materiality of any specific transaction, event, or condition.* "What's that?" It is a judgment on the part of the audit firm as to whether such an item has sufficient importance to meaningfully affect the validity of management's representations. As you can imagine, this judgment is based on professional standards, experience, precedent, and a fair amount of regulatory direction. "But you didn't say what's material." That's right. I didn't, and I can't because it will vary with the situation and the enterprise. Two examples:

1. A million-dollar error by a giant global enterprise in calculating or reporting its revenue, when discovered after the opinion is issued, may be too small to warrant withdrawal of the attestation and a restatement of the company's condition for that period. (That doesn't mean that the company's reporting precision is permitted to be limited to the closest million.) That same million-dollar error could mean life or death for a dot.com.
2. Following the same logic, a theft of several thousand dollars from a company's assets may or may not require a separate comment. However, if the theft was committed by a member

of the company's executive committee, the added impact on the governance of the organization would put it in higher relief.

The point of all this is to show that the scope and orientation of the financial audit process may not always make it the best vehicle for the types of B2B assurance you are looking for. It will cover some portions of the waterfront, but not all.

If that's the case, what other matters should be covered by B2B assurance processes? We can group the topics several different ways:

A sample of other B2B e-Trust-related *regulatory* matters:

- Privacy
- Data protection
- Equal economic opportunities
- Consumer protection
- Intellectual property rights
- Interstate and transborder commerce
- Tax and customs concerns
- Antimonopoly (Is a netexchange or netmarket a cartel?)
- Defense and public safety
- Ecology
- On-the-job health and safety
- Racketeering/money laundering

Other *enterprise and cross enterprise* e-Trust assurance matters:

- Governance and structure
- Business processes from end to end
- Applications across entities
- Data quality
- Management across entities
- Policies, agreements, standards
- Human resources
- Suppliers and outsourcers
- Business infrastructure
- Business process management
- Project performance

- Crisis management
- Security

Technology-related e-Trust assurance matters:

- Network infrastructure
- Nodes, paths, traffic types, end points,
- Network technologies
- Protective technologies
- Certificate and registration authorities
- Architecture and design
- Technical standards
- Process centers
- Compatibility and interface concerns
- Development, test, and deployment
- Data management and data quality
- Intrusion, virus and denial of service detection and response
- Availability and disaster recovery
- Staff competence and certification

CONTROL OBJECTIVES, STANDARDS, AND OTHER METRICS

OK, so we've established the major forms an assessment can take and said something about scope. What do you use for metrics when you apply these assessments to the areas under examination? As we said, in the financial audit, the major question is whether generally accepted accounting principles are being met. However, in just about every type of assessment we also have to ask whether approved objectives of control have been established by management, and how well are they being met. *They are management's objectives that must be set and met by them and corroborated by the auditor.* On the financial side of things, an established body of control objectives usually applies. Of course, management gets a lot of help from the control specialists and auditors in setting them up. But nothing much happens unless and until there is agreement on both sides about the objectives.

We sometimes shorthand these objectives with titles like "separation of duties, multiple levels of control, complete and comprehensive transaction records, or appropriate protective methods." Under each of these are developed a more specific set of questions and considerations that should be tailored to the enterprise in question and answered in a level of detail appropriate for the scope.

Now comes the interesting question (at least to me): What are the control objectives for a B2B environment, and how do we establish them? (That's two questions.) For the typical business entity managing an extranet, the enterprise-related *business control* objectives would probably remain essentially the same. You would probably put additional stress on quality, process and data integrity, authorization, accountability, and nonrepudiation. Certainly, the mutuality, demonstrability, and reciprocity factors must be accounted for.

However, your *application* and *technology*-related control objectives would be more complex, ranging all over the nature and characteristics of network and the business process centers. Application controls would speak to how the business control objectives are met within the implementations, and also how the applications themselves are controlled and protected. Technology objectives would concentrate on reliability, integrity, consistency, and resistance to attack. Appropriate and complete control objectives are critical, but that is another and very different book.

But what of the netexchange and the netmarket, with their more complex structures and relationships? Are their control objectives simply the sum of the objectives of all the players, or are there new and overarching ones that need to be established as well? Is a different viewpoint required? I believe it is. A B2B relationship is best evaluated as a functioning network—not just the topology and technology, but all the network functions, especially the business processes.

Developing B2B control objectives is not a trivial exercise. Simply consider the number of enterprises and their supporting professional services groups that will be involved in reaching agreement. It should make the process interesting. "Wait, Mr. Consultant, are you telling me that your profession hasn't developed a common set of objectives to deal with this B2B animal?" At a high level of abstraction, of course. But the specifics of each B2B will force tailoring as we descend from the more generic to specific requirements and ultimately to framing individual questions. We're all working to expand the literature and guidance on this area, but as we've noted before, individual B2Bs, even within the same industry context, may be quite different. This difference will apply to some of their control priorities.

Regulations and Standards

Now, if control objectives developed by the players themselves were the only metrics we had to deal with, life would still be complicated but manageable. However, no B2B operates in a regulatory or professional vacuum. So we must also look to the external world for additional guidance on measurements. As we told you in Chapter 12, this will come in a variety of ways, especially for international or global B2Bs.

Summing Up on Metrics

So, where does this leave us? With at least three major classes of yardsticks for a B2B.

1. The applicable control objectives of the individual or collective members
2. The control objectives of the B2B itself as a functioning network-based process
3. The regulations and standards that apply to 1 or 2 above

The saving grace, if there is one, is that the there are many sources at your disposal.

RESPONSIBILITIES

Let's dispose of regulatory or professional standards audits immediately. Whether it's the Controller of the Currency; Public Utilities Commissions; the National Transportation Safety Board; laboratory, institutional, or professional accreditation entities; the Internal Revenue Service; or their international or global equivalents; they are there and must be accommodated. The difference is in most B2B situations there will be more of them simply as a result of the business combinations. They will have differing and sometimes conflicting requirements, not just on assurance objectives and metrics but on how and by whom the assessment will be performed. They may also just appear as preemptive strikes. As you formulate your B2B excursions, look at this area for potential storm warnings and variable winds. You can't do too much to change the weather, but you can ride it out effectively with a little preparation and foresight.

Assurance Processes Management Can and Should Control

We decided that relying solely on the financial audits of the B2B members or an incorporated netexchange or netmarket wasn't sufficient or entirely appropriate for e-Trust purposes. What are some others? By this point in our discussion, we may have given you the false impression that we believe accountants run the only assurance game in town. Clearly, this is not the case. If we have given insufficient attention to other sources, we are about to make amends in the rest of this chapter. The fact is that many different agencies are at the B2B's disposal, and each one can operate separately or in concert. *The major difference is that their scopes and timetables are set by management.*

Internal audit, for example, has its own responsibilities and agendas. Here again, we have the interesting issue of internal auditors acting for each separate member or in concert for the B2B or both. Internal audit was not set up to shadow or duplicate the functions of the external auditors. They might assist and supplement, as necessary, in financially material areas, but they can't be allowed to bias or influence the external audit. Their primary mission and value is to assess and report on a much wider range of matters significant to management. Their priorities are set and approved by management and often the audit committee of the board of directors. They may range over regulatory compliance, security, privacy, and internal accounting and reporting processes. The missions, number, and specific skills of the internal audit group vary widely from enterprise to enterprise. They may report to the CFO but they sometimes report directly to the CEO. Needless to say, they have an important and wideband role in e-Trust assurance.

Information security management also has an extremely important role to play. In addition to security administration, incident handling and reporting, policy and guideline development and participation in application, system and network design, development and deployment, many information security groups also maintain a strong review and assessment process of their own. Many enterprises are building up this group for the specific purpose of dealing with networked environments. They should.

External sources of assurance. We're back! "That didn't last long." This time we're in our role as consultants and we have lots of company. Clearly, the nature of B2Bs and e-Trust as we've been presenting it can create a very broad and variable array of assurance requirements. Frankly, no one individual or organization has a lock on all the expertise required. Consulting alliances and subcontracts are becoming common in these areas. Another form of coopetition.

In today's marketplace, technology and process specialties abound. Selection of consultants to conduct assessments is not an easy proposition, and knowledge is only one criteria. Assessments by an outside party can be disruptive if they are not properly managed and if the consultant is not sensitive to the time and resource constraints under which the client is operating. Data gathering should be done as much as possible on a one-stop shopping basis. Daily social gab fests with clients while the meter is running is frowned on by management. Consultants trying to preemptively take over systems for online tests will frighten operations managers to death. (To say nothing of what it might do to the consultant.) Client staffs often assume that consultants who are conducting assessments are out to pin scalps to the wall, and we have to be sensitive to that attitude. That's one reason we try not to use the word *audit* to describe assurance work, because the word has developed a punitive connotation in many circles. In short, the work ethic, management skills, attitude, and professional efficiency of the consultant counts for a great deal. Knowledge can be gained. It's more difficult to change attitudes or work ethics.

B2B as Amplifier (and Fuzz Box)

Now project all we have said above into a B2B environment where multiple enterprises, multiple managements with their own concerns, priorities, and agendas, possible multiple regulatory agencies, and multiple audit and consulting groups are called upon to collaborate, cooperate, or at least coexist. Here, I submit, is the B2B assurance area that needs strongest attention, starting from the first day an extranet, netexchange, or netmarket first appears as a twinkle in some visionary's eye. These combinations call for assurance groups to provide imaginative approaches, effective but flexible management, cool heads, and a willingness to compromise when it's permissible but to demonstrate strong professional courage when it's not. Respect for the collective and individual clients' concerns and costs, coupled with a damping down of finger pointing and intellectual and organizational competitiveness are musts. The only scorecard should be the measure of benefits for the client(s).

The closest analogy I can muster up is not a great one. Consider the current image of most multilawyer, multiplaintiff, or multidefendant lawsuits. They are usually not pretty. The assurance professions cannot afford for their own sakes or their clients' sakes to let B2B environments become battlegrounds or noise generators. It will not come without major professional effort on our parts. (End of sermon.)

REVIEW CYCLES, PRIORITIES, AND FREQUENCY

We can speak to this topic rather rapidly, but don't ignore it. Therein lies chaos and unpreparedness.

Cycles and Cyclists

Clearly, time cycles are the historically preferred mode of assurance scheduling. They still work well. The complication comes when you add target identification to the mix. Gone (or almost gone) are the site or computer-based cycles. "Let's look at our Paducah center's IBM systems E and F in March." Systems E and F may have been running the entire financials for the enterprise or producing the menus for the cafeteria. What was running on them was less important than what they were—technological objects in need of protection and scrutiny.

Most of that approach, thankfully, has been displaced by a business process view that says (very like external audit), let's concentrate on the controls and security of the supply chain or HR information process. These are much more valuable views for senior management. (A real CEO quote: "I really wonder about those guys. They probe and accumulate all kinds of information, but they never tell me anything useful.") The loss of integrity in System E's operating system becomes more poignant and pressing if I know it's jeopardizing our entire JIT inventory program.

Cycles are dictated by more than target characteristics and importance. They reflect resource availability, logistics (that's my fifth trip to Angola this year), and the expected level of change in the environment. High frequency of change and high importance of business process equals short cycle times.

Triggers and Events

But today, cycle plans for e-Trust assurance have their primary value in ensuring that nothing escapes review over time. Increasingly we are relying on triggers and events as assurance project initiators. A simple list for a B2B will make the concept of triggers self-evident:

- New partners
- New applications, especially across network boundaries
- New technology
- New organization
- New regulations
- New vulnerabilities and threats
- An incident

- My personal favorite—a memo from the chairman, CEO, or audit committee on a subject that has caught their interest

Once again, however, there's that complicating factor inherent in B2Bs. You may not always directly observe these arrivals, especially if they primarily involve your partners. Nonetheless, you may feel the impact. Back to our mantra. Coordinate and collaborate.

METHODS, PROCEDURES, MECHANISMS, AND PERFORMANCE STANDARDS

I remember once being told by an executive during a competitive bid, "All you guys have methodologies. That's no differentiator." Actually, he was wrong, and I could have told him so, proving my point with devastating and withering logic abetted by countless examples, leaving him dumbfounded and ashamed and leaving me without the engagement. (No, I didn't.)

Methods matter, a lot, whether we are talking about external consultants or internal groups. Assurance methods bring consistency, logic, structure, quality, completeness, and a basis for communication to the process. They can sure speed things up. They are not all the same, nor are they a substitute or crutch for consultant knowledge, competence, and experience. I am not about to parade the complete Deloitte & Touche Secure e-Business Technology Assurance Methodology before you. (It is only slightly longer than its title.) We would, of course, be more than happy to discuss our methodologies with you directly at any level you choose.

For the moment, let's take as given that methodologies exist, they are not all the same, they are important, and they should not be devalued as differentiators. Let us also take as given the fact that methodologies are not the sole province of consultants or auditors. For the very same reasons noted above, your own assurance staffs should develop or adapt them and evaluate the results, critically.

Instead, let's focus on several developments that are changing the assurance methodology landscape and have an important bearing on B2B e-Trust. Fact: Complex, network-based systems are proliferating. Fact: The B2B technology, applications, and service arenas are changing, expanding, and contracting at a bewildering rate. Fact: There is a shortage of skilled and experienced assurance professionals. Fact: The impact of a security, control, or trust failure can be significantly amplified in B2B environments.

Fact: We need some new as well as supplemental techniques to keep ahead of the power curve. (That's aviator talk.)

If all of those facts have a bearing on our ability to create e-Trust, then we have a few choices for improvement. We can broaden the base of participants. We can use new techniques and we can use technologies. Let's illustrate each one.

Self-Assessment

Is this not foxes guarding henhouses territory? Not if the assessments are properly designed, tested, implemented, supervised, and evaluated. They have the added value of using the expertise of the parties involved in the process to be assured and it also makes them a part of their own evaluation process. They can work well. I have had the opportunity to help design and evaluate network-related self-assessments for several large organizations. Some entities use them as supplements—stretching out the formal assessment cycle and not driving overworked assurance personnel into the ground. Some have gone the next step and actually substituted them in certain higher confidence areas. Our profession is spending more time designing and less time performing audits and assessments in many areas. Obviously, if handled correctly (and that's a big if), self-assessment can leverage your assurance power dramatically.

Sampling

A little known fact about the audit profession is they sometimes get to do some pretty unglamorous stuff. (Our recruiters will kill me.) I'm not talking about checking figures. I'm talking about counting and valuing things. If you want to send young audit practitioners into spasms of despair, simply walk up behind them and gently whisper "physical inventories" in their ears.

Every auditor I know (and for this reason alone I am thankful I am not one) has a physical inventory horror story. It is the KP of the profession. Measuring the real versus reported contents of oil tanks; counting tools on a gigantic shop floor; watching product move through an assembly or packaging line; counting vehicles in freezing or sweltering temperatures. You get the idea. Not only is it a pest, it is time consuming and not very cost effective. Only in recent years have tax authorities and professional standards and other groups concerned with methods begun to accept statistical sampling as a legitimate substitute for nose counting. These techniques are effective, quite sophisticated, and rigorously monitored. No one wants to go back to counting bags of onions.

Can these techniques be used in some of the complex environments we're addressing? Take data quality as a case in point. Are we really going to check each record and data field to accept or reject a terabyte-sized file? Even with computers, that's a chore. But if we set the parameters and sample size intelligently, we can create a go–no go trigger for accepting or rejecting large volumes of information from an outside source. I hear your facile brain whipping up all sorts of objections, and many of them are quite valid. This technique is more often used as a supplement or first-round analysis. Failure rates, rejected passwords, alarms, virus attacks, and any number of other indicators can be subjected to statistical analysis. Remember, B2Bs usually mean large—large volume, large value, large user base, large number of nodes and paths, large opportunities for mistakes and attacks, and, unless we get smarter, large costs for e-Trust assurance.

Intrusion Detection and Attack and Penetration Assessments

Intrusion detection is concerned with the detection, reaction to, and successful resolution of an actual attack on network-based systems. Intrusion detection *assessments* examine the effectiveness, completeness, timeliness, and appropriateness of the intrusion-detection methods that a network-based environment has in place. Like most assessments, recommendations for any necessary improvement are the primary objective.

Attack and penetration is a methodology for modeling and simulating network attack scenarios and determining through diagnostic analysis what vulnerabilities may have been revealed, as well as suggesting elimination or mitigation. Neither will expose all potential vulnerabilities, but they are effective weapons for the overall B2B assurance arsenal.

As you might expect, these two related approaches are given a great deal of attention in Internet-related environments. They should. They are important. But they need to be put in proper perspective. Too many executives faced with the need for B2B assurance zero in on these two activities to the exclusion of all others as they search for the best way to make the problem go away. Some organize strictly internal programs to maintain control and confidentiality over the activities. If you have the resources and capabilities to manage these areas on your own, by all means do so.

But if you elect to choose outside assistance, be careful. Often swayed by the media's predilection for "gee whiz" stories of intrusion, viruses, and denial of service, many of those concerned executives have turned to "reformed" hackers and electronic vandals to assist them in detecting and preventing attacks. This is roughly equivalent to putting criminals in law enforcement because they have experience in committing crimes. We feel that there are many responsible and capable organizations that can assist you cost-effectively in these programs without rewarding the people who created the problems in the first place. We consider ourselves to be a major player in this area.

The Twelve Commandments of Attack and Penetration Engagements
(adapted from Deloitte & Touche internal documents)

1. Engagement teams will consult with Firm national leadership for proper terms and conditions for proposals, engagement letters, and business terms.
2. Engagements will be initiated only after a full understanding and agreement is reached between the client and the engagement team concerning objectives, scope, constraints, timing, tools, reports, participants, and conditions.
3. Penetration testing shall only be performed by qualified personnel.
4. Client must authorize and consent to all testing, without limitation, including permission from third parties.
5. Clients must adequately back up all systems to be tested.
6. Clients shall provide a 'trusted agent' to participate in all testing.
7. Testing shall only be performed from authorized user accounts.
8. At no time shall testing be performed from an individual's private line.
9. Consultants shall only use approved and properly licensed tools.
10. Tools must be wiped of nonessential data, scanned for viruses, and verified before use.
11. Results and observations will be fully documented and strictly controlled.
12. Reports will be provided only to those client representatives explicitly authorized to receive them.

We believe that penetration testing is an important tool in the B2B environment. It should be used carefully and responsibly, and its results should be weighed in the context of other assurance data and methods. Major operational or investment decisions should seldom if ever be made strictly on A&P results alone.

REPORTING

So what is there to say about reporting assessment results that hasn't been said a hundred times before? Similar things to what we have been saying above: We need new techniques for the same reasons. For a single, typical, modestly structured B2B, multiply the number of enterprises by the number of managers concerned by the number of processing environments by the number of business processes by the number of trust subjects by the number of professional and internal assurance groups involved by an average of only two reports each, and you get an immense paper, e-mail, graphics, and even video deluge. Once again, we have the choice of doing it smarter, drowning in paper, or not doing all that's necessary.

Now add the load of individual incident reports and forensic analysis, and the pile gets higher. Let's look at some of the choices.

There's no argument that formal reports are necessary, but they, too, can be streamlined. Oddly enough, there's one approach that often backfires—the standardized report form, designed for consistency, comparative analysis, ease of reading, and preparation. How can you dislike the idea? I love the idea. I'm not very fond of many of the implementations I've seen.

The first abnormality is the all-inclusive form. Cover everything by including everything, whether it's relevant or not. Leave the respondent to determine whether this applies or not. A good index of one of these is the number of times N/A appears in the average response. Such forms are designed not for ease of use but ease of creation and handling once returned. In other words, make everyone spend more time than they need to, so a few administrators and assurance professionals can spend less.

These are even more pernicious in their website form where you may end up paging back and forth infinitely. Let's face it: Flipping paper is still often easier than flipping screens. On the opposite end of the spectrum, of course, is the blank sheet of paper (blank screen), stream of consciousness variety. "Report on Phenomenon X!" What do you wanna know? These forms are bad enough when they are used to gather data. They are even worse when they are then carried over into impressive and endless graphs and commentaries for management representing every data point, meaningful or not.

Once again, B2Bs are big. Everyone has his or her own pet ways of data gathering and reporting. Some are willing to die for their forms. (All right, you chaps, over the top and let's give our all for old Form #2345-7-08 Rev 6 Dated 9-22-86 in quadruplicate or its electronic cousin, whatever.htm.) As we mentioned several times in our discussions on bureaucracy in the previous chapter, lean and mean B2B will not come naturally. We're going to have to work for it. A bas les formes! (Yes, I know, that doesn't quite translate.)

Lest you think I am in favor of reporting anarchy, I am not. I would submit that some of our existing reporting methods are anarchic. Let's examine several more requirements before we wrap things up. As you can see, you're getting to the last pages of the book. I, on the other hand, have not reached that point yet. This book was not written entirely in front to back chapter order, so I still have to go back and write some more stuff that you've already read.

Quick Response

With the transaction velocity, status change, and the sheer breadth of B2Bs, timeliness is almost on a par with accuracy in our report requirements list. If you can't get it where it's supposed to go, it's not going to help. One of the major culprits to be overcome is the multiple sign-off. We use e-mail to speed up a report and it sits in an approver's inbox for three days before it gets released to the next approver. The delays in store and forward techniques are in the Store, not the Forward. It's not technology, it's discipline and process. A year ago, I started putting "Critical" on everything I sent to see if it improved turnaround time. It didn't. I guess everyone else had learned that trick before me. If we are going to build e-Trust, we need responsive reporting systems. Each entity has its own culture and a B2B will have many. A cooperative effort to make both intra- and interenterprise reporting efficient is an absolute necessity.

Log and Sensor Evaluations

This one may sound a bit silly to the nontechnician, but the purpose behind an alarm is not to sense an anomaly and go off. It is to send meaningful information to an appropriate system or individual for remedial action and analysis. You network managers know what I mean. I can remember participating in a security review of a fair-sized multisite network and being regaled with the number, strategic locations, sensitivity, and accuracy of the various sensors and alarms installed throughout the net. Someone then asked—"And then what happens?" The conversation turned downhill rapidly. We should not be in the business of creating howling car alarms that everyone ignores.

"Reporting by Exception"

This has been the Shangri La of reporting since the scribes worked for the Pharoahs. (Two cultures in one sentence, not bad.) It has to be taken out of the wish list category and put into the "do something about it category." Part of the issue is building sufficient trust in the security and controls system that we can, in turn, use it to support e-Trust—without constantly scanning in every nook and cranny. Reporting by exception causes "agita" among many members of the controls profession. I submit that we will get it one way or the other. We either design it to produce true exceptions—whether through analysis mapping, fuzzy logic or statistical analysis—or we'll get it via the far more dangerous mode of pursuing whatever you happen to pick out of a melee of undifferentiated messages. Now, that gives me agita.

Anticipatory Reporting

Sounds like an oxymoron but it's not. It simply means using more of our reporting mechanisms and predictive smarts to get ahead of possible problems. Early warning alerts, out-of-norm analysis, scenario playing—A&P is a form of predictive reporting—incident analysis and projection. All these and a lot more belong in B2B controls and in the hands of people who can use them meaningfully.

B2B is coming—sooner than you think. As late as 1995, little serious B2B was conducted on the Internet. Six years later, billions of dollars in transactions cross the Internet—daily. B2B (2C2B2C) is different. This is the tough period. We're in a state of transition, with one foot in the past and one foot in the future.

Query: Which way are we facing?

22

On with the Game

Obviously, our dance hall queen from Chapter 1 wouldn't have been sitting at the table if she didn't want to play poker. But she had her conditions for playing or cashing in, and one of them was trust. That's the final message we want to leave with you.

e-TRUST! IT'S AN ESSENTIAL

If you come away from this reading experience with any message at all (of course we hope you've gotten quite a few), we'd like it to be a sense of changed priorities. A sense of becoming different.

We believe that, if you haven't already done so, at some point sooner than you think, you and your organization will be taking the plunge into serious B2B activity. Not because it's fashionable, or some "techie" or venture manager talked you into it. Or some wild man competitor got there first. You're smarter than that. You're going to see a path to increased growth and profit that just won't be available any other way. But in the process, you should realize that you will be making a serious commitment not only to being significantly different—both from many of your contemporaries and from your prior self—but also to maintaining and expanding those differences.

After careful analysis and testing of alternatives and downsides, you'll probably be ready to make a significant commitment to external, interactive, high-volume, network-supported B2B and B2B2C processes. Before you take that step or even if you're already up to your knees in e's, please put up a sign somewhere in your line of sight that says, "e-Business As Usual Means Service, Quality and Trust."

Make sure everyone else in your organization buys into that motto, not as a slogan but as a basic business imperative. Then extend your reach and make sure your external partners share your priorities before you commit. Push e-Trust as hard as you can, because it doesn't come naturally, even if it is essential.

OUT FROM THE DUSTBINS AND MILLPONDS

For years, security and controls were treated in most business enterprises as somewhere between Cinderella and the Ugly Duckling. We should point out that the Fairy Godmother seldom showed up, and very few security millponds became Swan Lake. Only in recent times, especially with the advent of networks and huge databases, have most enterprises become conscious of the major threats and risks that lay both inside and outside the firewalls. And so, they developed self-defense systems, many of which were quite effective, as long as you stayed inside. Behind the bunkers, things could be relatively serene. Unfortunately, it's difficult to successfully engage in B2B strictly from behind walls and opaque interfaces.

HISTORY IS NOT ALWAYS A RELIABLE INDICATOR OF THE FUTURE

We're moving on now to the next stage in electronic business where bunkers and moats are inhibitors as well as protectors. In order to exploit the new opportunities, you are moving your business processes out into the open; turning some of them over to third parties; increasing your dependency on other organizations and other infrastructures. At the same time, many of your e-Business partners are doing the same thing with you. Your trust processes need to fit and support this new world.

NEW BUSINESS OPPORTUNITIES, NEW RELATIONSHIPS

The technology's here and expanding rapidly. Yes, we know. Some of it, you could do without. At the moment, it's a mixed blessing at best. But aversion, avoidance, and delay won't work. If Orville and Wilbur Wright had foreseen being penned in a crowded jet all day in a snowstorm at

Detroit Airport, they might have smashed their models and prints, folded their tent, scratched Kitty Hawk off their itinerary, and gone back to building the better bicycle. But somebody else would have invented the airplane (and airline dinners and airline lavatories and airport waiting rooms). B2B is here, and while it may still be in the Cinderella stage in some industries and environments, we believe it's going to the ball.

We urge you to capitalize on the opportunities that B2B provides. But don't rely strictly on the old trust, security, and control approaches when you play in this new game. Build business environments based on each player's willingness and ability to continuously demonstrate to all the other players' satisfaction that the game is honest, open, following the rules, and properly controlled. Don't be different for it's own sake but for your own sake. As we said at the start, you need a winning strategy and tactics (when to hold 'em and when to fold 'em), plenty of resources, reflexes, skill, and yes, luck. We wish you the best of luck. Just don't put your trust in it.

Glossary

Glossary terms are listed by acronym if commonly used, otherwise by name. See text, especially Chapters 2, 6, 7, 8, 12, 13, 18, 19, and 21, for additional topical definitions.

Accountability: The ability to identify, determine the nature of, and validate the business or personal responsibility for a process or information object.

Anonymity: The quality of being unknown or obscure. cf. Privacy and Confidentiality

Assurance: Assessment programs and methods that create the required levels of confidence about the areas under consideration for the benefit of parties concerned.

ASP (Application Service Provider): Third-party entities that centrally manage and distribute software-based services and solutions to customers across a wide area network. In essence, ASPs are a way for companies to outsource some or almost all aspects of their information technology needs.

A&P (Attack and Penetration): Processes for identifying vulnerabilities and control weaknesses within an entity's information systems and networks by performing "true-to-life" penetration and exploitation testing.

Attest engagement: One in which a practitioner (e.g., a CPA acting within his or her professional competence as a CPA) is engaged to issue or does issue a written communication that expresses a conclusion about the reliability of a written assertion that is the responsibility of another party— providing an opinion formally corroborating management's claims about its own condition.

Audit: The formal, professional process employed by competent practitioners to produce an attestation or other statements of assurance.

Auditability: The ability to trace, validate, and record the flow of a process and its results through all of its intermediate and final stages.

B2B: Cooperative e-Business interactivity among business entities (e.g., supply chain management).

B2B2C: Cooperative e-Business among business entities that also involves one or more direct to the consumer services (e.g., travel services).

B2C: e-Business between a business entity and consumers (e.g., e-retailing).

Bandwidth: As it relates to network technology, bandwidth is a relative measure of network data capacity and speed.

Browser: A workstation base program (Netscape and Microsoft Internet Explorer are the two most popular) that acts as a translator, navigator, presenter, and facilitator between the user and other Web-enabled Internet sites.

Confidentiality: Protecting information assets that have *both* commonly recognized value as well as specific value to the entities concerned. Intellectual property, processes, and techniques are examples. *See also* Privacy and Anonymity.

Co-opetition: Environments where two or more business entities may simultaneously or over time be each other's customer, supplier, ally, and competitor.

CP (Content Provider): Sources, developers, or aggregators of intellectual materials.

CSP(Content Service Provider): Internet servicers that deliver key intellectual materials to facilitate e-business or other processes. May or may not be a CP.

CRM (Customer Relationship Management): All aspects of interaction a company has with its customers, be it sales or service related. A comprehensive suite of business processes and applications (usually Internet-based) to provide this support.

DMZ (Demilitarized Zone): Used by a company that wants to host its own Internet services without sacrificing unauthorized access to its private network. The DMZ sits between the Internet and an internal network's line of defense, usually some combination of firewalls and bastion hosts. Typically, the DMZ contains devices accessible to Internet traffic, such as Web, file transfer, or e-mail servers.

Domain Name: A unique alphanumeric name that is used to identify your presence on the Internet. It appears between the www web identifier and the user class suffix (net., org., com., biz., edu., fr., ru., and others). The suffix permits multiple uses of the same domain name for increased capacity but may cause confusion. For example, www.mybusiness.net and www.mybusiness.org are two totally different websites.

Dot.com: A type of Internet-based enterprise that is entrepreneurial, fast growth, highly leveraged, high-risk, technocentric, and in recent years often unsuccessful.

e-Business: Leveraging new and existing information technologies to interact, transact, and collaborate with members of an organization's entire value chain.

e-Commerce: Using the Internet primarily as a means of conducting sales transactions, especially for consumers.

e-Trust: Trust (see below) required in B2B, B2C, B2B2C, and related environments.

EDI (Electronic Data Interchange): A pre-Internet set of protocols, standards, and conventions under which businesses can conduct common transactions. It covers format, structure, and general procedures. EDI has been partially adapted to the Web.

EFT (Electronic Funds Transfer): A rich environment of network-based financial transactions underpinning e-Commerce, e-Business, and individuals through the intermediation of the global banking system. Not exclusive to the Internet.

Encryption: A process for making intelligible information unintelligible through the application of sophisticated mathematical conversion techniques. Obviously, to be useful, the process must be reversible (decryption).

ERP (Enterprise Resource Planning): A business management system that integrates all facets of the business, including planning, manufacturing, sales, and marketing.

Extranet: An access-controlled network in which one party opens its inner processes *directly* to a wider range of authorized outside partners and their networks in the interest of saving time or cost, facilitating business growth, protecting against competition, improving service image, improving accounting or record keeping, reducing duplication of effort, or mutually building toward a more comprehensive relationship.

Firewall: A system designed to prevent unauthorized access to or from a private network, especially intranets. It can be implemented in either hardware or software or a combination of both. The firewall examines each message entering or leaving the intranet and blocks those that do not meet specified security criteria.

GLBA (Gramm-Leach-Bliley Act) (U.S.): Establishes security as a valid subject for regulatory control and audit. The Act applies to all companies that "appear financial in nature." Many states have written or are considering strong supplements to this law.

HCFA (Healthcare Financial Administration) (U.S.): Renamed in June 2001 as the Centers for Medicare/Medicaid Services (CMS or CMMS). Supervises security provisions for Medicare and Medicaid.

HIPAA (Health Insurance Portability and Accountability Act) (U.S.): HIPAA was designed to assure health insurance portability, reduce healthcare fraud and abuse, guarantee security and privacy of health information, and enforce standards for the electronic transmission of health information.

HTTP (HyperText Transfer Protocol): A special protocol by which Web-based servers and work stations intercommunciate and activate Web functions. The format "http://www.someplace.com" identifies itself to an Internet server as a hypertext-formatted address, with a Web-enabled location, using the http protocol. Not all Internet activities are http-based.

HTML (HyperText Markup Language): Format and programming rules that are used to build Web pages and to program and communicate through the http protocol. HTML and many of its derivative languages support links to other documents, as well as graphics, audio and video files.

Integration: As used in this book, refers to business processes, systems, applications, and technologies working together appropriately and cost-effectively.

Internet: A global network connecting millions of computers. At the end of 2000, the Internet had more than 400 million users worldwide, and that number is still growing rapidly.

Intranet: An access-controlled network, based on Internet data and transmission protocols, belonging to an organization, often a corporation, and accessible only by the organization's authorized members, employees, or other individuals such as contractors.

ISP (Internet Service Provider): A company that provides access to the Internet, usually for a monthly fee.

Intrusion detection: The detection, reaction to and successful resolution of an actual attack on network based systems. *See also* A&P.

LDAP (Lightweight Directory Access Protocol): A set of protocols that supports TCP/IP for accessing information directories . LDAP makes it possible for almost any application running on virtually any computer platform to obtain directory information, such as email addresses and public keys.

MIME and S/MIME (Multipurpose Internet Mail Extensions): A specification for formatting non-ASCII messages (graphics, audio, and video files) so that they can be sent over via Internet e-Mail. **S/MIME** supports encrypted messages.

NetExchange: An e-Business, Internet-based, intermediary environment where buyers and sellers with common interests can conduct business interactions. Usually structured around a specific industry, service set, or region.

NetMarket: An expanded e-Business environment that may be composed of multiple interacting NetExchanges as well as individual networks. Often combines industries, regions, and service sets. (e.g., a Global Travel and Entertainment Market).

Non-Repudiation: Non-Repudiation means that the execution and responsibility for a business transaction cannot be denied. In e-context, *Repudiation means to deny or seriously call into question the Existence, Nature, Participants, Content, Mode, Timing, Circumstances, or Authorization of a transaction, message, or other communication.*

PKI (Public Key Infrastructure): A system for publishing the public-key values used in public-key cryptography. There are two basic PKI operations. Certification is the process of binding a public-key value to an individual, organization or other entity, or to some other piece of information such as a permission or credential. Validation is the process of verifying that a certificate is still valid (see Chapter 18).

Portal: A website or service that offers a broad array of resources and services, such as e-mail, forums, search engines, and online shopping malls.

Privacy: Protection driven by the rights and desires of the information subject. The subject's rights may supersede either the inherent value of the information or the rights of the individual or entity in possession of or seeking possession of the information.

Process Integrity: (1). Ensuring that the process, application, or function does only what it's supposed to do (no more, no less) and does it correctly and within process specifications. (2) Ensuring that the process cannot be altered, copied, or destroyed except by authorized parties under authorized conditions. (3) Ensuring that the design, development, deployment, and maintenance functions maintain the integrity of the process as it is further modified, integrated or distributed over time. (4) Protecting the process from external influences such as service denials that would affect its timely and complete performance.

Protocol: A standardized mode of procedure or format. Accepted protocols are critical to interconnected, inteoperative environments like the Internet. Otherwise, chaos reigns.

Risk Assessment: An analysis of: (1) the potential threats to the entity and the likelihood of occurrence; (2) the current vulnerability of the entity to those threats; (3) the risks and potential damage associated with the current situation; (4) possible mitigation strategies and their value in reducing vulnerability and risk; (5) risk alternatives—for example, accept the risk as is, manage it down, or insure against the financial consequences if you can get coverage (see Chapter 21).

SAS 70: A specialized form of third party review (see Chapter 21).

S-HTTP (Secure HTTP): Whereas SSL creates a secure connection between a client and a server, over which *any amount* of data can be sent securely, S-HTTP is designed to transmit *individual messages* securely. *See* SSL.

SMTP (Simple Mail Transfer Protocol): A non-Web Internet e-Mail protocol.

SSL (Secure Sockets Layer): A protocol for transmitting private documents via the Internet. Web pages that require an SSL connection start with *https* instead of *http*. *See also* S-HTTP.

Standard: A definition or format that been accepted and approved by a recognized standards organization or accepted as a de facto standard by the industry.

Third party review: An assessment or audit conducted on behalf of a service entity (e.g., ASP, CSP, portal, service bureau, NetExchange, NetMarket) to be presented to the auditors of its customers, partners, and occasionally stakeholders. The service entity hires a professional firm to prepare and conduct an assessment of the service in question using rules and procedures accepted throughout the profession (see Chapter 21).

TCP/IP (Transmission Control Protocol/ Internet Protocol): The IP protocol deals with the structure, format, and processing of data packets. TCP enables two hosts to establish a connection and exchange streams of IP data.

Transformation: A procedure that takes disparate but related business applications throughout (or in major parts of) an enterprise and reconstructs and harmonizes them under a common business process umbrella.

Transitional Hybrids: Entities and processes with one foot in the technological and operational past and one or more feet scrambling into the future.

Trust: An ongoing interaction that establishes and maintains confidence between or among entities.

Trust Communities: A type of virtual community in which a high level of mutual trust is a critical or mandatory success factor.

URL (Universal Resource Locator): A Web-formatted Internet site address. Strictly speaking, only website addresses are URLs, but common usage is making "URL" synonymous with Internet addresses of any kind. Not to be confused with an individual's username provided by an ISP.

Virtual Communities: One that shares common interests, goals, processes, and characteristics and is brought together primarily through network connection.

VPN (Virtual Private Network): The Internet equivalent of a leased line arrangement usually enabled by the enterprises involved, not by the carrier. It is set up by hardware/software combinations at each end (gateway) of the specific link to be protected. VPN is called point-to-point protection and normally does not extend past the gateways into the supporting systems and servers.

WAP (Wireless Application Protocol): One of several protocols for enabling Web transactions on wireless devices such as Personal Digital Assistants (PDAs).

WebTrust: A family of assessment offerings and seals designed and developed jointly by the AICPA (American Institute of Certified Public Accountants) and CICA (the Canadian Institute of Chartered Accountants) specifically to inspire trust in Web-based environments (see Chapter 21).

World Wide Web: A subset of Internet servers that support specially formatted documents. The Web was designed to make graphical presentation and overall navigation easy on the Internet.

XML (Extensible Markup Language): As the name suggests, provides a much wider range of formatting, conversion, and access options than HTML, making the Web a much more compatible user interface for PC, server, and mainframe applications. It also facilitates the integration of Web-based data repositories into business systems.

Index